ANGER AND FORGIVENESS

Anger and Forgiveness

Resentment, Generosity, Justice

Martha C. Nussbaum

OXFORD
UNIVERSITY PRESS

OXFORD
UNIVERSITY PRESS

Oxford University Press is a department of the University of Oxford. It furthers the University's objective of excellence in research, scholarship, and education by publishing worldwide. Oxford is a registered trade mark of Oxford University Press in the UK and in certain other countries.

Published in the United States of America by Oxford University Press
198 Madison Avenue, New York, NY 10016, United States of America.

Library of Congress Cataloging-in-Publication Data
Names: Nussbaum, Martha Craven, 1947–
Title: Anger and forgiveness: resentment, generosity, justice /
Martha C. Nussbaum.
Description: New York: Oxford University Press, 2016. | Includes
bibliographical references and index.
Identifiers: LCCN 2015038395 | ISBN 978-0-19-933587-9 (hardcover: alk. paper) |
ISBN 978-0-19-933588-6 (ebook (updf)) | ISBN 978-0-19-933589-3 (ebook (epub))
Subjects: LCSH: Anger. | Forgiveness.
Classification: LCC BJ1535.A6 N87 2016 | DDC 179/.9—dc23 LC record available at
http://lccn.loc.gov/2015038395

9 8 7 6
Printed by Sheridan, USA

To the memory of Bernard Williams (1929–2003)

I agree to share a home with Pallas Athena . . .
For the city I make my prayer,
prophesying with a gentle-temper,
that the sun's radiant beam may cause
blessings that make life flourish
to spring up in plenty from the earth.

—Aeschylus, *Eumenides* 916–26[1]

The gentle-tempered person is not vengeful, but inclined to sympathetic understanding.

—Aristotle, *Nicomachean Ethics*, 1126a1–3

We must look the world in the face with calm and clear eyes even though the eyes of the world are bloodshot today.

—Mohandas Gandhi, August 8, 1942, reported in Jawaharlal Nehru,
The Discovery of India, ch. 1, p. 38

Contents

Acknowledgments   *xi*

1. Introduction: Furies into Eumenides   *1*
2. Anger: Weakness, Payback, Down-Ranking   *14*
3. Forgiveness: A Genealogy   *57*
   Appendix: *Dies Irae*   *89*
4. Intimate Relationships: The Trap of Anger   *91*
5. The Middle Realm: Stoicism Qualified   *137*
6. The Political Realm: Everyday Justice   *169*
7. The Political Realm: Revolutionary Justice   *211*
8. Conclusion: The Eyes of the World   *247*

Appendix A: Emotions and *Upheavals of Thought*   *251*
Appendix B: Anger and Blame   *256*
Appendix C: Anger and Its Species   *261*

Notes   *265*
Bibliography   *293*
Index   *303*

Acknowledgments

My first thanks are to the Sub-Faculty of Philosophy at Oxford University, for the invitation to present the John Locke Lectures in the spring of 2014. I am very grateful, too, to the *Indian Express* for an invitation to write on the theme of forgiveness apropos of Narendra Modi and the 2012 Naroda Patiya convictions, which turned my attention to this topic and led me to choose it as the theme of the Locke lectures—although I totally changed my view of the topic once I began working on it. For conversations that shaped my thinking early in the process of working on the topic, I am grateful to Justin Coates, Saul Levmore, and Saikrishna Prakash, and for comments on drafts of the various chapters I am grateful to Kelli Alces, Marcia Baron, Corey Brettschneider, Thom Brooks, Daniel Brudney, Emily Buss, David Charles, Justin Coates, Rachel Condry, Sarah Conly, Roger Crisp, Julian Culp, John Deigh, Rosalind Dixon, David Estlund, Jeremy Goodman, Paul Guyer, Richard Helmholz, Todd Henderson, Aziz Huq, Terence Irwin, Will Jefferson, Sharon Krause, Alison LaCroix, Charles Larmore, Brian Leiter, Katerina Linos, Alex Long, Jonathan Masur, Richard McAdams, Panos Paris, Eduardo Penalver, Ariel Porat, Eric Posner, Sara Protasi, Richard Sorabji, Nick Stephanopoulos, David Strauss, Kevin Tobia, Jeremy Waldron, Gabrielle Watson, Laura Weinrib, and David Weisbach. I am especially grateful to Saul Levmore for several rounds of patient and illuminating comments. Three work-in-progress workshops at the University of Chicago Law School and a series of seminars at Brown University were wonderful ways of getting critical comments on drafts. I am grateful to Albie Sachs for illuminating discussions about South Africa. For extremely valuable research assistance I owe thanks to Emily Dupree, Nethanel Lipshitz, and Dasha Polzik. I would also like to thank Emily Dupree and Nethanel Lipshitz for their help in creating the index.

It is fitting that I dedicate this book to the memory of my teacher and friend Bernard Williams, whose example of a life lived with daring and integrity in philosophy matters to me more than I can say. It is perhaps not surprising, given the nature of teacher-student relations, that I have spent a good part of my recent career rebelling against many of the ideas Williams conveyed in his later work. Here I find myself, somewhat surprisingly to myself, drawn inexorably in a Williamsesque direction, so to speak, recovering some of the sense of fellow feeling that I had long ago—although I am sure Williams would find much to disagree with. It is tragic that I cannot express those discoveries to him today.

ANGER AND FORGIVENESS

1

Introduction

Furies into Eumenides

At the end of Aeschylus' *Oresteia*, two transformations take place in the archaic world of the characters, transformations that the fifth century BCE Athenian audience would recognize as fundamentally structuring their own world. One transformation is famous, the other often neglected. In the famous transformation, Athena introduces legal institutions to replace and terminate the seemingly endless cycle of blood vengeance. Setting up a court with established procedures of reasoned argument and the weighing of evidence, an independent third-party judge, and a jury selected from the citizen body of Athens, she announces that blood guilt will now be settled by law, rather than by the Furies, ancient goddesses of revenge. But—and this is part and parcel of her famous transformation of the Athenian community—the Furies are not simply dismissed. Instead, Athena persuades them to join the city, giving them a place of honor beneath the earth, in recognition of their importance for those same legal institutions and the future health of the city.

Typically this move of Athena's is understood to be a recognition that the legal system must incorporate the dark vindictive passions and honor them. Thus the great Hellenist Hugh Lloyd-Jones concludes, "Far from wishing to abolish the prerogatives of the Erinyes, Athena is anxious to conserve them."[1] The suggestion is that the retributive passions themselves remain unaltered; they simply have a new house built around them. They agree to accept the constraints of law, but they retain an unchanged nature, dark and vindictive.

That reading, however, ignores the second transformation, a transformation in the nature and demeanor of the Furies themselves. At the outset of the trilogy's third drama, the Furies are repulsive and horrifying. Apollo's Priestess, catching a glimpse of them, runs in such haste that, an elderly woman, she falls and "runs" on all fours (*Eumenides* 34–38). They are not women but Gorgons, she exclaims. No, not even Gorgons, since these have no wings.[2] They are black, disgusting; their eyes drip a hideous liquid, and they snore a fearsome blast. Their attire is totally unfitting for civilized gatherings (51–56). Shortly afterwards, Apollo depicts them as vomiting up clots of blood that they have ingested from their prey (183–84). They exist, he says, only for the sake of evil (72). They belong in some barbarian tyranny where it is customary to kill people arbitrarily, to mutilate and torture them (185–90).[3]

Nor, when they awaken, do the Furies give the lie to these grim descriptions. As Clytemnestra's ghost calls them, they do not speak, but simply moan and whine: the text mentions *mugmos* and *oigmos*, noises characteristic of dogs. Their only words, as they awaken, are "get him get him get him get him" (*labe labe* etc.), as close to a doggy hunting cry as the genre allows. As Clytemnestra says: "In your dream you pursue your prey, and you bark like a hunting dog hot on the trail of blood" (131–32). If the Furies are later given articulate speech, as the genre demands, we are never to forget this initial characterization.

What Aeschylus has done here is to depict unbridled anger.[4] It is obsessive, destructive, existing only to inflict pain and ill. In its zeal for blood it is subhuman, doglike. The Greeks were far enough removed from fancy domesticated dog breeds and close enough to raw scenes of canine killing to associate the dog, consistently, with hideous disregard for the victim's pain. Even the idea of vomiting up the blood of victims is a quite literal depiction of doggy behavior.[5] The smell on the Furies' breath is the smell of half-digested blood, the same smell from which one might turn in revulsion today after witnessing unbridled canine behavior.[6] Apollo's idea is that this rabid breed belongs somewhere else, in some society that does not try to moderate cruelty or limit the arbitrary infliction of torture—surely not in a society that claims to be civilized.

Unchanged, these Furies could not be part and parcel of a working legal system in a society committed to the rule of law.[7] You don't put wild dogs in a cage and come out with justice. But the Furies do not make the transition to democracy unchanged. Until quite late in the drama, they are still their doggy selves, threatening to disgorge their venom (812), blighting the land and producing infertility (812). Then, however, Athena—who has already set up her legal institutions without them—persuades them to alter themselves so as to join her enterprise.[8] "Lull to repose the bitter force of your black wave of anger," she tells them (832–33).[9] But of course that means a very profound transformation, indeed a virtual change of identity, so bound up are they with anger's obsessive force. She offers them incentives to join the city: a place of honor beneath the earth, reverence from the citizens. But the condition of this honor is that they abandon their focus on retribution and adopt a new range of sentiments. In particular, they must adopt benevolent sentiments toward the entire city and refrain from stirring up any trouble within it—especially not civil war, but also not premature death or any intoxicating angry passion (850–63).[10] Indeed, they are required to invoke blessings upon the land (903 ff.). The deal is that if they do good and have and express kindly sentiments, they will receive good treatment and be honored. Perhaps most fundamentally transformative of all, they must listen to the voice of persuasion (885, 970). All of this, needless to say, is not just external containment: it is a profound inner reorientation, going to the very roots of their personality.

They accept her offer and express themselves "with a gentle-temper" (*preumenōs*, 922).[11] They prohibit all untimely killing (956). Each, they declare, should give love (*charmata*) to each, in a "mindset of common love" (*koinophilei dianoiai*, 984–85). Once again: these sentiments are utterly foreign to their previous doggy identity. Not surprisingly, they seem to be transformed physically in related ways. They apparently assume an erect posture for the procession that concludes the drama, and they receive crimson robes from a group of female escorts (1028–29)—the crimson robes that resident aliens wear in the city festival of the Panathenaia. They have become women, rather than beasts, and "resident aliens" in the city. Their very name is changed: they are now The Kindly Ones (Eumenides), not The Furies.[12]

This second transformation is just as significant as the first, indeed crucial to the success of the first. Aeschylus suggests that political justice does not just put a cage around anger, it fundamentally transforms it, from something hardly human, obsessive, bloodthirsty, to something human, accepting of reasons, calm, deliberate, and measured. Moreover, justice focuses not on a past that can never be altered but on the creation of future welfare and prosperity. The sense of accountability that inhabits just institutions is, in fact, not a retributive sentiment at all, it is measured judgment in defense of current and future life. The Furies are still needed, because this is an imperfect world and there will always be crimes to deal with. But they are not wanted or needed in their original shape and form. Indeed, they are not their old selves at all: they have become instruments of justice and welfare. The city is liberated from the scourge of vindictive anger, which produces civil strife and premature death. In the place of anger, the city gets political justice.

There is still room for awe: for would-be criminals and fomenters of civil strife are on notice that bad deeds will not go unpunished. Thus, the faces of the Eumenides are still described by Athena as fearful (990). But legal accountability is not mayhem; indeed, being precisely targeted, measured, and proportional, it is mayhem's opposite. Moreover, accountability for past acts is focused on the future: on deterrence rather than payback.

Aeschylus is not a philosophical theorist of punishment, and he leaves a lot of questions for later exploration. For example, is there a type of retributivism that can meet his constraints? Punishment must forgo the *lex talionis*, but is there a type of retributivism that is compatible with rejecting that idea? Or must society, as Socrates and Plato believed, and much of popular Greek thought with them, embrace an altogether different theory of punishment, one based upon deterrence and general utility?[13] There are hints of the latter approach, but no clear statement.

Another liberation goes unexplored, but invites our imaginations: it is the liberation of the private realm. In the old world of the Furies, the family and love, familial and friendly, were burdened by the continual need to avenge something for someone. The need for retaliation was unending, and it shadowed all relationships, including those fundamentally benign, such as Orestes' relationship with Elektra. Revenge made it impossible for anyone to love anyone. (The hideous musical world of Richard Strauss's opera *Elektra* is perhaps the most indelible realization of this Aeschylean/Sophoclean insight. There's not one note, one phrase, that is not bent and twisted by the distorting weight of revenge.)[14] But now law takes over the task of dealing with crime, leaving the family free to be a place of *philia*, of reciprocal good will. It's not that there are no more occasions on which people are likely to feel anger: but if they are serious, they are turned over to law, and if they are not serious, why should they long trouble reciprocal concern? (As we shall see, that dichotomy is too simple, since the intense love and trust of intimate relationships may still give legitimate occasions for painful emotions such as grief and fear, whether or not law has stepped in.) As Aristotle will later say, the gentle-tempered person (his name for the virtue in the area of anger) is not vengeful, but, instead, inclined to sympathetic understanding.[15] Law gives a double benefit: it keeps us safe without, and it permits us to care for one another, unburdened by retributive anger, within.

Notice, in particular, that law permits us to care about wrongs done to friends and family members, without spending our lives consumed with angry emotion and projects of retribution. Most of the anger in the pre-law world that Aeschylus depicts had little to do with the actual living people: it tracked past wrongs done to long-ago ancestors, or, occasionally, one's parents or relatives. Thus the *Agamemnon* opens with the past, in the form of the Chorus's anguished depiction of the long-ago slaughter of Iphigeneia—which Clytemnestra will shortly avenge. And as soon as Aegisthus enters, late in the play, rather than speaking at all about himself or what he cares about, he launches into the gruesome saga of his father Thyestes, who was duped into eating the flesh of his own children by Agamemnon's father Atreus. People don't get to exist as themselves: they are in thrall to a past that burdens them. Anger about wrongs done to oneself is transformed by law too, as we shall see, but perhaps the largest change law effects is to give people a way of caring about others that does not involve exhausting vicarious retributive projects.[16]

This book is not about ancient Greek ethics, but it takes its inspiration from the Aeschylean picture I have just sketched—from the idea that political justice offers a thoroughgoing transformation of the moral sentiments in both the personal and the public realms. But I shall go further than Aeschylus, arguing that anger is always normatively problematic, whether in the personal or in the public realm.[17] At the heart of my argument is an analysis of anger, which I present in chapter 2. Concurring with a long philosophical tradition that includes Aristotle, the Greek and Roman Stoics, and Bishop Butler, I argue that anger includes, conceptually, not only the idea of a serious wrong done to someone or something of significance, but also the idea that it would be a good thing if the wrongdoer suffered some bad consequences somehow. Each of these thoughts must be qualified in complex ways, but that's the essence of the analysis. I then argue that anger, so understood, is always normatively problematic in one or the other of two possible ways.

One way, which I call the *road of payback*, makes the mistake of thinking that the suffering of the wrongdoer somehow restores, or contributes to restoring, the important thing that was damaged. That road is normatively problematic because the beliefs involved are false and incoherent, ubiquitous though they are. They derive from deep-rooted but misleading ideas of cosmic balance, and from people's attempt to recover control in situations of helplessness. But the wrongdoer's suffering does not bring back the person or valued item that was damaged. At most it may deter future offending and incapacitate the offender: but this is not all that the person taking the road of payback believes and seeks.

There is one case, however, in which the beliefs involved in anger make a lot of sense, indeed all too much sense. That is the case that I shall call the *road of status*. If the victim sees the injury as about relative status and only about that—seeing it as a "down-ranking" of the victim's self, as Aristotle put it—then indeed it does turn out to be the case that payback of some sort can be really efficacious. Lowering the status of the wrongdoer by pain or humiliation does indeed put me relatively up.

But then there is a different problem: it is normatively problematic to focus exclusively on relative status, and that type of obsessive narrowness, though common enough, is something we ought to discourage in both self and others.

That's the core of my main argument in a nutshell, but of course all these ideas must be unpacked and defended. Anger may still have some limited usefulness as a *signal* to self and/or others that wrongdoing has taken place, as a source of *motivations* to address it, and as a *deterrent* to others, discouraging their aggression. Its core ideas, however, are profoundly flawed: either incoherent in the first case, or normatively ugly in the second.

I then arrive at a crucial concept that I call the *Transition*. Most average people get angry. But often, noting the normative irrationality of anger, particularly in its payback mode, a reasonable person shifts off the terrain of anger toward more productive forward-looking thoughts, asking what can actually be done to increase either personal or social welfare. I explore the course of reflection that leads to this future-directed thinking, which I prefer. (I interpret the transition undergone by the Furies to be this type of Transition, but that is not essential to my argument.) The Transition is a path that can be followed by an individual, but it may also be, as in Aeschylus, an evolutionary path for a society.

I also recognize a borderline case of genuinely rational and normatively appropriate anger that I call *Transition-Anger*, whose entire content is: "How outrageous. Something should be done about that." This forward-looking emotion, however, is less common, in that pure form, than one might suppose: most real-life cases of Transition-Anger are infected with the payback wish.

In the core chapter and subsequent chapters, armed with this analysis, I then tackle three commonplaces about anger that bulk large in the philosophical literature, as well as in everyday life:

1. Anger is necessary (when one is wronged) to the protection of dignity and self-respect.
2. Anger at wrongdoing is essential to taking the wrongdoer seriously (rather than treating him or her like a child or a person of diminished responsibility).
3. Anger is an essential part of combatting injustice.

I grant that anger is sometimes instrumentally useful in the three ways I have mentioned. But this limited usefulness does not remove its normative inappropriateness. Nor is it as useful, even in these roles, as it is sometimes taken to be.

Four subsequent chapters (4, 5, 6, and 7) develop this core argument further in four distinct domains of life. A good inquiry into these matters should distinguish several different realms of human interaction, asking carefully what human relations are proper to each, and what virtues are proper to each of these relations. The realm of deep personal affection (whether familial or friendly) is distinct from the political realm; it has distinct virtues and norms, where anger and judgment are concerned. My argument will be structured around this division of realms.

First, in chapter 4, I investigate the role of anger in intimate personal relationships, where it is often thought that anger, though sometimes excessive or misguided, is a valuable assertion of self-respect, and that it should be cultivated, particularly by people (and women are the example so often given) who are inclined to have a deficient sense of their own worth. I argue against this line of thinking, suggesting that the values distinctive of personal intimacy not only do not require anger but are deeply threatened by it. Of course serious damages and breaches of trust do occur, and they are often occasions for short-term anger and long-term grief. But grief for a loss is preferable, I shall argue, to an ongoing determination to pin the loss on someone else—both instrumentally, being better for the self, and intrinsically, being more appropriate to the nature of loving human relations. Though short-term anger is understandable and human, it is rarely helpful, and it certainly should not dictate the course of the future.

I next investigate (in chapter 5) what I shall call a "Middle Realm," the realm of the multitude of daily transactions we have with people and social groups who are not our close friends and are also not our political institutions or their official agents. A great deal of resentment is generated in the Middle Realm, from slights to reputation to that unpardonable sin—mentioned already by Aristotle—in which someone forgets your name. In this realm, I make a different argument from the one I advance for the intimate realm, where I recommend strong emotional upset, albeit grief and not anger. Here, I argue that the Roman Stoics, whose culture was unusually disfigured by resentments in the Middle Realm, are entirely correct: the right attitude is to get to a point where one understands how petty all these slights are, and one not only doesn't get angry but also does not grieve. The damage simply is not serious enough. Seneca never quite got there, but he records his self-struggle in a way that offers good guidance. (Thus I shall be following Adam Smith in holding that the Stoics give sound advice except when they tell us not to care deeply for our loved ones, family, and friends.)

But that cannot be the entire story, for of course, although a great deal of daily anger does deal with trivia such as insults and incompetence, sometimes damages in the Middle Realm are extremely serious: stranger-rape, murder by strangers, and so forth. These cases are not like the petty irritations and insults with which Stoic texts and daily life are typically filled. Here is where the insights of Aeschylus become so important. In such a case, the thing to do is to turn matters over to the law, which should deal with them without anger and in a forward-looking spirit. Although serious matters in the personal realm may also be turned over to law, they leave, and appropriately so, a residue of deep emotion (grief, fear, compassion) that are integral to a relationship of love and trust. In the Middle Realm, by contrast, there is no point to any ongoing relationship with the malefactor, and law can assume the full burden of dealing with the wrong.

I turn next to the Political Realm. In this realm, the primary virtue is impartial justice, a benevolent virtue that looks to the common good. It is first and foremost a virtue of institutions, but it is also, importantly, if derivatively, a virtue of the people who inhabit and support these institutions. But what sentiments animate and support justice? Here, once again, it is often held that anger is important, as a sentiment vindicating the equal dignity of the oppressed and expressing respect for the human being as an end. I divide my treatment of the Political Realm into two parts: everyday justice (chapter 6) and revolutionary justice (chapter 7).

In the case of everyday justice I shall argue that the pursuit of justice is ill-served by a narrow focus on punishment of any type, but especially ill-served by criminal law retributivism, even of a sophisticated sort. Above all, society should take an *ex ante* perspective, analyzing the whole problem of crime and searching for the best strategies to address it going forward. Such strategies may certainly include punishment of offenders, but as just one part of a much larger project that would also include nutrition, education, health care, housing, employment, and much more. Although I shall not be able to carry out, here, the wide inquiry into social welfare that is really demanded, I offer at least an idea of what it would look like, and I then look more narrowly at criminal punishment as one tiny sliver of that enterprise.

But what about revolutionary justice? Here it is often believed that anger can be both noble and essential, helping the oppressed to assert themselves and pursue justice. I argue, however, following the theoretical writings of Mohandas Gandhi and Martin Luther King, Jr., that anger is not only not necessary for the pursuit of justice, but also a large impediment to the generosity and empathy that help to construct a future of justice. Anger may still have limited utility in the three instrumental ways I have identified (as signal, as motivation, and as deterrent), but it is crucial that the leader of a revolutionary movement, and many of the followers, be strange sorts of people, part Stoic and part creatures of love. Nonetheless there have been such leaders and followers, as the thought and life of Nelson Mandela demonstrate. And maybe they are not so strange after all, since human life does contain surprising stretches of joy and generosity, qualities that go well with the project of building something better than what exists already.

This clean division of realms is too simple, of course, because the realms intersect and influence one another in many ways. The family is a realm of love, but it is also a political institution shaped by law, and it contains many wrongs (such as rape, assault, and child abuse) that the law must take extremely seriously. Slights in the workplace (for example) are Middle Realm wrongs, but they may also be instances of racial or gender discrimination, of harassment, or of tortious negligence, thus bringing them within the ambit of the law, and of the sort of carefully limited Transition-Anger (the Eumenides in their new basement abode) that is proper to political wrongs. Moreover, our relationships with colleagues, unlike relationships with strangers on airplanes and on the road, are ongoing relationships that have at least some weight and significance: so they lie between the full intimacy of love and friendship and the forgettable encounter with a rude seatmate. Furthermore, as I have already emphasized, serious crimes against the person, such as assault, rape, and homicide by non-intimates, are serious wrongs and also legal offenses in the Middle Realm. The proper attitudes toward these wrongs, in their different aspects, will take a lot of sorting out.

Equally important, the Political Realm is not simply a realm of impartial justice. If a nation is to survive and motivate people to care about the common good, the public realm will need some of the generosity and the non-inquisitorial spirit that I think of as proper to the personal realm, where keeping score of all one's wrongs may be carried too far and poison the common endeavor. That, really, is the core of Aeschylus' insight: that instead of exporting to the city the vindictiveness and bloodthirstiness of the family at its worst, the city should draw on the bonds of trust and the emotions of loving generosity that characterize the family at its best.

Although my central topic is anger and its proper management in the three realms, my project also has a subtheme, which involves a critical examination of one prominent candidate to replace anger as the central attitude in the area of wrongdoing. This substitute attitude is forgiveness, and its candidacy is vigorously championed in modern discussions. The concept of forgiveness is strikingly absent from the *Eumenides*, as, indeed, (I would say) from all of ancient Greek ethics,[18] but it is so central to modern discussions of anger that one cannot approach the topic without grappling with it extensively. I therefore propose to do so here, addressing the familiar contention that forgiveness is a central political and personal virtue. At the end of the day we will be close, in at least some crucial respects, to where Aeschylus left us—but after clearing away a great deal that intervening centuries have bequeathed. Thus we will be able to see more clearly what the insights of the *Eumenides* might offer to a modern world. Let me now introduce that subsidiary theme.

We live in what is often described as a "culture of apology and forgiveness."[19] A cursory Amazon book search turns up scores of titles. Most are works of popular psychology and self-help. Frequently they couple the idea of forgiveness with that of a "journey" or a "road." Taking this journey, usually guided by a therapist, the wronged person moves from some terrible place of pain to a lovely place of transfiguring happiness. My favorite such title is *Breaking Night: A Memoir of Forgiveness, Survival, and My Journey from Homeless to Harvard.*[20] Imagine that. From the horrors of homelessness, and the anger one can imagine that life evoking in a young person, this same young person, embarking on the journey of forgiveness, arrives, at last, at the most coveted of all earthly destinations.

Forgiveness is "a very 'in' topic,"[21] with many defenders in both politics and philosophy. Leading political figures extol its potential benefits, and even leaders who never spoke about forgiveness at all are lauded for their alleged focus on forgiveness, an unsurprising but unfortunate aspect of the many memorials of Nelson Mandela—who, as we shall see, did not use that concept, and framed his efforts in different terms.[22] A growing philosophical literature, meanwhile, addresses the place of forgiveness among the virtues and its potential benefits in both personal and political relations.[23] One finds dissenters, but typically in the direction of greater interpersonal harshness, as the dissident philosophers reassert the benefits of retribution and "getting even."[24] Jeffrie Murphy's fine dissident study, for example, repeatedly asserts the S. J. Perelman *bon mot*: "To err is human, to forgive, supine."[25] Nobody seems to be interested in criticizing forgiveness from the other side, so to speak—arguing, as I shall here, that, in its classic transactional form at any rate, forgiveness exhibits a mentality that is all too inquisitorial and disciplinary. This, however, is to get ahead of our story: first we must understand the "journey" on which forgiveness invites us to embark.

The "road" of forgiveness begins, standardly, in terrible anger over a wrong one has suffered at the hands of another. Through a typically dyadic procedure involving confrontation, confession, apology, and "working through," the wronged person emerges triumphant, unburdened from angry emotion, her claims fully acknowledged, ready to bestow the grace of her non-anger. That is what I shall call "transactional forgiveness," and it is both enormously influential historically and very common today. It is plausible to think of it as the canonical form of forgiveness in today's world.[26]

As chapter 3 will demonstrate, these procedural aspects of forgiveness have their origin in, and are organized by, a Judeo-Christian worldview, especially as structured by organized religion, in which the primary moral relationship is that between an omniscient score-keeping God and erring mortals. God keeps a record of all our errors, a kind of eternal list, the *liber scriptus* that greets the dead at the last judgment.[27] Then if there is enough weeping, imploring, and apologizing—typically involving considerable self-abasement—God may decide to waive the penalty for some or all transgressions and to restore the penitent person to heavenly blessings. The abasement is the precondition of the elevation.[28] The relationship between one human and another is then, in a second stage, modeled on the primary relationship, so as to incorporate its motifs of list-keeping, confession, abasement, and indelible memory.

This constellation of sentiments and actions is, as such, absent in ancient Greco-Roman ethics, although that tradition does contain some valuable attitudes in the general neighborhood of forgiveness— gentleness of temper, generosity, sympathetic understanding,[29] pardon, and, importantly, mercy in punishing—into which translators and commentators sometimes inject the forgiveness journey. All these notions, however, I shall argue, are in crucial ways distinct from the modern notion of forgiveness, and available to one who rejects the guidance of that notion.[30]

There is something remarkably unpleasant in the confessional idea of groveling and abasement—even, I would say, when one imagines any God whom one could revere, but certainly when one thinks about one's friends, family, and fellow citizens. Indeed it is very hard (as chapter 3 will show) to reconcile the emphasis on these attitudes with the idea of unconditional love that inhabits the same tradition. And there is also something remarkably narcissistic in the idea of a drama that revolves around oneself, the wrong one has suffered, and the gift of atonement one is offered. (The astonishing narcissism of the *liber scriptus*, where the record of the entire universe prominently contains one's own name, is replicated in the interpersonal realm.) In short, forgiveness of the transactional sort, far from being an antidote to anger, looks like a continuation of anger's payback wish by another name.

Some thinkers in a loosely Judeo-Christian tradition improve on the core ideas of transactional forgiveness by departing significantly from them, and I shall find both Bishop Butler and Adam Smith valuable sources. (Even though Butler uses the term "forgiveness," what he says has less to do with the score-keeping mentality I deplore than with sheer generosity and humanity. And Smith, interestingly, avoids the term "forgiveness" altogether, substituting the useful Ciceronian term "humanity.") I shall also argue in chapter 3 that both Jewish and Christian texts and traditions contain alternatives to transactional forgiveness, in which generosity, love, and even humor replace the grim drama of penance and exacted contrition. Two alternatives are salient. The first is *unconditional forgiveness*, the waiving of angry feelings by the wronged person's own free choice, without exacting a prior penance. The second, which I like even better, is *unconditional love and generosity*. I examine the biblical credentials of each and examine them as moral alternatives.

On the whole, I shall be arguing that Nietzsche's instincts are sound when he sees in prominent aspects of Judeo-Christian morality, including its idea of transactional forgiveness, a displaced vindictiveness and a concealed resentment that are pretty ungenerous and actually not so helpful in human relations. He goes wrong, however, by not seeing the multiplicity and complexity in these same traditions. Both Judaism and Christianity contain all three of the attitudes I consider.

We should remain alert, then, to the fact that not everything that is called by the name "forgiveness" has the features of transactional forgiveness. Once the term is in general use as a virtue, writers steeped in the Judeo-Christian tradition have a way of attaching it to whatever they favor in that general area of life.[31] Sometimes it would not even be correct to find *unconditional* forgiveness there: what is called "forgiveness" is best understood as some type of unconditional generosity. Thus not everyone who praised Nelson Mandela for "forgiveness" really meant to associate him with transactional forgiveness, and perhaps not even with unconditional forgiveness (which presupposes angry feelings that are being waived). They might have used the term to describe the type of generosity that, as I shall argue, he actually instantiated. But it is also clear that many do endorse attitudes of transactional forgiveness as the appropriate ones for the South African reconciliation process, as did Desmond Tutu in the last chapter of his book *No Future Without Forgiveness*, with its detailed discussion of contrition, apology, humility, and absolution—although Tutu carefully and accurately refrains from imputing these notions to Mandela or indeed to the procedures of the Truth and Reconciliation Commission.[32]

As I proceed through the steps in my argument, then, I first investigate the claims of anger in each realm, and then ask whether transactional forgiveness, as classically defined, is the replacement we need. I argue that the Judeo-Christian "virtue" of transactional forgiveness is not a virtue in any of the three realms. In the personal realm, the whole machinery of confession, apology, and forgiveness is retentive, unloving, and quite often vindictive in its own way. The offer of forgiveness, though seemingly so attractive and gracious, all too often displays what Bernard Williams, in a different context, called "one thought too many," that is, a list-keeping, inquisitorial mentality that a generous and loving person should eschew. Bishop Butler warned of the narcissism of resentment, and I shall argue that the "journey" of forgiveness all too often gives aid and comfort to that narcissism. The personal realm at its best is characterized by a generosity that gets ahead of forgiveness and prevents its procedural thoughts from taking shape. In a very real sense, love does mean never having to say you're sorry. The fact that this was said in a lightweight popular novel (albeit one written by a fine classical scholar) does not make it false.[33] Apologies can sometimes be useful, but as evidence of what a future relationship might hold, and whether such a relationship might be fruitful.

The Middle Realm, similarly, contains a significant role for apology as evidence that, going forward, the offending worker or boss can be trusted; it is a useful device that smooths the way for respectful interactions after a breach. But the desire to extract apologies from others as a kind of payback or "down-ranking" haunts this realm as well, and we should beware of it.

Although at times apology will play a valuable role in political reconciliation, political apologies turn out to be distinct from transactional forgiveness in important ways.[34] Often they are signals of trustworthiness going forward, and expressions of a set of shared values on which trust may be based. Moreover, since humiliation always threatens to undermine reconciliation, it is sometimes important to avoid the whole issue of apology, as the Truth and Reconciliation Commission wisely did. The focus should be on establishing accountability for wrongdoing, as a crucial ingredient of building public trust, on expressing shared values, and then on moving beyond the whole drama of anger and forgiveness to forge attitudes that actually support trust and reconciliation.

What values promise such support? Generosity, justice, and truth.

2

Anger

Weakness, Payback, Down-Ranking

> We feel calm toward those who humble themselves before us
> and do not talk back. For they seem to acknowledge that they are
> our inferiors. . . . That our anger ceases toward those who hum-
> ble themselves before us is shown even by dogs, who do not bite
> people when they sit down.
>
> —Aristotle, *Rhetoric* 1380a21–25

I. Anger: The Missing Link

Anger has a twofold reputation. On the one hand, anger is taken to be a
valuable part of the moral life, essential to human relations both ethical
and political. Typical, and highly influential, is Peter Strawson's famous
argument that the "reactive attitudes and feelings," of which "resentment"
is a central case, play a major role in our dealings with one another and
are integrally bound up with the very idea of human freedom and responsibility.[1] Other philosophers have insisted on anger's close connection to
the assertion of self-respect and to protest against injustice.[2]

On the other hand, the idea that anger is a central threat to
decent human interactions runs through the Western philosophical tradition—including the political thought of Aeschylus' time,[3]
Socrates and Plato,[4] the Greek and Roman Stoics, the eighteenth-
century philosophers Joseph Butler and Adam Smith, and numerous
more recent contributors. As Butler notes, "No other principle, or
passion, hath for its end the misery of our fellow creatures"[5]—and he
is therefore troubled that God has apparently implanted anger in our
human nature. The same idea of anger's destructiveness is prominent
in non-Western traditions (Buddhism and some varieties of Hinduism

14

especially).[6] Today the idea of anger as disease has generated a large contemporary therapeutic literature, in which it is the apparently inexorable grip of anger that prompts intervention (or advice for self-help). It is because anger is felt as such a problem in the moral life that the project of forgiveness takes on such central importance, and forgiveness is typically defined in terms of a moderation of angry attitudes.

Both of these contentions might be correct: anger might be a valuable yet dangerous tool in the moral life, prone to excess and error but still a source of irreplaceable contributions. (So Butler thought.) On the other hand, it is also possible that one of these contentions is far better grounded than the other. So I shall argue here. But it is highly unlikely that we will make progress unraveling these issues unless we first have a clearer understanding of what anger is.

Recent philosophers, on the whole, spend little time analyzing the emotion. Typical, and highly influential, are Strawson's reference to a class of "reactive attitudes and feelings" including guilt, resentment, and indignation, all of which track the relation of another's will to us;[7] and R. Jay Wallace's highly abstract, albeit valuable, characterization of a class of "reactive emotions" in their relation to evaluation.[8] Even in contexts where it might seem to matter greatly what attitude is in question, philosophers all too often follow Strawson's lead.[9] Meanwhile, cognitive psychologists have provided rich materials for a detailed analysis of anger's elements,[10] but since providing definitions is not their project they typically do not arrange those materials into a philosophical account.

Agreeing with most traditional philosophical definitions of anger, I shall argue that the idea of payback or retribution—in some form, however subtle—is a conceptual part of anger. I then argue the payback idea is normatively problematic, and anger, therefore, with it. There are two possibilities. Either anger focuses on some significant injury, such as a murder or a rape, or it focuses only on the significance of the wrongful act for the victim's relative status—as what Aristotle calls a "downranking." In the first case, the idea of payback makes no sense (since inflicting pain on the offender does not remove or constructively address the victim's injury). In the second, it makes all too much sense—payback may successfully effect a reversal of positions—but only because the values involved are distorted: relative status should not be so important. In the process of defending these contentions, I recognize a borderline species of anger that is free from these defects, and I describe, and recommend, a transition from anger to constructive thinking about future good.

II. Anger: Cognitions, Feelings, Eudaimonism

Like all the major emotions, anger has a cognitive/intentional content, including appraisals or evaluations of several distinct types.[11] Often, it involves not simply value-laden appraisals, but also beliefs.

Furthermore, the appraisals and beliefs involved in anger are what I call "eudaimonistic": they are made from the point of view of the agent, and register the agent's own view of what matters for life, rather than some detached or impersonal table of values. Even when anger involves issues of principle, of justice, or even global justice, this is because the angry person has managed to incorporate such concerns into her conception of what matters in life. Such incorporation into the "circle of concern"[12] need not precede the event that triggers the emotion: a vivid tale of woe (such as Adam Smith's example of the news of an earthquake in China) can arouse compassion for people we never met and about whom we have no antecedent concern.[13] However, unless a firmer structure of concern either exists already or is established, the emotion will be a will-o'-the-wisp: a distraction closer to home makes us forget entirely about the distant people.

The eudaimonism of the emotions is a key idea, too, in the modern psychological literature. Thus Richard Lazarus, in his magisterial *Emotion and Adaptation*, one of the most influential works of experimental psychology in the late twentieth century, speaks of the major emotions as focused on "core relational themes," themes of importance for the person's "ego-identity."[14] Like Smith's account and mine, Lazarus's treatment emphasizes that causes and principles can be objects of emotions—but only when and if a person has ascribed personal importance to them.

Anger is typically accompanied by a wide range of bodily changes and subjective feeling-states. Bodily changes of some type are always present when people are angry, and, after all, the thoughts involved in anger are themselves bodily changes.[15] Subjective feelings of some type are typically present as well, but they are likely to be highly varied (both within a person at different times and across people), and they may be entirely absent if anger is not conscious. Just as the fear of death can lurk beneath the threshold of consciousness and yet influence conduct, so too with anger, in at least some cases. It is a familiar experience to become aware that one has been angry at someone for some time, and that this hidden anger has influenced one's behavior.

The bodily changes and subjective feelings often associated with anger, though important in their way, have too little constancy for them to be included in the definition of anger, as necessary conditions of that emotion.[16] For some people, anger feels like boiling in the neighborhood of the heart (as Aristotle says). For others, it may feel like a throbbing in the temples or a pain at the back of the neck. And in some cases it simply is not felt, like a lurking fear of death. One job of therapy is to discover hidden anger. Although at times the therapeutic process (badly managed) manufactures anger where it was not present before, there are surely many cases of genuine discovery.

III. Elements of Anger

What is anger's distinctive content? A good starting point is Aristotle's definition. Although it will turn out to be too narrow to cover all cases of anger, it helps us dissect its elements.[17]

Anger, Aristotle holds, is "a desire accompanied by pain for an imagined retribution on account of an imagined slighting inflicted by people who have no legitimate reason to slight oneself or one's own" (*Rhetoric* 1378a31–33). Anger, then, involves

1. Slighting or down-ranking (*oligōria*)
2. Of the self or people close to the self
3. Wrongfully or inappropriately done (*mē prosēkontōn*)
4. Accompanied by pain
5. Involving a desire for retribution

By twice repeating "imagined" (*phainomenēs*), Aristotle emphasizes that what is relevant to the emotion is the way the situation is seen from the angry person's viewpoint, not the way it really is, which might, of course, be different.

Anger is an unusually complex emotion, since it involves both pain and pleasure: Aristotle shortly says that the prospect of retribution is pleasant. He does not clarify the causal relationships involved, but we can easily see that the pain is supposed to be produced by the injury, and the desire for retribution somehow responds to the injury. Moreover, anger also involves a double reference—to a person or people and to an act. Using non-Aristotelian terminology to make this issue explicit: the *target* of anger is typically a person, the one who is seen as having inflicted damage—and as having done so wrongfully or illegitimately. "I am angry *at* so-and-so." And the *focus* of anger is an act imputed to the target, which is taken to be a wrongful damage.[18]

Injuries may be the focus in grief as well. But whereas grief focuses on the loss or damage itself, and lacks a target (unless it is the lost person, as in "I am grieving for so-and-so"), anger starts with the act that inflicted the damage, seeing it as intentionally inflicted by the target—and then, as a result, one becomes angry, and one's anger is aimed at the target. Anger, then, requires causal thinking, and some grasp of right and wrong.[19]

The damage may be inflicted on the person who, as a result, feels anger, or it may be inflicted on some other person or thing within that person's circle of concern.

The least puzzling parts of Aristotle's definition, from the vantage point of contemporary intuitions, are its emphasis on pain and its emphasis on wrongful damage. How exactly does the wrongful act of another cause pain to the self? Well, presumably, the person sees (or believes) that something about which she cares deeply has been damaged. The item damaged must, indeed, be seen as significant and not trivial, or pain will not be a consequence. This pain is, up to a point, not dissimilar to the pain felt in grief. It tracks the perceived size of the damage. Nonetheless, the pain of anger typically makes internal reference, as well, to the (believed) wrongful act of another person: the pain of seeing one's child murdered just feels different from that of losing a child to accidental death. (Aristotle often emphasizes that pleasure and pain themselves have an intentional content: the pain, then, is pain *at* the injury that has [as the person believes] been inflicted. It's that specific sort of pain.)

As for wrongful injury: even though we experience frustration when someone inadvertently damages us, we only become angry when we believe (rightly or wrongly) that the damage was inflicted by a person or persons, and in a manner that was illegitimate or wrongful. Lazarus gives the example of a store clerk who ignores a customer because he is busy talking on the phone. The customer will feel wrongly slighted, but if she learns that the reason for the phone call was a medical emergency involving the clerk's child, she will no longer be angry, because she will see that it was legitimate to give the phone call priority.[20] We aren't always so reasonable, of course, but what matters is how we see the situation: we are angry only if we *see* the damage as illegitimate. (This need not be a notion of *moral* wrong: just some type of wrongfulness.)

Notoriously, however, people sometimes get angry when they are frustrated by inanimate objects, which presumably cannot act wrongfully. This sort of behavior was reported already by the Stoic philosopher Chrysippus, who spoke of people biting their keys and kicking their door when it doesn't open right away, and hurling a stone against which one has stubbed one's toe, all the while "saying the most inappropriate things."[21] In 1988, the *Journal of the American Medical Association* published an article on "vending machine rage": fifteen injuries, three of them fatal, as a result of angry men[22] kicking or rocking machines that had taken their money without dispensing the drink. (The fatal injuries were caused by machines falling over on the men and crushing them.)[23] Do such familiar reactions show that anger does not require the idea of wrongful damage? I see no reason to think this. We tend to think that we have a right to expect "respect" and cooperation from the inanimate objects that serve our ends, and in the moment we react as if they were bad people, since they clearly are not doing "their job" for us. We quickly realize that this doesn't make sense—most of the time.

Butler suggests that there can be a species of anger, "sudden anger," when something thwarts or opposes us, and that this type does not require the thought of a wrong.[24] I doubt, however, that Butler has actually identified a distinct species of anger. Suddenness by itself will not do that: for once judgments of value become deeply internalized, we will become angry very quickly at a wrongful attack on what we love. When someone pulls a gun on your child, you don't stop to think. Nor is it obvious that angry people are aware that a "thwarting" is not a real wrong: consider those vending machines. At most, we should concede to Butler that there may be a type of anger that is inchoate, prior to full-fledged causal thinking and thus prior to a real judgment of wrong. Infants, for example, fly into a rage when their needs are not met. And yet our increasing knowledge of the cognitive sophistication of young infants makes it plausible to ascribe a vague inchoate judgment of the form, "I ought to have this, and my parent is withholding it."[25] On the whole then, with some borderline cases in early infancy, Aristotle's insistence on wrong holds up.[26]

More problematic, at least initially, is Aristotle's restriction to "oneself or one's own": for surely we may have anger when a cause or principle one cares about has been wrongfully assailed, or when a stranger is the victim of an unjust aggression. Yes indeed, but that (claims the Aristotelian) is because in that case it has become part of one's circle of concern. In other words, "oneself or one's own" is just a way of alluding to the eudaimonistic structure that anger shares with other emotions. This response seems correct: just as we grieve not about every death in the world, but only the death of those who are dear to us, so we get angry not at any and every instance of wrongdoing in the world, but only those that touch on core values of the self. As with other emotions, a vivid episode may jump-start the response by moving a distant object into the circle of concern. If, instead of Adam Smith's tale of an earthquake in China (which jump-starts compassion), we hear a vivid tale of a genocide in a distant country, then we may be aroused to anger on behalf of the slaughtered people, even if they were not antecedently of concern to us. But Smith's point holds: so long as the emotion lasts, so long those people have to be of concern to us. If the concern ceases (because, for example, we become diverted by pressing concerns closer to ourselves), so does the emotion.

More problematic still is Aristotle's reference to a "slighting" or "down-ranking." We immediately associate this with the values of an honor culture, where people are always ranking themselves against one another, and where the central case of wrongdoing is indeed a down-ranking. Surely, we are inclined to say, many damages involve cherished projects without being seen as diminutions of status. Subsequent Greco-Roman philosophy modifies Aristotle's condition, as I have already done. Seneca defines anger in terms of a "wrongful harm," rather than a "slighting."[27] The canonical Stoic definition speaks of a belief that one has been wronged.[28]

Has Aristotle simply made a mistake? I shall argue that he has, but not as large a mistake as one might think: he has captured a style of thinking that is very common in anger, though not omnipresent.

First, the mistake. Defenders of Aristotle try to defend his definition by referring, once again, to eudaimonism. Thus Lazarus, attempting to give a general definition, and not one pertaining only to honor cultures, applauds Aristotle's definition, because it captures this very general idea of an injury to the self's cherished projects.

Lazarus's defense, however, is clumsy. Not every eudaimonistic injury (meaning injury to something seen by the agent as important) involves a personal down-ranking. Injuries to causes or principles are typically eudaimonistic without involving the thought of a low ranking of the self. Even when anger's focus is an injury to a beloved person, the angry person usually does not think that the damager is trying to belittle her. She has a sense of eudaimonistic injury (the injury looms large from the viewpoint of her values and concerns), without a sense of personal diminution. So Aristotle's account is too narrow.

The idea of down-ranking proves more explanatorily fertile, however, than we might at first suppose. There is something comical in the self-congratulatory idea that honor cultures are in another time or at least another place (such as, putatively, the Middle East), given the obsessive attention paid by Americans to competitive ranking in terms of status, money, and other qualities. Even the idea that "honor killings" are an artifact of specific (Middle Eastern? Muslim?) cultures needs rethinking. The rate of intimate partner violence is slightly higher in Italy than in Jordan,[29] and we may safely say that a sense of manly honor and competitive injury is involved in many killings of women in many countries.[30] Empirical psychologist Carol Tavris's wide-ranging study of anger in America finds ubiquitous reference to "insults," "slights," "condescension," "being treated as if I were of no account."[31] People remain intensely concerned about their standing, now as then, and they find endless occasions for anger in acts that seem to threaten it.

From now on I shall call this sort of perceived down-ranking a *status-injury*. The very idea of a status-injury already includes the idea of wrongfulness, for, as Aristotle notes, diminution of status is usually voluntary: if someone acted accidentally, I won't perceive that as diminishing my status. (Remember the store clerk who had an urgent phone call.)

We should, however, broaden the scope of Aristotle's account to include the many cases in which people behave in a denigrating or insulting way without being consciously aware that this is what they are doing. When the target of such behavior (status-related denigration in the workplace, for example) reacts with status anger, he need not think that his boss consciously intended the insult. But he probably does need to think something else: that the remark is part of a pattern of belief and conduct, a policy regarding the status of employees, that the boss has adopted and for which he is accountable.

Anger is not always, but very often, about status-injury. And status-injury has a narcissistic flavor: rather than focusing on the wrongfulness of the act as such, a focus that might lead to concern for wrongful acts of the same type more generally, the status-angry person focuses obsessively on herself and her standing vis-à-vis others.

In connection with such injuries, both Aristotle and Lazarus emphasize the relevance of personal insecurity or vulnerability: we are prone to anger to the extent that we feel insecure or lacking control with respect to the aspect of our goals that has been assailed—and to the extent that we expect or desire control. Anger aims at restoring lost control and often achieves at least an illusion of it.[32] To the extent that a culture encourages people to feel vulnerable to affront and down-ranking in a wide variety of situations, it encourages the roots of status-focused anger.

IV. Anger and Payback

What is anger's aim? The philosophical tradition concurs in holding that there is a double movement in the emotion; this double movement, from pain inflicted to striking back, is so prominent that ancient taxonomies classify anger as an emotion that looks forward to a future good, rather than as one that responds to a present bad—although, once they say more, they acknowledge that it has both aspects. Aristotle emphasizes that the forward movement characteristic of anger is pleasant, and that anger is in that sense constructive and linked to hope. The imagined payback is seen as somehow assuaging the pain or making good the damage.[33]

But how exactly does this work? How does pain lead to the sort of lashing out, or striking back, that we associate with anger in at least many cases? And why would someone who has been gravely wounded look forward with hope to doing something unwelcome to the offender? If we had a non-cognitive account of anger, there would be nothing further to say: that is just the way hardwired mechanisms work. But ours is not that type of account, so we must try to understand this puzzle. For it is a puzzle. Doing something to the offender does not bring dead people back to life, heal a broken limb, or undo a sexual violation. So why do people somehow believe that it does? Or what, exactly, do they believe that makes even a little sense of their retaliatory project?

First, however, we had better make sure that the philosophical tradition is correct in holding that a wish for payback is a conceptual part of anger. It is pretty impressive that so many first-rate thinkers, from Aristotle and the Stoics to Butler and Smith to recent empirical psychologists such as Lazarus and James Averill should agree on this. They have thought long and hard about the concept, and it would be surprising if they had made an obvious error. Still, let us think again. Anger is not the only emotion that contains a double movement. Many emotions contain a backward-looking appraisal while also having associated action tendencies oriented toward a future goal.

Compassion, for example, looks at the bad fate that has befallen someone else; but it also has an associated future-directed action tendency. When I feel compassion for a person who is suffering, I often imagine helping that person, and in many cases I do it. Daniel Batson's research shows that this tendency toward helping behavior is quite powerful, if the helpful action is ready at hand and not very costly. But the connection between compassion and helping is typically understood as contingent and causal, rather than conceptual. Philosophical definitions of compassion (from Aristotle and the Stoics through Smith and Rousseau to Schopenhauer) do not suggest that the helping tendency is part and parcel of the emotion, something without which one could not be said to experience compassion.[34] I think this is probably correct: the connection is indeed causal and external rather than conceptual and internal. We can feel compassion for people even when there is nothing to be done for them: people who have been drowned in a flood, to take just one example, or distant people whom we can imagine no way of helping.

With anger, however, the future-oriented aim is standardly thought to be part of the emotion, something without which there is pain of some sort, but not anger. (Butler, we recall, holds that anger's internal goal is the misery of our fellow humans.) We must figure out, first, whether this is correct—whether there really is a conceptual connection in this case, and not simply a causal connection as in others. Second, we must figure out how, more precisely, the pain is connected to the strike-back response.

Let's be clear, first, about what the claim is. The claim is not that anger conceptually involves a wish for violent revenge; nor is it that anger involves the wish to inflict suffering oneself upon the offender. For I may not want to get involved in revenge myself: I may want someone else, or the law, or life itself, to do it for me. I just want the doer to suffer. And the suffering can be quite subtle. One might wish for a physical injury; one might wish for psychological unhappiness; one might wish for unpopularity. One might simply wish for the perpetrator's future (your unfaithful ex's new marriage, for example) to turn out really badly. And one can even imagine as a type of punishment the sheer continued existence of the person as the bad and benighted person he or she is: that is how Dante imagines hell. All that I am investigating here (and ultimately accepting, with one significant qualification) is that anger involves, conceptually, a wish for things to go badly, somehow, for the offender, in a way that is envisaged, somehow, however vaguely, as a payback for the offense. They get what they deserve.

So let's investigate this, considering a range of different cases. And let us start from a basic scenario: Offender O has raped Angela's close friend Rebecca on the campus where both Angela and Rebecca are students. Angela has true beliefs about what has occurred, about how seriously damaging it is, and about the wrongful intentions involved: O, she knows, is mentally competent, understood the wrongfulness of his act, etc. (I choose rape rather than murder, in order to leave Angela with a wider range of possible actions and wishes than would typically be the case with murder. And I choose a friend in order to give Angela more latitude about how to position herself toward the offense and the offender.) Most rapes take place in the context of intimate relationships. But because for me this domain has special complexity, involving issues of trust and grief that relations with strangers do not, let me imagine the case as a (conceptually simpler) stranger-rape, or at any rate not rape in the context of an ongoing intimate relationship involving trust and deep emotion.

Case 1. Angela feels pain at Rebecca's rape. She feels that her circle of concern, what she deeply cares about, has been severely damaged, and she believes, correctly, that the damage was wrongful. She now take steps to mitigate the damage: she spends time with Rebecca, she makes efforts to support her in therapy, in general she devotes a great deal of energy to mending Rebecca's life—and thus to mending the breach in her own circle of concern. So far, Angela's emotion appears to be grief/compassion, and I think the standard definitions are correct when they suggest that it is not anger, even though the occasion for the grief is a wrongful act. We should notice that in this case the primary focus of Angela's emotion is the loss and pain caused to Rebecca, rather than the criminal act itself, and to that extent her emotion seems to have Rebecca, not the rapist, as its target.

Case 2. Angela feels pain at Rebecca's rape, etc. She does all the things that she did in Case 1, thus expressing her compassion. But she also focuses on the wrongfulness of the act, and her pain includes a special pain directed at the wrongful act—to some extent distinct from her pain at Rebecca's suffering. This additional pain leads her to want to do something about that wrongfulness. So Angela forms a group to support rape victims, and she gives money to such groups. She also campaigns for better public safety measures to prevent rape and for better treatment of the problem of sexual violence on her campus. (Again, I abstract from the special complexities of rape in the context of intimate relationships involving trust and love.) Should we call Angela's emotion anger because it focuses not only on Rebecca's pain but also on the wrongfulness of the act, and has an outward movement aimed at something like a righting of the wrong? It is an interesting case, but I think that we typically would not call Angela's emotion anger. I am inclined to see it as a type of morally inflected compassion— not very different, really, from a compassion for one hungry acquaintance that leads me to campaign for better welfare support for all. As in Case 1, the emotion does not have the offender as its target; its target is Rebecca, and other women in Rebecca's position. The offender comes into it only because stopping similar harms is Angela's goal for the future. Angela is thus thinking of general utility (and in Case 2 the Utilitarian idea of anger's limits appears for the first time).

Case 3. Angela feels pain, etc., as in Cases 1 and 2. As in Case 2, she focuses on the wrongfulness of O's act, and she may campaign for general measures to prevent that sort of damage in future. But she also focuses, this time, on O. She seeks to mend the damage by making the offender suffer. Because her circle of concern is damaged, she wants something to happen to O (whether through legal or extralegal means). Here we finally seem to have arrived at anger, as the philosophical tradition understands it: a retaliatory and hopeful outward movement that seeks the pain of the offender because of and as a way of assuaging or compensating for one's own pain.

The question now is, Why? Why would an intelligent person think that inflicting pain on the offender assuages or cancels her own pain? There seems to be some type of magical thinking going on. In reality, harsh punishment of the offender rarely repairs a damage. Adding O's pain to Rebecca's does not do anything to ameliorate Rebecca's situation, so far as one can see. In a TV interview after his father's murder, Michael Jordan was asked whether, if they ever caught the murderer, Jordan would want him executed. Jordan sadly replied, "Why? That wouldn't bring him back."[35] This eminently sensible reply is rare, however, and perhaps only someone whose credentials in the area of masculinity are as impeccable as Jordan's would dare to think and say it.[36]

Ideas of payback have deep roots in the imaginations of most of us. Ultimately they probably derive from metaphysical ideas of cosmic balance that are hard to shake off, and that may be part of our evolutionary endowment.[37] Indeed the first preserved fragment of Western philosophy, the famous words of the Greek thinker Anaximander, dating from the sixth century BCE, is based on just such a powerful analogy between the institution of punishment and the alternations of the seasons: they are said to "pay penalty and reparation" to one another for their sequential encroachments, as the hot and dry drive out the cold and wet (not so successfully, however, in Chicago). We think this way naturally, for whatever reason. Many cherished literary works contain such ideas of "comeuppance," which give us intense aesthetic pleasure.[38] Whether the pleasure we take in such narratives derives from antecedent cosmic-balance thinking or whether narratives of this sort (the entirety of the detective-story genre, for example) nourish and augment our tendency to think in such ways, we cannot say. Probably both. But we do think in such ways, and we do take pleasure in narratives in which the doer suffers, purportedly balancing the horrible act that occurred. Aesthetics, however, like our evolutionary prehistory, can be misleading. Our satisfaction does not mean that such ways of thinking make sense. They really do not. Raping O does not undo the rape of Jennifer. Killing a killer does not bring the dead to life.[39]

This brings us to an alternative to this type of magical thinking which at first seems rational: a focus on the idea of personal slighting or diminution.

Case 4. Angela is pained, etc. She believes that O's bad act is not only a wrongful act that seriously damaged someone dear to her, but also an insult or denigration of her. She thinks something like, "This guy thinks that he can insult my friend's dignity with impunity, and, insofar as he thinks this, he thinks that he can push me around—that I'll just sit by while my friend is insulted. So he diminishes me and insults my self-respect." Here the connection between pain and retaliation is made through the Aristotelian idea that the eudaimonistic ego-damage O has inflicted is a kind of humiliation or down-ranking. No matter how implausible it is to read O's act as a down-ranking of Angela (given that O doesn't know Angela, or even Rebecca), Angela sees O's harm to her friend as an ego-wound that lessens Angela's status. She therefore thinks that lowering O through pain and even humiliation will right the balance.[40]

Many cultures, past and present, think this way all the time. In most major sports we find an emphasis on retaliation for injury, and players are thought wimpy and unmanly to the extent that they do not strike back so far as the rules permit (and a little beyond that). Even though it is obvious that injuring one player does not take away the injury to another, it is a different story if one focuses not on injury but on ranking and humiliation: the retaliatory hit is plausibly seen as taking away the humiliation of the first hit. Slighting in the sense of diminution reaches a broad class of cases, even if not all cases where anger is involved. It is very easy for people to shift mentally from a eudaimonistic concern (this is part of my circle of concern, what I care about) to a narcissistic status-focused concern (this is all about me and my pride or rank). In such cases, a retaliatory strike-back is thought symbolically to restore the balance of status, manliness, or whatever.

Jean Hampton, whose analysis is very close to mine, puts it this way: if people are secure, they won't see an injury as a diminishment; but people are rarely this secure. They secretly fear that the offense has revealed a real lowness or lack of value in themselves, and that putting the offender down will prove that the offender has made a mistake.[41] I feel her account does not cover all the cases: more straightforwardly, people may simply care a great deal about public standing, and they can see quite clearly that to be pushed around has indeed diminished that. Even in her subset of the cases, the fear she describes is much more plausible if the value people care about is relative status, which is easily damaged, than if it is some inner worth or value, which is not.

All of a sudden, the retaliatory tendency makes sense and is no longer merely magical. To someone who thinks this way, in terms of diminution and status-ranking, it is not only plausible to think that retaliation atones for or annuls the damage, it is actually true. If Angela retaliates successfully (whether through law or in some other way, but always focusing on status-injury), the retaliation really does effect a reversal that annuls the injury, seen as an injury of down-ranking. Angela is victorious, and the previously powerful offender is suffering in prison. Insofar as the salient feature of O's act is its low ranking of Angela, the turnabout effected by the retaliation really does put him down and her (relatively) up.

Notice that things make sense only if the focus is *purely* on relative status, rather than on some intrinsic attribute (health, safety, bodily integrity, friendship, love, wealth, good academic work, some other achievement) that has been jeopardized by the wrongful act, and that might incidentally confer status. Retaliation does not confer, or restore, those things. It's only if she thinks purely in terms of relative status that she can plausibly hope to effect a reversal through a strike-back that inflicts pain of some type on the offender. (Thus people in academic life who love to diss scholars who have criticized them, and who believe that this does them some good, have to be focusing only on reputation and status, since it's obvious that injuring someone else's reputation does not make your own work better than it was before, or correct whatever flaws the other person has found in it.)

It's clear that Angela need not think that the injury she has suffered is a down-ranking. That is why Aristotle's definition is too narrow. Indeed, in this case it seems odd for her to do so, given that O is a stranger who does not know her connection with Rebecca. But this way of seeing injury is very common, and very common even in cases where people are eager to deny that this is really what is going on.[42] That is why Aristotle's definition is helpful.

At this point I must introduce a distinction that will be important in later chapters. There is a special status that good political institutions rightly care about: equal human dignity. Rape can be seen, plausibly, as a dignitary injury, not just an injury to bodily integrity. It is right for legal institutions to take this into account in dealing with rapists and rape victims. However, notice that equal dignity belongs to all, inherently and inalienably, and is not a relative or competitive matter. Whatever happens to the rapist, we should not wish his equal human dignity to be violated any more than we approve his violation of the victim's dignity. And it is most important to see that pushing his dignity down does not push the victim's up. Dignity is not a zero-sum game; in that way it is utterly different from relative status.[43]

Suppose Angela does not think this way, but stops at Case 3. Then, insofar as her emotion is anger and not simply some combination of grief and compassion, she does initially wish some sort of bad result for the offender, and she does initially think (magically) that this will set things right, somehow counterbalancing or even annulling the offense. It is human to think this way. However, if she is really focusing on Rebecca and not on her own status-injury, she is likely to think this way only briefly. Magical fantasies of replacement can be very powerful, but in most sane people they prove short-lived. Instead, she is likely to take a mental turn toward a different set of future-directed attitudes. Insofar as she really wants to help Rebecca and women in Rebecca's position, she will focus on the responses characteristic of Cases 1 and 2: helping Rebecca get on with her life, but also setting up help groups, trying to publicize the problem of campus rape, and urging the authorities to deal with it better.

One of these future-directed projects may well involve the punishment of O. But notice that, insofar as Angela is thinking sanely and rationally about what will make the world a better place for rape victims, she will view the punishment of O very differently from the way she viewed it in Case 4. There she saw punishment as "payback" or retribution—or perhaps, more specifically, as a down-ranking or humiliation of O, which effected a reversal of positions between her and O: women (and Angela above all) on top, bad men (and O in particular) on the bottom. Now, however, she is likely to view the punishment of O in the light of the future good that could actually be achieved by punishment. This can take several forms: specific deterrence, incapacitation, general deterrence (including deterrence through public expression of important values), and, possibly, instead or in addition, the reform of O. But her pursuit of future good might also take the form of creating a better society with better educational institutions and less poverty, thus deterring crime *ex ante*. All this remains to be discussed in chapter 6.

V. The Three Roads: The Transition

In short, an Angela who is really angry, seeking to strike back, soon arrives, I claim, at a fork in the road. Three alternatives lie before her. Either she goes down what may be called the *road of status*, seeing the event as all about her and her rank, or she takes the *road of payback* and imagines that the offender's suffering would actually make things better, a thought that doesn't make sense. Or, if she is rational, after exploring and rejecting these two roads, she will notice that a third road is open to her, which is the best of all: she can focus on doing whatever would make sense, in the situation, and be really helpful going forward. This may well include the punishment of O, but in a spirit that is ameliorative and/or deterrent rather than retaliatory.[44]

What is really wrong with the road of status? Many societies do encourage people to think of all injuries as essentially about them and their own relative ranking. Life involves perpetual status-anxiety, and more or less everything that happens either raises one's rank or lowers it. Aristotle's society, as he depicts it, was to a large extent like this, and he was very critical of this tendency, on the grounds that obsessive focus on honor impedes the pursuit of intrinsic goods. The error involved in the first road is not silly or easily dismissed. Still, the tendency to see everything that happens as about oneself and one's own rank seems very narcissistic, and ill suited to a society in which reciprocity and justice are important values. It loses the sense that actions have intrinsic moral worth: that rape is bad because of the suffering it inflicts, and not because of the way it humiliates the friends of the victim. (Remember that we are talking about a *pure* status-injury, not one in which status is an incidental concomitant of some more substantial attribute.) If wrongful injuries were primarily down-rankings, they could be rectified by the humiliation of the offender, and many people, certainly, believe something like this. But isn't this thought a red herring, diverting us from the reality of the victim's pain and trauma, which needs to be constructively addressed? All sorts of bad acts—murder, assault, theft—need to be addressed as the specific acts they are, and their victims (or the victims' families) need constructive attention; none of this will be likely to happen if one thinks of the offense as all about relative status rather than injury and pain.

An apparent exception proves instructive. Discrimination on grounds of race or gender is often imagined as an injury that really does consist in down-ranking, so there is a tendency to think it can be rectified by bringing the injurer low. But this idea is a false lure. What is wanted, as we've already said, is equal respect for human dignity. What is wrong with discrimination is its denial of equality, as well as its many harms to well-being and opportunity. Reversing positions through down-ranking does not create equality. It just substitutes one inequality for another. As we shall see, Dr. King wisely eschewed this way of framing the racial issue.

So the road of status, which makes "payback" intelligible and after a fashion rational, is morally flawed. It converts all injuries into problems of relative position, thus making the world revolve around the desire of vulnerable selves for domination and control. Because this wish is at the heart of infantile narcissism, I think of this as a *narcissistic error*, but we can also ignore that label and just call it the *status error*. If Angela takes the first road, then, her anger makes sense, but she commits a (ubiquitous) moral error.

If Angela chooses the second road, by contrast, the *road of payback*, she does not embrace narrow and defective values; she values things that are really valuable. But she engages in magical thinking, which is normatively objectionable in a different way, since we all want to make sense to ourselves and to be rational. The idea that payback makes sense, counterbalancing the injury, is ubiquitous and very likely evolutionary. Still, what else may make people cling to it? One factor is surely an unwillingness to grieve or to accept helplessness. Most of us are helpless with respect to many things, including the life and safety of those we love. It feels a lot better if we can form a payback project and get busy executing it (suing the bad doctor, depriving one's ex of child custody) than to accept loss and the real condition of helplessness in which life has left us.

Payback, thus, often has a psychic function. If people are culturally sold on the idea that payback is good, they will feel real satisfaction when they get it. Often this satisfaction is called "closure."[45] But of course the fact that a cultural teaching constructs patterns of sentiment that become real should not make us embrace a deception—especially when life will soon disabuse us of our error. Malpractice litigation does not resurrect the dead, nor does a punitive divorce settlement restore love. Indeed, in both cases the payback project likely jeopardizes future happiness rather than advancing it. And even if people feel overwhelming delight when they have retaliated against the aggressor, that pleasure gives us no reason to endorse or make law around such sadistic and malicious preferences.[46] People can learn to feel pleased by many bad things (racial discrimination, domestic violence, child abuse) and by many silly fantasies (the thought that their cat channels the spirit of a beloved ancestor). These pleasures should be neither here nor there when we perform a normative evaluation.

So, if Angela cares about rationality, she will soon see little point in payback, and she will shift, very likely, to the third road, focusing on creating future welfare. This will be so whether she focuses on the particular offense and offender or whether, as often happens, she focuses on the class of similar offenses. For a corollary of taking the third road is likely to be a tendency to focus on the general rather than the particular. If one is thinking about Rebecca and what will really be helpful to her, it is natural to focus not only on therapy for her and specific deterrence, incapacitation, and perhaps reform for her rapist, but also on preventing future offenses of this sort, both for her and for others.

Followers of the road of status, too, can generalize: for people can come to attach status-importance to general causes. A person full of status-focused rage because her child has been raped may form a group to prevent sex offenders from living in neighborhoods where families live, *seeing this cause as a way of lowering the status of sex offenders and raising the status of good people like herself.* How exactly is this symbolic retaliatory "lowering" different from what the person who takes the third road would imagine and attempt? The status-focused person zeroes in on rank and lowering: thus it is very important to her that sex offenders suffer humiliation and that she and her sort are seen as virtuous and good. The non-status-focused person will consider what actually promotes social welfare—and this will lead her, once again, to a different approach to punishment, which may combine deterrence (specific and general) with incapacitation and reform. It all depends on what helps people.[47] It is clear that sex offender registries serve the interests of narcissistic rage. It is much less clear that they serve any of the three goals of punishment that the non-status-focused person prefers. So, even though both become attached to general causes as ways of carrying out their future-directed projects, they will approach these causes in a different spirit, and very likely choose different causes as a result.

The third road, which I recommend, seems, and is, welfarist, and this may be surprising to readers, given my criticisms of some forms of Utilitarianism elsewhere. But the errors that I have elsewhere imputed to Utilitarianism need not be made by the person who takes this road: she does not need to hold that all goods are commensurable; she does not need to ignore the boundaries between persons; and she does not need to deny that some good things are so much more important than others that they should enjoy a special protected status. She can, that is to say, be Mill rather than Bentham (see chapter 6). And welfarist ideas about the correct response to wrongdoing (already supported by Smith and endorsed by Butler independently of the Utilitarians)[48] grew out of a justified critique of a culture suffused with status-consciousness and a virulent payback mentality. The topic of punishment will occupy us in chapter 6, and I describe there the form of welfarism I endorse; for now the idea of promoting social welfare appears in a general form, as the natural outgrowth of Angela's rational deliberation.

I am saying something very radical: that in a sane and not excessively anxious and status-focused person, anger's idea of retribution or payback is a brief dream or cloud, soon dispelled by saner thoughts of personal and social welfare. So anger (if we understand it to involve, internally, a wish for retributive suffering) quickly puts itself out of business, in that even the residual focus on punishing the offender is soon seen as part of a set of projects for improving both offenders and society—and the emotion that has this goal is not so easy to see as anger. It looks more like compassionate hope. When anger does not put itself out of business in this way—and we all know that in a multitude of cases it does not—its persistence and power, I claim, owes much, even perhaps everything, to one of two pernicious errors: either to a fruitless focus on magical ideas of payback, or to an underlying obsession with relative status, which is the only thing that really makes sense of retaliation as ordinarily conceived.

So, to put my radical claim succinctly: when anger makes sense, it is normatively problematic (focused narrowly on status); when it is normatively reasonable (focused on the injury), it doesn't make good sense, and is normatively problematic in that different way. In a rational person, anger, realizing that, soon laughs at itself and goes away. From now on, I shall call this healthy[49] segue into forward-looking thoughts of welfare, and, accordingly, from anger into compassionate hope, the *Transition*.

I have imagined the Transition in personal terms, and these cases remain to be further examined in chapters 4 and 5, where I discuss betrayal and harm in intimate relationships and in the Middle Realm. But to clarify further what I mean by the Transition, let us consider a case in which it takes a political form. For it has often been thought (including by me, in many earlier writings) that anger provides an essential motivation for work to correct social injustice. So let us look carefully at just one case, the sequence of emotions in Martin Luther King, Jr.'s "I have a dream" speech.[50] King begins, indeed, with an Aristotelian summons to anger: he points to the wrongful injuries of racism, which have failed to fulfill the nation's implicit promises of equality. One hundred years after the Emancipation Proclamation, "the life of the Negro is still sadly crippled by the manacles of segregation and the chains of discrimination."

The next move King makes is significant: for instead of demonizing white Americans, or portraying their behavior in terms apt to elicit murderous rage, he calmly compares them to people who have defaulted on a financial obligation: "America has given the Negro people a bad check, a check which has come back marked 'insufficient funds.'" This begins the Transition: for it makes us think ahead in non-retributive ways: the essential question is not how whites can be humiliated, but how can this debt be paid, and in the financial metaphor the thought of humiliating the debtor is not likely to be central. (Indeed it looks counterproductive: for how will such a debtor be in a position to pay?)

The Transition then gets under way in earnest, as King focuses on a future in which all may join together in pursuing justice and honoring obligations: "But we refuse to believe that the bank of justice is bankrupt. We refuse to believe that there are insufficient funds in the great vaults of opportunity of this nation." No mention, again, of torment or pay-back, only of determination to ensure payment of what is owed, at last. King reminds his audience that the moment is urgent, and that there is a danger of rage spilling over: but he repudiates that behavior in advance. "In the process of gaining our rightful place, we must not be guilty of wrongful deeds. Let us not seek to satisfy our thirst for freedom by drink-ing from the cup of bitterness and hatred.... Again and again, we must rise to the majestic heights of meeting physical force with soul force."

So the "payback" is reconceived as the paying of a debt, a process that unites black and white in a quest for freedom and justice. Everyone benefits: as many white people already recognize, "their freedom is inextricably bound to our freedom."

King next repudiates a despair that could lead either to violence or to the abandonment of effort. It is at this point that the most famous section of the speech, "I have a dream," takes flight. And of course, this dream is one not of torment or retributive punishment but of equality, liberty, and brotherhood. In pointed terms, King invites the African-American members of his audience to imagine brotherhood even with their former tormentors:

> I have a dream that one day on the red hills of Georgia, the sons of former slaves and the sons of former slave owners will be able to sit down together at the table of brotherhood.
>
> I have a dream that one day even the state of Mississippi, a state sweltering with the heat of injustice, sweltering with the heat of oppression, will be transformed into an oasis of freedom and justice. . . .
>
> I have a dream that one day, down in Alabama, with its vicious racists, with its governor having his lips dripping with the words "interposition" and "nullification"—one day right there in Alabama little black boys and black girls will be able to join hands with little white boys and white girls as sisters and brothers.

We have only to contrast this speech with the vision of payback in the *Dies Irae* (ch. 3) or the book of Revelation to see the magnitude of King's departure from one standard trajectory of anger in the Christian tradition—albeit following another strand in that same tradition.

There is indeed anger in this speech, initially, and the anger summons up a vision of rectification, which naturally takes, initially, a retributive form. But King gets busy right away reshaping retributivism into work and hope. For how, sanely and really, could injustice be made good by retributive payback? The oppressor's pain and lowering do not make the afflicted free. Only an intelligent and imaginative effort toward justice can do that. This is what I mean by the "Transition," a movement of mind we shall study more fully in subsequent chapters.[51]

We notice something further: once the Transition gets under way, there is no room for a familiar type of forgiveness, which we'll study in chapter 3. The payback mentality often wants groveling. What I call "transactional forgiveness" exacts a performance of contrition and abasement, which can itself function as a type of payback. (Often, too, the payback mentality is combined with a focus on status, in the form of abasement and lowness.) The Transition mentality, by contrast, wants justice and brotherhood. It would do no more good for Governor Wallace to moan and grovel than for him to burn in hell: these things do not produce justice, and they are restorative only in the magical thinking characteristic of anger's initial pre-Transition phase. In the Transition, one comes to see that the real issue is how to produce justice and cooperation. Rituals of forgiveness might possibly be thought useful to this end, and in chapter 7 we shall encounter such arguments. But King has no room for them: he wants reconciliation and shared effort. To these political issues we shall return.

Lest, however, the idea of the Transition should seem too lofty or remote, too connected to the almost saintly figure of King, let me add a more homely example, which shows the Transition embodied in American popular culture and in the conduct of, perhaps surprisingly, an iconic "manly man." In the 1960s TV show *Branded*, Chuck Connors plays such a classic Western figure, Jason McCord—courageous, loyal, yet aloof and alone. In the first episode, he meets a dying man in the desert and saves his life by giving him water and even carrying him on his own horse—only to find himself held up at gunpoint at an oasis, as the duplicitous Colbee takes McCord's horse and leaves him to walk across the desert, very likely to die in the attempt. Colbee explains that he has to do this because he has a wife and two daughters, and so he has to live—and to get to town in time for his daughter's birthday! McCord survives, and meets up with the Colbee family in town. A friend urges him to anger and confrontation. McCord really is angry, and he walks toward Colbee resolutely, as Colbee's two little daughters play around him with their hoops. McCord, looking at the family, then has a second thought; he turns around and walks away. As he does, he says over his shoulder, with a wry smile, "Happy Birthday, Janie."

Here's a very flawed and yet somehow heroic character choosing the general welfare (in the form of the well-being of this family) over anger—after an initial very human period of rage. He is stronger than his anger, and that is part of what makes him a truly heroic man.[52]

Before moving on, however, we must return to Bishop Butler, for he suggests a good role for anger that needs to be pondered. According to Butler, who finds anger pretty appalling, it nonetheless has this value: it expresses our solidarity with wrongs done to other human beings.[53] Human beings have a general desire to see wrongdoers punished. This desire is felt to a higher degree when we, or people we care about, are victims, but it is felt to some degree as a purely general matter. It is a good thing if justice and social order become objects of concern to all of us; so the anger that reacts to a wrongful disruption of that order is highly useful, reinforcing concern and binding human beings in a useful sort of solidarity. I shall shortly make some concessions to this argument, discussing anger's instrumental role. But Butler claims more: he claims that the payback thought itself, and anger including that thought, have normative value, containing the idea of general human concern.

First, we ought to question Butler's empirical claim that human beings have a general desire to see wrongdoers punished that leads them to seek solidarity with the human species as a whole. I've said that the desire for payback probably expresses an innate evolutionary tendency. But Paul Bloom's examination of the desire for payback in young infants does not support Butler: Bloom finds that the payback wish does not link young humans to the human species as a whole. As children develop, a very powerful tendency to care narrowly and to demonize strangers makes moral thinking develop narrowly and unevenly. Most of humanity remains outside the child's circle of concern, and often strangers are seen as harmful and deserving of punishment just because they are strangers.[54]

Even to the extent that Butler is correct, however, what he does not explain is why solidarity is aided by the desire to inflict pain and suffering on the wrongdoer (which he takes to be essential to anger, and it's what he means by punishing). We could agree that the disruption of social order is bad and that the desire to protect people from wrongful damages is good, without buying into the payback idea or thinking, magically, that returning pain for pain achieves anything. Butler's suggestion is free of the status error, but it does not avoid the payback error; indeed, it is simply a high-minded form of the latter. The best form of solidarity with other human beings would surely focus on doing something constructive to promote human welfare, not on a project doomed to incoherence and futility.

This much, however, is right and important: human welfare is served by taking note of wrongful acts and establishing public standards of accountability for them. Truth and accountability promote welfare, by

announcing to all what society takes seriously and what we are committed to protecting. With Butler, then, my argument favors denunciation
and protest when wrongful acts occur—and, after that, whatever policies
can be shown to have a likelihood of discouraging those acts going forward. Victims are right to demand acknowledgment and accountability,
and societies are right to offer it. I discuss this question in chapters 6 and 7.
For now, however, we may turn to an emotion that does appear to contain what Butler wanted from anger, without anger's defects.

VI. Transition-Anger, a Rational Emotion; Anger's Instrumental Roles

There are many ways in which anger can go wrong. The person may
be mistaken about the target: O did not do what Angela thinks he did;
another person, P, was the rapist. The angry person may also go wrong
about the event that is anger's focus: O was there, but did not rape
Rebecca. The person may also be mistaken about the appraisals of value
involved. Aristotle remarks that people often get angry when someone
forgets their name, and this plainly is a confused response. (Either the person has a bizarre view of the importance of names, or she has interpreted
this forgetfulness as a more general slighting of her own importance.)
I discuss such errors in chapter 5.

Often, however, the facts and the relevant appraisals are correct: the
wrongful act occurred, it was intentionally inflicted by the target, and it
inflicted a serious damage. I introduce here a further piece of terminology:
in such cases, anger is "well-grounded." I refuse to call this sort of anger
"justified," because, as I've argued, anger conceptually contains the payback wish, and that is normatively problematic. So "well-grounded"
means that everything but that one part of anger's cognitive content is
well-established.

Even if anger avoids such errors, however, it still founders on the
shoals of payback. It is here that I introduce a major exception to my thesis
that anger always involves, conceptually, a thought of payback. There are
many cases in which one gets standardly angry first, thinking about some
type of payback, and then, in a cooler moment, heads for the Transition.
But there are at least a few cases in which one is there already: the *entire*
content of one's emotion is, "How outrageous! Something must be done
about this." Let us call this emotion *Transition-Anger*, since it is anger, or
quasi-anger, already heading down the third fork in Angela's road. One
might give it some ordinary-language name, such as Jean Hampton's
"indignation,"[55] but I prefer to segment it cleanly from other cases,
since I think a lot of cases we call "indignation" involve some thought

of payback. So I prefer the clearly made-up term. Transition-Anger does not focus on status; nor does it, even briefly, want the suffering of the offender as a type of payback for the injury. It never gets involved at all in that type of magical thinking. It focuses on social welfare from the start. Saying, "Something should be done about this," it commits itself to a search for strategies, but it remains an open question whether the suffering of the offender will be among the most appealing.

Is Transition-Anger a species of anger? I really don't care how we answer this question. Such special borderline cases are rarely handled well by conceptual analysis. It's certainly an emotion: the person is really upset. And it appears distinct, though subtly, from compassionate hope, since the focus is on outrage. The person says, "How outrageous," not "How sad," and entertains forward-looking projects focused on diminishing or preventing wrongful acts. What is important is how rare and exceptional this pure forward-looking emotion is. Angry people very rarely think in this way from the start, not wanting ill to befall the offender, even briefly (except as a means to social welfare, should a dispassionate inquiry show that it is indeed that). It is much more common to get angry first and then head to the Transition, than to be there already, focused on social welfare. The retaliatory instinct is deeply human, no doubt through both evolutionary tendency and cultural reinforcement. It is only exceptional individuals who are there already, in major issues affecting their welfare. Such presence of mind typically requires long self-discipline. Thus, one could imagine that King's own emotion was Transition-Anger, while the emotion constructed in his speech, for his audience, is brief (standard) anger and then a turn to the Transition. In what follows I shall use the special term Transition-Anger when that is what I mean, and if I use the bare word "anger," that is not what I mean: I mean the familiar garden-variety emotion, about whose conceptual content Aristotle and Butler are correct.

Transition-Anger will be very important in thinking about political institutions. But it is not totally absent in daily interactions. One place it often flourishes is in parents' relationships with their young children. Their behavior is often outrageous, and yet parents rarely want payback. They just want things to get better. If they are wise, they choose strategies designed to produce improvement. Garden-variety anger, wishing ill to the offender, is in tension with unconditional love. Transition-Anger is not, because it lacks that wish for ill.

Transition-Anger may also be found when people get angry at a violation of an important principle, or at an unjust system.[56] Not all such anger is Transition-Anger: for the payback wish is subtle, insinuating itself in many places, like the snake in the garden. Sometimes people who say they are angry at a violation of a principle want the violators to suffer in some fashion for what they have done. Sometimes people who get angry at the injustice of a system want to "smash the system," to bring chaos and pain down around the heads of the people who upheld it. If, however, the entire content of the person's anger is "This is outrageous, and how shall things be improved?" or "This is outrageous, and we must commit ourselves to doing things differently," then the anger is indeed Transition-Anger.

To illustrate the subtlety of this distinction, let's focus on a common case: people think that it is outrageous that the rich do not pay more taxes to support the welfare of the poor. They are indignant at a system that seems to them unjust. Let us simply stipulate that their empirical analysis is correct: if the rich pay more taxes, this will indeed help the poor. (Of course it's not obvious that this is true.) And let us grant, as well, what seems obvious: the rich will be upset and pained by such a change if it occurs. Now let us imagine two proponents of this change. P focuses on social welfare. Outraged by injustice, he wants to produce a more just society. He doesn't think that the likely suffering of the rich should stop us from doing what is right, but he doesn't want that suffering. Indeed, to the extent that it might create political resistance to his project, he would rather that there was no such suffering. Q, by contrast, wants the beneficial change, but she also likes the idea of the rich suffering, as a payback or comeuppance for their arrogance and greed. They *deserve* to suffer, she thinks, and the goal of her anger is at least in part the justified (as she sees it) pain of the rich. P's anger is pure Transition-Anger. Q's anger is the usual mixed bag that is garden-variety anger. It might move toward the Transition sooner or later, but it also might not. Unfortunately, real political actors, including voters, are rarely as pure as P.

What good can be said of (garden-variety) anger, in the end? Anger has three possibly useful instrumental roles. First, it may serve as a *signal* that something is amiss. This signal can be of two sorts: it can be a signal to the person herself, who might have been unaware of her value-commitments and their fragility; and it can be a signal to the world, a kind of exclamation point that draws attention to a violation. Since the latter role can be equally well played, and often better played, by a non-angry performance of anger, as chapter 5 argues, I shall focus here on the former role. Anger embodies the idea of significant wrongdoing targeting a person or thing that is of deep concern to the self. While one could have that idea of significant injury without anger—with, and through, grief and compassion—those two emotions do not contain the idea of wrongfulness, which is anger's specific focus. (It is for that reason that Butler, for all his animadversions against the passion, attempts to defend its social utility, with the mixed results that we have seen.) Nor, importantly, do those two emotions contain the thought that something needs to be done, which, as I've argued, is a conceptual part of anger, though usually in the defective form of the payback thought. The experience of anger can make a previously unaware person aware of her values and the way in which another's wrongful act can violate them. For example, a person who is in a hierarchical relationship may not realize how unfairly she is being treated, until she has an experience, or repeated experiences, of anger. If the experience helps her to decide to protest, or in some other way to improve her situation, then it is useful.

The signal anger sends is pretty misleading, since it embodies an idea of payback or retribution that is primitive, and that makes no sense apart from magical thinking or narcissistic error. So it is a false lead to that extent, and the angry person is always well advised to begin moving beyond anger as soon as possible, in the direction of the Transition. Still, it can be a useful wake-up call.

We see this in King's speech (addressed to a public some of whose members might have been incompletely aware of the ills of racial oppression): he does indeed encourage anger at the behavior of white America, acknowledging the magnitude of the wrongs done and the way in which they affect everyone's well-being. But then he immediately turns his audience away from the payback thought that inevitably surfaces, toward a different picture of the future. Managed by such a skillful entrepreneur, anger can be useful, and King always conceived of his project as active and militant, pitted against complacency. Perhaps it's even more useful in cases where the wrongdoing might have slid along barely noticed, beneath the surface of daily life, and only the emotion directs the person's attention to its presence.

Closely linked with the idea of anger as signal is the idea of anger as *motivation*. The Greek Stoics were often charged with robbing society of motives to pursue justice by their insistence that anger is always mistaken. They responded that people can be moved by principles, without the emotion, and that such principle-based motivations are more reliable than anger, which is likely to run amok.[57] In their own terms, their reply was unsuccessful: for they actually believed that injuries other people can inflict are not serious wrongs, so they really had no resources for addressing them, or motivating others to do so. The Stoics would have held that the values expressed in King's speech are altogether erroneous; but then they are bound to hold that his protreptic to pursue justice is also inappropriate.

Things are otherwise with my own critique. In my view, anger is often appropriate enough with respect to its underlying values, and the love and grief that focus on these same values are often fully appropriate; the problem comes with the idea of payback. That idea is, I argued, a conceptual part of anger (except in the rare borderline case of Transition-Anger), and no doubt it is part of what motivates people, at least initially. The intensity of the emotion and perhaps, too, its magical fantasy of retribution are part of what get people going, when otherwise at least some people might simply fail to act (or, without anger's signal, even fail to notice the wrongdoing or its magnitude). Love is not always enough, though often it is. But once they get going, they had better not follow anger's lure all the way to fantasized retribution. It does not make sense, unless one errs in a different way, focusing disproportionately on status-injury.

Returning to King's example, one might imagine a future of payback, in which African-Americans would attain power and inflict retributive pain and humbling on white Americans. Society abounded with such ideas, despite the fact that payback of that type would have made things no better and a lot worse. King's altogether superior stance was that the Transition is only a heartbeat away, since only cooperation will really solve the nation's problems. Still, anger was a useful motivational step along the road—for a very brief time, and carefully managed. I do not believe that anger is necessary as a motivation to pursue justice, but I still believe it can often be useful, a part, probably, of our evolutionary equipment that usefully energizes us toward good ends—unless things go astray, as they so often do.[58]

Non-anger, however, does not entail nonviolence. We shall investigate this issue in chapter 7, but I note here that, despite Gandhi's strictures against violence, both King and Mandela more convincingly argue that violence in self-defense is justified, and indeed (in Mandela's case) that violent tactics may prove instrumentally necessary even without a self-defense context. Nonetheless, as we shall see, both King and Mandela insisted that violence be wielded in a spirit of non-anger, and with Transition thoughts of future cooperation.

Finally, anger may be a *deterrent*. People who are known to get angry often thereby deter others from infringing on their rights.[59] Here one can only say that the way anger deters is not likely to lead to a future of stability or peace; instead, it is all too likely to lead to a more devious aggression. And there are many ways of deterring wrongdoing, some of which are much more attractive than inspiring fear of an explosion.

Anger, in short, has a very limited but real utility, which derives, very likely, from its evolutionary role as a "fight-or-flight" mechanism. We may retain this limited role for anger while insisting that its payback fantasy is profoundly misleading and that to the extent that it makes sense it does so against the background of diseased values. The emotion, in consequence, is highly likely to lead us astray.

But isn't anger an irreplaceable avenue of expression for people who are not especially verbal and conceptual?[60] It might be objected that my proposal sounds all too much like that of the upper-middle-class (ex)-WASP academic that I certainly am, schooled from childhood to "use your words," and discouraged from strong direct emotional expression. I simply deny the charge. First of all, my proposal is not Stoic. As we'll see, it does not discourage the experience or strong expression of grief, compassion, and a host of other emotions. But in any case it seems just wrong to portray lower-class or less educated people as inexpressive or crude, lacking avenues of communication that do not involve lashing out. The music and art of poor people through the ages, in many cultures of the world, is astonishingly expressive of a wide range of emotions. At the same time, in my experience it is people with an overweening sense of their own privilege who seem particularly prone to angry displays. In my gym, I will avoid mildly asking another member if I can work in on a piece of equipment, fearing an explosion, to the extent that I observe that this person is privileged, youngish, and male. On the road, it is drivers of expensive SUVs who tend, again in my anecdotal experience, to behave as if they owned the road. So I think the objector asks a good question, but one to which there is a good reply.

The tendency to anger and retaliation is deeply rooted in human psychology. Believers in a providential deity, like Bishop Butler, find this fact difficult to explain, given its irrationality and destructiveness.[61] For those who do not share Butler's framework, however, it is much less difficult to understand. Anger brings some benefits that may have been valuable at one stage in human prehistory. Even today, vestiges of its useful role remain. But beneficent forward-looking systems of justice have to a great extent made this emotion unnecessary, and we are free to attend to its irrationality and destructiveness.

VII. The Anger of God

If anger is so compromised, why has it standardly been imputed to God or gods, who are supposed to be images of perfection? The first thing to say is that it has not, in fact, always been so imputed. Buddhism is non-theistic, but the most perfected humans, bodhisattvas, are free from anger. Hindu texts emphasize that anger is a disease that a pious person should strive to avoid.[62] In both Epicurean and Stoic thought, the gods lie outside the mistakenly competitive and status-obsessed societies that spawn destructive angers. As Lucretius says of the gods, "Needing nothing from us, they are not ensnared by (our) grateful offerings, nor are they touched by anger."[63] In Greco-Roman religion the gods are not ideals for mortals at all, just flawed beings with outsized powers, so Lucretius is basically saying that this is what a truly perfect being would be like.

This idea of a god's impassivity is the mainstream one in Hellenistic and post-Hellenistic Greco-Roman thought.[64]

Indeed, it is virtually only in the Judeo-Christian tradition that we find the idea that God is both exemplary and angry. The Christian author Lactantius (240–320), advisor to Constantine, the first Christian emperor, wrote a work entitled *On the Anger of God* (*De Ira Dei*), in which he attacks both Epicureans and Stoics, saying that there is no reason to worship a God who doesn't need our attention and love, and doesn't get angry when it is withdrawn. Moreover, he continues, if God never gets angry we don't need to fear God, and that would do away with all religion. Such arguments do not address the Epicurean and Stoic contention that a perfect being would not have anger; they simply amount to the claim that religion as we know it requires the idea of an angry God.[65]

But key texts in both Christianity and Judaism are inconsistent and complicated on the topic of God's anger.[66] For the most part, the Jewish God is imagined as a "jealous" God who wants to be ranked number one in the attentions and affections of the Jewish people, who have other options for their worship. Repeatedly, the relationship is compared to a marriage. There are other men, and a bad wife will allow herself to be lured away from her husband by the money and power of these rivals, forgetting to put her husband in an exclusive first place; so too God wants to be in an exclusive first place vis-à-vis the other gods, who are trying to lure the Jewish people away.[67] Indeed, the text is suffused with very standard payback thoughts about the status-injury that either the other gods or the unfaithful people inflict upon God, and the gruesome comeuppance they will soon get. Those other gods and the *goyim* who follow them will get countless plagues and diseases, and the unfaithful people themselves will be tormented or even destroyed. All of this will constitute a lowering or humbling of these people or peoples, by comparison to God.

This is the status-focused thinking so common in anger, but with this difference: that God can make all these things happen. (And notice that, God being God, God cannot really be personally injured by a human act, *except with respect to status*. God cannot be murdered, or assaulted, or raped. So, insofar as God is angry, this anger is extremely likely to be status-focused anger.)

There are, however, times when God focuses more purely on the intrinsic wrongfulness of harmful acts—particularly, but not only, in the prophetic books, and especially in their discussions of greed and the ill-treatment of strangers. These offenses are taken to be wrongful in themselves, not only as offenses against the status of God. In such cases, God is angry not because of a status-injury, but because what humans do and suffer is of deep and intrinsic concern to God. Lactantius observes that when God gets angry at wrongful acts of humans to one another, this is a way of showing concern for the good and just, and promoting their interests. He makes two distinct points: first, that punishment as a result of God's anger incapacitates wrongdoers, thus clearing the way for the good and just; and, second, that the fear of divine punishment deters wrongdoers, thus keeping the world safer for the good and just.[68]

We can see that Lactantius—correctly summarizing one prominent strand in the biblical portrait of divine anger—becomes a proto-Utilitarian, thinking of the role of anger in forward-looking welfarist terms. We can agree that anger is sometimes a useful deterrent, and that punishment can promote welfare by incapacitating—although it is not so clear why anger is required, as opposed to well-designed institutions. At any rate, this picture of God's anger is quite different from the status-focused picture that Lactantius presented earlier (correctly summarizing other biblical texts). And we can see that this sort of benevolent anger is more likely than the other sort to move in the direction of the Transition. Thus, although payback of all sorts is imagined even in what we might call welfarist contexts, the texts frequently move, rather quickly, to an imagined future of peace, cooperation, and reconciliation, and God urges humans to make this future happen.

In short, the Jewish God's anger has all the varieties and complexities of human anger, and all the same problems and prospects.

When we move to Jesus we have the daunting problem already explored in our previous chapter: the texts give dramatically different pictures of Jesus' attitude to erring mortals. Certainly many texts in the New Testament embody terrible payback wishes. The book of Revelation, for example, jolts uneasily from thoughts of the vindication of the meek and mild to the most gruesome fantasies of destruction visited on those who don't acknowledge the new religion. But what about the Jesus of the Gospels? It has long been observed—and was compellingly argued by Augustine in *The City of God*—that the emotions of Jesus are genuine emotions, embodying all the vulnerability of a mortal human being for whom pain and loss matter terribly. Thus Jesus was not a good Stoic. Augustine, however, focuses on grief and joy, and a human being may have those without anger. So, does Jesus get angry? One key text, unfortunately, contains a textual crux at precisely this point. At Matthew 5:22, Jesus says, "I say to you that every person who gets angry at a brother is liable to judgment." But some manuscripts add the word "randomly" (*eikēi*) at this point, making Jesus condemn only ungrounded anger.[69] And Jesus displays anger at least once, in the well-known scene in which he throws the moneychangers out of the temple. Even this, however, is not decisive.

A remarkable account of this passage is offered by the Utku Eskimo people studied in Jean Briggs's *Never in Anger*, one of the most compelling works of descriptive anthropology in the twentieth century.[70] The Utku believe that anger is always childish, and a threat to the intense cooperation required for group survival in a very adverse climate. Although anger in children is tolerated and even indulged, both the experience of anger and its outward manifestation are viewed as extremely inappropriate in adults. Briggs was searching for a way of finding out whether they disapproved of the emotion itself or only its outward expression; so, given that they were devout Christians, she asked them about the money-changing scene. It was clear that the incident disturbed them. As good Christians, they felt that they had to endorse Jesus' behavior; but it did not fit with their picture of adult good character. They adopted an ingenious solution. Jesus, the Utku chieftain told her, did scold the moneychangers, but not out of real anger: he did it "only once," in order to improve them, because they were being "very bad, *very bad*, and refusing to listen to him."[71] Their picture of Jesus as moral ideal was incompatible with ascribing real anger to him—although, notice, they allowed the idealized Jesus to use anger-behavior as a wake-up call.

Were the Utku imagining our idea of Transition-Anger and distinguishing it from (garden-variety) anger? I think it's more likely that they are thinking of Jesus as giving a performance without having any emotion in the anger family—a possibility that is open to those who want to deter without risking going down a wrong path. (We'll investigate this idea in chapter 5.)

Biblical texts are written for people many of whom need simple messages. The idea of an angry God may, in such cases, be not only a useful internal signal of where wrongdoing is located and a deterrent to wrongdoing, but also a useful source of motivation to correct social problems (imitating God in intensity of concern). Still, the potential for distortion is huge, when God and his anger are considered a moral ideal for humans. Therefore the texts that depict a brief anger leading to a constructive Transition are definitely to be preferred, as is the Utku's sage interpretation of Jesus.

VIII. Anger and Gender

Americans are inclined to associate anger with male gender norms. From athletes to politicians, males who do not display anger at an affront are denigrated and thought weak. A famous example took place during the presidential campaign of 1988. In one of the televised debates, Democratic candidate Michael Dukakis was asked, "Governor, if Kitty Dukakis [his wife] were raped and murdered, would you favor an irrevocable death penalty for the killer?" Dukakis replied, "No, I don't, and I think you know that I've opposed the death penalty during all of my life."[72] Dukakis was already under fire for his prison-furlough program, which famously led to the temporary release of convicted murderer Willie Horton, who committed a rape and assault while on furlough. Dukakis's lack of passionate anger in his response to the question about his wife reinforced a public perception that he was unmanly. (His relatively short stature, probably five feet, six inches, did not help.) The manly man would display controlled and yet palpable rage, and would affirm a desire for payback in the form of capital punishment.

In keeping with this norm, little boys in America are often encouraged and not criticized when they manifest anger, whereas little girls are taught compassion and empathy.[73] Even in infancy, children's emotions are labeled in accordance with their believed gender.[74] Thus, the crying of a baby labeled female is typically interpreted as fear, while the crying of a baby labeled male is typically interpreted as assertive anger. Babies are also held and played with differently, in accordance with their perceived gender, "girls" being cuddled and sheltered, "boys" being bounced in the air and treated as active. It is thus no wonder that many adults follow these cultural scripts. It is surprising, indeed, that there are so many dissenters. And yet, even in the Wild West, one finds heroes (like Jason McCord) who forgo revenge.[75]

These gender norms, which connect anger to power and authority, womanly non-anger to weakness and dependency, make many women think that they need to school themselves in anger to right the balance and assume their full equality as agents. The female defender of non-anger is put on the defensive, as if she were defending foot-binding or corsets.

It is with great interest, then, that the defender of non-anger turns to ancient Greece and Rome, where gender norms operated very differently.[76] These cultures do not go all the way to an Utku, or Stoic, commitment to non-anger. But many of their members do accept the full Stoic position that anger is never appropriate; and even dissenters are likely to view retributive anger as a danger and a disease, and a propensity to anger a corrigible flaw.[77] Not surprisingly, gender norms follow general norms: males are understood to be rational beings who are capable of restraining their rage and rising above it, perhaps utterly getting rid of it. Females are taken to be inferior creatures who indulge in the doomed and fruitless projects of retributive payback, with great harm to both self and others. Indeed, the position for which I argue here, describing it as "radical," is not at all radical in Greece and Rome, and anger's futility and childishness is well understood. So males, who are understood to be (normatively) adults and reasonable, are pretty non-angry (normatively, at least), and females, paltry and childish, show by their addiction to anger how silly and dangerous it is.

These cultural differences show us that however hardwired a tendency to anger may be, social norms play a large part in giving people instructions about how to cultivate themselves. If anger is seen as childish and weak, that does not mean it will disappear; but people who aspire to dignity and rationality try to avoid its call.

An insightful point about gender is repeatedly made in the Greco-Roman texts. Anger is conceptually linked to helplessness. One reason why women so often turn out to be the angry ones is that they are disproportionately unable to control the things they need and want to control. Thus there are far more openings for injury, and more temptations to seize upon revenge as an imagined restoration of lost control. Medea, whose anger we'll discuss in chapter 4, is a paradigm of helplessness run amok. Alien, jilted wife, with no rights over her own children, she loses everything in one betrayal. Her outsize zeal for payback is related to the size of her loss, as she attempts to substitute retaliation for mourning. Her story tells us that even where norms do not encourage female anger, asymmetrical female helplessness may breed it; and I believe this is true. The extent to which an American woman will focus obsessively on payback in divorce litigation, for example, may often be proportional to her lack of other avenues for moving into a productive future, such as a career and confidence in her own talents. This sort of anger, however, is hardly a sign of womanly dignity and strength.

Medea's story also suggests that where we encounter outsize male anger, we ought to ask whether helplessness lurks somewhere in the background. American males are certainly privileged by contrast to females: but they are by no means secure. What they are expected to control, on pain of dishonor, is so vast. They must be high achievers, big earners, fit bodies. And they must always focus on status relative to other males. The competitive struggle is exhausting, and almost never winnable. Shame is the almost inevitable result, and shame can feed anger.[78]

All human infants are to some degree narcissistic, inclined to think that they ought to be omnipotent. Deeper even than gender is the phenomenon of human helplessness combined with the expectation of control. The very status of human infancy—cognitively very competent, physically totally powerless—is a cauldron of anger. So both genders can be expected to have many occasions for anger, which gender norms vary and inflect but do not remove. One way cultures affect anger in male and female is by the creation of normative emotion-scripts. Another way, however, is by the differential manipulation of helplessness: what does each gender think it ought to control, and how reliable is its access to that control? The apostle of non-anger can learn from this. One thing that needs to be done is to write new scripts for both males and females, in which anger appears as weak and childish, non-anger, and allies such as interdependence and reciprocity, as strong. (To some extent at least, the Greeks and Romans did this.) But another, very different thing that needs to be done is to give people access to the things they rightly value and protect those things from damage.

IX. Anger and Other "Reactive Attitudes": Gratitude, Grief, Disgust, Hatred, Contempt, Envy

Because it has become common to treat anger as one of a long list of "reactive attitudes," without much attention to finer points of difference among them, the next step in our clarification of anger must be to distinguish it from its relatives. As we have seen, anger[79] involves a belief that the target's act has wrongfully inflicted damage on something within one's circle of concern. I've argued that it also includes a wish for the doer to suffer, somehow.

The first relative we must consider is anger's first cousin, gratitude. The two emotions are typically held closely together in philosophical discussions, from the Greek Epicureans and Stoics through to Spinoza, and beyond. Gratitude, like anger, has both a target (a person) and a focus (an act): it is a pleasant emotion responding to the apparently intentional beneficent act of someone else, which is believed to have affected one's well-being in a significant way. Gratitude is typically taken to contain a wish to benefit the other party in return, so it is often classified, along with anger, as a retributive emotion. It seems to point backward, and it seems to treat the beneficent wish as a sort of payback wish. One might then wonder whether anyone who criticizes anger as I have been doing is bound in consistency to repudiate gratitude. So thought the Epicureans, imagining the rational gods as free of both emotions.

I address this question in detail in my chapters on intimate relationships and on the "Middle Realm," coming to slightly different conclusions in the two cases about the normative propriety of gratitude. But we can make three preliminary observations. First, the primary reason for the repudiation of gratitude by philosophers from Epicurus and the Stoics to Spinoza is not its payback idea: it is, rather, that (according to these thinkers) gratitude and anger both betray an unhealthy need for the "goods of fortune," which we cannot really control. But I do not accept that Stoic position, since I hold that it is right to care deeply about at least some people and things outside oneself, whose actions one cannot control. The second point to make is that gratitude wishes for good and anger for ill, and this creates a strong asymmetry between the two emotions. One may think that special scrutiny is needed for an emotion that purposes ill, without being so vigilant and censorious about the wish for good, given that beneficence is usually too scarce in all our lives. Third, gratitude, though in a way retrospective, is often part of a system of reciprocity that has important forward-looking aspects, and which, as a whole, contributes to welfare. Anger's ongoing system, in the pre-Eumenides world of Aeschylus, did not create welfare; instead, it tied unwilling present-day people to a past that disserved their interests. Thus, although gratitude and anger are cousins in a sense, there are significant asymmetries that may be used to justify differential assessment.

Although *grief* is not standardly classified as a reactive attitude, it is so close to anger that we need to begin by commenting on its differences. Grief, like anger, focuses on a damage to the self (or the self's circle of concern). This loss is painful, and that pain is a key similarity between the two emotions. Grief, however, focuses on an event—which may be an act done by a person, but may also be a natural event, such as death or a disaster in nature. And its focus is on the *loss* brought about by this event. Even if the event is thought to be caused by a person, the loss, not the perpetrator, remains its focus: it does not take the person as its target. If there is a target at all, it is the person who has died or departed. Nor is the idea of wrongfulness central to grief, since loss is loss whether or not wrongfully inflicted. For all these reasons, the action-tendency of grief is quite different from that of anger: grief seeks restoration of or substitution for that which was lost, whereas anger typically wants to do something to or about the perpetrator. Grief addresses the hole or gap in the self, anger the wrongful infliction of that damage by the target.

Grief and anger may of course be co-present; at times it may be difficult to separate them. Often a grieving person tries to blame someone for the loss, even when blame is not warranted, as a way of regaining control or asserting dignity in a situation of helplessness. Indeed, the turn to anger may function psychically as a way of restoring the lost person or object. In such cases, grief can be deflected into an unusual intense anger, in which all the energy of love and loss is turned toward persecution, as in the mania for malpractice litigation in American health care, or as in my Michael Jordan example, where the TV commentator suggested to Jordan that the death penalty might somehow functionally replace Jordan's lost father and Jordan, rightly, rejected that suggestion, preferring to acknowledge his loss. One source of excess in anger, in fact, is a reluctance to grieve, thus acknowledging helplessness. The distinction between grief and anger therefore deserves the greatest possible attention, and we shall return to this theme in the following chapters. The laborious transactions of forgiveness often substitute for the helplessness of mourning.

But isn't grief itself tarnished by my critique of anger? Doesn't it wish to change the past, and isn't it to that extent objectionable? I believe the answer is no, though the question is important.[80] The fantasy of restoration that often accompanies grief is irrational if it persists and organizes large stretches of the person's life. But deep pangs of longing for the lost are ways of registering the immense importance of that lost person, and thus important ways of making wholeness and sense out of the narrative of one's life. Moving on without grief means having a disjointed or patchwork life, and so the most important reason for grieving is forward-looking: it draws attention to a very important commitment that should remain embedded in the narrative understanding that a person has of her own life, and communicates to others. It expresses a deep aspect of who that person is.

Anger is also distinct from four other "negative emotions" that focus on other people: disgust, hatred, contempt, and envy. All of these emotions, unlike anger, focus on relatively permanent traits of the person, rather than an act. (To recall my terminology: the *target* of anger is a person, but its *focus* is a wrongful act. In these other cases, the target is a person, and the focus is a more or less enduring trait of the person.) So they immediately raise a question that anger in and of itself does not raise: is it ever appropriate to have strong negative emotions toward a person's enduring traits? As we shall see, all three of these emotions are initially easy to distinguish from anger—but the distinction becomes blurred when anger is of the status-focused type.

Disgust is a strong aversion to aspects of the body that are seen as "animal reminders"—that is, aspects of ourselves that remind us that we are mortal and animal. Its primary objects are feces and other bodily fluids, as well as decay (especially the corpse), and animals or insects that are oozy, slimy, smelly, or in other ways reminiscent of the repudiated bodily fluids.[81] The core idea in disgust is that of (potential) contamination through contact or ingestion: if I take in what is base, that debases me. In a secondary phase, disgust properties are projected onto groups of humans who do not really have those properties: racial, sexual, religious, or caste minorities are portrayed as hyperanimal or hyperbodily, and are then said to be contaminants on the grounds that they are (allegedly) smelly, germy, etc. Societies then devise remarkable rituals of contamination-avoidance, policing the boundary between the dominant group and the animal by refusing to share food, swimming pools, drinking fountains, or sexual relations with those who are cast as surrogate animals.

So disgust and anger both involve strongly aversive tendencies directed at a target. Disgust does not exactly involve the idea
of a wrongful act, but blame often creeps in: the contaminating person or group is resented for daring to claim space, or to contact the
self-insulating person or group. Even when disgust and anger move
close to one another in this way, however, disgust is fantasy-ridden
through and through, in a way that anger is not. Anger can often be
well-grounded, by which term I mean that all of its elements are correct apart from the wish for payback. There really was a wrongful act,
the perpetrator really did that act, and it is as important as the angry
person thinks it is. Disgust, by contrast, involves fantasy from the get-
go: its core idea is, "If I avoid contact with these animal reminders
I will protect myself from being/becoming animal." This is of course
nonsense, though a type of nonsense that has been very important to
people in many times and places. Disgust is thus suspect as a whole
category in a way that anger need not be: it centrally involves false
beliefs ("I am not an animal," "I do not excrete and smell," "Only *those*
people have smelly animal bodies"). Anger may involve true beliefs—
up to the point of the payback idea.

Because disgust focuses on the person rather than a bad act, its
action-tendency is also different from that of anger: the disgusted person
seeks separation, rather than retaliation or retribution—although separation may at times involve great harshness and coercion (such as that of
the apartheid and Jim Crow regimes), thus bleeding into the harshness of
the penal institutions associated with anger.

Despite these differences, disgust and anger have a great deal in
common—when anger is of the status-focused type. Anger heading
toward the Transition (rational anger, we might call it) focuses on a bad
act and seeks rectification in a way that promotes social good. Status-
focused anger, by contrast, reacts to a "down-ranking" or ego-injury
and seeks to diminish or lower the (alleged) perpetrator—*not*, note, the
perpetrator's deed—in order to right the balance. This common type of
anger lies close to disgust. It sees the other person as a malefactor, rather
than a slimy roach or beetle, but insofar as it wishes the "down-ranking"
of the other, it often involves representing the other as low or base; thus
its focus imperceptibly shifts from act to person. Thus projective disgust
and anger become very difficult to disentangle. On the one hand, disgust,
though directed at the person, is often triggered by allegedly wrongful
acts: sodomy is a triggering proxy for what some people find disgusting
about gay men.[82] On the other hand, insofar as anger seeks lowering, it
often slides over into a more general down-ranking of relatively stable
personal traits, rather than a temporary down-ranking of a person on
the basis of the wrongful act. (Criminals become a despised subgroup

and targets for disgust.) Thus the distinction between disgust and anger, which initially seems clear, turns out to be not clear at all—when the anger in question is of the status-focused sort.

Hatred is another negative emotion that focuses on the entirety of the person, rather than a single act. Although anger is directed at a person, its focus is an act, and when the act is disposed of somehow, anger could be expected to go away. Hatred, by contrast, is global, and if acts are involved it is simply because everything about the person is seen in a negative light. As Aristotle remarks, the only thing that will really satisfy hatred is that the person cease to exist (1382a15). If we think that hatred— an intensely negative attitude to the entire being of another person—is always a bad emotion to have, we are not required to think this about anger, which is fully compatible with liking or even loving the person.

Once again, however, things are not so easy. Transition-Anger has virtually nothing in common with hatred: it looks forward to good for all. The anger of a person who undergoes the Transition, focused on an act and aiming at social good, is also easy to distinguish from hatred. The person wants wrongdoing to cease, but may continue to love the person and wish her well. The minute the payback wish gets into the picture, however, things are more complicated: wanting payback looks like a kind of hatred of the person, since it clearly is not a constructive reparative act.[83] And if the person chooses the road of status, the distinction is blurred there too: she seeks to lower or humiliate the person, and that project easily segues into a negative attitude toward that person, not just a deed. People who want to lower others typically want the lowering to last.

Contempt is another "reactive attitude" that is frequently associated with anger. At the outset, once again, the two emotions seem very different. Contempt is an attitude that views another person as low or base, usually on account of some enduring trait or traits for which the person is taken to be blameworthy.[84] It presents "its object as low in the sense of ranking low in worth as a person in virtue of falling short of some legitimate interpersonal ideal of the person."[85] Of course the ideal may or may not be really legitimate, and the person may or may not really fall short of it. In many cases, contempt is not addressed to failings of ethical character, but, instead, to lack of social standing, or wealth, or position. Thus the imputation of blameworthiness (which distinguishes contempt from condescending pity) is often mistaken: people often blame the poor for their poverty, thinking it a sign of laziness, and have contempt for them on that account. But it seems right to say that contempt usually involves the thought, right or wrong, that the person is somehow to blame for the characteristics that are contempt's focus—even if they are just forms of weakness for which people are actually not responsible.

Contempt is thus like anger in having both a focus and a target: its focus is a trait or traits, and its target is the person seen as low because of those traits. In both cases, the target is a person. But the focus of anger is an act, that of contempt a relatively stable trait or traits.

We may leave to one side the interesting question whether contempt for another person is ever morally justified.[86] (One significant issue is that contempt frequently underestimates human fragility and the difficulty of developing good traits in an imperfect world.) What we can now observe is that, with contempt as with anger, distinguishing the two emotions is easy when we are dealing with Transition-Anger or anger leading toward the Transition. In both of these cases anger has nothing to do with a low ranking of the person, remains focused on the act, and ultimately seeks future good. It is also relatively easy to distinguish contempt from anger that takes the road of payback, since contempt lacks a payback idea, and seems to have no associated action tendency. (Thus there could be a sort of character-anger that would treat the person's whole self-formation as a wrongful act, but it would remain different from contempt.)

The distinction is far less easy when we consider status-focused anger, which seeks the down-ranking of a person in retaliation for the down-ranking inflicted on the self by an act. Still, there is an interesting difference of dynamic. In contempt, the starting point is the alleged low-ness of the person: the person is thought to lack some good characteristic, whether moral or social. The negative attitude responds to the perception of lowness. With status-focused anger, by contrast, the negative attitude responds to something about oneself—the lowering allegedly inflicted by the act on which anger focuses—and then the emotion seeks to put the emotion's target, a person, into a low position. Indeed, the person is not initially thought to be low at all, but powerful and capable of inflicting damage. So the two emotions end up in the same place, so to speak, but through a very different dynamic.

Envy and its close relative *jealousy* resemble anger in being negative emotions directed at a person or persons.[87] Envy is a painful emotion that focuses on the good fortune or advantages of others, comparing one's own situation unfavorably to theirs. It involves a rival, and a good or goods appraised as important; the envier is pained because the rival possesses those good things and she does not. As with anger, the good things must be seen as important not in some abstract or detached way, but for the self and the self's core sense of well-being.[88] Although envy, unlike anger, does not involve the idea of a wrongful act, it typically involves some type of hostility toward the fortunate rival: the envier wants what the rival has, and feels ill will toward the rival in consequence. If the advantages are thought to have been unfairly gained, envy and anger draw very close, and envy may engender similar payback thoughts, similarly unhelpful. As with anger, it is only where the focus of envy is on relative position alone, not any more tangible advantages, that the payback can actually improve the envier's situation: and that narrow focus has normative problems similar to those involved in anger. A focus on relative position is extremely common in envy. Indeed, two psychologists who have produced a fine systematic study of the emotion end up defining it in terms of positional goods: "The object of envy is 'superiority,' or 'non-inferiority' to a reference group or individual."[89]

Jealousy is similar to envy: both involve hostility toward a rival with respect to the possession or enjoyment of a valued good. Jealousy, however, is typically about the fear of a specific loss (usually, though not always, a loss of personal attention or love), and thus about protection of the most cherished goods and relationships of the self. Its focus is on the rival, seen as a potential threat to the self. Although there may be as yet no (known) wrongful act, jealousy can easily shade over into anger at the rival for (allegedly) intending such an act. Payback wishes and actions are a common result. Unlike envy, jealousy is rarely about relative position alone: it typically stays focused on important goods, and that is why it is so difficult to satisfy, since security with respect to important goods is almost never available.[90]

This brief exploration informs us that anger is a distinct emotion, but difficult to distinguish from quite a few others—especially when it takes what I have called the *road of status*. Anger does have something going for it: it can be what I've called *well-grounded*, as disgust cannot. But its characteristic payback wish (which it shares with envy and jealousy, but not with grief) is deeply problematic. We need to keep our eye on these fine distinctions as we move forward.

X. Anger's Gatekeeper: The Gentle Temper

How might someone become less prone to the errors of payback fantasy and/or status-obsession, and more prone to make the Transition? Adam Smith offers one very useful proposal, and Aristotle's discussions of anger and the associated virtue of "gentleness of temper" offer two more.[91] All three are variants of the idea that avoiding anger requires becoming less wrapped up in the narcissistic wounds of the ego.

In general, Smith's procedure is to figure out the proper degree of any passion by imagining the response of a "judicious spectator," who is not personally involved in the events. This device, he says, is particularly needed in the case of anger, which more than most emotions "must always be brought down to a pitch much lower than that to which undisciplined nature would raise them."[92] The spectator, he argues, will still feel anger when he contemplates injuries done to another person. But his anger will be tempered, first by his distance and non-involvement—and second, interestingly, because he has to consider the situation of the person against whom anger is directed, and this thought of the other will block demands for revenge.

In other words, when we move outside of narcissistic self-involvement, we are aided in two ways: first, we don't have the bias inherent in thinking that it's all "about me," and, second, we have to consider everyone's welfare, not just that of the wronged party. Smith's judicious spectator is thus a device that promotes the Transition from excessive ego-involvement to general social concern. It is an imperfect such device: as we saw, people can become ego-invested in their friends' suffering, or even in general causes. But Smith has the right idea: as a proto-Utilitarian, he moves from concern for the ranking of the fragile self toward more general and constructive social concern.

Aristotle makes a complementary suggestion: we avoid inappropriate anger through positional thinking, assuming the point of view of the person who has offended us. Aristotle does not share my view that garden-variety anger is always normatively inappropriate. But he does think that error falls far more often on the side of too much / too often rather than too little. Therefore, he gives the virtuous disposition a name that suggests extremely little anger: "gentleness" (*praotēs*, 1125b26–29).[93] The hallmark of *praotēs* is good reasons: The gentle-tempered person "is typically undisturbed and is not led by passion except as reason dictates" (1125b33–35). Nor is he afraid to incur disapproval on that account: "He gives the appearance of going wrong in the direction of deficiency: for the gentle-tempered person is not vengeful, but inclined to sympathetic understanding (*suggnōmē*)" (1126a1–3).[94]

What Aristotle says, then, is a person who sees things from the point of view of others, understanding what they experience, is unlikely to desire payback. What is the connection? First of all, this sort of mental displacement can weed out some errors about blame: we may be able to see that the person was negligent or even just mistaken, rather than fully culpable.[95] We may also be able to appreciate mitigating factors such as duress of various types, or the pressure of conflicting obligations. Such discoveries might block anger from forming altogether. This point connects to Aristotle's observation about good reasons: participatory imagining helps us figure out which reasons are and are not good, and how strong they really are.

But even if anger turns out to be grounded in true facts, taking the time to see things from the other person's viewpoint can potentially block or counteract the two errors we have discovered in anger. First, it makes us think hard about payback and what it can and cannot achieve.

Thinking of the other person getting retributively clobbered makes us wonder whether that really does anyone any good, and we may well start to see the error in this familiar type of magical thinking. Second, displacement also counteracts the narcissistic tendency to focus on one's own status, thus aiding the Transition. Sympathy steers anger in the direction of a balanced focus on harm and correction of harm, rather than on personal down-ranking, with its connection to revenge. Retribution is made a lot easier by a mindset that sees the other person as a mere obstacle to one's own status, a thing. Sympathetic understanding already steers thought in the direction of general social good.

And while we are heading there, we might note, sympathetic understanding makes it a lot easier to get there. When you can understand your adversaries, you are much more likely to be capable of devising constructive projects that include them—an issue I'll discuss in chapter 7 in relation to the career of Nelson Mandela.

Aristotle's other valuable insight concerns the importance of a light-hearted and playful temper. In the *Rhetoric* he observes:

> People are gentle when they are in an opposite condition to those who get angry: when they are at play, or laughing, or feasting, or feeling prosperous or successful or satisfied, and in general when they are enjoying freedom from pain or pleasure that does not harm others or decent hope. (1380b2–5)

These comments are unexplained, but let us look into them. Why should people in all these conditions be less inclined to inappropriate anger?[96] All the named conditions, it turns out, conduce to a diminished emphasis on narcissistic vulnerability. I have suggested that people often grab onto anger and payback fantasies in order to exit from an intolerable condition of vulnerability and helplessness. People who feel prosperous or successful or satisfied are not likely to take a setback as a terrifying type of helplessness. Similarly with those who are free from pain, or enjoying some non-harmful pleasure. (Recall King's concern that despair would lead to violent retaliation.) When someone looks to the future with "decent hope"—by which Aristotle seems to mean the hope characteristic of a decent or fair-minded person (not, therefore, a hope of riding roughshod over others), he is less vulnerable to payback wishes—or to competitive anxiety.

But what about being at play and laughing? Those seem the most obscure of the items on the list, and yet they may be potentially the most revealing. First, what does he mean by "at play" (*en paidiai*)? Aristotle certainly cannot be talking about competitive sports, where people are highly prone to anger (and this is a staple of Greek society and Greek philosophy, not just a modern issue).[97] But *paidia* does not mean athletic competition, it means a sort of relaxed and playful activity, of which the games of children (*paides*) are an example. By coupling it with laughter, he gives us a sense of the subset of playful activities he has in mind. The ego at play, playing around (and *paidia* is often contrasted to what is serious), has a way of not taking itself too gravely; in such a condition, the ego is worn lightly and slights loom less large. Play is also a way of coping with anxiety and helplessness: as children we learn to manage potentially exhausting fears through drama and games. Instead of grasping onto other people and insisting that they assuage our terror, the person at play is relaxed and confident in the world and able to allow other people to exist as who they are. Play helps with both payback anger and status anger: people at play are less likely to be rigidly focused on their standing, and they are also less likely to need the useless project of payback to assuage their anxiety.

Aristotle is not Donald Winnicott: he does not have a theory of play.[98] But he has an insight that leads in Winnicott's direction: play is a set of stratagems by which the ego grows strong enough to live in a world with others. This idea fits with the concept of the Transition: for, I said, anger in sane people has a way of laughing itself out of existence. If one is already in a frame of mind prepared to take oneself lightly or even to laugh at oneself, the Transition is ready to hand.

What is the point of talking normatively about anger? If it really is a deep-seated tendency left over from our evolutionary prehistory, what is the possible use of this critique? The use, I believe, is threefold. First, even tendencies that cannot be altered can be bracketed as sources for public policy. Thus, behavioral psychology, noting certain quirks of the human mind, allows us to see them for what they are, just quirks, and to think about more rational ways to make policy. For example, if we understand that people have a tendency to what psychologists call the "availability heuristic," that is, to thinking of a single salient example and judging other cases in the light of that, we will see why intuitions about risk might need to be balanced by some type of detached cost-benefit analysis. Or, as I've argued concerning disgust, if we see that human beings have a strong tendency to subordinate and exclude others by projecting disgust-properties (bad smell, animality) onto them, we can be alert to the dangers of stigma and subordination in our society and refuse to base public policy on an emotion whose normatively defective foundations have been laid bare.

But, second, the tendency to anger appears to be only partly evolutionary, and at least in part cultural and role-specific. Or rather culture makes a difference in the further development and expression of the tendency, if such there is. There is considerable variation across cultures in the valorization of anger—the Utku lying at one extreme, and the Greeks and Romans a good deal closer to them than modern Americans. Within a single culture there is also great variation, as we've noted with regard to gender. Some subcultures—Stoics, Gandhians—may also deviate from a larger cultural pattern. Observing this elasticity, we can set ourselves to educate children to emulate models we take to be good and rational.

Finally, there is at least some room for self-change, even in an adult. Seneca describes the patient self-examination through which he works, nightly, on his own anger. If he does not claim complete success, he at least makes progress. And perhaps more time for self-examination would permit even more progress. Nelson Mandela claims he achieved a great deal during his twenty-seven years of imprisonment. Most of us, fortunately, will not have such lengthy stretches of solitude and inactivity; but that does not mean that no progress can be made.

3

Forgiveness

A Genealogy

Ingemisco tamquam reus;
Culpa rubet vultus meus:
Supplicanti parce, Deus.

I moan like a guilty criminal,
My face blushes with my fault.
Spare me, God, your suppliant.

—*Dies Irae*, thirteenth-century hymn

Blinded by his tears and by the light of God's mercifulness he bent
his head and heard the grave words of absolution spoken and
saw the priest's hand raised above him in token of forgiveness.

—James Joyce, *Portrait of the Artist as a Young Man*, ch. 4

I. Forgiveness and Genealogy

Now I turn to my ancillary theme, forgiveness. As with anger, we need
a working account of forgiveness, and Charles Griswold has admirably
provided one. Forgiveness, he argues, is a two-person process involving
a moderation of anger and a cessation of projects of revenge, in response
to the fulfillment of six conditions. A candidate for forgiveness must

1. Acknowledge that she was the responsible agent
2. Repudiate her deeds (by acknowledging their wrongness) and herself
   as their author
3. Express regret to the injured at having caused this particular
   injury to her
4. Commit to becoming the sort of person who does not inflict injury
   and show this commitment through deeds as well as words
5. Show that she understands, from the injured person's perspective, the
   damage done by the injury
6. Offer a narrative accounting for how she came to do wrong, how that
   wrongdoing does not express the totality of her person, and how she
   is becoming worthy of approbation.[1]

(I do not defend this as a perfect analysis, but it is good enough to give us a place to begin.) Let us call this the classic account, to indicate its centrality and longevity.[2] But I shall henceforth refer to it as "transactional forgiveness," in order to contrast it with alternatives that lack this conditional structure. As we shall see, each of these elements has a long Judeo-Christian history, and together they form a familiar package. Investigating the history of that group of elements will help us better understand their moral role and will also help us see more clearly how alternative approaches deviate from this one.

In the case of anger, my procedure was straightforward: I examined the components of anger, discussed their role, and, by investigating a variety of cases, argued that it contains hidden defects and irrationalities. With forgiveness I feel the need to proceed in a more indirect way, by considering the Judeo-Christian history of the concept. Why?

When a philosopher proposes to investigate a concept by delving into its history, she will immediately be warned of "the genealogical fallacy." Seeking the nature of something by looking to its origins is typically thought to be an unreliable way to study something. Often, this warning is wise. For example, we can understand some features of human psychology by looking at their evolutionary origins, but we had better not think that this gives us a complete understanding. In constitutional law, the idea that we understand the meaning of a provision fully by looking at what the framers meant by it is, if believed by some, still intensely controversial. Even originalists should not simply presume that originalism is correct.

As Nietzsche understood, however, there are times when historical investigation is illuminating, and I shall be using the idea of genealogy in Nietzsche's sense.[3] What Nietzsche thinks about morality, and what I think about forgiveness, is that there are certain norms that are so honored and so central to people's discourse and daily lives that their precise contours are not studied with clarity. An aura of sanctity surrounds them. Habit, too, makes them difficult to see. So, I suggest, it is with forgiveness. Because we are so used to the idea, we think we don't need to pause to define it precisely and disengage it from various related attitudes. Because our culture so reveres it, we shrink from examining it in a critical spirit. Thus we may be slow, for example, to recognize elements of aggressiveness, control, and joylessness that lurk within it.

History defamiliarizes. It reminds us that things could be, and indeed sometimes were, otherwise. Here, it reminds us that forgiveness, a cherished modern concept, was initially introduced, and persisted for millennia, in connection with a range of religious attitudes and practices; it got its sense from that embeddedness. We may ultimately conclude that the entire conceptual legacy is worthy of our endorsement. We may also conclude that some aspects of forgiveness can be detached from this network and are to be valued on their own. But we may, by contrast, find ourselves noticing that some features that fit naturally in their original religious setting are actually not such a good fit if we should reject key aspects of that framework. If we notice such a lack of fit, we will be at least skeptical of whether we can in fact retain a kernel of forgiveness while discarding the traditional husk. We will never get to this point of critical seriousness, however, if we continue to feel that forgiveness is as natural as the air we breathe, or the water in which, if we were fish, we would be swimming around.[4] I believe that some aspects of forgiveness may survive their separation from a particular framework within which the transactional concept developed—but it remains to be seen which ones, and with what result.

Michel Foucault made a similar argument about the modern institution of punishment.[5] Foucault maintained that we accept certain pieties about punishment habitually and without scrutiny. In particular, we like to think that the cruel public punishments known in former times have now been replaced by a milder set of practices involving incarceration and reform. Indeed, we are so enamored of the idea that the reform of offenders through prison is a gentle and progressive practice that we are slow to recognize the punitive, controlling aspects of even the most apparently benign of prisons.[6]

In the case of forgiveness, one phenomenon we shall repeatedly observe is the tendency to use the word for whatever attitudes one thinks good in the management of anger. This tendency confuses, and it also makes criticism difficult: "forgiving" is just an all-purpose term of commendation in the general neighborhood of dealing with wrongdoing. Another tendency we shall observe, to some extent in tension with this one, is to drag in a lot of baggage historically associated with Judeo-Christian forgiveness as though it must all be part and parcel of the vague good thing one has already introduced. Take Desmond Tutu's *No Future without Forgiveness*, which I shall discuss in detail in chapter 7. Having introduced "forgiveness" in a vague normative manner, as whatever the positive generous reconciling attitude might be, Tutu then without further argument goes on to associate with it a whole panoply of religious attitudes, such as confession, contrition, and absolution. Suddenly "forgiveness" becomes Christian transactional forgiveness, and has an extremely definite content, but the slippage is not noticed because readers are so steeped in these Christian attitudes and concepts.

I shall be arguing that the Judeo-Christian tradition, being complex, also offers us two alternative attitudes that deserve our attention. I will spend much of this chapter on *transactional forgiveness*, the type of conditional forgiveness that Griswold's definition well describes. *Transactional forgiveness* is the central theoretical concept in medieval and modern Jewish philosophy (drawing on some biblical texts but ignoring others), and it is one of three highly influential attitudes in the Christian tradition, and the one that the organized church tends to prefer and codify. But some less codified parts of the Jewish tradition and some well-known parts of the Christian tradition also introduce two different attitudes. One I shall call *unconditional forgiveness*; the other I shall call *unconditional love and generosity*. We shall see that these alternatives, and particularly the latter, have a great deal to offer. And both are prominent in biblical texts, in both the Old and New Testaments. Nonetheless, it is not possible to avoid the fact that for a great deal of the history of organized Judeo-Christian religion, *transactional forgiveness* has held the center of the stage, with large consequences for both political and personal relations.

Let us, then, examine the Judeo-Christian tradition of *transactional forgiveness* in a Nietzschean spirit.

II. *Jewish* Teshuvah: *Keeping Score of Acts and Omissions*

Jewish *teshuvah*, or repentance—and its associated attitude of forgiveness—has a long and complex history. Many biblical texts, especially in the prophetic books, discuss and exemplify a wide range of relevant acts and attitudes that a later tradition codifies. These texts are not systematic, and they do not form a theory or a canonical set of practices. Ideas of transactional forgiveness are prominent.[7] But, as we shall see in section V, they coexist, not fully codified, with texts that suggest ideas of unconditional forgiveness and unconditional love. Nor is the Talmud systematic, and I shall discuss its insights on the topic only later, when I investigate dissident traditions.[8]

A subsequent rabbinic tradition, however, codified these ideas, defining authoritatively what *teshuvah* is and how it should be performed.[9] The leading voices in this tradition are the great twelfth-century thinker Maimonides,[10] whose *Hilchot Teshuvah* (*The Laws of Repentance*) form part of the first book of his magisterial *Mishneh Torah*; and the thirteenth-century Yonah of Gerona, whose *Shaarei Teshuvah* (*The Gates of Repentance*) is the most extensive codification of *teshuvah*.[11] Contemporary Jewish theological discussions of *teshuvah* in such authorities as Joseph Dov Soloveitchik and Holocaust historian Deborah Lipstadt hew very closely to these texts.[12]

As one can see from the titles of these works, the organizing concept is that of *teshuvah* or repentance, rather than forgiveness; but forgiveness is the ultimate goal of the process, and it plays a crucial organizing role. Initially, however, the accent is on the activity of the wrongdoer, rather than the victim. A primary reason for this emphasis is that *teshuvah* is above all a process undertaken by erring human beings in relation to God and God's anger. Ethical prescriptions are given to the transgressor, and not, of course, to God. There is an ancillary account of how *teshuvah* works in relation to other human beings; as we shall see, human-human *teshuvah* is distinct and unmediated, and one cannot fulfill its obligations simply by repairing one's relationship with God. Nonetheless, every bad act toward a human being is also, and above all, a wrongdoing toward God, and the relationship of the wrongdoer to God is given considerably greater emphasis, both ritually and textually, than are human-human relationships. Yom Kippur is aimed entirely at repairing one's relation to God, although mention is made of the separate need to atone for wrongs against humans. The text of Yonah is virtually silent about human-human atonement, mentioning it only briefly and toward the end of a four-hun- dred-page work. Soloveitchik's authoritative contemporary account dis- cusses human-human *teshuvah* only fleetingly. Maimonides gives human *teshuvah* a proportionally greater emphasis—but only because the *teshu- vah* section of his work is very short, since the ethical commandments that occupy most of Yonah's work occur in other parts of Maimonides' great treatise.

The framework of *teshuvah* is the very long list of commandments that the observant Jew is required to keep. Yonah divides these into "positive," commandments requiring one to do something, and "nega- tive," commandments requiring one not to do something. In other words, there are sins of omission, typically lighter, and sins of commission, vary- ing in gravity but always grave. These commandments cover the entire terrain of life. Some are central moral or religious requirements; others are "fences," commandments whose function is to keep the potential sin- ner further away from a possible site of sin. (An example of a "fence" is the commandment that a male must not touch a married woman in any way at all: this commandment creates distance between the poten- tial sinner and the possibility of a serious sexual offense.) Even though violation of a "fence" is a lighter transgression than violating the primary commandment, however, it is still a violation, for which *teshuvah* must be undertaken. Moreover, both deliberate and accidental violations require *teshuvah*.[13]

The fabric of life is thus suffused with occasions for *teshuvah*. Constant vigilance is required, and *teshuvah* itself is certain to be needed very often, given the number of laws and the ease of transgressing. Indeed one might say that one function of the entire framework of *teshuvah* is to fill up the fabric of life with thought about one's relationship to God. The period between Rosh Hashanah and Yom Kippur, and the Yom Kippur ritual itself, are the primary occasions for gathering up all the year's occasions for repentance.[14] Still, Maimonides envisages *teshuvah* taking place all through the year. Yonah remarks that the entire process is like a fortification, which protects one from future sin.

Some sins are forgiven by God immediately on repentance. For others, the sinner will have to wait until the next Yom Kippur. For yet others, forgiveness follows only after one suffers further tribulation. For some particularly grave sins, the repentant sinner is not forgiven until death.[15] (For sins against other people, as we'll see, further conditions obtain.)[16]

The first requirement of *teshuvah* is confession. Maimonides insists on a personal and specific verbal confession (in addition to the communal confession recited on Yom Kippur). Confession to God should be done in private, but it must take an articulate verbal form. Soloveitchik explains that this is because emotions and ideas "become clear, and are grasped only after they are expressed in sentences bearing a logical and grammatical structure" (91–92). When the transgression is against another person as well as God, confession must be public as well as verbal. "For the *teshuvah* of one who is so arrogant as to conceal his acts of rebellion rather than disclose them is incomplete."[17] Soloveitchik says that one reason for this requirement is that the sinner must "clear the name of his fellow-man that has been muddied, and effectively remove the stigma he applied to him" (80). (He thus appears to hold that wrongdoing is a diminution of the victim, a position interestingly close to Aristotle's emphasis on "down-ranking.")

But confession is only a first step. The sinner must then take steps to chart a course that will avoid the sin in the future. This course must begin with sincere regret and a commitment not to repeat the sin. God "discerns all hidden things," and yet the statement of regret should also be made verbally (publicly if another person is involved, secretly if only God is involved). Maimonides and Yonah both use a telling image that, since it appears in both texts, and is so unusual, betrays its origin in a common source: the person who confesses verbally but does not have sincere regret is like someone who seeks purification in a *mikvah* (ritual bath) while holding a vile reptile: he won't be purified until he gets rid of the reptile. True *teshuvah*, Maimonides summarizes, is "no longer committing a sin one once committed, not thinking of committing it anymore, and affixing to his heart the commitment never to do it again."[18]

Extremely helpful in this process is a general attitude of mind that is "submissive, humble, and meek."[19] Worry is also extremely helpful, in keeping one fixed on the ease with which sin may be committed. (Maimonides remarks that the sound of the *shofar* is a metaphor for spiritual alertness.)[20] The culmination of successful *teshuvah* would be to be in the presence of the same temptation with similar opportunities for sin—and to refrain from sinning.[21] However, this cannot be strictly a requirement, since one can perform *teshuvah* and receive forgiveness right up until the moment of one's death—and there are many sins one can no longer commit when on the verge of death.[22] The constant awareness of impending death is a great help in the *teshuvah* process.[23]

Teshuvah pertains not to wishes or desires but to acts and omissions-to-act. The inner world is important because it is both a cause of transgression and a valuable part of the *teshuvah* process. As Yonah puts it, stirring up a tempest in oneself is very useful in distracting one from pleasure and the evil inclination. And "fences" often address the inner world: withdrawing from occasions that stimulate desire is part of the avoidance of sin.[24] However, even here it is the related acts and omissions that are of the essence: desire is not itself a sin, but only a cause or an effect of sin. Similarly, where other humans are concerned, only acts and omissions count, not wayward wishes, except insofar as they tend to produce bad acts.

Turning now to offenses against other people, we find that human-human *teshuvah* has, up to a point, a non-derivative status. Although every crime against another person is also a crime against God, repenting before God and receiving God's forgiveness does not suffice to square one's score with another human being. Nor, indeed, does monetary compensation or restitution of the property (in the case of property crime) suffice.[25] Instead, one must approach the other person directly, confess the fault publicly, express regret and a commitment not to do this sort of thing again—to change the course of one's life in regard to that whole area of sin. And then the victim must accept the apology. "For even after the transgressor pays the victim what is owed him, the victim must still become favorably inclined toward him, and the transgressor must ask him for forgiveness." Yonah remarks that compensation and restitution do not reach the victim's shame and distress: only an appeal for forgiveness can do this.

Here we finally arrive at human forgiveness, in something like our canonical sense: a change of heart on the part of the victim, who gives up anger and resentment in response to the offender's confession and contrition. The *teshuvah* process contains all the elements of Griswold's core definition. Even empathetic understanding of the victim's suffering, though not greatly emphasized, is present in the account of why restitution alone is insufficient. And the process culminates in the victim's willing abandonment of resentful feelings and projects.

Forgiveness, the Jewish tradition holds, is a virtue. The victim should not bear a grudge, but should be readily appeased and slow to anger. (Maimonides remarks that Gentiles are always holding grudges: a forgiving disposition is the hallmark of the Jew.)[26] If, however, the victim is initially obdurate, the transgressor should come to him with three friends and implore him for forgiveness. If the answer is still no, he should come with a second and a third group of (different) friends, all making persuasive arguments. At that point, the shoe is on the other foot: the obdurate victim becomes a transgressor. An exception is made for the teacher-pupil relationship: if the victim was the transgressor's teacher, he will have to go back "as many as a thousand times." (There is apparently no point at which an unforgiving teacher becomes culpable.) Special rules obtain for apology to someone who has died, and for restitution to people whom one does not know personally.[27] On the whole, however, the process is ritualized and quite coercive: either forgive, or you become the transgressor.

In the discussions of human-human *teshuvah* there is no explicit mention of worry, abasement, or humbling oneself. These attitudes are appropriate to the relationship with God. It would not be difficult, however, for them to become endemic to the human-human encounter too—given that every offense against another human is also, at the same time, an offense against God and thus an appropriate occasion for these attitudes. At any rate, given that anxiety and abasement are supposed to be ubiquitous features of each person's life, they are bound to be present in human relations, whether or not they are clearly directed toward the other person. And anxiety is likely on the victim's side as well, since he is commanded, on pain of sin, to change attitudes that can be very difficult to change.

When one compares this structured account, fixed by tradition over many centuries, to Griswold's philosophical definition, one gains new understanding, and this new angle of vision is the purpose of genealogy. In Griswold's contemporary account, a structure that is initially at home within an all-encompassing religious way of life has been extracted from it whole, so to speak, as if it could and should remain exactly the same even in the absence of those life-permeating commitments. Whether this is so or not would appear to require detailed argument, but the familiarity of the whole idea makes people feel that they can dispense with argument.

Let us continue, however, pondering the structure in its original context, asking what it promises for both personal and political relations. The more we understand the tradition, the better will be our ability to ask questions about the truncated version.

In Jewish *teshuvah*, both personal and political relations are reduced to a very small part of life. The relationship to God is primary, suffusing everything. The political as such is not even mentioned, and the personal either occupies a very small space in the text (as in Maimonides and Yonah), or virtually no space (as in Soloveitchik). And it is not simply that human relations occupy very little space in canonical texts on *teshuvah*. It is perfectly clear that the result, and indeed the purpose, of the life-suffusing process is to sideline them, rendering them secondary. Even if human forgiveness cannot be fully achieved by squaring one's account with God, the whole transaction takes place in the context of a primary commitment to God that fills up the whole of life, structuring it in its most intimate details. The combination of the large number of positive and negative commandments, including the many "fences," with the injunction to constant worry and mindfulness means that there is simply not much room to look at or care for another human being as such, and certainly no space at all for spontaneity, passion, or play. Indeed, the life this process organizes seems remarkably anxious and joyless, albeit within a tradition whose capacity for joy and humor is so clearly one of its great virtues.

Particularly striking, in the light of our Aeschylean starting point, is the absence of any sense that the political makes a difference. Unlike personal relations, which are at least mentioned, political relations are not mentioned at all—not even in Soloveitchik's contemporary treatise. Anger is not transformed by political justice, since it is God's anger and God's justice that really matter. Even in a just and law-governed society, then, the wrongdoer bears exactly the same burden of worry, confession, and potential divine wrath as in a pre-legal society.

How, in this tradition, is a human victim's anger allayed? Not by any active generosity on the part of the victim, who is instructed to wait for an apology and supplication accompanied with protestations of change and non-renewal, as well as restitution where this is appropriate. At this point, the victim is to be non-grudging, but not before. Indeed, there is a strong suggestion that preemptive generosity on the part of the victim would be a great error, short-circuiting the mandated work of the *teshuvah* process. Certainly God demands of us the full procedure, constantly iterated, and human beings are not encouraged to be more careless or frivolous than God. If eventually yielding, victims are encouraged to be initially quite tough, and to that extent the transgressor is forced into postures that are extremely elaborate and uncomfortable: imagine rounding up a series of three distinct groups of three friends, all of whom must know the intimate details of the transaction and be prepared to intercede in it.

At the conclusion of the process, moreover, there is also no room for generosity or spontaneity: forgiveness is a requirement of religious law and should not be freely given.

Interpersonal relations, then, are doubly burdened: first and foremost, by constant preoccupation with transgression against God, which takes most of life's space; second, by the demands of the public *teshuvah* process within these relations themselves. Given the large list of ways in which one person may offend another, the demands of interpersonal *teshuvah* are themselves extremely onerous, taking space that might otherwise be taken by happier things. These burdens are the sort of thing that Athena was keen to remove; the *teshuvah* process does not contemplate their removal, but intensifies them. That is no mistake: it is its purpose.

Section VI will present some alternative voices from the Jewish tradition that (like some biblical texts) suggest a different viewpoint. Now, however, continuing the narrative of what I've called *transactional forgiveness*, let us turn to the main lines of a related Christian tradition.

III. Christian Transactional Forgiveness: Score-Keeping in the Inner Realm

The Christian tradition is many things. So too, of course, is the Jewish tradition. But in that case, at least when we are dealing with the philosophical texts of Orthodox Judaism, there is remarkable constancy over time. Christianity was heterogeneous from the start, with a plurality of founding texts and increasing diversity over time and space. A genealogy of our sort cannot exhaustively delve into all relevant scholarly disputes about the authors of the Gospels, or about differences between Jesus and Paul, or even, except very generally, about differences between Catholic and Protestant doctrines of forgiveness, and among various types of Protestantism. Instead, my genealogy of *transactional forgiveness* aims at extracting, as with Judaism, a familiar structure of remarkable ubiquity and persistence, recognizable across time and space, and formative of modern culture in ways of which we are often unaware. It will focus on the organized church, which may well have departed from its origins, as so often happens with organized religion. But it is the organized church that overwhelmingly influences daily life and culture. After describing schematically a mainstream Christian transactional version of the *teshuvah* process, I shall turn to two alternatives within this tradition, prominently attested in the biblical text, which offer attractive possibilities.

To begin with, we must dispense with the erroneous but ubiquitous view that the Jewish tradition is punitive while the Christian tradition is merciful. As we have seen, the Jews said just the opposite: the *goyim* hold grudges, whereas Jews have a principled way of laying anger aside. Both claims of superior mildness are equally false. The Christian tradition has enormous resources for punitiveness (one need only consider the book of Revelation), and the Jewish tradition certainly encourages strict accounting and laborious penance. Indeed, as we shall see, there is, not surprisingly, great continuity between the two traditions, with Christianity on the whole going further in a similar direction.

Transactional forgiveness is surely not absent from the Gospels, although it is not as prominent as the organized church would lead one to expect. A major statement is Luke 17:3–4: "if your brother wrongs you, reprove him; and if he repents, forgive him. And if he wrongs you seven times a day, and seven times a day he turns to you saying 'I repent,' you shall forgive him."[28] Another authoritative text is Acts 3:19: "Therefore repent, and be converted, so that your sins may be blotted out, when the times of refreshing come from the face of the Lord." Moreover, the entire practice of baptism initiated by John is characterized as a "baptism of repentance for the forgiveness of sins" (Mark 1:4, Luke 3:3). This phrase is plausibly construed as meaning that there is no baptism without repentance:[29] in Matthew 3:8 John upbraids the Pharisees and Sadducees who come for baptism because they had not already repented. Baptism is probably not meant to be sufficient for God's forgiveness: only Christ's death on the cross will achieve that; but baptism does seem to be necessary.[30] Thus forgiveness, while involving Christ's free act of grace, is also deeply transactional.

These ideas are not the only ones we find in the Gospels, as we shall see. But they shape the early rituals of what became the Christian church, and it is not surprising that, much later, the organized church codified them and made much of them. Thus, whatever baptism was in the early church, it quickly became an entry condition for promised salvation. And the forgiveness of sins it offers was, and still is, envisaged as transactional through and through: the child's sins are remitted conditionally on an expression of contrition and renunciation by the parents and/or godparents.[31]

But since transactional forgiveness, though present in the Gospels, is above all a construction of the organized church, let us now focus on a much later text—the *Dies Irae*, the medieval poem that records Christian views about the Last Judgment and that held for centuries a central place in the Requiem Mass (prior to Vatican II, when it was removed).[32] The *Dies Irae* is just one of many ritual texts about penance and forgiveness. More or less all of its structure is already present in Tertullian's second century CE *De Paenitentia*.[33] But its imagery has been common pedagogical currency in many places and times. (For example, more or less all of it is in the sermon delivered to the Dublin schoolboys imagined in Joyce's *Portrait of the Artist as a Young Man* [1916], a sermon that clearly tracks closely a sermon or sermons heard by Joyce in his youth.) And it neatly encapsulates a widespread set of ideas and practices in Christian forgiveness.

The *Dies Irae*, "Day of Anger," depicts a world suffused by divine anger, human fear of divine anger, and humble pleas for forgiveness. Part of the idea behind the hymn is that the person who sings or hears it never knows whether actual forgiveness will occur, since if one is singing or hearing that hymn, one is not yet dead and may always sin again. One can only hope, and continue imploring.

The day of wrath is a day of universal cataclysm: the whole world is in flames and ashes. A trumpet calls the dead to judgment. The judge is arriving, to judge everything strictly. A book is brought out, containing the entire record from which judgment will take place. "Whatever is hidden will appear, nothing will remain unavenged." The transgressor (still alive, the singer of the hymn) then wonders what on earth he will say on that day. Guilty, like a criminal, he imagines himself blushing before the throne of judgment. He knows that his prayers are unworthy. Still, he hopes for a totally unjustified forgiveness. He implores, low and in suppliant posture, his heart as contrite as ashes. When the damned are burned up, he asks to be forgiven and thus spared, citing Jesus' incarnation for the sake of humanity.

In many respects, this is the *teshuvah* process in (anticipatory) postmortem form. Confession, apology, pleas, contrition, a chronicle of one's bad acts—all are here. Even the determination to change and not to repeat the sin, although hard to inject into the postmortem context, is still present theologically, in classic depictions of Purgatory, where the souls, once saved by divine forgiveness, must learn by painstaking labors and eons of habituation to undo their attachment to their besetting sins. And God is depicted, as in Judaism, as a demanding and an angry God, who, nonetheless, if sufficiently supplicated, may opt for forgiveness, in the sense of turning from anger and not exacting the merited punishment. As in Judaism, again, the primary relationship is that with God, and the primary victim and forgiver is God.

The Catholic sacrament of penance (virtually unchanged since Tertullian's *De Paenitentia*) makes the continuity with Jewish *teshuvah* especially clear, with its precise analogues to each stage of the *teshuvah* process.[34] Penance requires verbal confession, then contrition (defined by the sixteenth-century Council of Trent as "sorrow of heart and detestation for sin committed, with the resolve to sin no more"). Thus, penance is void if the transgressor is simply going through the motions. Following contrition and confession—if the priest is satisfied that these are complete enough—is absolution, accompanied by the assignment of a penance, "usually in the form of certain prayers which he is to say, or of certain actions which he is to perform, such as visits to a church, the Stations of the Cross, etc. Alms deeds, fasting, and prayer are the chief means of satisfaction, but other penitential works may also be required."[35] Restitution to the human victim or to the community may also be commanded at the discretion of the priest, although these human compensations are less frequently assigned than forms of prayer.

The penance ritual is thus continuous with *teshuvah*. In a good deal of mainstream Protestantism, things are less structured, and yet not fundamentally dissimilar. There is no anointed intermediary to hear the confession and assign the penitential tasks, but transgressors are still urged to confession, contrition, and penance. The Anglican Church has a communally recited confession, and other denominations have other analogues. In evangelical Christianity, it is common for a public confession of sin, accompanied by contrition and self-abasement, to be followed by a communal invocation of divine forgiveness.

Another striking similarity between the two traditions is the incorporation of a ritualized type of forgiveness at periodic intervals. The sins against God that one sincerely repents at Yom Kippur are moot. Even Maimonides, who urges that the transgressor confess them again, does so only as a device of warning and memory. With transgressions against other people too, *teshuvah* mandates a determinate ending. So it is, as well, in the Catholic ritual: one should confess at regular intervals, and if one has been sincere and exhaustive, one receives forgiveness for all the sins committed during that interval. This guarantee is less secure in Protestantism, which leaves the business of forgiveness to the relationship between transgressor and God. Still, there is a communal form of absolution in Anglican ritual; similar forms exist in other denominations. The evangelical idea of being "born again" is a variant of the idea of absolution.

In the transition from Judaism to Christianity, however, several important changes in the forgiveness process have taken place.

First, the independent human-human forgiveness process, already de-emphasized in Judaism, simply drops away: all forgiveness is really from God (sometimes mediated by clergy). If you square your relationship with God, then the other person is by definition satisfied, and you do not need to engage in separate negotiations with that person.[36] Catholic confession makes this explicit: the priest, in God's name, can absolve you from an interpersonal transgression, and you do not need to do or say anything to the other person, unless the priest tells you to do so. Usually, however, penance is not very other-directed, but takes place primarily through prayer. The eschatology of Purgatory is again instructive here: people who are habitually stingy, or imperious, or deceitful, but who manage to get into Purgatory through absolution, can have eternity to work on their character and improve it, without having to interact with the real living people whom their acts have harmed. Thus, unlike *teshuvah*, Christian forgiveness is essentially a God-directed process, whether in the form of the Catholic sacrament or in some other form. Humans do not face humans (apart from clergy) directly; they turn to God.

A second difference concerns the scope of sin. In Jewish *teshuvah*, the site of sin is an external act or omission to act. Desire is relevant as a cause of good or bad action, but is not in and of itself an act to be judged.[37] In the Christian tradition, it is famously otherwise. Jesus indicts the Jewish tradition for its narrow focus on acts. "You have heard, 'You shall not commit adultery.' But I say to you that anyone who looks at a woman in such a way as to desire her has already committed adultery in his heart" (Matthew 5:27). The inner world is now open to view as a site of recalcitrant quasi-acts,[38] to be excavated through memory and confessed. Indeed, in Tertullian's *De Paenitentia* sins are divided into two basic categories: sins of the body and sins of thought or mind. Both require penance, but the latter are held to be more fundamental.[39]

At this point, we can introduce the important philosophical account of penance and confession by Michel Foucault that has recently been published as *Mal faire, dire vrai*, based on lectures that Foucault presented in Louvain in 1981.[40] Foucault's historical account of the confessional has a number of defects, among which is its complete neglect of the Jewish tradition; but it has undoubted insight and importance. Whereas my account has been largely synchronic, Foucault argues that it is worth studying these practices diachronically. Passing rapidly over Tertullian and other early developments,[41] he locates the primary development of confessional practices in a fourth- to fifth-century monastic tradition, arguing that it is this tradition that later gets codified and legalized.[42] His developmental inquiry dovetails with my synoptic account in emphasizing certain features of the monastic tradition as pivotal. First, he emphasizes the asymmetry of power relations: the listener has the upper hand, and the speaker is abased. Second, he stresses the endlessness of confession: there is no exhausting it; one never reaches a point at which one can be confident that one has ferreted out and truthfully confessed every hidden sin. Third and most important, he insists, persuasively, that the whole process is a practice of self-abasement, self-obliteration, and shaming, as the inner world is exposed to the community (or, later, the confessor).

If through such practices Christianity expanded our awareness of the inner world, as is often said (especially with reference to Augustine's *Confessions*), it is also true, as Foucault rightly emphasizes, that obsessive awareness of the inner world greatly magnifies the occasions for sin, and extends sin, too, into the domain of the uncontrollable. Augustine's torment over his nocturnal emissions is not simply torment over an impure act; it is torment over inclination itself, which burrows down into the depths of the personality. Similarly, souls in Purgatory atone not for an unabsolved act—if there were such, they would be in hell instead—but for standing flaws of desire and inclination: for being lustful, gluttonous, etc.[43] The inner realm, however, is messy and ungovernable; to the extent that confession and apology focus on that, they focus on something that is unlikely ever to be brought into a satisfactory ordering. Thus the mood of Christian confession is always one of intense sorrow and terrible fear and shame, and the shame pertains to one's whole being, not just to a set of bad practices.

One marvelous depiction of the terrifying nature of this process is Joyce's, describing sixteen-year-old Stephen's reaction to the sermon he hears:

> Every word of it was for him. Against his sin, foul and secret, the whole wrath of God was aimed. The preacher's knife had probed deeply into his disclosed conscience and he felt now that his soul was festering in sin. Yes, the preacher was right. God's turn had come. Like a beast in its lair his soul had lain down in its own filth but the blasts of the angel's trumpet had driven him forth from the darkness of sin into the light. The words of doom cried by the angel shattered in an instant his presumptuous peace. The wind of the last day blew through his mind, his sins, the jewel-eyed harlots of his imagination, fled before the hurricane, squeaking like mice in their terror and huddled under a mane of hair.

The horrendous sins are sexual fantasies (as well as acts of masturbation and, occasionally, intercourse with prostitutes). The extraordinary cruelty of giving teenage boys such lectures about their ungovernable mental lives is combined with a type of prurience all too real.[44] A key to the disciplinary power of the church, indeed, is its fixation on fantasy, which cannot be governed, which is always disobedient. As the preacher continues (of Lucifer): "He offended the majesty of God by the sinful thought of one instant and God cast him out of heaven into hell for ever." The quest for forgiveness that sends Stephen ultimately to a priest to confess is born of abject terror and intense self-loathing. He vomits, just thinking of his own mind. The account makes us wonder—as is its intent—how anyone who grew up in that tradition could become able to love anyone, much less a woman. (*Ulysses*, and particularly its final chapter, are Joyce's answer to that question, since if Joyce is Stephen Daedalus he is also Leopold Bloom.)

Finally, by comparison to the standard picture of transactional forgiveness in Judaism, the Christian transactional forgiveness process places a far greater accent on humility and lowness, as essential features of the human condition. Jewish *teshuvah* urges worry and discourages pride and confidence; but the tradition never claims that the human being as such is low and base and has no worth. A core of human self-respect remains intact, and perhaps even, with it, a love of the body.[45] These attitudes dissolve utterly beneath the keen gaze of a certain sort of Christian self-scrutiny. Yes, flesh is indeed worthless, and you are consequently worthless. This theme is prominent from the very beginning of the transactional forgiveness tradition. Thus much of Tertullian's *De Paenitentia* is spent describing the process of *exomologēsis*, a discipline in which the penitent outwardly acknowledges his lowness by self-mortifying practices, including fasting, weeping, groaning, self-prostration, filthy clothes, and a commitment to sorrow.[46] *Exomologēsis* is held to be a necessary condition of restoration to God.

Where is interpersonal forgiveness in this set of transactions? Although the Christian transactional tradition, like the Jewish transactional tradition, makes all forgiveness essentially God-directed, the process of penance is also widely understood to offer a model of interpersonal relations, based on confession, apology, and ultimate forgiveness. The countless thinkers in this tradition who offer the penance process as a model for interpersonal reconciliation are following indications in the text, as well as applying the general idea that we are to model our own conduct on the conduct and teachings of Jesus. Nor is it surprising that the attitudes of shame, self-disgust, and apology that we've encountered in human relations to God would turn up in interpersonal relations, shaping ways of dealing with sexuality and other important human matters.

As in Judaism, then, we have forgiveness, but at the end of a process involving abasement, confession, contrition, and penance. In contrast to Judaism, the process requires acknowledging that one is fundamentally low and of little worth and putting oneself, imaginatively, into the midst of a spectacle of the most savage retribution. It also requires opening the most hidden recesses of desire and thought to the searching eye of another, whether priest, congregation, wronged party, or only the eye of God.

It's no news to say, as I have, that this strand of Christianity (only one among many, but a prominent one) juxtaposes an ethic of forgiveness with an ethic of spectacular retribution. One can see this same combination in the book of Revelation, where the triumph of the mild lamb is immediately followed by visions of horrible torment for the lamb's enemies. Usually, however, the two aspects are held to be in tension with one another. Rarely are they taken to be complementary. What my genealogy suggests, however, is that the forgiveness process itself is violent toward the self. Forgiveness is an elusive and usually quite temporary prize held out at the end of a traumatic and profoundly intrusive process of self-denigration. To engage in it with another person (playing, in effect, the role of the confessor) intrudes into that person's inner world in a way that is both controlling and potentially violent toward the other person's self. It's like the old story about child abuse: the abused all too often becomes an abuser. In this case, the inquisitorial role is given strong normative support, in the idea that this is how God acts toward us.

Could one avoid this problem by simply adopting a more limited account of sin? This is like the question whether Jewish *teshuvah* would lose its life-enclosing character if there were just not so many commandments. The answer is not yet clear, and we must later return to this possibility. But what changes, exactly, would one introduce? Would one simply exempt the inner world? That would be a truly enormous change. It is of the essence of the tradition to scrutinize and control the wayward self, prominently including the inner world. Would we instead retain some scrutiny of inner acts, but exempt seemingly harmless fantasies, such as teenage sexual fantasies? Well, again: the tradition would have to be hugely changed to forgo all scrutiny of the sexual realm, and at least some scrutiny of wishes and fantasies is a pretty important part of the scrutiny of that realm that the organized church has traditionally endorsed.

Nietzsche saw the following link between the punitive and the kindly aspects of the Christian tradition: to the extent that Christians felt themselves incapable of worldly success on the terms set by competitive pagan cultures, they invented a new form of success, namely being mild and humble. Then, in a reversal of values and expectations, they envisage the triumph of these meek values over pagan values, in a very literal sense: the humble are exalted in the afterworld, the formerly proud are damned and tortured. They thus satisfied their original impulse for competitive triumph, albeit only in the realm after death.[47]

There is some truth in this picture, but I would like to suggest a different connection between Christian transactional forgiveness and Christian harshness, which fits better with Christianity's Judaic roots. The forgiveness process is itself a harsh inquisitorial process. It demands confession, weeping and wailing, and a sense of one's lowness and essential worthlessness. The penitent is tormented simply by penitence. The person who administers the process is controlling and relentless toward the penitent, an inquisitor of acts and desires—even if in the end forgiveness is given. If we now imagine the process transferred from the priest-penitent relation to the person-person relation, so that the role of the priest is played by the human victim of transgression, the process asks us to sit in judgment on one another, confessing and being confessed to—even when in the end the wronged party will forgo anger. The *teshuvah* process accords a certain dignity and self-respect to both parties, who can preserve their privacy of thought and desire. The two parties meet expecting something good of one another. In Christian forgiveness, by contrast, the drama of lowness and fear has been amped up so high that there seems to be no room for personal dignity or self-respect. Lowness seems just right, and the victim is encouraged to enjoy the spectacle of this groveling as an intrinsically valuable part of the forgiveness process, as it doubtless is in its priest-penitent form. We see this drama played out daily when marriages dissolve, to cite just one example.

This type of connection between forgiveness and harshness is not repudiated, but strongly endorsed, in the tradition itself. The *Catholic Encyclopedia* confronts the charge that the penance/confession process is too harsh. This view is called "strange," and the following rebuttal is given: "[T]his view, in the first place, overlooks the fact that Christ, though merciful, is also just and exacting. Furthermore, however painful or humiliating confession may be, it is but a light penalty for the violation of God's law."

We might summarize this part of our inquiry by saying that transactional forgiveness, far from providing an alternative to the two errors in anger that chapter 2 diagnosed, actually involves both. The payback error turns up in ideas of cosmic balance or fittingness that frequently inhabit the process: the victim's pain somehow atones for pain inflicted. Equally ubiquitous is the error of narrow status-focus. Because the whole process is modeled on God's relationship to erring mortals, and God is not vulnerable to any injury but a status-injury, the forgiveness process between humans also focuses unduly on status, suggesting that lowness and abasement compensate for a lowering or status-offense that the offender has inflicted.

One might now try to argue that the intense pain and humiliation characteristic of the forgiveness transaction was necessary, at a time in human history, to burn into the consciousness a sense of the importance of morality. At a time when people lived lives of casual hedonism, as parodied in the tale of the Golden Calf, the painful discipline of *teshuvah* created a people distinctly moral and worthy of morality—and the Christian internalization of the process deepened the moral personality yet further. Such is in essence Nietzsche's diagnosis: for, far from holding that moral heedlessness is good and Christian ethics inferior, he holds that Christianity was necessary in order "to breed an animal with a right to make promises," and thus an important ingredient of the good person, even if inadequate on its own. But we should also ask whether the right way to educate a heedless being is to inflict humiliating and painful discipline. Such has been the common idea of child-rearing in many places and times. But it is quite possible that moral sadism breeds more sadism rather than generosity and virtue. At any rate even that Nietzschean story does not justify continued reliance on the transactional forgiveness process. It gives us no reason not to seek attitudes that move to the Transition and pave the way for a constructive future. Far more promising in this regard are the alternative traditions now to be investigated.

IV. Unconditional Forgiveness

Transactional forgiveness, present in some biblical texts, has become deeply embedded in church practices and, thence, in many aspects of personal and political relations. It is thus no surprise to find both historians of thought (e.g., David Konstan) and philosophers (e.g., Charles Griswold) asserting that this is the full or complete account of what forgiveness is. Nonetheless, the Gospels clearly offer a different model as well. So far as the words and example of Jesus are concerned, this model is more prominent than the transactional model.

The Hebrew Bible already contains some instances of unconditional forgiveness, forgiveness that rains down freely on the penitent, without requiring an antecedent confession and act of contrition. Numbers 14:18–20 does refer to God's great capacity for retribution, but it also credits God with what appears to be spontaneous mercy and forgiveness: "Pardon, I beseech thee, the iniquity of this people according unto the greatness of thy mercy, and as thou hast forgiven this people, from Egypt even until now. And the Lord said, I have pardoned according to thy word." A clear and extended case is Psalm 103, in which God is merciful, gracious, and forgiving, apparently without being supplicated. God still gets angry, but he "does not keep his anger for ever."[48]

This strand is significantly developed in the Gospels. In Luke 5, Jesus pronounces to a man with palsy, "Your sins are forgiven"—much to the consternation of the Pharisees, who object that only God has the power to forgive sins. But the key example is Jesus himself: for he gives his life in order to remit the sins of human beings. At the Last Supper, Jesus says that the wine is his blood, "which is shed for many, toward the forgiveness of sins" (26:28). On the cross, similarly, Jesus asks unconditional forgiveness for those who have put him to death: "Father, forgive them, for they know not what they do" (Luke 23:33–34).[49] Apparently following Christ's example, Stephen, in Acts, says as he dies, "Lord, lay not this sin to their charge" (7:60). So there is a powerful tradition of unconditional forgiveness that Christians are asked to follow (although, since it is not clear that Jesus is ever angry, this unconditional forgiveness lies further from transactional forgiveness than do the Jewish models, where God is angry but gives up anger).

It should come as no surprise that the organized church has tended to appropriate and alter this emphasis, making the forgiveness of Jesus look far more transactional and less unconditional than the text by itself suggests. For once the body and blood become a sacrament with human officiants, they can be and often are refused to sinners of various sorts—typically one must perform a confession and receive absolution before being admitted to the sacrament. And of course, once Jesus is no longer in the world, unconditional forgiveness cannot be offered directly by the words of Jesus to the sinner, so the organized church becomes Christ's intermediary, speaking on Christ's behalf; and the organized church rarely forgives without a transaction.

We must also mention the role of baptism: Bash, a contemporary Anglican theologian and prelate, finds the entirety of Jesus's procedure in the Gospels implicitly transactional, because he emphasizes John (the Baptist)'s apparent insistence that repentance must precede baptism. Although Jesus, at least in these passages, simply offered forgiveness without insisting that the person be baptized or even become one of his followers, the organized church cultivates the belief that "unconditional" forgiveness has at least one huge condition: that one accept Jesus as one's savior and undergo the (transactional) ritual of baptism, a ritual that requires explicit renunciation of sin and wickedness, typically by the godparents of the child.[50]

It is no surprise that a human institution seeking authority over human beings should prefer to attach conditions to the powerful offer of remission. Still, it is important to state that Jesus, at least in some passages, does not do so.

According to the unconditional-forgiveness model, then, we should, like St. Stephen, forgive those who wrong us even when they do not make any gesture of contrition. Doesn't this model solve all the problems associated with transactional forgiveness? Well, insofar as unconditional forgiveness is still understood as a waiving of angry emotion (as it is in the Jewish texts and in most human instances, though perhaps not in the case of Jesus), there is still the question whether anger was an appropriate response in the first place. Perhaps it would have been better still not to have been dominated by resentment even temporarily. Unconditional forgiveness in human relations is rarely free from some type of payback wish, at least at first.

Another issue is the direction of attention: unconditional forgiveness remains backward-looking and not Transitional. It says nothing about constructing a productive future. It may remove an impediment to the future, but it does not point there in and of itself.

And this leads us to a further problem: sometimes the forgiveness process itself channels the wish for payback. The person who purports to forgive unconditionally may assume the moral high ground in a superior and condescending way—secretly thinking, "You ought to be groveling, whether you are or not." Or, a slight variant, he or she may want through the forgiveness process itself to get a moral advantage and inflict a humiliation on the offender. This attitude itself has biblical precedent. In Romans 12, after insisting that his addressees should live in peace with one another, and should not go about avenging one another's wrongs (but should remember that God said, "Vengeance is mine, I shall repay"). Paul then concludes, "Therefore, if your enemy is hungry, feed him; if he is thirsty, give him drink: for in so doing you will heap coals of fire on his head" (12:20). Paul first makes clear that the recommended forgiving treatment of enemies does not abandon the project of payback, since the believer is asked to clear the field for God to do the avenging.[51] And then, second, Paul also suggests that the good behavior and forgiving demeanor of the believer *is itself a punishment* of the offender, establishing the believer's superiority and dishing out some sort of pain or humiliation. That's an all-too-easy thought to have, even without Paul's encouragement.

In short, unconditional forgiveness has some advantages over transactional forgiveness, but it is not free of moral danger. The minute one sets oneself up as morally superior to another, the minute one in effect asserts that payback was a legitimate aim—but one that I graciously waive—one courts the dangers of both the road of status (inflicting a status-lowering on the offender) and the road of payback ("coals of fire"). One also runs the risk of assuming a moral prerogative that is originally that of God, and that seems a problematic role for a human being in this religious tradition to assume. Those Pharisees who criticized Jesus had an important point, which we miss only because we are focused on their failure to acknowledge that Jesus *is* God. And Paul knows that his addressees need to be warned against taking up God's role.

Does unconditional forgiveness point to the Transition? Not stably. Unconditional forgiveness is still about the past, and it gives us nothing concrete with which to go forward. It just wipes out something, but entails no constructive future-directed attitude. It might be accompanied by love and good projects—or it might not.

There is, however, a version of unconditional forgiveness that lies very close to unconditional love and generosity, lacking any nuance of superiority or vindictiveness. This sort of unconditional forgiveness was remarkably displayed by the survivors of the racially motivated shooting in a Charleston, South Carolina, church on June 17, 2015. Invited by the judge in charge of the bond hearing to make statements on behalf of each victim, family members addressed the defendant, Dylann Roof (who has confessed). Most uncommonly in so-called "victim impact statements," they did not express any vindictiveness or payback wish. Nor did they express anger—except, in one case, to admit it as a defect: "I'm a work in progress, and I acknowledge that I am very angry." But universally, while expressing profound grief, they offered Roof forgiveness, wished for God's mercy, and insisted that love is stronger than hate. "She taught me that we are the family that love built."[52] No concrete Transition is envisaged, and the only future mentioned is one of God's mercy at the final judgment. Perhaps the situation offers little room for the Transition. And yet there is something Transitional in its spirit, in the idea that love will prevail over hate and that a world can be reconstructed by love.[53] This brings us to our third possibility: unconditional love.

V. A Counter-Strand: The Prodigal Son, Mahler's Religion of Love

Christianity has many strands. The transactional strand has been enormously influential, particularly in and through the organized church. The alternative idea of unconditional forgiveness is not without its own moral risks and shortcomings. There is, however, a further counter-strand in at least some parts of the Gospels, and in some later Judeo-Christian thinkers. Often this counter-strand is called an ethic of "unconditional forgiveness." But the strand that interests me is best called not forgiveness at all, but an ethic of unconditional love. As we shall see, it departs altogether from judgment, confession, contrition, and consequent waiving of anger.

In the Sermon on the Mount, Jesus says, "Love your enemies, and pray for those who persecute you" (Matthew 5:44–45). Luke reports him as saying, "Love your enemies, do good to those who hate you" (Luke 6:27). The Gospels make numerous other references to the central importance of freely given love.[54] No conditions are mentioned. In these passages Jesus definitely does not say, "Love your enemies if they apologize" (although he does often elsewhere speak of conditional forgiveness, as we've seen). And he also does not seem to speak even of unconditional forgiveness, since there is no mention of waiving a prior anger. Love is a first response, not a substitute for a prior payback wish. In still other cases where translations of the Bible refer to forgiveness, the Greek seems to speak of love instead.[55]

Paul is, if anything, even clearer. Ephesians 4:31–32 insists: "Let all bitterness (*pikria*) and ill temper (*thumos*) and anger (*orgē*) and shouting and blasphemous speech be put away from you, along with every vice."[56] So anger is not just condemned: it seems to be counted as intrinsically a vice. This would of course entail that a forgiveness preceded by anger is not fully virtuous, it is just a remediation of a prior vice. And in the famous discussion of love in 1 Corinthians 13, we find Paul stating, similarly, that love "does not become angry (*paroxunetai*) and does not keep score of wrongs done." It could not be clearer that this view rejects both conditional forgiveness and unconditional forgiveness as fully adequate norms, recommending, instead, a love that bypasses anger altogether.

Especially important for our purposes, since it deals with love in the context of someone else's wrongdoing, is Jesus' parable of the Prodigal Son in Luke 15, which is standardly understood as an example of forgiveness. The larger context does indeed contain a reference to forgiveness, in the standard conditional and transactional mode. Two chapters *later*, Jesus says: "If your brother wrongs you, rebuke him; and if he repents, forgive him. And if he wrongs you seven times in a day, and seven times turns to you saying, 'I repent,' you shall forgive him" (17:3–4).[57] The two briefer parables that precede the story of the Prodigal Son, however, make reference only to loss, and to joy at rediscovery: the shepherd rejoices at finding the lost sheep, the prudent housekeeper rejoices at finding her lost piece of silver.

Now let us turn to the story of the son:

> A certain man had two sons: And the younger of them said to his father, Father, give me the portion of goods that falleth to me. And he divided unto him his living. And not many days after the younger son gathered all together, and took his journey into a far country, and there wasted his substance with riotous living. And when he had spent all, there arose a mighty famine in that land; and he began to be in want. And he went and joined himself to a citizen of that country; and he sent him into his fields to feed swine. And he would fain have filled his belly with the husks that the swine did eat: and no man gave unto him.
>
> And when he came to himself, he said, How many hired servants of my father's have bread enough and to spare, and I perish with hunger! I will arise and go to my father, and will say unto him, Father, I have sinned against heaven, and before thee, and am no more worthy to be called thy son: make me as one of thy hired servants. And he arose and came to his father.
>
> But when he was yet a great way off, his father saw him, and he was seized by a surge of emotion (*esplanchnisthē*), and he ran, and fell on his neck, and kissed him. And the son said unto him, Father, I have sinned against heaven, and before thee, and am no more worthy to be called thy son. But the father said to his servants, Bring forth the best robe, and put it on him; and put a ring on his hand, and shoes on his feet: And bring hither the fatted calf, and kill it; and let us eat, and be merry: For this my son was dead, and is alive again; he was lost, and is found. And they began to be merry.

Now his elder son was in the field: and as he came and drew nigh to the house, he heard music and dancing. And he called one of the servants, and asked what these things meant. And he said unto him, Thy brother is come; and thy father hath killed the fatted calf, because he hath received him safe and sound. And he was angry, and would not go in: therefore came his father out and entreated him. And he answering said to his father, Lo, these many years do I serve thee, neither transgressed I at any time thy commandment: and yet thou never gavest me a kid, that I might make merry with my friends: But as soon as this thy son was come, which hath devoured thy living with harlots, thou hast killed for him the fatted calf. And he said unto him, Son, thou are ever with me, and all that I have is thine. It was meet that we should make merry, and be glad: for this thy brother was dead, and is alive again; and was lost, and is found.[58]

We must carefully distinguish two points of view in the story: that of the son, and that of the father. The son does resolve to confess sin and to express contrition, and at least his words communicate this resolution. It is left utterly unclear whether the son is sincere. He has ample instrumental motivation in his hunger, and the story suggests that he is going through a calculation rather than really changing his life. The phrase translated "came to himself," much discussed by translators, might possibly allude to a true self to which the prodigal is returning, but nothing in the story has suggested a prior good self. The phrase would just as easily, I think more easily, mean "contemplating," "turning within," "deliberating."

But the son is in any case not the focus of the story. The focus is on the reaction of the father, and this reaction certainly cannot be described as forgiveness, whether transactional or unconditional. The father sees his son coming from a great distance. He recognizes him. At this point he cannot possibly know what the son is going to say or what his attitudes are. He just sees that the son he has believed dead is actually alive, and he is seized by a violent surge of strong emotion. The Greek *esplanchnisthē* is a rare and extremely emphatic term, which means, literally, "his guts were ripped out," or even "his guts were devoured."[59] The father, then, feels strong pangs—of a type of intense love that involves strong bodily feeling, as might often happen with a parent who feels that his own body and life are tied to this child. He runs to the son and embraces him, utterly without asking him any questions. There is no statement of forgiveness and no time for forgiveness. Even after the son makes his statement of repentance—*after* the father's embrace—the father does not acknowledge the issue of contrition at all, but goes straight ahead with his joyful plans for celebration.

Moreover, when the good son who has done everything right gets annoyed at this celebration of his inferior brother, the father does not say, "Look, he repented and I have forgiven him." Instead—while reassuring this son of his continued love and support for him, in words suggestive of ongoing intimacy ("You are always with me")—he just says, "I'm so happy that he is still alive." In short, there is no reference to forgiveness in this story, and no reference to contrition either, except in the possibly unreliable statements of the son. To call the father's attitude canonical forgiveness, one has to impute something like the following thought process to him: "I see my son coming. If he is coming back, this must mean that he has learned his lesson and repented. Since he has repented, I will let go of my anger and forgive him." Even to call it unconditional forgiveness, we have to imagine the father thinking about his resentment, and choosing freely to give it up. But of course there is no such thought process in the story, and no reference, even, to anger. Such a thought process would have been that of a different father, more calculating and controlling. This father is taken over by love.

To understand this story, in short, we ought to put aside our ideas of transactional forgiveness, whether Jewish or Christian, and even an idea of an unconditional forgiveness without contrition, which would still require the deliberate putting aside of anger. This story concerns the depths and the unconditionality of parental love. What is so great about this father is precisely that he does not pause to calculate and decide: he just runs to him and kisses him. He has no thought for wrongs done to himself; his only thought is that his son is alive.

Such a father might still, at some later time, talk to the son about his life's course. Unconditional love is fully compatible with guidance; indeed, since the father wishes well to this son, he is almost certain to give him advice so that his life will go better henceforth. The direction of his emotion is Transitional: his love points to a future, and that future will almost certainly contain advice. The initial impulse toward the son, however, does not come from advice or calculation.

In the surrounding context, Jesus is speaking of God's relationship with sinners. At least the possibility is held out, then, of a love that is itself radical and unconditional, sweeping away both forgiveness and the anger that is its occasion, a love that embarks upon an uncertain future with a generous spirit, rather than remaining rooted in the past.[60]

Such a picture of divine and human love is offered, almost two millennia later, in our other dissident Judeo-Christian text, Mahler's Resurrection Symphony.[61] I call the work Judeo-Christian because Mahler, a Jew, converted to Christianity for social reasons, though he remained quite heterodox in his religious attitudes, particularly in relation to the Christian majority.

A deliberate continuation of a long Christian tradition of pondering an "ascent" of love, Mahler's work—with texts partly borrowed and
mostly written by himself—deals with the Last Judgment and the *Dies
Irae*, in what Mahler understood to be a radically subversive manner.
Although Mahler never remained content with the verbal programs he
wrote for his symphonies, he was repeatedly drawn to such verbal formulations. Here is the account of the final movement of the symphony
that he wrote for the Dresden performance of 1901:

> The voice of the Caller is heard. The end of every living thing
> has come, the last judgment is at hand and the horror of the day
> of days has come upon us. The earth trembles, the graves burst
> open, the dead arise and march forth in endless procession. The
> great and small of this earth, the kings and the beggars, the just
> and the godless, all press forward. The cry for mercy and forgive-
> ness sounds fearful in our ears. The wailing becomes gradually
> more terrible. Our senses desert us, all consciousness dies as the
> Eternal Judge approaches. The last trump sounds; the trumpets
> of the Apocalypse ring out. In the eerie silence that follows, we
> can just barely make out a distant nightingale, a last tremulous
> echo of earthly life.
>
> A chorus of saints and heavenly beings softly breaks
> forth: "Thou shalt arise, surely thou shalt arise." Then appears
> the glory of God! A wondrous, soft light penetrates us to the
> heart—all is holy calm. And behold—it is no judgment—there
> are no sinners, no just. None is great, none is small. There is no
> punishment and no reward. An overwhelming love lightens our
> being. We know and are.[62]

There are many reasons to connect this symphony with Mahler's ongoing suffering from hostility and misunderstanding at the hands of the
dominant, and strongly anti-Semitic, Christian music-culture of Vienna
in his day. Indeed, he records that the inspiration for the final movement
came to him while attending the funeral of Hans Von Bülow, an anti-
Semitic German conductor who had been particularly hostile to him. So
the context, at any rate, is one in which we might expect forgiveness to
play a role. We could even say that it is Mahler's attempt at a Requiem
Mass. (A lifelong conductor of opera and symphonic music, Mahler was
intimately familiar with this genre.)

Whatever is "happening" in this final (fifth) movement, however, it
is radically unconventional in the Christian culture of the Requiem Mass.
As Mahler's biographer Henri-Louis de La Grange says, with understate-
ment: "It has been pointed out that the very concept of resurrection is
essentially foreign to the Jewish faith, but the idea of a last judgment with
no judge and no recognition of Good and Evil is just as unorthodox for a

Christian."[63] (Note a crucial misstatement: Mahler does not say that there is no good and no evil; rather, that there is no judgment dividing people into "sinners" [damned] and "just" [saved].)

Immediately before the fifth movement, in the short fourth movement, whose entirety is a song, entitled *Urlicht* ("Original Light"), Mahler has dramatized the journey of a child who sets out on a quest to alleviate human need and suffering. This child comes to a "wide road" (and note that the road of sin, in traditional Christian metaphor, is the one that is wide). An angel appears and tries to "warn her off" (*abweisen*) that road. But the child now bursts out passionately, "Oh no! I will not allow myself to be warned off!" (*Ich liess mich nicht abweisen*). This drama, and the accompanying music—in which the child's outburst introduces, for the first time in the movement, characteristic Mahlerian chromaticism—alludes to Mahler's own contest with Christian music-culture, and the way in which the "angels" of that culture warn him off from a path of emotion and unconventional creativity that he feels he must take. (This "path of sin" was also identified, by Mahler's enemies, with the "Jewishness in music" that Wagner had already famously repudiated.)[64] Setting what is in effect his own dramatic first-person point of view for a passionate contralto voice,[65] Mahler alludes to themes of androgyny and receptivity that surface often in his writings, and expresses his refusal to yield before convention. At the same time, he insists that his unconventional journey is motivated by compassion for human need. He will not abandon that quest.

The refusal, however, is not angry: it is just determined. The child says, I'm going to go my own way and not permit you to stop me. (I'm tempted to call its spirit Transitional.) The music expresses passionate longing, but not any sort of resentment.

Thus, when we arrive at the last movement, which Mahler connects with his enemies through the story of Von Bülow's funeral, we should expect no conventional resolution, no standard *Dies Irae* as in the many Requiem Masses Mahler knew and conducted. We do indeed find, in both verbal program and music, the first part of the *Dies Irae*: the fear, the urgent plea for forgiveness, the last trumpet. But then something fundamentally different happens. Mahler gleefully draws our attention to this surprise. There is actually no judgment after all, only a chorus of people singing softly. There is no punishment and no reward, only an overwhelming love. "We know and are." The ensuing text, sung by the chorus and two solo female voices, draws attention to the fact that the ongoing creative life of the loving person, including its passionate erotic love ("the hot strivings of love"), is its own reward.[66]

Here, we might say, is the Prodigal Son in eschatological form. But this would be subtly wrong, for there is actually, it turns out, no eschatology here either: there is a replacement of eschatology by this-worldly love. There is no heaven, no hell, no judgment at all. Just love and creativity.

Where, if anywhere, is forgiveness in this world? The theme of wrongdoing and opposition was introduced into the story of this symphony by Mahler himself, and no doubt he was strongly inclined to anger against Von Bülow, who had been especially hostile to him at a crucial stage in his career, when he was trying to get his First Symphony performed. Having struggled to find a way of ending this Second Symphony (including, he says, a search through "all of world literature, including the Bible"), Mahler tells us that he finally came up with the idea for the closing movement while listening to the choir sing an ode by Klopstock at Von Bülow's funeral. But in reality the Klopstock ode is a banal set of pieties, and Mahler keeps very little of the original text, writing most of the words himself, and all the music. So it seems pretty clear that the profound meaning of the Klopstock ode lay more in its occasion than in its content: there is something about overcoming resentment going on.

How, though, is anger overcome? It is like the father in the story: the anger simply disappears, and love surges up.[67] The persona whom Mahler depicts as the "hero" of the symphony doesn't ask for apology, and he also doesn't decide to forgive without apology. He simply goes on living as a loving and creative person, refusing to be "warned off" from his creative path—and overwhelming love simply drowns out resentment. Asking, "Shall I forgive my enemies?" would have implied that anger is still speaking, demanding to be heard. Instead, creativity and love have silenced it. The "wings I have won in the hot strivings of love" carry the creative hero to a light "that no eye has ever seen." If one can venture a bold interpretation, this "unseen" light appears to be music itself.[68]

In short, there are two ways a creative person might react to a struggle against adversity. One way would be to remain focused on the wrongs one has suffered, and on the possibility that the wrongdoers will weep and moan and express contrition. This type of reaction is common enough, but isn't it petty? The path mapped out by Mahler is, instead, to keep on being oneself and doing one's work, not wasting time on angry thoughts and feelings, but just giving whatever one has to give.

As de La Grange says, the whole idea of resurrection is un-Jewish. But in fact there is no after-worldly resurrection here. Instead, we are speaking of an earthly love that rises above anger and is its own reward. Perhaps this is also un-Jewish, if we are thinking of the *teshuvah* process. And yet such an attitude is perhaps more compatible with the Jewish emphasis on the worth of this-worldly striving than with the Christian eschatology of lowness and penitence that is Mahler's primary target. From the start, the voices sing with strength, dignity, and passion.

Mahler emphasizes the centrality of music to his entire idea of active love. We should not take this as simply a statement of personal predilection. We are invited to think about the role of music in human life, and even in religion. Music expresses many emotions, but it is surprisingly rare to find music expressing, as a predominant organizing structure (as opposed to brief episodes), vindictive anger and simmering resentment.[69] At any rate, the type of unconditional love and joy that Mahler's symphony offers and to which it draws our attention is characteristic of the way in which music can impart to human relations, whether in a religious context or not, a sense of joy and shared delight, thoroughly bodily and consisting of vibrations, breaths, and movements, that simply rise above anger and humiliation. How could music in fact repudiate the body with shame, except by destroying itself?[70] Indeed, one could go out on a limb and say that even when first-rate music expresses the verbal agenda of the *Dies Irae* (as, for example, in the *Requiems* of Mozart and Verdi), its corporeal nature and its passion—its generous outward movement of the breath—tend to negate that process and to gesture toward a more humane and more loving way of life.[71]

In both of our dissident examples, we see reasons for anger, and probably, in the past, actual anger. But in the reconciliations depicted, there is no allusion to a past of anger. Not only is there no structured *teshuvah* or penance process, with its multiple conditionalities, there is also no forgiveness in any recognizable form at all, even unconditional. There is just love, silencing anger. This theme cannot be fully developed at this stage, but it gives us at least a sense of what options might be open to one who looks askance at the whole forgiveness idea.

VI. Dissident Voices in the Jewish Tradition

The Jewish tradition, too, has dissident voices. To do justice to the tradition's complexity and to avoid appearing to support the stereotype that contrasts Christian mercifulness with Jewish harshness and conditionality, let us now introduce them. As with the Prodigal Son, so here: the dissident voices appear in stories, which need to be carefully read.

The classic transactional account prompts a variety of questions that subsequent interpreters ponder. Isn't the ritualized account of *teshuvah* too unyielding? Can such complex interpersonal matters be structured by law, and doesn't law at times deform them? Do the rules promote reconciliation, or do they actually often impede it, by forcing attention backwards and constructing an obsessive search for blame? Three stories from the Talmud meditate on these complexities, told one after another in the text.[72] The first two go as follows:

> R. Jeremiah injured R. Abba. R. Jeremiah went and sat at R. Abba's doorstep. When R. Abba's maidservant poured out wastewater, some streams of water were sprayed on R. Jeremiah's head. He said, "they have made me into refuse," and he read, as pertaining to himself, the verse, "God lifts up the needy from the refuse heap." R. Abba heard him and went out to him. He [R. Abba] said to him, "Now it is I who must appease you."
>
> When a certain person injured R. Zera, he [R. Zera] would go by and study before him and invite himself into his presence, so that the injurer would come and appease him.

Both the first and the second stories short-circuit the formalistic process of supplication, in favor of a forward-looking and generous relationship. In the first, sheer chance intervenes before R. Jeremiah gets a chance to confess and implore. The maid's careless act of sprinkling him with waste-water evens the playing field: neither is above the other, each has wronged the other, so they may as well just make amends without playing the "who's to blame" game. (Notice that there isn't even a confession.)

The first story, then, presents an alternative model for human relations, suggesting that a search for the first offender often yields to harsh and unyielding behavior, while an admission that each has no doubt offended one another in some way paves the way for constructive thinking that moves past the wrong and looks forward. In the second story, R. Zera doesn't play the traditional retentive role of the injured, waiting for the injurer to come to him. Instead, pretending to study, he actively goes out of his way to create, flexibly and generously, conditions for apology and reconciliation.

It's clear that these two stories do not represent transactional forgiveness. What about unconditional forgiveness? I don't think so. Unconditional forgiveness requires that the wronged party have angry feelings first, and then choose to waive them. In the first story, we simply know too little about the feelings of the wronged R. Abba. His decision to come out might involve either unconditional forgiveness or unconditional generosity. In the second, we can be pretty sure that R. Zera is not harboring anger: his calm strategic behavior is indicative of active generosity and love.

The third story, however, is the most complex of all:

> A certain animal slaughterer injured Rav. [The slaughterer] did not come [to Rav] on the eve of the Day of Atonement. Said Rav, I will go and appease him. R. Huna met him. He said, "Where is my master going?" He said, "To appease so-and-so." [R. Huna] said to himself, Abba [that is, Rav] is going to kill a man. Rav went and stood over him. The slaughterer was seated, cleaning

the head [of an animal]. He raised his eyes and saw him [Rav].
He said to him, "Abba, go: I have no dealings with you." While
he was still cleaning the animal's head, a bone let fly from it,
struck the slaughterer's neck, and killed him.

In the most obvious and frequent interpretation of this story, the slaughterer dies because he has behaved obdurately, failing to apologize to
Rav.[73] Rav, by contrast, has behaved well, seeking out the injurer himself,
an especially generous act given the social and class difference. (So Rav's
behavior, in my terms, would be unconditional forgiveness.)

However, the idea that this is a generous act is shaken by R. Huna's
reaction, and Huna was Rav's greatest student. Huna does not see the
initiative as an act of great generosity. He sees it as an act of violence
that will lead to death. Not an act of grace but an act of aggression.
As Moshe Halbertal writes, "The story forces us to confront squarely
the ambivalence between sanctity and narcissism that inheres in
any act of grace." Rav is aware that the slaughterer has missed the
time appointed for apology, so he goes to him—and it seems that he
is going in a state of high dudgeon, in order to *extract* the apology.
For R. Huna sees something in his demeanor—he is too enraged, or
too determined—that makes him see the visit as violent. And indeed
Rav's demeanor to the slaughterer turns out to be very different from
R. Zera's sensitive and indirect offer of an opportunity for apology: he
stands over him, backing him into a corner, thus provoking the ensuing fatal confrontation.

What an alternative interpretive tradition has seen here is the aggressiveness sometimes inherent in the demand for apology, and the great
difficulty of distinguishing between aggression and sensitivity, when
we're dealing with imperfect human beings. Even unconditional forgiveness can be tainted with narcissism, aggression, and assumed superiority.
Think how often—in a marriage, in relations between children and
parents—people do in effect stand over another person, sanctimoniously
demanding apology—until somehow a bone flies off and a serious injury
occurs. I'm with Moshe Halbertal when he argues that these stories com-
plement the formal tradition of *teshuvah*, making us see that real *teshuvah*
among human beings is always too complex to be fully captured in legalistic formulations, because it always involves a story involving real people involved in a complex and multiply fallible human relationship.

The suggestion of all three stories is that there is something wrong
with sticking to the classic account of transactional *teshuvah*, given the
imperfect nature of human beings and their complicated motives. In the
first story, the maid's chance action made both men see that they were
both imperfect, and had better try to raise each other up to create something a little better than before—something that the legalistic account,

with its emphasis on who's the first offender, did not invite. The second story suggests that it's all too easy for victims to be self-righteous and wait for propitiation, secure in the feeling that they are the wronged party. Instead, the gentle act of paving the way for apology, making it easy and natural, almost a nonevent, is a better harbinger of good relations to come.

And the third goes even further, seeing that even an unconditional act may have its problems. When one is wronged, the suggestion is, it is extremely easy to be wrapped up in oneself and to feel that it's outrageous that the other person doesn't come to beg for forgiveness. But that stance, saying, "I am important and you have wronged me, so why haven't you come to me?" can easily become narcissistic aggression and lead to great harm. Human beings are, so to speak, narrative creatures, full of mixed motives, so they need to remember the likelihood of hidden narcissism, through a sensitive reading of both self and other. Parties who harp constantly on who did the first wrong, and ask all the time for acknowledgment of their own moral superiority, may be choosing a doomed and violent path—even if they are right. At any rate, the Talmudic author suggests that people should take a hard look at the motives behind their righteous self-assertion, and ponder stories such as these. If they do, they may conclude that the best question to ask is not, "Who is more wronged?" but, instead, "How might reconciliation be achieved?"

The Jewish tradition, too, is complex. Its counterproposal is a cousin of Christian counter-traditions, less focused on an upsurge of strong emotion and more intent on altering the complicated transactions in which individuals or groups engage, shifting from a fruitless "blame game" to a future-directed process of reconciliation. Both traditions make clear the pitfalls that lie in even an unconditional type of forgiveness; both commend Transitional thinking and a generosity that makes this sort of thinking easier.

VII. Acknowledging Human Vulnerability?

A merit often claimed for forgiveness is that it involves an acknowledgment of human vulnerability. Griswold, contrasting forgiveness with "perfectionist" philosophies, argues that the forgiveness process comes to terms with, and treats with sympathetic understanding, the flaws that are endemic to human life.[74] Griswold is contrasting forgiveness, which acknowledges that one has been deeply hurt by another, with moralities in which one strives to live in such a way that nothing others can do will inflict a deep hurt. Such Stoic norms are indeed too rigid, I shall argue, at least in the realm of intimate personal love and friendship, where we should live in a way that opens us to the possibility of loss and grief.

I agree with Griswold, then, that we should be ready to acknowledge significant losses. But there is a long step from loss to anger, and still another long step from being angry to engaging in the transactional forgiveness process. We must examine those steps in each of our three realms. For now, let us only note that the transactional forgiveness process is perfectionistic and intolerant in its own way. The list-keeping mentality that it engenders is tyrannical toward human frailty, designedly so. We must constantly scrutinize our humanity, and frequently punish it. At least the Jewish tradition limits the scrutiny to things that a person can be expected to control. The transactional strand of the Christian tradition contains no such limitation and is consequently exactly as punitive toward the everyday as Joyce intuitively feels it to be. Moreover, in its exacting control over wayward desires and thoughts, the transactional strand of the Christian tradition is highly continuous with (and influenced by) the very Stoicism Griswold criticizes. Stoic philosopher Epictetus' instruction, "Watch over yourself as if an enemy is lying in wait,"[75] could easily have been said by many a Christian thinker—or by many a parish priest.

Appendix: *Dies Irae*

Dies irae! Dies illa	Day of wrath. That day
Solvet saeclum in favilla	Will dissolve the world in ashes
Teste David cum Sibylla!	As witnessed by David and the Sibyl.
Quantus tremor est futurus,	How great a tremor there will be,
Quando iudex est venturus,	When the judge will come
Cuncta stricte discussurus!	To investigate everything strictly.
Tuba mirum spargens sonum	A trumpet, scattering an amazing sound
Per sepulchra regionum,	Through the burial-chambers of the world,
Coget omnes ante thronum	Will compel all to come before the throne.
Mors stupebit, et natura,	Death will be silent with awe, and nature,
Cum resurget creatura,	When creation will arise
Iudicanti responsura.	To reply to the judge.
Liber scriptus proferetur,	A written book will be brought forth,
In quo totum continetur,	In which everything is contained
Unde mundus iudicetur.	From which the world will be judged.
Iudex ergo cum sedebit,	Therefore, when the judge will sit,
Quidquid latet, apparebit:	Whatever is hidden will appear:
Nil inultum remanebit.	Nothing will remain unavenged.

Quid sum miser tunc dicturus?
Quem patronum rogaturus,
Cum vix iustus sit securus?

What shall I say then, wretch that I am?
What advocate shall I ask for,
When even the just may not be safe?

Rex tremendae maiestatis,
Qui salvandos salvas gratis,
Salva me, fons pietatis.

King of fearful majesty,
Who freely saves those who are to be saved,
Save me, source of compassion.

Recordare, Iesu pie,
Quod sum causa tuae viae:
Ne me perdas illa die.

Remember, kind Jesus,
That I am the reason for your journey
Do not destroy me on that day.

Quaerens me, sedisti lassus:
Redemisti Crucem passus;
Tantus labor non sit cassus.

Seeking me, you sat in weariness,
You redeemed me by enduring the Cross.
Let such effort not be in vain.

Iuste iudex ultionis,
Donum fac remissionis
Ante diem rationis.

Just judge of vengeance,
Make a gift of remission,
Before the day of reckoning.

Ingemisco, tamquam reus;
Culpa rubet vultus meus;
Supplicanti parce, Deus.

I moan like a guilty criminal.
My face blushes with my fault.
Spare me, God, your suppliant.

Qui Mariam absolvisti,
Et latronem exaudisti,
Mihi quoque spem dedisti.

You who absolved Mary,
And heard the thief,
Have given hope to me, too.

Preces meae non sunt dignae:
Sec tu bonus fac benigne,
Ne perenni cremer igne.

My prayers are not worthy:
But you, being good, act kindly:
Do not burn me in eternal fire.

Inter oves locum praesta,
Et ab haedis me sequestra,
Statuens in parte dextra.

Grant me a place among the sheep,
And separate me from the goats,
Setting me on your right hand.

Confutatis maledictis,
Flammis acribus addictis:
Voca me cum benedictis.

When the wrongdoers are confounded
And thrown into the sharp flames,
Call me with the blessed.

Oro supplex et acclinis,
Cor contribum quasi cinis:
Gere curam mei finis.

I implore, bent down, a suppliant,
My heart as contrite as ashes,
Show concern for my end.

4

Intimate Relationships

The Trap of Anger

Do you acknowledge your wife?

> —Seneca, *Medea* 1021: Medea to Jason, as she throws
> the murdered children down from the roof

He tried to let reason rise to the surface—how hard he tried.

> —Philip Roth, *American Pastoral*: Swede Levov, learning
> from his estranged daughter Merry, the "Rimrock Bomber,"
> that she has murdered four people

I. Vulnerability and Depth

Betrayed wife, abandoned mother, she says that her anger is morally right, and the audience is likely to agree. She invokes Juno Lucina, guardian of the marriage bed, protector of childbirth, to come to her aid. But since her anger demands misery for Jason, she also calls on a darker group of divinities:

> Now, now be near, goddesses who avenge crime, your hair foul with writhing serpents, grasping the black torch in your bloody hands—be near—as once, dread spirits, you stood about my marriage bed. Bring death to this new wife, death to her father, to all the royal line. (Seneca, *Medea* 13–18)

Medea's anger seems both justified and hideous. Before long, she murders her own children, in order to inflict the maximum pain on Jason—despite the fact that their death also deprives her of love, a fact of which she has long since lost sight. She tosses their bodies down to him from the roof on which she stands, the "last votive offering" (1020) of their marriage. Now finally, she says, he must acknowledge the presence of his wife. Punishment accomplished, she feels her dignity and self-respect restored. "Now I am Medea," she exclaims (910). "My kingdom has come back. My stolen virginity has come back. . . . Oh festal day, o wedding day" (984–86).[1]

Medea's story is all too familiar. Few betrayed spouses murder their children to hurt their betrayer, but many certainly aim to inflict pain, and these efforts often have heavy collateral damages. Even when self-restraint prevents the enactment of anger's wishes, ill will seethes within, just hoping for some bad outcome for the wrongdoer and his new family. And so often that ill will sneaks out after all, in litigation, in subtle deflection of children's affections, or maybe only in an unwillingness to trust men again, which Medea aptly expresses through her fantasy of restored virginity.

But many will say that her payback wish is justified—so long as it does not go quite to the extreme point of crime. In the intimate domain, even people otherwise sympathetic to a critique of anger often hold that anger is morally right and justified.[2] (I used to hold this view.) People, and women especially, should stand up for themselves and their diminished status. They should not let themselves be pushed around. They owe it to their self-respect to be tough and uncompromising.[3] Maybe, just maybe, if the wrongdoer apologizes with sufficient profuseness and self-abasement, some restoration might possibly be imagined—or not. And if not, the ritual of apology and abasement can become its own reward.

Life is too short. That is in essence what I shall say in this chapter. And we could stop there. Nonetheless, since this is philosophical argument, I won't stop there. Instead, following the lead of chapter 2's analysis of anger, I shall ask about the role of both anger and forgiveness in intimate relationships, and how my previous account of payback, status anger, and the Transition applies in this domain. I shall focus on anger involving parents and adult children, anger between spouses or partners, and anger at oneself.[4]

I shall try to accomplish four things in this chapter. First, I'll describe the features of intimate relationships that make them require special treatment, where anger is concerned. Second, I'll argue that in this special domain a Stoic response is usually inappropriate and that emotions such as grief and fear are often appropriate—but not anger, apart from Transition-Anger. Third, I'll respond to the claim that anger is essential in order to assert one's self-respect and stand up for one's dignity when one has been seriously wronged in this realm. And fourth, I'll answer the related claim that anger is necessary (in this realm) in order to take the other person seriously: that a non-angry response does not show sufficient respect for the wrongdoer. Along the way, I'll attend to related issues concerning forgiveness, and also to the issues of empathy and playfulness, which I've tentatively marked out as playing a productive role.

Here's where we are. I have argued that the conceptual content of anger includes the idea of a wrongful act against something or someone important to the self, and that anger (with one important exception) also includes, conceptually, the idea of some sort of payback, however subtle. This being the case, even when a serious wrongful act has really been committed, anger is ethically doomed, in one of two ways. Either the victim imagines that payback will restore the important thing that was damaged (someone's life, for example)—but this is metaphysical nonsense, however common and deeply engrained in human cultures, in literature, and, probably, in our evolutionary equipment. Or the person imagines that the offense is not really about life, or bodily integrity, or other important goods, but is a matter of relative status only: it is what Aristotle calls a "down-ranking." In this case, the payback idea does after all make a grim sort of sense, since lowering the wrongdoer does relatively raise up the wronged. But this emphasis on status is normatively defective. A rational person will therefore reject both of these flawed roads, which I call the *road of payback* and the *road of status,* and will rapidly move toward what I call the Transition, turning from anger to constructive thoughts about future welfare.

There is one species of anger, I argued, that is not flawed in these ways. I call it Transition-Anger, because, while it acknowledges the wrong, it then moves forward. Its entire cognitive content is, "How outrageous. That should not happen again." Transition-Anger, a borderline case of anger, is not as common as we might at first think. So often the wish to return pain for pain sneaks in, contaminating it.

Let's also recall another piece of terminology. Anger is "well-grounded" when all of its cognitive content is correct apart from the payback idea: the person is in possession of correct information about who has done what to whom, that it was wrongful, and also about the magnitude of the damage that has been wrongfully done. It is something worth being intensely concerned about. Anger in intimate relationships, I'll argue, is often well-grounded.

II. Intimacy and Trust

What is special about intimate relationships? Four things, I believe. First, they are unusually pivotal to people's sense of what it is for their lives to go well, to their *eudaimonia,* to use Aristotle's term. The other person, and the relationship itself, are cherished component parts of one's own flourishing life—and the relationship weaves its way through many other elements of life, in such a way that many pursuits become shared pursuits, and goals shared goals.[5] A rupture thus disrupts many aspects of one's existence.

Second, such relationships involve great vulnerability because they involve trust. Trust is difficult to define, but one can begin by saying, with Annette Baier,[6] that it is different from mere reliance.[7] One may rely on an alarm clock, and to that extent be disappointed if it fails to do its job, but one does not feel deeply vulnerable, or profoundly invaded by the failure. Similarly, one may rely on a dishonest colleague to continue lying and cheating, but this is reason, precisely, *not* to trust that person; instead, one will try to protect oneself from damage. Trust, by contrast, involves opening oneself to the possibility of betrayal, hence to a very deep form of harm. It means relaxing the self-protective strategies with which we usually go through life, attaching great importance to actions by the other over which one has little control. It means, then, living with a certain degree of helplessness.

Is trust a matter of belief or emotion? Both, in complexly related ways. Trusting someone, one believes that she will keep her commitments, and at the same time one appraises those commitments as very important for one's own flourishing. But that latter appraisal is a key constituent part of a number of emotions, including hope, fear, and, if things go wrong, deep grief and loss. Trust is probably not identical to those emotions, but under normal circumstances of life it often proves sufficient for them. One also typically has other related emotions toward a person whom one trusts, such as love and concern. Although one typically does not decide to trust in a deliberate way, the willingness to be in someone else's hands is a kind of choice, since one can certainly live without that type of dependency, and Stoics do.[8] In any case, living with trust involves profound vulnerability and some helplessness, which may easily be deflected into anger.

A third distinctive feature of intimate relationships pertains to breakdown scenarios. The damage involved in the breakdown of an intimate relationship, because it is internal and goes to the heart of who one is, cannot fully be addressed by law, though people certainly try. Even though, as I've said, most forms of wrongdoing are in some sense irreparable (the murdered person cannot be brought back, rape cannot be undone), nonetheless a decent legal system does relieve people of much of the practical and emotional burden of dealing with such cases, by incapacitating the wrongdoer and deterring future wrongs. It thus assists what I've called the Transition. When someone you love harms you, however, even though in cases of violence or fraud one should turn to the law for assistance, the relationship is sufficiently central to one's well-being that the law cannot exhaust the emotional task of dealing with it. Beyond a certain point there is really no place to go, except into your own heart—and what you find there is likely to be pretty unpleasant. So there is something lonely and isolating about these harms; they involve a profound helplessness. Once again, this helplessness can easily be deflected into anger, which gives the illusion of agency and control.

A fourth feature might point in a more constructive direction, although all too often it doesn't: We typically form intimate relationships with people we like. We choose our spouses, and even though parents do not choose their children or children their parents, there is typically, in cases that are not really awful, a symbiosis that produces liking on both sides, though adolescence certainly obscures this. Most other people in the world, by contrast, are not people with whom one would choose to live. It's pretty easy to find them irritating, or off-putting, or even disgusting. How many people who sit next to one by chance on an airplane are people with whom one would be happy living in the same house for an extended period of time? But a spouse, a lover, a child—these people are welcomed, and there usually remains something nice about them that is not utterly removed by whatever it is they have done. The target of anger is the person, but its focus is the act, and the person is more than the act, however difficult it is to remember this. This nice something could become another knife to twist in the wound of betrayal (to the extent that a person is appealing, it's harder to say good riddance), but on the other hand it could also be a basis for constructive thought about the future—in a restored relationship or some new connection yet to be invented.

We now need to figure out how, in this special domain, anger and forgiveness properly figure. Is anger often well-grounded? If so, might it ever be fully justified? What becomes, or should become, of its fantasies of payback? Do people owe it to their self-respect to get angry and to be uncompromising (as so many suggest)? Or is anger more likely to be an impediment to constructive forward-looking projects and healthy relationships, a narcissistic "dance" in which one indulges at the price of not trying to figure out what the real problems are?[9] As Bishop Butler notes, "[C]ustom and false honor are on the side of retaliation and revenge . . . and . . . love of our enemies is thought too hard a saying to be obeyed."[10] But we don't have to agree with custom.

Such breakdowns typically, and rightly, involve deep grief, and grief needs to be dealt with. Grief is amply warranted: intimate relationships are very important parts of a flourishing life. (Here the Stoics are wrong.) But grief, and the helplessness it typically brings with it, are usually not well addressed by allowing anger to take the center of the stage. All too often, anger becomes an alluring substitute for grieving, promising agency and control when one's real situation does not offer control. I shall argue that the way to deal with grief is just what one might expect: mourning and, eventually, constructive forward-looking action to repair and pursue one's life. Anger is often well-grounded, but it is too easy for it to hijack the necessary mourning process. So a Transition from anger to mourning—and, eventually, to thoughts of the future—is to be strongly preferred to anger nourished and cultivated.

And what of forgiveness? Is forgiveness of the classic transactional sort a healthy and morally admirable process, or is it, all too often, a covert form of retaliation? Even at its mildest and most morally valuable, might it not be (to use Bernard Williams's phrase, in a different context) "one thought too many," a labored deflection from a spirit of generosity and spontaneity that is more valuable still?[11]

And if the standard transactional sort of forgiveness turns out to have serious defects, might there be a type of unconditional forgiveness, a struggle within the self to free oneself from corrosive anger, that does have considerable moral value?

Let me concede at the outset three points in favor of anger that I already conceded in chapter 2. Anger is often useful as a signal (to oneself and/or to others) of a problem; thus it is a good idea to attend to one's angry responses—bearing in mind many of them are unreliable, signs of misplaced social values or a warped concern with status. In some cases, anger may give motivational strength to action, though this is least true in the personal realm, where inactivity is not likely to be a major problem. and where anger can surely motivate people to do things both good and bad. A person's capacity for anger can also be a deterrent to another person's bad behavior—although a relationship of trust that sustains itself only through fear of the other party's anger is doomed already.[12] But even when these modest positive roles are present, anger should always be promptly transcended in the direction of the Transition.

III. False Social Values: Shaming and Control

Anger in intimate relationships often goes astray through a host of false social values concerning what a wrongful act is, or how serious it is. For example, the search for independence and even sheer pleasure in childhood has often been viewed with extreme disapproval. Similarly, many cases of anger in marriage involve expectations shaped by unjust gender roles; women's search for independence and equality, in particular, has been found very threatening by men. It is often difficult to disentangle cases in which anger is inappropriate because the person has violated some bad social norm but has not done anything really wrong, from cases in which there is a genuine wrongful act. After all, we are all creatures of our place and time, and our own intuitions about how children should talk to their parents, how much independence they ought to have at various ages, when sexual activity ought to begin, how wives and husbands should pursue career aspirations and divide domestic labor—all these are contingent and fallible. We feel we see clearly what was wrong with parents, and spouses, of an earlier era, when they got angry at things that we now think appropriate or at least permissible. But we know that we don't know what later generations will find wrong with our own attitudes and values. We must try to make the distinction between anger that is not well-grounded because the values involved are bad, and anger that is problematic simply because it is anger. But we know in advance that our distinction is fallible.

One ubiquitous source of cultural error involves hierarchy and status. Parents all too often think of children as disorderly beings who ought to learn their place—which is way below the parent! Many defective social norms in marriage involve something similar: a husband is angry because his wife has a job, or earns a good income, or wants him to share the housework. Such social norms frequently use the fear of the "superior" party's anger as an enforcement mechanism, and rituals of forgiveness and atonement are very often used to establish status asymmetry.

Status-obsession is only partly a cultural construct; narcissism and anxiety are endemic to human life, and intimate relationships are one place they are especially likely to surface, because of the great vulnerability they involve. When people establish hierarchies and try to control others, they are often enacting universal human tendencies in a world of helplessness. Thus even in the most enlightened of cultures the "road of status" is a constant temptation. Although such cases of anger are not well-grounded, they are so ubiquitous and so often endorsed by the authority of culture that we should not simply brush them aside, but be on the lookout for them as we analyze cases of anger that initially seem to be well-grounded. Often, when we look more closely we will find that what makes anger persist and fester is a hidden thought about status.

Norms pertaining to intimate relationships are among the most controversial and uncertain in human life. It does seem clear, however, that there are some instances of anger in intimate relationships that are well-grounded, because a genuinely wrongful act has occurred. Getting angry at abuse, violence, betrayal—but also incivility, or failure of concern and support—is often well-grounded. Although the Stoics hold that no human relationship is worth getting upset about, and although I shall agree with them concerning the more casual interactions that characterize the "Middle Realm," I do not agree here. Friendship, love, and family relationships are all genuinely important goods, and worth caring about deeply. So wrongful acts that take place in the context of these relationships of intimacy and trust are worth serious concern. Often they will be appropriate occasions for fear, hope, joy, and grief, and anger is at least well-grounded. I shall focus on such cases.

IV. Parents' Anger at Children: The Prodigal Daughter?

Children make their parents angry. They are rude, unwashed, disobedient, lazy. They don't do their homework. They don't help around the house. They also do some things that are seriously wrong: telling lies, stealing, breaking promises, bullying other children. Sometimes they damage their own future, for example by drug abuse. And sometimes, albeit more rarely, they commit very serious crimes. So anger is likely to play a significant part in even the best parent-child relationships.

In addition to the status error I have already mentioned (focusing unduly on hierarchy), parent-child relationships also involve a significant cultural danger in the area of payback. For long stretches of time, in many domains of Euro-American culture, the relationship between parent and child, at least in some quarters, was modeled on the imagined relationship between an angry God and the young sinner, often against a background of a belief in innate sinfulness. Thus Mr. Murdstone, David Copperfield's stepfather, regards a boy as exactly like "an obstinate horse or dog," who must be made to obey through pain.[13] David's entire life soon becomes a series of episodes of anger, punishment, and (failed) atonement. Mr. Murdstone may be fiction, but his attitudes were common enough during the Victorian era—and for a long time after it, particularly in the world of the English public school. George Orwell's essay "Such, Such Were the Joys" describes as typical his experience as an eight-year-old child boarding at St. Cyprian's School, where parental surrogates made him feel that he had to atone for sin more or less constantly. He wet the bed, and that was said to be evil, so the young Orwell grew up feeling that he had a propensity to evil that could not be checked or controlled, even by the frequent beatings, since he had no idea how to stop wetting the bed. Thus, he learned that he was constantly the object of (allegedly) justified anger, and he constantly had to do penance.[14]

Such attitudes were evidently so common that Anthony Trollope can depict as idiosyncratic Dr. Thorne's ideas about children, showing us the rule through the rarity of the attractive exception:

> Among the doctor's attributes, not hitherto mentioned, was an aptitude for the society of children. He delighted to talk to children, and to play with them. He would carry them on his back, three or four at a time, roll with them on the ground, race with

them in the gardens, invent games for them, contrive amuse-
ments in circumstances which seemed quite adverse to all manner of delight.... He had a great theory as to the happiness of
children.... [H]e argued that the principal duty which a parent
owed to a child was to make him happy. Not only was the man to
be made happy—the future man, if that might be possible—but
the existing boy was to be treated with equal favour.[15]

Where Dr. Thorne's heretical views did not prevail, anger was ubiquitous
in parenting, a repressive and controlling anger that took any independent movement to be a wrongful act.[16]

Modeled on a problematic conception of divine anger, this conception
of parental anger involves both anger and forgiveness/penance based on
misplaced cultural values. Nor did it have the instrumental value often
claimed for it. Control through fear of anger and even violence turns out
to be a very ineffective method of deterrence (Orwell wets the bed all the
more, David Copperfield can't remember his lessons when Murdstone
is glaring at him), and it is certainly, as Annette Baier says, the sign of a
diseased relationship of trust, if we can even speak of trust. We should
therefore put such misplaced-values cases to one side when investigating
more plausible instances of parental anger. But we must bear in mind, as
we do so, that such ideas, in a more subtle form, infect many good cases
of parental anger.

The relationship between parent and child, when they know each
other and live to at least some extent together,[17] has huge significance
for the well-being of both. For parents, children are commonly deeply
wanted and loved. They are also a parent's surrogate future, a way of
being immortal and contributing to the world. They can, however, also
impede parents from attaining well-being in other areas (work, friendship), draining energy and resources, and thus constraining their pursuits of other goals—a likely occasion for anger, particularly when
children prove ungrateful. For children, meanwhile, parents are sources
of life, nourishment, health, and security, of education, values, and support, financial and emotional. Since matters of such great importance for
well-being are involved, the relationship is, on both sides, one of enormous vulnerability.

Trust between parents and children is multiform, and constantly
evolving. When infants are born they have no say in the matter of trust;
they depend utterly on parents,[18] and have to entrust them with their
well-being, whether parents are trustworthy or not. Children seem, as
well, to have a kind of natural trustingness, which leads them to bond
with parents unless there is very serious abuse or neglect.[19] These attitudes evolve over time, as do the expectations they ground.[20] On the one

hand, children become progressively more aware of what they can and can't expect from their parents, and typically see reasons for confidence and gratitude that had been taken for granted before. But at the same time, children become more skeptical and withholding, no longer willing to entrust everything about themselves to parents. This gradual withdrawal of naïve trust is a part of growing up, but it can be painful to the parent, who feels increasingly helpless.

The parent-child relationship is inherently directed toward the child's future, and this future-directed focus is auspicious, where anger is concerned, suggesting ways in which rational parents might move quickly to the Transition, or experience from the start only Transition-Anger. But a focus on the future also has its pitfalls, since supporting a future is sometimes difficult to distinguish from trying to control that future, particularly in the context of a parental fear of helplessness, as children move beyond their control. Many sources of parent-child anger lie here, as children choose a future that is different from the one the parents imagine for them—and one that may not include the parent as a central figure. At the same time, despite these pitfalls, one of the best things about the parent-child relationship, where anger is concerned, is that both parties know the relationship is going to change. Spouses often do not know or expect this. Parents, by contrast, are prepared for upheavals, and children are positively eager for them.

Many stages in parent-child relationships interest me, but some involve complicated worries about the extent to which children are full moral agents at different stages of their lives. So I shall focus, instead, on children who are indubitably full moral agents if anyone is, that is, young adults living apart from their parent or parents.

The more independent adult children become—and of course this is desired, in a sense—the more complete the parent's helplessness becomes, since no amount of advice or persuasion can really control the outcome, even in ways that are highly desirable. If, as I've suggested, anger is often a mask for and deflection of helplessness, a way (not a very smart way) of reasserting control, we can expect anger to be particularly common when children move out. The combination of intense love and complete helplessness is greater by far than in spousal relations, where people usually share deliberations. Indeed, a spousal relationship is unlikely even to be formed at all if people don't like thinking about the future together.

On the other hand, there are aspects of the parent-child relationship, at this stage of life, that augur well for an anger-free future. Although the parent-child relationship is not like a love marriage, and in a way is more like an arranged marriage, in that neither has really chosen the other, early symbiosis and long sharing of habits and experiences create both many similarities of outlook and many deep bonds—as both remember trips, jokes, conversations, birthdays, other holidays, all sorts of shared formative experiences, and the sheer physical intimacy itself of hugging and close physical proximity, and, often, the memory of early nursing and holding. Such shared experiences sometimes give anger new fuel— how could you do this to me when we've shared this and this? But they also create a basis for movement beyond anger to a reinvented future.

One further distinction remains to be made. When parents deeply love their children, wish them well, and are not in the grip of a distorted conception of the parent-child relationship, there are two distinct ways in which they get angry. Hard though it is in practice to distinguish these, we must try. One involves vicarious ego-investment: the child is seen as an extension or continuant of the parent, a way of fulfilling parental aims. The other involves concern for the child's well-being, present and / or future. The two overlap, since a central parental aim is often to have a successful and happy child.

Ego-investment need not be malign, and it can lead to intense attention and concern, as awareness of mortality makes people grasp at whatever seems to give them a hope of defeating death.[21] Still, it can easily become infected by a concern for control, since not all possible futures for a child are futures that parents will endorse as continuations of themselves. From ego-investment comes much anger about choices of careers, religions, partners. It takes a lot of maturity and inner calm to think that the best continuant one might have might be a free person who forges his or her own way. Moreover, investment in an ego-ideal, though not necessarily competitive, is all too likely to be infected by status-concerns: parents want a child who gets into a college at least as good as those that accept other people's kids, a child who looks at least as attractive as other people's children—a child who is a source of pride to the parent, rather than shame. Such anger is not well-grounded. Even though some cases of ego-investment are benign, involving good values, we would do well, then, to focus on cases in which the parent is clearly focused on the child's flourishing.

Young adult children do things that involve harm to either self or others. Parents who are not unduly preoccupied with status and control will find anger well-grounded in many such cases. This type of anger frequently fits the model of chapter 2: the parent gets angry, thinks briefly that the offending child should suffer, or atone—and then, seeing that this does not quite make sense in the situation, shifts his or her thoughts toward the future, asking what type of constructive project might improve the situation. Often, too, the parent is one step ahead, having Transition-Anger rather than the garden-variety emotion.

In making this Transition, both of Aristotle's insights prove helpful. Empathy with one's child, which parents often attain to a high degree, helps the parent think of the child's path productively, rather than focusing on useless thoughts of payback. And the sense of humor and play mentioned by both Aristotle and Dr. Thorne is also a great help. Relaxed interaction with children often cuts off anger before it can fester, and helps even the well-grounded sort of anger reach a reciprocally productive resolution.

The Transition, however, is not always easy to access, and anger here is very human. Indeed we might be tempted to think a parent who never got angry was weird, and not fully involved in the relationship. When a child's bad act is very serious, harming self or others in a way difficult to repair, parents who deeply love the child and who feel profoundly vulnerable in the light of the centrality of the child in their whole scheme of goals and plans will be strongly inclined to anger. The question is whether this anger can ever be fully justified—including its wish for some type of payback or suffering, however subtle.

It is difficult, but essential, to separate grief and disappointment from anger. When one wishes a child well there are many occasions for a sense of loss and sadness, but loss and sadness are not anger. They lead to thoughts of helping or restoration, or, if these are not possible, to mourning. Anger, I've argued, is inseparable from some retributive wish, however refined. I've said that anger, like grief, is sometimes well-grounded, but that its wish for payback makes no sense and does no good, and a reasonable person will see this pretty quickly. But we need to test this on a difficult case, in which an adult child's bad acts produce well-grounded anger in the parent, anger that might initially seem rational and appropriate, and in which some sort of grief is surely appropriate. So: The Prodigal Daughter.

Philip Roth's *American Pastoral* portrays a gifted, successful, and decent man who is hit by terrible bad luck. Seymour "Swede" Levov, star athlete, successful businessman, married happily to a beautiful and decent woman (a former Miss New Jersey), delights in his gifted, albeit eccentric and emotionally complicated, daughter Merry. At first the trouble seems nothing more than familiar adolescent rebellion, angry protests against the Vietnam War and the system that created it. Then one day Merry bombs the local post office, killing an innocent bystander. After years on the run, and after killing three more people, she is rediscovered by her father, hiding in a squalid room, living a life of self-inflicted penance as a Jain ascetic. (As her father soon grasps, the asceticism is self-destruction rather than any positive religious commitment, since she interprets the Jain idea of *ahimsa* in an absurd manner, refusing to wash for fear of "harming the water," etc. "The words sickened him, the flagrant childishness, the sentimental grandiosity of the self-deception" [250].)

How could anger not be well-grounded in such a case, anger of so many kinds? The Swede is angry at her murders, angry at her self-destruction, angry at the way she inflicted so much pain on her family, both by her actions then and by not getting in touch with them for so many years. And he asks himself, as he always would, this reasonable man, "What does a reasonable man say next? . . . What does a reasonable, responsible father say if he is able still to feel intact as a father?" (249).

The Swede does indeed feel anger, and he does denounce Merry, "as angry as the angriest father ever betrayed by a daughter or son, so angry he feared his head was about to spew out his brains just as Kennedy's did when he was shot" (256). He even briefly violates his own "injunction against violence," which he has "never before overstepped" (265)—tearing her Jain veil from her face and commanding her to speak, and then, when she won't, prying her mouth open by force. It is clear that he does in that moment want her to feel the pain that her actions have inflicted on others. His lifelong commitment to reasonableness briefly goes by the boards. And the reader certainly feels, initially, that his anger is appropriate.

But then, something interesting happens. Love, grief, and helplessness take over from anger. First, he acknowledges that he is in fact helpless: "You protect her and protect her—and she is unprotectable. If you don't protect her it's unendurable, if you *do* protect her it's unendurable. It's all unendurable. The awfulness of her terrible autonomy" (272). And then, telling his brother Jerry about the meeting, he simply breaks down in an unprecedented outpouring of grief:

> And now he is crying easily, there is no line between him and his crying, and an amazing new experience it is—he is crying as though crying like this has been the great aim of his life, as though all along crying like this was his most deeply held ambition, and now he has achieved it, now that he remembers everything he gave and everything she took, all the spontaneous giving and taking that had filled their lives. (279)

Describing his brother to the writer Nathan Zuckerman (whose imagination gives us most of the narrative), Jerry Levov says that the Swede's problem was that he did not stay angry: anger would have given him distance and control. " 'If he had had half a brain, he would have been enraged by this kid and estranged from this kid long ago. Long ago he would have torn her out of his guts and let her go.' " It is Jerry's theory that the Swede " 'will not have the angry quality as his liability, so doesn't get it as an asset either' " (71–72). Anger is a way of not being helpless, seizing control, and in this case anger would have given him the banishment of a source of unendurable pain. Without anger, he's stuck with unconditional love. (He keeps visiting Merry in secret until she dies.) And love is both helpless and intensely painful. (Jerry, by contrast, has "a special talent for rage and another special talent for not looking back" [72].)[22] Jerry's proposal is, in effect, that the Swede should form a payback wish that consists basically in saying "good riddance": if you behave this way, I'll withdraw my support and love.

In the Swede, by contrast, the payback fantasy of anger fades rapidly in the face of the overwhelming love and grief that assail him. It just seems to have nothing to say to the love, makes no sense in connection with it. Indeed. So, we have the Transition, in this case in a terribly painful form in which there is little to be done. He can only visit her and go on expressing love. There's no apology, and there's really no question about forgiveness on the agenda, whether conditional or unconditional. There's just painful unconditional love.

The novel's stance (or Zuckerman's) toward the Swede is profoundly ambivalent. His unwavering commitment to reasonableness, generosity, and love strikes Zuckerman as both tragic and comic. These don't do him any good, the suggestion is; they are even ridiculous, since this is not a reasonable or loving or generous universe. My own stance is not ambivalent.[23] He is a generous and admirable father, in the worst of circumstances, and his story is rather like a Greek tragedy, in which the protagonist's virtues still "shine through," despite the blows of fortune that assail him. Reasonableness and generosity do not remake an intrinsically meaningless universe, but they have their own dignity.

It seems clear in this case that the parent's own self-respect does not require anger. Even Jerry doesn't say that: he just says that comfort and sanity require anger. But our other question seems more pressing: doesn't the non-angry parent insult the child by refusing to take her seriously? I think the point is mistaken, but it needs to be answered. The Swede would surely be condescending if he treated Merry's actions as the actions of a baby or a person of diminished capacity. Crediting the child with full agency is indeed necessary for respect; that, in turn, requires acknowledging the serious wrongfulness of her acts, and this entails at least Transition-Anger. The question is whether full-fledged anger, along with its wish for pain, is also entailed by respect. What's wrong with a set of emotions whose content is "You did something very seriously wrong; I am upset about it because I love you and want you to flourish and do good things. I see you as someone who is capable of much better than that act, and I hope you will put that act behind you and do better in the future"? I think this set of emotions, which is the Swede's (though with little hope) surely takes the (adult) child seriously, but it isn't sufficient for garden-variety anger. If some individual child thinks that he or she is being condescended to by being approached non-angrily in this spirit, that is a misunderstanding, though hardly an uncommon one, and it must be dealt with as such. Children often think that they have established an equal footing by making the parent (or other adult) lose control and behave badly; but who wants, really, that type of equality?

To summarize: parental anger at adult children often goes wrong by taking what we have called the road of status. When it does not make that error, or some other cultural error, it more rarely falls into the other trap, of focusing on payback, where payback would be utterly useless and unproductive. The reason parental anger is prone to these errors is the profound helplessness the relationship with an adult child involves: anger is a vain attempt at seizing control.

Roth's Swede, however, still poses unsettling questions for me. As readers we certainly sympathize with his anger, and I would say that we like him better because he becomes briefly angry. Had he preserved his cool, we might have thought the less of him. Mightn't a totally non-angry response have been not quite fully human—as if the pose of being a WASP, penetrating to his very core at last, had deprived him of some part of his humanity? So is it better, given that we are all human, that we do become briefly angry, when seriously provoked, before heading for the Transition? The payback wish is futile and senseless, and isn't there something weird and not quite human about rising entirely above it, in intimate relationships? I find this question troubling. On the whole, I think the answer is "no." Grief and love are enough vulnerability to establish one's full human credentials.

Another question left on the table concerns forgiveness. The Swede's case was pretty hopeless, and some unconditional attitude was his only possibility, whether of love or unconditional forgiveness. But is trans-actional forgiveness of an erring adult child a good thing, and, if so, forgiveness of what sort? Certainly we do not want forgiveness of the Murdstone variety, where angry emotions are waived after rituals of atonement that are themselves retributive and sadistic. Unfortunately, Murdstone forgiveness is all too common. In the best case, though, where there is a demand for contrition in connection with a really wrongful act, uncontaminated by status-hierarchy or undue desire for control, of what use are the apology and the ensuing forgiveness? Certainly they are not useful, or morally valuable, if they serve to abase or humble the adult child before the parent's anger. On the other hand, an apology can be useful evidence that the adult child understands the wrongfulness of his or her action, and asking for it can be a way of reinforcing attention to such matters in the future. So apology can aid the Transition. The parent's "forgiveness" is also useful if it is a way of reestablishing trust: you disappointed my expectations, but I will hope again, because I love you and you've given me evidence that there is reason for hope. We'll start afresh, and I won't hold this over your head. But this is forgiveness in quotes, because there is no reason to connect this sensible parental attitude with the waiving of angry emotion. Indeed, such a parent might well not be angry at all, just disappointed or sad.

Let us now return to the Swede. Was his attitude unconditional forgiveness, or unconditional love? And what difference does this distinction make? He was briefly angry. But in unconditional forgiveness we would have had a decision to waive angry feelings, and the attitude would be primarily backward-looking, not necessarily accompanied by positive love and concern going forward. Furthermore, the stance of the forgiver, as I have argued, is often tinged with a hierarchical assumption of moral superiority. In the Swede, instead, we see unconditional love welling up and displacing all thought of anger; it's the Transition, albeit in a tragic mode. There is no decision, and no sense of superiority, so immersed is he in the (hopeless) love that he feels.

In general, the whole ritual of apology and forgiveness is a bit grim and labored, and very likely hierarchical, in a relationship where love and generosity can and should dominate. If parents are forgiving all the time, even unconditionally, it is likely that something has gone wrong, some failure to delight in the child's positive achievements, some retentive insistence on score-keeping, and rituals of authority. When a parent actually says the words, "I forgive you," what is going on? It's here that I feel that the Bernard Williams idea of "one thought too many" is useful. The words "I forgive you" seem pretty overelaborate, by contrast to "Don't worry about it," or "Forget about it." They also seem pretty self-focused, expressing the parent's own emotional state, rather than useful sentiments on behalf of the child.

V. Children's Anger at Parents

Adult children also get angry at their parents. They resent parental authority, they feel the need to seize autonomy by emotional confrontation. Anger, indeed, is woven into the relationship, because the child, trying to be independent, naturally resents the very existence and competence of the parent, and good parents are almost more intolerable than bad parents (a point beautifully made in Roth's novel). In adolescence this anger is typically strategic: children do what Jerry Levov has done all his life, they use anger as a tool to effect separation, even if they are not aware that this is what they are doing. In the case of children, this is usually a benign strategy, and temporary. Still, its effects linger. The power imbalance is hard to shake off, and there is anger inherent in that, which can persist all through life. The very existence of the parent can seem like a wrongful act, a denial of equal status. It is never easy to relate to the parent as a whole person, rather than a total context for life and a looming threat to autonomy.

This anger is at bottom status anger. And often it takes the zero-sum form that Aristotle depicts: the one who feels inferior reacts to slights by imagining a payback that makes her superior and the (formerly superior) parent inferior. Whenever parents do something that is thoughtless, or rude, or disrespectful, a well-grounded anger at the wrongful act tends to get hugely inflated by this lingering status-anxiety. It is thus an occasion for comedy (but also much real suffering) that parents often perceive themselves as doing only good, while children perceive them as constantly aggressing against their autonomy—and the truth is often somewhere in between. (Think of the comic mother Marie in the TV comedy *Everybody Loves Raymond*—played with wonderfully egregious zest by Doris Roberts—who simply cannot understand why her efforts to help and advise are greeted with such hostility by her two sons and, especially, her daughter-in-law.)

What is really at stake is respect for separateness and autonomy. This is what children imagine is being withheld, and what parents either deliberately or unconsciously withhold—or just fail to see that they are perceived as withholding it. Withholding it is indeed wrong, and in that sense anger can be well-grounded. Still, anger, particularly with its likely admixture of status-anxiety, often makes things worse. What would be really useful would be to express the concern frankly and try to work with the parent to figure out a respectful relationship with the right sort of space. But the asymmetry inherent in the history makes this very hard. It is extremely difficult for children to see the world from the point of view of parents, as whole and fallible people, rather than thinking of them as magical and huge.

Where do anger and forgiveness fit in? Both are expressed, all the time—and sometimes the anger is well-grounded. Still, it is likely to be inflated, as I've said, by status-anxiety, and the forgiveness of the parent, correspondingly, is likely to be infected by gloating at control and new superiority. And even were this not the case, following the lead of anger and its promise of self-respect is usually counterproductive.

In *The Dance of Anger*, psychologist Harriet Lerner describes an adult daughter in Kansas whose frequent migraine headaches and constant anger revolve almost entirely around her mother—even though the mother, living in California, visits only once a year. The mother is always present, but things get much worse when she actually turns up:

> During her therapy sessions, she would describe the horrors
> of the particular visit to which she was being subjected. With

despair and anger in her voice, she would recite her mother's crime sheet, which was endless. In vivid detail, she would document her mother's unrelenting negativism and intrusiveness. During one visit, for example, Maggie reported the following events: Maggie and Bob had redecorated their living room; mother hadn't noticed. Bob had just learned of his forthcoming promotion; mother didn't comment. Maggie and Bob effortfully prepared fancy dinners; mother complained that the food was too rich. To top it all off, mother lectured Maggie about her messy kitchen and criticized her management of money. And when Maggie announced that she was three months pregnant, mother replied, "How will you deal with a child when you can hardly make time to clean your house?"[24]

(This really could be Doris Roberts, but then it would be funny. . . .) Of course things go from bad to worse when the baby is born, in predictable ways. Maggie wants Lerner to say her anger is justified, and to sympathize with her; and of course her anger is at least what we have called well-grounded. Its "payback" wish seems mild—only that the mother will go away. But what lies within that wish may be less mild. Moreover, the pain of separation for the mother is all too evident.

Lerner's point is that asking who's to blame and for what, keeping a crime list, is rarely a useful thing to do. Even trying to figure out how far the anger is well-grounded is likely to be counterproductive. Indeed, in this case it positively obstructs useful change. What Maggie had never done was to speak calmly about her goals and to let her mother know the limits she believes compatible with her independence. That would take work, and it would be risky, because things would then have to change. Cycling round and round in the predictable "dance" is a lot easier, because it means not having to address fundamental issues. So anger becomes a deflection from the constructive job of working out a reciprocal adult relationship. It is not just non-Transitional, it is anti-Transitional.

Finally, as tensions around how to deal with the baby become fraught, with Lerner's encouragement Maggie finally breaks the predictable pattern. "Maggie's heart was beating so fast, it occurred to her that she might faint. She realized in a split second that it would be easier to fight than to do what she needed to do."[25] What she needs to do is not to talk angrily about independence and maturity but to *be* mature. And so, for the first time, she speaks to her mother calmly and firmly. Her mother stands amazed. "Maggie felt as if she had stabbed her mother with a knife."[26] At first her mother goes right back to the old pattern of intrusive criticism, but Maggie stands firm, while again and again her mother tries "to draw Maggie back into fighting in order to reinstate their earlier, predictable relationship." When her mother slams the door, "Maggie had the terrifying fantasy that her mother was going to kill herself and that she would never see her again. Suddenly, Maggie noticed that her own knees were shaking and she felt dizzy. . . . Maggie was beginning to leave home."[27] And her mother too, terrified of being abandoned, is just barely beginning to comprehend that there can be closeness without blame and counter-blame.

Lerner makes two excellent points in this fascinating chapter. First, she shows that anger is often a way of not solving the real problem, of cycling it round and round. (And of course, the forgiveness that would follow one of these routine fights would be just another part of the ritual. We see this clearly when it's an abusive spouse, just not when it's us.) It's like a game with repeat play, and in this case each repetition makes things worse for both. Like all rituals, this one is rooted in the past. Especially in the child-parent relationship, playing out the anger ritual locks both parties into a posture of no-change, and positively deflects them from examining what they need to do and what would really solve the problem. Indeed it compounds the problem, by focusing attention on what is bad in the other, rather than on what might be good.[28]

Second, Lerner emphasizes that anger is easy and reasoning about the future is hard, because repeating a problem is easier than solving it. It is very challenging, when two people are close, to renegotiate a relationship that will include both genuine separateness and real love and intimacy. Change is scary, whereas going through the familiar routine, even if painful, is less scary.

Let us now return to our questions about respect and self-respect. I think here the question about respect is the clearer of the two: we are not inclined to say that Maggie's new calm manner toward her mother is condescending or disrespectful. Indeed it seems that it is only now, after forgoing anger, that Maggie finally sees her mother as a whole and separate person, and can treat her with respect as such. Does Maggie fail to respect herself, when she puts aside her anger at her mother's encroachments? Actually, as Lerner argues, she is now stronger and more self-respecting. She has given up the crutch of the anger game, and she is able to stand up for herself in a productive way, forging true reciprocity for the future.

As for empathy and playfulness: both were utterly lacking in the "dance of anger." With the calm renegotiation comes the beginning of real thought in Maggie about the mother's point of view, her ongoing need for closeness. The two are still too tentative to tease one another or be playful, but we can observe that the rigidity of the former relationship, while humorous from the outside, made humor on the inside utterly impossible. (The role of repetition and rigidity in humor is notorious.) After the renegotiation, things are more relaxed, and humor might possibly begin to emerge.

As the two start talking about limits, independence, and a new future, what place is there for forgiveness? Clearly there is no place for forgiveness of the classic transactional sort. Indeed, to the extent that apologies and demands for forgiveness—or even spontaneous offers of forgiveness—become prominent, we would be right to feel that the old "dance" was continuing. Maybe Maggie will need something in the neighborhood of forgiveness to wean herself from her angry feelings—but maybe not. Maybe thinking about her wrongs, and how to forgive her mother for those wrongs, would be a way of not moving on with the constructive job. Anger will be dissipated far more effectively by a new mode of interaction than by meditative exercises about forgoing anger.

We have been talking about an ongoing relationship, and about trivial wrongs—albeit wrongs that cause real suffering. What about the truly terrible things some parents do to their children? Things such as abandonment, neglect, and abuse?[29] Often, in such cases, the parent is no longer around in the child's life, and the child is held captive by feelings of resentment. In such situations, a type of internal forgiveness, meaning a liberation of the self from angry and punitive wishes, can be very important, and I shall discuss this sort of forgiveness further in section VIII. Even in such cases, however—especially when the parents are not monsters but deeply flawed and yet basically loving people—a kind of generous letting-go is often more promising than delving into anger and pursuing forgiveness.

A case in point is a best-selling memoir that is touted as a "memoir of forgiveness"—but it really is no such thing.[30] Liz Murray was the child of two drug-addicted hippie parents. The parents were in a sense extremely loving, but as their use of both cocaine and heroin increased, they could not be effective parents. Her mother sold Liz's winter coat, her birthday money, even a Thanksgiving turkey a local church had given them. The two girls were often hungry, and because they were unwashed and lice-ridden, they were bullied at school and stopped going. Along the way, her mother contracted AIDS, and Liz and her sister spent much of their time nursing her—until she died, and the father, failing to pay rent, moved to a homeless shelter. Liz lived on the streets.

The memoir is primarily about Liz's decision to take her life into her own hands, educate herself, and go back to school. It culminates in her winning a New York Times Scholarship to attend Harvard, where she began her studies in 2000. Because her father also had AIDS, she took time off to care for him (an episode not discussed in the memoir, which ends with the scholarship). She graduated in 2009, and is currently a motivational speaker.

How do anger and forgiveness figure in this terrible story? Liz shows us clearly that her parents really loved her. She does not appear to harbor a grudge or to have a difficult struggle with angry feelings— toward them. She does report a lot of anger toward people who denigrate her attempts to educate herself. One obtuse welfare caseworker, for example, taunts her when she talks about her Harvard interview, not believing her. Liz gets really mad. "Blood rushed to my cheeks, and I stormed out" (309). And her anger is very well-grounded. The welfare system behaves pretty badly through most of the memoir. Still, Liz does not waste any time on connecting with her anger or understanding it or even dealing with it. She just goes on with her life, in the spirit of the Transition: "That's okay, I thought, pushing open the double doors and exiting that miserable office. That's okay, because despite my caseworker's disbelief, I did have an interview with a Harvard alumnus that afternoon. In fact, my schedule that day was packed" (309).

So far as her father is concerned, she does report one brief episode of forgiveness, but it is significant for what it omits. On Liz's eighteenth birthday, her father tells her that he has AIDS:

> When the cake arrived, glowing with eighteen candles, they both sang me happy birthday and Daddy gently squeezed my hand below the tabletop—one awkward touch with his own shaky hand. . . . In his gesture, I could feel him reaching out to me across our distance, assuring me silently, "*I know, Lizzy, and I'm with you.*" I couldn't take my eyes off him, I was captured by this image: my father clapping his hands before the smoke of my extinguished birthday candles, so vulnerable and still full of life right in front of me, for now. I wanted to grab on to him, to protect him from AIDS. I wanted to make this stop happening to our family, to keep him safe and to make him healthy again.
>
> I did not make a wish over my candles. Instead, I chose to forgive my father, and made a quiet promise to work on healing our relationship. I wouldn't make the same mistake that I'd made with Ma, I would be there for him through this. We would be in each other's lives again. No, he hadn't been the best father, but he was my father, and we loved each other. We needed each other. Though he'd disappointed me countless times through

the years, life had already proven too short for me to hold on to that. So I let go of my hurt. I let go years of frustration between us. Most of all, I let go of any desire to change my father and I accepted him for who he was. I took all of my anguish and released it like a fistful of helium balloons to the sky, and I chose to forgive him. (294–95)

Liz forgives her father, she says. But what she lets go of, as she tells the story, is disappointment, "hurt," and "anguish." It is not anger. Indeed we can see from the opening description that she loves him intensely, and he her. They have been estranged, because she could not endure the repeated disappointments: but her position (like that of Swede Levov) was that of grief and helplessness, together with a wish to control his choices that she increasingly realizes to be doomed. There's no bitterness, no resentment, no wish for payback—before or after. So what forgiveness means to her is letting go of grief at his failure to be someone different, and taking on the far more difficult task of supporting and caring for him as the person he is (rather as Swede Levov takes on the job of visiting Merry and trying to care for her until she dies).[31] If she wants to call this forgiveness, fine, but it is very different from forgiveness in the classic transactional mode (there's no apology, indeed she renounces concern with whether he regrets his prior actions), and different, as well, from the sort of unconditional forgiveness (if one wants to call it that) that one might have if one is very angry, and lets anger go. There's no Transition, because there is no anger and no payback fantasy. She is as focused on the future as she can sensibly be, given that her father does not have long to live.

It is not surprising that as a motivational speaker Liz Murray's message is about taking control of your own life and building your own future, not trying to make excuses by blaming others, and not expecting to be able to control others. Her memoir goes in the opposite direction from those therapies that urge people to delve into their inner anger—even if that is supposed to be a prelude to healing. When the time seems to have come for anger, she just doesn't give anger the time of day.

There are problems in Liz Murray's approach to life (insofar as she gives advice to others): It is all about the individual will, and it neglects politics. Some people really can will and discipline themselves into success, but these people are the lucky exceptions. Others may really need therapeutic assistance in order to avoid or exorcise anger. More important still, if the problems Liz encounters are really to be solved, society itself has to change. The inhumanity and inefficiency of the social welfare system should be addressed not by Stoic detachment, but by political change. That issue awaits us in chapters 6 and 7. For now, I focus on her relationship with her father as a personal relationship, bracketing the impact of institutions.

VI. Gratitude and Reciprocity

At this point it is time to revisit our discussion of anger's good-payback cousin. As I said in chapter 2, gratitude is typically regarded as a first cousin of anger: given a high evaluation of some things or persons beyond our control, we will naturally feel anger if someone wrongfully damages those things, but gratitude if there is intentional benefit. Both, say the Stoics, betray an unwise dependency on the goods of fortune, and in chapter 5 I will basically agree with this critique in the Middle Realm, admitting gratitude as legitimate only in a narrow range of settings in which it is just a nice windfall and does not betray an unwise dependency.

Toward intimate relationships, however, my position is not Stoic: I insist on their great importance for people's well-being, despite their considerable vulnerability. Indeed they appear to be constituent parts of well-being.[32] And yet I argue that full-fledged anger is never appropriate. What, then, of gratitude, with its wish to benefit the other, analogous (apparently) to anger's wish for payback?

The first and most obvious point to make is that doing good is always in short supply and hardly requires a justification. So a suspicious scrutiny of motive and coherence of thought seems uncalled for. Even if the person benefited others because of some incoherent fantasy, we should probably say, "So much the better."

In intimate relationships, where gratitude is closely akin to love and registers a person's delight at the benefits that her parent, or child, or lover has conferred on her, the pleasant emotion seems to have more going for it than that: it seems to be a constituent part of the relationship itself, which is not exhausted by reciprocal benefit, but includes that as a prominent component. And this sort of gratitude is above all forward-looking, though not merely instrumental. Parents don't care for their children only in order to receive care in return in their old age, though this is important. They would care for their children even if they knew they would long outlive them. But the care is part of constructing a valuable relationship that will endure over time, in which exchanges of many sorts of care and benefit figure. And even though strictly speaking a child's gratitude looks back to care received, it too has a forward-looking function, whether or not the child is aware of this: the emotion contributes to the relationship's depth and stability. So gratitude, including its wish for good, seems not only defensible but very important.

Attention, however, must be paid to counterfactuals. There may be a gratitude that has the following inner form: "I am very happy right now because you have benefited me, given that I love and trust you and am consequently extremely vulnerable to your actions. I feel grateful, and I want to benefit you. But this vulnerability means that if you should ever betray me and act badly, I will be furious and want you to suffer." Gratitude sometimes, even often, takes this form. The attitude that is defensible, and constitutive of a healthy loving relationship, is gratitude without this implicit threat, gratitude that is compatible with generous onward movement in case of a betrayal or rupture. I think the reciprocal gratitude of children and parents is often of this more generous form. Perhaps one reason for this healthy situation is that both parties expect the child to become somewhat independent, not vulnerable to the very core; and parents understand themselves to be preexisting people with a core that antecedes the child and would survive the child's bad deeds. Such limits to vulnerability are, I believe, healthy, and they make gratitude healthy.

Now let us study the strains and betrayals of intimate spousal relationships, where the conditional threat-laden type of gratitude is, unfortunately, all too common—perhaps because a core of personal identity, not utterly vulnerable to the other party's bad behavior, is not always stably present.

VII. Lovers and Spouses: Strains

Marriage[33] involves enormous trust. Unlike (at least some instances of) the trust parents have in their children, this trust is not merely strategic and pedagogical. Spouses entrust one another with many important aspects of their lives, including sexual responsiveness,[34] financial security, care for a home, and, often, care for children. To some extent, trust is codified in contractual form, particularly if there is a "prenup," but also in explicit marital vows, if the parties take these ritual utterances seriously, or promises outside of ritual. Many other aspects of marital trust are understood implicitly, and it would be a very untrusting marriage that relied on explicit promises for everything—although it would also be a bad marriage if the parties didn't clarify their commitments and expectations in certain important areas such as having children and sexual monogamy. Because the couple pursues jointly some of the most important life goals of each, these goals themselves become shared goals and are shaped by the partnership.

The vulnerability involved in such a relationship therefore goes very deep. It is quite different from parents and children: parents want all good things for and from their children, but they also know that life is a lottery, and you really never know what child you are going to get. Parents also don't plan their whole lives assuming some specific input from a child: the child-rearing relationship is understood as temporary, and as not being a fulcrum for all of one's friendships, career choices, and so forth. With spouses it is different: the partner is thought to be a known quantity, at least in many respects, and the terminus of the trusting relationship is typically thought to be death, even if people know that half of marriages end in divorce. As is typically not the case with parents and children, the relationship is taken to be basic to one's choices in other important areas of life, financial, employment-related, and geographical. Even though it would still be possible, and, I believe, highly desirable, to preserve a core sense of oneself as a person who could continue no matter what, this is often difficult to achieve, and it is always difficult to strike a balance between this healthy self-preservation and a kind of self-withholding that is incompatible with deep love.

Some minor wrongs in a marriage may be occasions only for disappointment: they undermine expectations, but they don't really undermine trust. Thus if one person is always late, that may be annoying, but it won't feel like betrayal, unless punctuality has assumed unusual importance in the relationship, or unless unpunctuality is plausibly read as a sign of something deeper, such as a lack of respect. Many inconsiderate or harmful acts, however, cut deeper, and are occasions for well-grounded anger because they involve a significant betrayal.

Before we can talk of well-grounded anger, however, we need to be aware that here, as with children, false social values play a huge role in conditioning people's expectations and behavior. Ideas about how women should behave have been particularly distorted by the demand for a complete surrender of autonomy. Many cases of anger in current relationships result from a cultural hangover: one party expects things to be as they always used to be, the other wants them to be as she thinks they really should be. Of course it is a separate question whether, once two parties have made a bad bargain, they ought to stick to it: clearly there is something problematic in agreeing to forgo a career and then getting angry at the other person later when one realizes that one has done just that. But at least in that case we can say that the normative framework is part of the problem: one party is angry because he expects ongoing conditions of hierarchy and injustice.

Like marital anger, forgiveness between spouses often embodies false social values. The idea that a woman who has sex before marriage is impure and unacceptable is one idea that hoodwinks many people into thinking about forgiveness when what has really gone on is harmless behavior outside of accepted social norms, or even victimization. The idea that people should atone all their lives for a premarital "sin"—by being separated from their children and given a low image of themselves— is a staple of the nineteenth-century novel. A particularly ugly case is depicted in Hardy's *Tess of the d'Urbervilles*, where Angel Clare's confession to Tess that he has had premarital sex is greeted with prompt forgiveness, but her confession of her own rape and abuse by Alec causes him to leave the marriage.[35]

In order to study "pure" cases of wrongdoing internal to the intimate relationship, we need to focus on cases that do not involve such false cultural values, so far as we can tell with our limited vision. But we need to bear in mind that problematic cultural norms are often hard to distinguish from a more general status-anxiety, which we do need to confront as a central part of our concern. Indeed it is often difficult to tell whether a spouse who resents his spouse's independence is angry as a result of culturally deformed social expectations or as a result of personal insecurity and status-anxiety—and often it's both.

First, let's look at strains in an ongoing relationship. There are likely to be many, as time goes on, since we are dealing with two people with different goals (to some extent), trying to figure out how to balance autonomy and shared life. It's clear that there will be more strains when people are inflexible and intolerant, seeing every divergence from what they want as a threat. Aristotle's reminder about the playful and gentle temper is important here: that background approach to life makes it much less likely that people will find themselves constantly angry.

Anger will also be more common when one or more of the parties feels a lot of insecurity, because so many things can seem threatening, including, indeed, the sheer independent existence of the other person. (Proust makes the point that for a deeply insecure person, the other person's very independent will is a source of torment and, often, rage.) A good deal of marital anger is really about this desire for control—and since such projects are doomed, that sort of anger is likely to be especially hard to eradicate. Intimacy is scary, and it makes people helpless, since deep hurt can be inflicted by the independent choices of someone else; so, as with other forms of helplessness, people respond by seeking control through anger. People never dispel their own insecurity by controlling someone else or making that person suffer, but many people try—and try again. Furthermore, people are adept rationalizers, so insecure people seeking control are good at coming up with a rational account of what the other person has done wrong, just as Maggie's mother was good at giving an account of Maggie's failings, even though what she really wanted was a daughter who would remain a child and not grow up.

Harriet Lerner proves an insightful guide here as well. Let's look at a case from her book that does involve some real wrongdoing: failure

INTIMATE RELATIONSHIPS   117

of respect, failure to listen, failure to allow independence. Our question, like hers, will be: what is the good of anger, and indeed of apology and forgiveness, in such a situation?[36]

Sandra and Larry went to Dr. Lerner together for therapy. Both were deeply committed to their marriage. But they had some very serious problems. Lerner's first observation was that when Sandra spoke she put her hand in front of her face so that she couldn't see Larry: and then delivered her indictment. Larry is a workaholic. He neglects the kids and Sandra. He leaves the housework and kids all to her, and then fails to sympathize with her emotions when something goes wrong. He gets angry at her for being emotional and needy. Then, suddenly, he will take charge and do something for the kids without consulting her (for example, buying an expensive present). He doesn't know how to talk. When she advances, he retreats, opening a book or turning on the TV.

What does Larry have to say? Lerner observes that he is just as angry as Sandra, but speaks in a cold controlled voice. Sandra doesn't support him. He works hard all day, and comes home to find a lot of complaining. "'I walk in the door at six o'clock, and I'm tired and wanting some peace and quiet, and she just rattles on about the kids' problems or her problems, or she just complains about one thing or another. Or, if I sit down to relax for five minutes, she's on my back to discuss some earthshaking matter— like the garbage disposal is broken.'" Despite the deep love and commitment that Lerner later uncovers, all the two appear to share is blaming.

We can see that, although cultural expectations do shape this relationship, the anger of each is well-grounded, to some extent. Nor is it just about status: it concerns important goods. Larry lacks respect for Sandra's work, as this brief extract makes clear: he thinks it is all trivial stuff, and he is the one who does the real work. He also doesn't appreciate her isolation and her need for companionship. Sandra, for her part, probably does not imagine with empathy how tired Larry may be after a day at work. When he has a real problem at work (being passed over for a promotion), she blames him again—for not being openly angry enough!

Another background issue is the behavior of Larry's parents: very wealthy, living abroad, they don't respect Sandra, and don't show interest in seeing their new granddaughter. As usual, Sandra gets emotional and blames them, which causes Larry to clam up, retreat, and defend them.

At a more abstract level, Lerner learns that Sandra has become the one who voices emotions, and Larry is the calm rational one. This division of emotional labor may have worked early on, but it has become a dysfunctional pattern, as Larry never learns to recognize his own emotions, and Sandra over-emotes in ways that are not helpful. Above all, the two spend most of their time assigning blame for their various quarrels, in particular by a triumphant search for "who started it."

As with Maggie and her mother, anger and blame, even if well-grounded in a way, have become a self-perpetuating "circular dance," which impedes real understanding and progress. As with Maggie again, progress begins by breaking this cycle and taking constructive forward-looking action. One day Sandra calmly asks Larry to put the children to bed one night so that she can go to a yoga class. "When a pursuer stops pursuing and begins to put her energy back into her own life—without distancing or expressing anger at the other person—the circular dance has been broken" (61). Such behavior could become manipulative. But if it is honest and not cold or angry, a declaration that a person wants to do something for herself rather than blaming the other person because she doesn't have what she wants can prove productive, Lerner argues. It's a much longer story, and it contains reversals, but the theme continues: anger resulted from seeking superior position through blame, rather than simply cultivating an independent life, Transitionally. Even to the extent that anger is well-grounded, it is a deflection of attention from the underlying problem: Sandra needs an independent life, and Larry needs to cultivate his ability to care for others.

With Lerner's assistance, both arrive at what I have called the Transition: rather than punishing the other for their problems, they see that they both want to solve the problems, and that turns them constructively toward the future. As in the stories of Maggie and Liz Murray, simply realizing that you can take charge of your own life is a key Transitional point. Trying to get something by controlling someone else didn't work, and it built up resentment. Depending more on oneself takes the pressure off the relationship. "Thus," Lerner concludes, "she can talk to Larry without hostility and let him know that she is needing to do something *for* herself and not *to* him" (65). Oddly (since the contexts are so different), it's like our King example again: okay, anger is well-grounded, but let's not dwell on that and wallow in blame, let's look to the future and figure out what will work and what we can live with. In effect, we want accountability (stating clearly what the important values are) without a constant focus on liability: the "blame game" deflects attention from a constructive resolution.[37]

What about apology and forgiveness? Along the way, there are many apologies, and these were part of the "circular dance." They didn't serve a constructive function. If forgiveness means just not wallowing in anger, they do extricate themselves from that swamp—but not by anything that seems to be sensibly called "forgiving," since forgiving looks backward and not forward. Is going to a yoga class forgiving? Is forgiving having a calm discussion of how they will handle the in-laws' next visit? It seems not, unless one is determined to call everything good by that name.

We often hear that women, in particular, need to connect with their anger. Hieronymi urges us all to be "uncompromising," meaning that we should continue to maintain three things: that the wrongful act was wrong, that the wrongdoer is a member of the moral community, and that one is oneself a person who ought not to be wronged.[38] She seems to think that these three propositions entail anger. But who is more self-respecting? The Sandra who keeps dredging up every wrong, trying to pin blame on Larry (however justifiably, in a way), or the Sandra who simply gets on with her life and invites him calmly to go along? Anger looks like a childish and weak response, not an expression of self-respect. We may preserve Hieronymi's three claims, minus anger's payback wish. But we need to add to them a focus on constructing the future, rather than continuing to wallow in the wrongfulness of the past.

Larry and Sandra were guilty of no major wrongs, and that is one reason why their relationship, deeply unhappy at the start, was reparable. Sometimes, however, although the relationship continues, a terrible discovery comes to light that undermines the edifice of trust on which the relationship is built. We'll talk about erotic betrayals and breakup in the next section: but not all betrayals of trust are of this sort. When people marry, they trust one another not only to stick to the sexual terms they have agreed on, but also to be decent honest people playing a certain sort of role in the community. In the nineteenth century, a woman in particular, entrusting her entire livelihood and status to her husband, trusted him to be the person she believes him to be, and not a criminal. When a sordid past comes to light, betrayal and pain are the inevitable result—as in George Eliot's account of the marriage of the Bulstrodes in *Middlemarch*. This case will show us a lot about forgiveness by understanding what is achieved by its absence.[39]

Harriet Vincy has married the wealthy banker Nicholas Bulstrode, thinking him to be what he appears to be, a pious and honorable man. Bulstrode, however, built his fortune on shady financial dealings; when Raffles threatens to expose him, Bulstrode connives in Raffles's death. All of this is finally revealed to Harriet, and it becomes clear to her that Bulstrode will lose all his fortune and position. What we might expect from her is terrible and fully well-grounded anger, followed either by forgiveness or not. Retribution, indeed, is what Bulstrode himself expects—both from his wife and from God. What he actually finds is very different:

> It was eight o'clock in the evening before the door opened and his wife entered. He dared not look up at her. He sat with his eyes bent down, and as she went towards him she thought he looked smaller—he seemed so withered and shrunken. A movement of new compassion and old tenderness went through her

like a great wave, and putting one hand on his which rested on the arm of the chair, and the other on his shoulder, she said, solemnly but kindly—

"Look up, Nicholas."

He raised his eyes with a little start and looked at her half amazed for a moment: her pale face, her changed, mourning dress, the trembling about her mouth, all said: "I know," and her hands and eyes rested gently on him. He burst out crying and they cried together, she sitting at his side. They could not yet speak to each other of the shame which she was bearing with him, or of the acts which had brought it down on them. His confession was silent, and her promise of faithfulness was silent. (ch. 74)

Like the father of the prodigal son, Harriet does not appear to feel anger at all. Instead, she sees her husband's enormous vulnerability, and she feels a compassion that is related to the tenderness she has felt for him all along. (Perhaps tenderness has blossomed into compassion precisely because of his new vulnerability. The earlier Bulstrode didn't give her much room to care for him.) When he looks up, he does not see the punitive angry face he has expected. Nor, indeed, does he see the face of someone who assumes moral superiority in order to forgive. Instead, he sees that she has put on a garment indicative of mourning: she regards this as a great, and shared, sorrow, not as occasion for blame. Her dress announces that she is with him in sorrow, and that sorrow and shame are fully shared. She even sees shame as having been brought down "on them." Bulstrode does "confess," but Harriet, instead of forgiving, simply promises "faithfulness." She doesn't even want to hear him say what he has done.

Is there forgiveness in this scene? I can't find it. We are given no idea what Harriet's view of his crime is, except that she is prepared to continue loving him and to share his lot. It is like the story of the Prodigal Son: love and generosity get ahead of the angry response, and thus there is no struggle with angry emotion. It seems that it is only by a strained extension that one would call this "forgiveness," perhaps in the grip of the idea that any gentle and non-resentful response to a loved one's wrongful act deserves that name. But really, it is just unconditional love.

VIII. Lovers and Spouses: Betrayal, Breakup

A large share of the popular literature on forgiveness focuses on marital breakup, and, in particular, breakup occasioned by erotic betrayal. Not all betrayals lead to breakup; we are greeted every day, it seems, by erring politicians whose partners announce that they have forgiven and who then stand loyally and/or stupidly by their mate. But often breakup is the consequence. Whether or not the relationship ends, these violations of trust go deep and create great pain. Anger is often well-grounded—and yet it also damages all parties (the angry person, the target, and children or others who absorb collateral damage). Anger is such a large and corrosive problem that much of the literature focuses on how to manage it so that it does not destroy one's entire life. And it is especially here that there's a widespread feeling that, bad though anger is, people (and women especially) owe it to their self-respect to own, nourish, and publicly proclaim their anger. If a particular woman doesn't, she is accused of being weak, or lacking self-respect. Generosity and acceptance are regarded as major failings. The erring partner, meanwhile, has to establish standing in the community by proclaiming that he is seeking forgiveness, has confessed and expressed contrition, etc. The betrayed spouse is expected to demand no less.

Once again, anger at marital betrayal has a bad cultural history, which punishes the straying person excessively, particularly if female. *The Scarlet Letter* shows us society's anger bearing down upon Hester from all sides—and there seems to be nothing to mitigate its assault. Theodor Fontane's heroine Effi Briest, like Hester, is excluded from society for a marital lapse (at age sixteen!) that would be venial in a male, and is not even received with love by her own parents. If this is anger without forgiveness, we certainly feel that anger with forgiveness would be a lot better. (Indeed, Effi's husband Instetten, discovering the lapse years after it occurred, is immediately inclined to unconditional forgiveness, before cultural values interfere, blocking this path.)

Sometimes social punishment crashes down heavily on a person who has only thought of doing something bad. In Anthony Trollope's *Can You Forgive Her?*, Lady Glencora is unhappily married to the rigid politician Plantagenet Palliser, who blames her for their infertility and cannot relate well to her witty fun-loving personality. She contemplates eloping with her earlier fiancé Burgo Fitzgerald, and goes so far as to dance with him at a ball. This is the crime to which the forgiveness in the title (ironically) alludes, and once again, although there is really no wrongful act at all, the answer seems to be that if the only other option to forgiveness is obdurate anger and social exclusion, then forgiveness is surely a lot better than that. (However, Trollope is one step ahead of the forgiveness game. Palliser, who, it emerges, really loves his wife and is not as stupid as one might have supposed, does not ask Glencora for an apology or offer her forgiveness, conditional or unconditional—both of which she would surely have found fatally insulting. Instead, he simply takes her off on a continental vacation, lovingly—and because she finds herself pregnant shortly thereafter, the marriage endures.) So: false social values are everywhere, when we consider the errors for which spouses are thought to require forgiveness. And let's also note, here too, that Plantagenet's non-anger does not fail to take Glencora seriously. Indeed, his love takes her far more seriously than anger would have, since the anger he was culturally expected to feel was about hierarchy and control of property, not about her at all.

The punitive and asymmetrical history of the marital breakup is not our theme. But it reminds us that, as in the case of children and parents, there is a deep need for status hierarchy in many if not most human beings; given the social power to do so, they treat an intimate as an inferior, a wayward child, a piece of property. Anxieties about power, status, and helplessness are endemic to human life, and certainly to marriages nearing dissolution. Often it is the more socially and economically powerless partner, likely to be the female, whom betrayal sends into a tailspin of grief and anger. Since such women are often at risk of losing not only love but also money and status, a tidal wave of helplessness makes them seize any chance to reestablish lost control. Anger and blaming look like appealing ways of achieving that aim. And because the betrayed spouse feels not only loss, but also humiliation, she feels a need to restore lost status as well. Thus the road of status and the road of payback are complexly intertwined and difficult to distinguish.

The story of Medea is a myth, and yet it resonates through the ages, because of its indelible portrayal of the depredations of marital anger. (In July 2013, a modern Hispanic retelling opened to a rave review in Chicago, later winning a major award for "best new work.")[40] Medea's story has some unusual features: she is an alien in Corinth (which the contemporary version renders using the issue of illegal immigration). She has left behind all her family and friends. And as an alien there is nothing she can do once Jason abandons her. Moreover, because he is marrying a wealthy member of the ruling elite, he will acquire custody of the children. So her helplessness is extreme. Nonetheless, the story is in a sense a very common one, since it revolves around the fact that Medea has lost the man she deeply loves, who has betrayed her for another woman. And many such women have abandoned their career plans, leaving them vulnerable in related ways.

There is no doubt that her deep grief is justified and that Medea's anger is well-grounded. Jason has behaved very badly, harming her with full knowledge of what his betrayal will do to her. He has in effect destroyed a large part of her self. Her repeated insistence that only anger restores her full sense of being herself, of being Medea again, makes a lot of sense—in a way. She feels the need to extrude him from her whole being, to create a self that does not contain him at all: hence her fantasy of restored virginity. And she goes further:

> If even now in my uterus there lies concealed some safety deposit from you, I shall examine the inside of my abdomen with a sword and draw it out on the iron. (1012–13)

In this fantasy of abortion, Medea expresses the thought that everything his and him must be forced out of her body. It must be sealed against his aggression.

Medea's anger would not be anger, it would just be grief, if it didn't contain some wish for Jason to suffer. As we can see, her thoughts about how to rid herself of him all involve violence and the infliction of pain. Grief-fantasies are not like this. What Medea would like is to be invulnerable (a virgin), and since he is inside of her, invulnerability for her means for him to be cut into ribbons. To be Medea herself, powerful, and for him to be helpless. The project of murdering the children has nothing to do with anger against the children: repeatedly she says that they are innocent and that she loves them. She just can't think of any other way to make him suffer. He does not love her any longer, so what she does by and to herself is a matter of indifference. But he loves them: they are his "reason for living" (547); hence, as she notes, "there is a space wide open for a wound" (550).

But the payback thought still doesn't make sense. She can't get back what she really wants and has lost. All she can achieve by payback is more pain for all. Medea's path is extreme. Often the retributive wish inherent in anger is more civilized, just a wish that the new relationship will fall apart, or the new partner will come to grief in some way. All too often, however, the children suffer, because they are indeed spaces of vulnerability in the betraying spouse's heart. None of this does anything at all to restore what was lost, and it usually makes life go worse for the betrayed.

Is Medea's problem simply that she goes too far? According to my analysis of anger, the problem lies deeper: it is inherent in the very idea that Jason's suffering can ameliorate or counterbalance her pain. One way or another, she can certainly arrange to make him suffer. But what good, actually, does this do? It does no good if she is focused on love. Not only does payback not give her love, it also makes her less capable of love and less likely to find love. So, insofar as her anger is well-grounded anger, she should reject the payback wish pretty quickly as a bad way of dealing with her predicament. At the play's end, she gets into a chariot drawn by scaly snakes and flies off into the sky. "This is the way I make my escape," she calls. But of course it is escape up into the sky only in the sense suggested by the road of status: she's put him down (temporarily) and herself relatively up. It is not escape from the actual predicament of having no spouse, no love, no conversation, no money, and no children.

So anger, while understandable and well-grounded, does no good and may do great harm. What about forgiveness? When people are feeling helpless and need to reestablish control, they can all too easily use the forgiveness idea to control the other person. It is horrible to think of the inside of those political marriages, where the politician has to grovel to the end of his days in order to secure a "forgiveness" that makes his continued public career possible. Sometimes transactional forgiveness does not have that taint. But it is so difficult to know oneself in such tumultuous circumstances, and it would be difficult to be sure that one was putting the other party through a ritual of apology for loving and pure reasons. I find myself hoping that the forgiveness stuff, in at least some cases, is just a charade for the American public, so hooked on Christian penance, and that something more constructive is actually happening on the inside. Even unconditional forgiveness seems too asymmetrical and past-focused: Mrs. Bulstrode did better with generosity.

Apology can certainly be useful evidence (as with children) that the wrongfulness of the behavior is understood, and thus a sign that a future relationship might be possible (whether marital or of some other type).[41] But demanding apology seems all too controlling, not too different from the Puritans hanging that A around Hester's neck.

What's the real problem? It is one of deep loss. Two selves have become so intertwined that the "abandoned" one has no idea of how to have fun, how to invite friends to dinner, how to make jokes, how to choose clothes even, if not for and toward the other one. So it's like learning to walk all over again, and that is particularly true of women without strong independent careers and social networks, since those who do have careers have many parts of their lives that have not been blasted by the betrayal, friends of their own who are not attached to the spouse, and lots of useful work to do. Children have all of their adolescence to learn, gradually, how to live apart from their parents, and they expect to do so all along. A betrayed spouse often has no preparation for separateness, and no skill at leading a separate life. I've so often seen recently separated women flummoxed by the sheer act of going out to dinner alone with a friend, not being part of a couple. Their whole self-definition was not as "Louise B." (her maiden name) but (as culture urges) as "Mrs. George C." Without George, she doesn't exist.

So that is the problem. It is easy, in that situation, to think that the best future is one involving some type of payback, since that future, unlike the future of self-creation, is easy to imagine. It's still intertwined with the other person. It is like not breaking up. You can go on being part of a couple, and keeping that person at the center of your thoughts.

But anger does nothing to solve such a person's real problems, and it positively impedes progress, for a number of reasons. First, it diverts one's thoughts from the real problem to something in the past that cannot be changed. It makes one think that progress will have been made if the betrayer suffers, when, in reality, this does nothing to solve the real problem. It eats up the personality and makes the person quite unpleasant to be with. It impedes useful introspection. It becomes its own project, displacing or forestalling other useful projects. And importantly, it almost always makes the relationship with the other person worse. There was something likable about the person, and even if marriage is no longer possible or desirable, some other form of connection might still be, and might contribute to happiness. Or it might not. But the whole question cannot be considered if angry thoughts and wishes fill up the mental landscape. Far from being required in order to shore up one's own self-respect, anger actually impedes the assertion of self-respect in worthwhile actions and a meaningful life.

What does seem like a reasonable demand (when the other party is still somehow on the scene) is that the wrongdoer acknowledge the truth: a wrong has been done. (This is what I shall say about political cases in chapters 6 and 7.) Being heard and acknowledged is a reasonable wish on the part of the wronged party, and asking for truth and understanding is not the same thing as asking for payback. Indeed, it often helps the Transition. However, often the *extraction* of acknowledgment shades over unpleasantly into payback and even humiliation, and this temptation should be avoided.

Because anger is a very large problem in contemporary life, a large therapeutic literature on "forgiveness" focuses on how people can free themselves from obsessive and corroding anger.[42] Typically the label "forgiveness" does not suggest that a transaction between two people is envisaged. Instead, the other person is usually entirely absent, and the effort of the therapist is to get the betrayed person to stop being dominated by anger. It is a struggle in the self to surmount negative and retributive wishes, fantasies, and projects (such as litigation, influencing children and friends, etc.).

In this process, a common device does involve changing the way the patient thinks of the betraying spouse: with empathy and understanding, not as a monster, and so forth. To that extent, the process has some links to the forgiveness process described by Griswold, albeit in a one-sided form, since the other person is not in the picture. It is thus a type of unconditional forgiveness, and as such is not free of the moral dangers inherent in that attitude: moral superiority, and an undue focus on the past. A further problem is that it is often hard to tell, reading these therapeutic texts, whether the goal is really forgiveness, or simply getting rid of anger by any feasible stratagem. If hypnosis worked, one feels that these therapists would use it, since they are not typically concerned with the moral value of forgiveness as such, only with its instrumental usefulness.

And is the forgiveness emphasis even instrumentally useful? Of course the therapists say so, but they would: it is their trade. We must remember that they have not tested the relative helpfulness of anger-therapy by contrast to other devices for restoring the self, such as work, friendship, shopping, exercise. Therapy invites the betrayed person to focus hours and hours of mental and emotional energy on the person who has left, when, as I've suggested, what she really needs to do is to learn how to go forward—to enjoy being alone, to cultivate a range of friendships and activities. It can be a crutch, keeping her leaning on the past, rather than on herself. Even though the person is gone, he really isn't, because every day brings some new drama concerning him. It will be said that no new projects will work until the person "works through" her anger. But working through grief is something that simply happens as life goes on: new ties replace the old, the world revolves less around the departed person. Is anger really different, and, if so, why? As with grief, as life moves on, the importance of the damage actually shifts. When we see a person for whom the dead person is still at the center of life five years later, we feel that a case of pathological mourning. New values replace the old. Anger ought to move on too: what was damaged, and the damage itself, become, as life goes on, much less important. Anger typically does not remain fixed like a tumor. Indeed the idea that it does, and that one must access and express one's buried anger, is one of the most damaging tales of therapy.[43] If anything, it is the therapeutic insistence on accessing buried anger that keeps it fixed and immovable, like a stone. The real issue is, after all, the loss, and how to move on from that.

In short, if a person is dominated by angry and punitive thoughts, something needs to be done about that, and a struggle within the self needs to be fought. Is the quest for "forgiveness" a useful form of that struggle? It's like struggling with loss of faith by thinking about God all the time. There is a lucrative profession of anger therapy, and so those therapists convince people that forgiveness (of the internal sort) is valuable. But maybe singing lessons, or going to the gym, or, more generally, focusing on areas of competence and self-esteem, and making new friends (a task that is not assisted by a persistent focus on anger and blame) would be better ways of throwing off the dead weight of the past.

Notice, too, that although these therapists typically avail themselves of one of Aristotle's good suggestions, focusing on empathy, they are far from taking seriously his other suggestion, about lightheartedness and play. Indeed when one reads a long series of such books, one gets a very strong impression of people who have never laughed. By dragging the patient into a grim and frequently lugubrious process they certainly discourage lightheartedness and they may impede any creative response to helplessness.

To sum up: Intimate relationships are perilous because of the exposure and lack of control they involve. Being seriously wronged is a constant possibility, and anger, therefore, a constant and profoundly human temptation. If vulnerability is a necessary consequence of giving love its proper value, then grief is often right and valuable. It does not follow, however, that anger is so. From my analysis it does follow that anger is often well-grounded: what has been harmed by another's wrongful act is truly important, and the other person really did act wrongfully. However, here as before, the payback wish characteristic of anger is a kind of magical thinking that makes no sense—if one remains focused on the genuine goods of love and trust, which payback cannot replace.

It will be said that this way of viewing breakups is cold and hyperrational, a refusal of love and vulnerability. I deny this. My view in this domain is not Stoic. Grief and mourning are legitimate and indeed required, when one loses something of such great value. And I even grant that, to the extent that what is damaged has value, anger has good grounds. It's just that it gives such bad advice. Indeed, I think the shoe is on the other foot. It is Medea, the angry person, who is trying to be invulnerable by devoting herself to projects of controlling others. Her anger is a way of sealing the self, not really mourning or accepting vulnerability.

IX. Anger at Oneself

Finally, we must talk about a relationship that is among the most intimate of all: our relationship to ourselves. In some ways, this is indeed a relationship of privileged intimacy: we are with ourselves every minute of every day, from birth to death, so we have a lot of evidence that others don't have. We also show ourselves things that we don't typically show others. And we appear to have capacities for changing ourselves that we don't have for changing the character or behavior of others.

To a great extent, however, the asymmetry is illusory. We may in some sense be "with ourselves" all the time, but we change, forget, evolve: so the actions of a youthful self may be far stranger to us than the actions of a friend today. We also deceive ourselves a lot; even when we don't, we are ignorant of many of our motives and patterns, and we are highly biased interpreters—one reason why Aristotle held that friends offer us a self-knowledge we can't get from ourselves.[44] Finally, we just don't notice lots of things about ourselves that others notice. We don't even have superior knowledge of our own bodies. We do see and feel some things that others don't, but others see us much more completely, so they have a lot of evidence that we don't have.

Still, the difference between self and other, if in many respects illusory, still has ethical significance. We're entitled to make decisions for ourselves (even our future selves) that we would not be entitled to make for others, except in special circumstances. Self-control can be carried too far, or become destructive, but in general it is a fine thing, whereas control over others is usually not a fine thing. Similarly, being tough with ourselves, or holding up very stringent standards, or making a rigid time-schedule, may be fine, if it works for a particular person; being similarly tough with others, even one's own children, is usually not so great. Even in small ways there is moral asymmetry. A person who works a lot may find that in order to relax she has to say to herself, "Now you have my permission to go read a mystery novel." That would be a pretty annoying way to talk to a friend, or a child—even, I think, quite a small child.

The first thing to say about self-anger is that Transition-Anger is common here, and a very important force for moral improvement. Noticing some substandard act (whether moral or nonmoral), one thinks, "How outrageous! I'd better make sure not to do that again." Since the act is judged outrageous against the background of ongoing aspirations and goals, the anger is basically forward-looking (if it is anger at all), and it is constructive. Rather than inflict pain on oneself as if it balanced, somehow, the damage done by one's act (whether to others or simply to cherished ideals), one simply resolves, going forward, to be watchful and do better.

A lot of anger at self, however, is accompanied by self-inflicted pain, which is a type of payback; and it is often thought that this pain is an important part of the moral life. This sort of self-anger is often called guilt, and guilt, indeed, encompasses a good deal of self-related anger. Guilt is a negative emotion directed at oneself on the basis of a wrongful act or acts that one thinks one has caused, or at least wished to cause.[45] It is to be distinguished from shame, a negative reaction to oneself that has a characteristic, or trait, as a focus. We can see that guilt parallels anger: both focus on acts.

This focus on acts, rather than the self, is auspicious, since separating the deed from the doer is a constructive aspect of moral (or nonmoral) change. Another promising aspect of guilt is that, focusing on an act, it typically focuses on damage to our relationships with others, an important and (unlike more or less permanent traits) a remediable aspect of our conduct.[46] The problem comes, as usual, when we focus on the wish for payback.

My previous analysis suggests the following analysis of anger at self: (1) genuine anger at self, even if well-grounded on account of the genuine wrongfulness of the action, always contains a wish for the suffering of the wrongdoer. (2) This retributive wish makes no sense as such, *if* the focus is on the seriously wrongful act for which it is supposed to be "payback": one's own suffering does not undo or "balance" whatever harm one has caused. (3) But if one thinks that the real issue is one of relative status, then the payback wish makes perfect sense: if one person is lowered, the relative position of the other really does go up. This narrow status-focus, however, is ethically problematic. (4) Therefore a rational person will remain focused on the harm that has been done or intended, but will steer clear of the futile thought of payback and seek to do something useful or good in the future to ameliorate the situation: hence the Transition.

Does this analysis make sense in the context of relations with oneself? (1), (2), and (4) appear to make perfect sense. It is (3) that seems at first blush mysterious. What is the zero-sum game here, when there is only one person involved? Well, now we must point to a further symmetry between self-self and self-other relations: both involve multiple entities. We don't need to buy any particular theory of the divided self, such as Plato's divided soul or Freud's triad of superego/ego/id, in order to feel that in cases of self-accusation different aspects of the personality are involved. Often, the commanding or judging self puts down the infantile pleasure-seeking self; sometimes the creative self wants to put down the rigid judgmental self; sometimes it's just a struggle between the present, highly focused self and a lax or inattentive former self. In any case, it isn't at all difficult, after all, to make sense of (3) in terms of an internal debate. You ate that extra bagel; now you must be put in your place.

So the parallel makes pretty good sense. What we need to ask is whether the theory developed so far is correct for this unusual case. Is anger a deflection from useful future-directed thought? And is forgiveness, similarly, for the most part a red herring?

Here's what I used to think.[47] Guilt at one's own aggressive or otherwise harmful actions and wishes is a major creative force in the moral life, because it leads to reparative activity. Following the psychoanalytic accounts of Klein and Fairbairn, I argued that our interest in other-regarding morality, and, in general, a good deal of creative human endeavors, are the outgrowth of a need to make reparations for aggressive wishes or acts committed or wished toward those who care for us. So guilt, although it may be excessive or even misplaced (as when soldiers feel guilt at the very fact of surviving their comrades),[48] is on balance a strongly positive force.

Moreover, guilt plays a pivotal role in moral development. Early on, young children are full of aggressive wishes, and sometimes actions, toward anything and anyone that blocks their pursuit of their own ends. Wrapped up in infantile narcissism, they are unable to accord to the needs of others any independent moral weight. However, because they have developed a kind of love for their caregivers, they come to a point in their development where they are able to see their own aggression as a problem. Suddenly, they realize that the very beings toward whom they wish destruction are the ones who care for them and comfort them. This realization is the occasion of a deep crisis in the personality, which might lead to a total shut-down—except that, at this point, morality comes to the rescue. What Fairbairn calls the "moral defense" is the idea that through adopting rules protecting the rights of others, children can atone for their aggression. By obeying these rules, they become able to forgive themselves. Melanie Klein adds to this the further idea that persisting anxiety about guilt makes people try throughout their lives to benefit humanity: guilt leads to cultural creativity.[49] So that is my earlier view.

Herbert Morris develops a related picture in a powerful and nuanced way.[50] Guilt involves inflicting pain on oneself, with the idea that this pain is owed. Pain, indeed, is one constituent of the emotion. This pain expresses "hostility to oneself." But that suffering is intrinsic to the idea of a world in which we all need to learn moral rules in order to live together in community. The wrongdoer isolates himself from the community by violating its rules. Fortunately, wrongdoing takes place in a world in which there is a well-understood path to reestablishing the torn fabric of community: "asking for and receiving forgiveness, making sacrifices, reparation, and punishment . . . have the significance of a rite of passage back to union."[51]

Here's what my teacher Bernard Williams thought. (I must reconstruct this somewhat conjecturally, because his animus against what he called "the morality system" is expressed in many contexts, but never developed as fully as one might wish.) The Kantian idea of morality as a system of prohibitions, held in place by guilt, is confining and repressive. It stifles creative aspiration and the pursuit of personal ideals. It is incompatible with the generosity and spontaneity of love. Williams admitted that moral rules have a legitimate role to play in the political domain, but he questioned the claim of ubiquity and supremacy made on their behalf in the ethical life.[52]

Sometimes one becomes able to acknowledge the full measure of truth in one's teacher's insights only after that teacher has died—in this case, lamentably and prematurely.[53] I now think that I was too influenced by the strongly Kantian views of certain psychoanalysts, and that what I said about guilt is highly problematic. We don't need self-inflicted pain to correct ourselves and help others. And we do not need the fear of the torments our own conscience will inflict, as a motive to pursue our ideals. A positive love of others, combined with compassion at their predicaments, seems a sufficient motive for moral conduct, and a much less problematic one. Indeed, if one can only pursue morality by lacerating oneself, one's devotion to morality is surely very incomplete. It's like Aristotle's distinction between self-control and virtue: if you find yourself fighting an inner struggle to prevent yourself from committing acts such as theft and murder, something has gone badly wrong somewhere. Admittedly we all commit errors against others: but love of them, and a desire to do better by them, seems more productive than guilt, which is all about oneself and not about them.

Like anger, guilt may often be well-grounded. But, like anger, if it is attended by the thought, "Things will be made right if I inflict suffering (on myself)," that thought is highly irrational and unproductive. As with other-directed anger: pain won't solve the real problem, if the focus remains on the real problem. It's only if the focus shifts to a status concern, in this case a wish for one's own self-abasement to counteract a putative self-aggrandizement, that the suffering of the self seems to do any good at all. But that's the wrong focus to have, since it is narcissistic and has nothing to do with others. If one retains the correct focus on the other, one may feel guilt and have a wish for one's own suffering, but one will quickly recognize the futility of that project and move toward the Transition. In this case, the Transition takes the highly reasonable form of redoubling one's attention to the rights and needs of others and figuring out what actions of one's own will make their lives better.

Does guilt promote creativity? This is one of those untestable empirical claims that seems true only because it is untestable and because it resonates with so much that Judeo-Christian culture has taught us. It's interesting to observe that the Greeks, who did not recognize guilt as an emotion worth talking about, thought that creativity was promoted by a wide range of motives, including love of virtue for its own sake and including, too, the desire to achieve a surrogate immortality. These positive motives seem sufficient to generate other-regarding and creative efforts. And they are more appropriate than guilt, which has an unpleasantly stifling and narcissistic aspect. If we think of love, whether between parents and children or between spouses, it seems that Williams is likely to be on the right track: guilt is the wrong motive and positive love and compassion the right motives. Guilt may well block or inhibit these other motives.

With young children, the case for a positive role for guilt seems stronger. Consider Nietzsche's judgment that guilt was productive in order "to breed an animal with the right to make promises"[54] (discussed in chapter 3). The picture is that children are like heedless animals, and only the infliction of pain can get them to notice morality and take it seriously. Whether pain is the best way to train horses and dogs can certainly be questioned, and it should! It has long been established that even in the case of a "wild" animal such as the elephant, positive reinforcement is much more effective than pain.[55] Scientists studying marine animals, too, have discovered that positive reinforcement is sufficient for teaching: they had to use this strategy, since whales and dolphins can just swim away if they don't like what is in the offing. By now this appreciation of the positive has extended to other species. So, our antiquated views of animal training are evolving rapidly.[56] Where humans are concerned, we now know a lot more than Nietzsche did about the psychology of infancy, and we know that infants are capable of both empathy and inchoate altruism, which oppose narcissism, albeit in a primitive form. We probably don't need the Fairbairn picture of an abrupt crisis in the self, in order to explain how selfish infants become capable of morality. But that also means that we don't need to rely on instilling guilt as a force in moral development. A positive focus on the rights and needs of others, and on developing compassion for their plight, seems both possible and better, because more about others and less about one's own inner drama. At the most, one should grant a partial role for Morris's picture: a pain at one's isolation from others (as when children are sent to think over their actions in their room) may prompt useful self-criticism and a wish to act in a way worthy of human relations that one prizes.

Williams thought (again, I'm to some extent putting words in his mouth) that the Christian idea of original sin was at the root of the way we look at guilt and punishment, and that this focus smelled of the Murdstone school of child-rearing: it was inherently repressive and self-hating, encouraging sadism in parents and masochism in their children—who no doubt, once grown, would turn into sadists in their turn. Although I still want to distinguish the Klein-Fairbairn psychoanalytic story from Williams's (rather extreme and incomplete) version of deontology, I now see a kinship between the two that I did not see earlier, and I would rather rely on love—as does my favorite among psychoanalysts, Donald Winnicott.

What about self-forgiveness? Well, if one is dominated by guilt, and thus by angry feelings toward oneself, then a practice of self-forgiveness is surely better than that. But the vigilance of this process, and its obsessive inward focus, appear stifling in their own way, and surely impede outward-looking concerns and activities. Rather than figuring out how to rid oneself of crushing feelings of guilt, whether conditionally or unconditionally, it might be better to look at the world in a different way all along, so that one would not be crushed by those feelings. Even if one is in that undesirable state already, it might be better to get out of it through mental focus on others, and by becoming active in other-directed projects.

At this point, it will be natural to object that our main problem, in today's world, is not too much self-anger, but too little. Public life is filled with people who have little reflective or self-critical capacity, and who don't hold themselves to a high standard. I agree with the statement of the problem, but not with the diagnosis. The problem is not too little guilt, it is too little compassion and too little love of justice. For all we know, some of the furtive behavior in which public officials ubiquitously engage may be an outgrowth of guilt. At any rate, getting more angry at themselves would not be the solution to the problem. At best, it would be a signal that a problem exists and possibly also a motivation to solve the problem. But it could also impede the outward future-oriented focusing that the problems of public life require. Guilt is a slippery motive, because only insecurely and contingently linked to the real goal, which is the welfare of others.

But what about the deterrent value of guilt? Surely at least some people avoid wrongdoing only because they know it will mess up their relationship to themselves, keeping them awake at night and marring daily enjoyment. Well, if this is how one is and can't be otherwise, then there's no more to say, and such a person had better avoid her own wrath. But it seems sad that any person should avoid wrongdoing for such purely negative and self-focused reasons. It's one thing to avoid coffee in the afternoon because one knows that one won't sleep well that night, but if what is avoided is an act with serious moral content, one would hope that the motive to avoid would be connected to morality's positive goals. As with trust in intimate relations with others, so with self-trust: a relationship of trust that depends on fear of anger is not a healthy relationship. If it is possible to cultivate more positive motives for behaving well, one should certainly do so, moving to the Transition as quickly as possible.

Some of these motives may include a kind of pain, the pain of not having been the sort of person one was aspiring to be, or having done something that was not really up to one's own standard. I think that sort of pain can feel like a kind of grief, a part of oneself that has gotten lost or gone missing. Like grief, it focuses outward toward replacement: I redouble my efforts to do the good thing, to be the sort of person I really aspire to be. That kind of pain (which we might call moral disappointment or moral loss, and which often accompanies Transition-Anger) may well motivate good conduct (and awareness of it may deter). But that's different from the self-inflicted punishment of guilt.

More generally: although self-torment is less morally objectionable than tormenting others, it is not terribly desirable either, and a more generous and constructive attitude toward one's imperfections seems preferable. Above all, one should care about the welfare of others because it is them, not because it is all about me and my own guilty conscience.

There is one further complexity to be addressed; like the rest of this section, it will require me to reformulate some of my previous views. Sometimes a person does something seriously wrong because of the pressure of circumstances. The case on which I want to focus is the well-known case of moral dilemma: circumstances are such that, whatever one does, one will do something seriously wrong. There are dilemmas of many types, and I have written about them over a long time period.[57] Like Bernard Williams, I have argued that it is not right to assimilate these conflicts to conflicts of belief, holding that if two obligations collide, at most one of them can be correct.[58] I have also argued, in a Williamsesque fashion,[59] that these situations are not correctly described by typical Utilitarian cost-benefit analysis, which poses only the question, "Which choice shall I make?" and fails to pose another very important question: "Is any of the available alternatives free of serious wrongdoing?" I argued that in the situations where the answer to the second question is "no," then, even if the agent landed in that terrible situation through no fault of his own, and made the best possible choice under the circumstances, he should still feel emotions of something like "remorse," connected to the fact that, even if under constraint for which he is not to blame, he himself did a morally repugnant act.[60]

Why does the insistence on negative emotion make a difference? In earlier work I offered three reasons. First, the pain of negative emotion reinforces moral commitments that are otherwise valuable, and reinforces, too, the unity and continuity of a person's character, showing that she is not a chameleon who changes with each situation. (Aristotle already used that animal as an image of ethical inconstancy!) Second, negative emotion may prompt reparative actions (the Kleinian strand mentioned above), such as reparations for some of the bad acts committed in a war.[61] Third, and of increasing importance to me over time, is a point well made by Hegel: taking note of the special "clash of right with right" that a tragic situation presents may help us to think well about the future, trying to create a future where such clashes do not face well-intentioned people.

I still believe that marking the difference between tragic choices and other situations of choice is extremely important, and that Hegel's forward-looking account of that importance, at any rate, is powerful. I think that one may also endorse the other two reasons for marking the distinction. But we must now ask what the right emotion is. Clearly grief and regret are not enough: for they do not differentiate between mere bad luck and this case of horrible, albeit co-opted, agency. On the other hand, I see no reason why guilt should be called for, if we understand guilt as I have so far in this section, as a kind of self-punishing anger. "Remorse" is a very unclear term, so we cannot use that without defining it further. What may work best is Williams's term "agent-regret," regret of a special sort focused on one's own wrongful act. We could combine this with a special sort of moral horror that a good person feels, when confronted with the necessity to violate a cherished moral norm, and perhaps with a profound sense of moral loss, the loss of one's consistency and full integrity as a morally good person. None of this requires self-castigation or self-anger. Or so it now seems to me.[62]

Later, in the political context, I shall insist that we need two things: truth, and reconciliation, i.e., acknowledgment of what was done, and then a move beyond it to a better future. That is what we need here too: a truthful acknowledgment that this was not just a hurricane or a wildfire, but a deed done intentionally by me, albeit in the worst of circumstances and under duress; and then, a strategy to move beyond the horror, of which Hegel gives us a useful idea.

X. Law in Family Relationships

The Eumenides relieved families of the never-ending burden of avenging long-ago crimes: that burden henceforth was assigned to impartial courts of law. Aeschylus' insight remains important. According to my account, intimate relationships are intrinsically important. So law cannot fully take over the grief and loss appropriately involved when serious wrongdoing takes place in such a relationship. But it can take over the burden of securing accountability for the wrongful acts that have taken place. A large proportion of serious offenses (rape, murder, child abuse or neglect, assault, theft, and many others) occur in intimate relationships, and when they occur, the law must get involved. If Aeschylus means to suggest that law fully deals with the wronged person's legitimate emotions, leaving no remainder, then he is mistaken. Unlike the irrational and rude people of the Middle Realm, those we love or have loved remain, properly, of deep emotional concern to us. But the involvement of law should surely diminish the temptation to prolonged anger and should assist agents in arriving at the Transition.

Often in the past, law has evaded this job, through the pernicious idea of a "private realm" in which the law has no legitimate business. Laws against crimes in the family remain seriously underenforced today. When the law is not doing its job, people who have been wronged in the intimate realm should protest and try to get the law to do its job better.

Liz Murray is misleading when she suggests that people should react to parental wrongdoing with will and effort alone, rather than by also demanding legal accountability.

This important job for law, however, does not entail that law should be a vehicle for victims' anger or deal with offenders in a retributive spirit. Accountability expresses society's commitment to important values; it does not require the magical thinking of payback. Better alternatives are discussed in chapter 6. Moreover, in the pre-law world, a lot of victim anger was not really about damage within an ongoing intimate relationship: it was about a hereditary burden of retribution that involved, often, people the current generation had never known and to whom it had no meaningful bond but the bond of retribution itself. This type of futile payback thinking can and should be completely eliminated. What Atreus did several generations back need not concern Orestes at all: it is not the type of deep emotional tie that warrants even love and grief. In such cases, the fact that the family is involved does not make the offense part of an intimate relationship: it may as well be, and it is, part of the Middle Realm, where law completely assumes the emotional burden of the wrong.

We are vulnerable in major ways because we love and trust others. Vulnerability often brings grief. And it often also brings great anger. This anger is sometimes well-grounded, but, unlike grief, it is never fully justified: either it contains an excessive focus on status or it embodies a payback fantasy that makes no sense. In both cases, while acknowledging truthfully the bad actions that have occurred, people ought to focus on the well-being of others and creating a future. Anger does not assist in this task. Forgiveness might sometimes assist, if the person is fighting a difficult internal struggle against anger, but it is likely that claims on its behalf have been exaggerated by those professionals (religious or clinical) whose trade it is to help people fight these struggles—so they need to represent the struggle as necessary and valuable. The way anger goes away in the Transition seems much more promising: one stops thinking about one's own inner states and starts thinking about how to do something useful, and perhaps even generous, for others.

5

The Middle Realm

Stoicism Qualified

Polonius: My lord, I will use them according to their desert.

Hamlet: God's bodykins, man, much better! Use every man after his desert, and who should 'scape whipping? Use them after your own honor and dignity.

—Shakespeare, *Hamlet*, 2.2

I. Anger Every Day

Seneca pays a visit to his suburban estate. The house is in very bad condition. He complains to the steward, but the steward says it's not his fault, it's just an old house. Since both he and Seneca know that the house was built by Seneca in his youth, Seneca takes this as a personal remark, whether careless or intentional. "Angry at him, I seize the first occasion to vent my irritation." It seems, he says, that you have neglected those plane-trees: they have no leaves, their branches are knotted and twisted, their trunks bare. They would never be in that condition if you had irrigated the roots and mulched the soil around them. But again the steward is too sharp for him: he swears—by Seneca's tutelary divinity, indeed—that he has done everything in his power. They are just old. Narrating the story, Seneca confesses to his correspondent Lucilius, *intra nos*, that he had planted those trees himself as a young man. So the steward's remark sounds like a reference to himself. Anger ascending, Seneca turns and stares at the nearby doorman. "And who is this decrepit old guy? The door is the right place for him: he's on his way out. Where did you hire him? Do you enjoy having a corpse around the house?" This time the steward doesn't need to say a word: the doorman does it for him. "Don't you recognize me? I'm Felicio, the son of the old steward Philositus. You and I used to play together, and you used to call me your little buddy."[1]

Everywhere Seneca turns, people allude to his age (or he thinks they do), insulting him (or he thinks they do). And Seneca, as luck would have it, is approximately sixty-seven, a very good age to write moral philosophy, if only it were not so easy to be provoked into inappropriate anger.[2]

Seneca's behavior is, of course, absurd. He overreacts to everything, and allows anger to dominate his day. In the process he insults others and makes a spectacle of himself, when he might have been gracious and generous, ignoring references to his age (if indeed they were that), and perhaps even *really* ignoring them within, and just going about his business. That's the point of the little comedy he has constructed out of his own silly behavior, and Lucilius (in this letter early in the collection) is supposed to understand the comedy as an advertisement for getting more deeply involved with Stoic philosophy, at his own similar age.[3] Maybe he shouldn't, since Seneca represents himself as prone to similar outbursts of inappropriate anger in the *De Ira*, written approximately twenty-five years earlier: so the practice of nightly self-examination depicted there has apparently achieved little. But we should not read either of these passages as literal biography; Seneca is using a fiction of himself to instruct, in both cases. (In what follows I take Seneca as a literary model, using a similar representation of myself to illustrate failings, at the same time illustrating, one hopes, a type of self-detachment and even self-teasing that are helpful in addressing these problems.)[4]

This chapter is about the domain of life that can be called the "Middle Realm," a realm in which much of our daily life is spent: in dealings with strangers, business associates, employers and employees, casual acquaintances, in short people with whom we are not involved in relations of intimacy and deep trust, but who are also people and not legal and governmental institutions. A great deal of anger is generated in this realm, over slights to reputation and honor, insults or fantasized insults, and some genuinely harmful and awful behavior. Seneca's *On Anger* depicts a typical Roman's day as a minefield. Go to a neighbor's house and you are greeted by a surly doorman who speaks rudely to you. Go to a dinner party and you discover that the host has seated you at a place at the table that others will view as insulting. And on it goes.[5]

It's not difficult to update, especially when most contemporary cultures, similarly, contain so many cues for outrage over diminished respect and, in addition, so much really rude and inconsiderate behavior. Just to choose a non-random example, flying anywhere is a minefield of Roman proportions. You are almost certain to encounter rude agents or flight attendants, sloppy procedures that inflict delay and hardship, fellow passengers who are too loud, too smelly, or given to irritating impositions.

My own pet peeve is large men, usually very out of shape, who grab one's suitcase without asking permission first and try to hoist it into the overhead rack—thus giving a Senecan prompt for outraged feelings of gender or age stigmatization. Many of the same things can be said about driving, although at least in that case the offending parties are not right next to one's own body, and are often rendered helpfully invisible by the circumambient armor of their badly driven SUVs. When one's loved ones do something bad, they have this mitigating aspect: they are our loved ones, and we like and choose them. Much of one's day, unfortunately, is spent with people whose company we do not choose. Anger is waiting just around the corner.

My own temptations to anger lie primarily in this domain, and I am far from non-angry, as subsequent examples will show. In fact I am often ridiculous, in much the way that Seneca is ridiculous. With people I love, I luckily find it pretty easy to move quickly to the Transition. Anxiety often, grief sometimes, but anger, fortunately, rarely and briefly. With irritating strangers, however, I find non-anger hard. Indeed, as with Seneca, mental effort helps little, although it must be said that, given the triviality of these interactions, I don't work on it very hard. Clearly, I should work harder.

The Middle Realm is a mixture of heterogeneous elements. It contains irritants and apparent insults that exist largely in the eye of the angry recipient; it contains real slights to honor and reputation; it also contains behavior that is by any reasonable standard rude or inconsiderate or hostile. And it contains, as well, some very serious wrongs, which affect one's own well-being or that of one's loved ones: improper termination of employment, negligent medical treatment, harassment on the job, theft, sexual assault, even homicide. It is not to be expected or desired that all these offenses would receive the same analysis. Nonetheless, some initial points can be made.

In general, I shall argue that in this domain the Stoics are basically correct: most of these things (though not the last group) are not worth getting upset about, and it's a mistake to make them the object of any serious emotional concern. Even grief about the bad relationship is not appropriate: here the analysis differs from my view about intimate relationships, in a way already mapped out by Adam Smith, who thought that the Stoics were right about lots of things, only not about the intimate realm.

Sometimes the mistake is one of false construal: people think something an insult because they are anxious or hypersensitive, and there is actually no reason to regard the situation in that light. Sometimes the mistake is a more serious one involving false social (or personal) values: people impute to a reputational or other slight a significance that is inappropriate. While false social values play some role in intimate personal relationships, as I've said, here they virtually dominate the scene. As my analysis of down-ranking concludes, people in most cultures are commonly obsessed with relative social status, and this focus is inappropriate. I shall argue that to the extent that any emotion at all is appropriate (apart from the cases of serious damage to well-being, which we'll treat separately), it is at best a Transition emotion. If the behavior is outrageous enough, then it's right to have the forward-looking emotional attitude, which I've called Transition-Anger, whose content is "How outrageous. Something should be done about this." But to have full-fledged anger, even briefly, seems quite inappropriate. Moreover, as Seneca likes to point out, not correcting that tendency will virtually guarantee that one's whole day is filled with anger, because there is so much behavior everywhere that is rude, inconsiderate, or in some other way subpar. Detachment is urgently needed if life is to go well.

But my position is not Stoic, even here, because I hold that important constituents of one's own well-being are vulnerable to damage by others who are not our friends and loved ones: health, bodily integrity, work, and the health, safety, integrity, and work of people whom one loves. It's appropriate, I hold, to care a lot about these things. But these things can be damaged by strangers and other non-intimates, so anger could be, if not justified, still well-grounded. In such cases, what I shall say is much more complicated. First, I shall argue that in these cases a sense of loss or grief is often appropriate, and indeed inevitable given a person's (appropriately) high evaluation of the damaged aspect of her well-being. But the (appropriate) grief has a different object from its object in intimate relationships. When one loves a friend or a child or a spouse, that relationship has intrinsic value, and one rightly grieves when it ends, whether by death or rupture. Relationships with strangers are not of intense importance, so one should not focus emotional attention on that person (the annoying sales agent on the phone, the rude seatmate, even the thief or assailant). If one's own health or livelihood has been damaged by such a person, that damage is a legitimate object of grief and upset, but the person is incidental—much though we tend to obsess about such people. So grief and upset, when appropriate, still have a different focus. As in the intimate cases, full-fledged anger, including the payback wish, is not appropriate, and for similar reasons—so one had better head for the Transition as rapidly as possible.

These cases, however, are not exactly like the intimate personal cases, because here there is a productive road to take: turn matters over to the law. We don't have to engage, even briefly, in pointless anger and fantasies of retribution against non-intimates who seriously harm us, because what they have done is either illegal or ought to be, if it is serious enough to be the appropriate object of strong emotion.

Law can't fully deal with the grief of such cases—that, as in the intimate cases, remains for the person herself. But law can deal with the idea that something must be done about the offender, thus rendering garden-variety anger redundant. The Transition is right in front of us, and Transition-Anger (or a Transition after a brief episode of real anger) has an immediate direction: That's outrageous, let's call in the law. There's no point in getting further embroiled, mentally and emotionally, with the unsavory stranger who has done the damage. Let the impartial agencies of law figure out how to do this in a socially productive way. In intimate cases too, one may sometimes need to call in the law, and violence in the intimate realm, like violence in the Middle Realm, should be and is illegal. But I have argued that the importance of an intimate relationship, in emotional terms, greatly outstrips any amelioration that law can offer. Such is not the case with the Middle Realm. We can forget about those offending strangers, and we need have no further dealings with them.

Indeed, it is above all in the Middle Realm that people need the Eumenides. Aeschylus makes things too simple by suggesting that these kindly goddesses solve the problem of having a homicidal mother or a father who has devoured your half-brothers in a stew. Complicated negotiations among intimates are rarely settled, and perhaps never fully settled, by the law. But if some stranger from Sparta has hacked up your father, there is no need to try to work out an appropriate future relationship with him. What you had better do is to mourn your father and turn the prosecution of the murderer over to the state.[6]

On the other hand, anger has a limited use as an attention-getter, and therefore a potential deterrent. Although I've criticized people who need the threat of anger to deter their friends' bad behavior, the same is not true of the virtual army of heedless, careless, and rude offenders who assail us in the Middle Realm. I'll argue that anger (or, even better, a carefully controlled performance of anger) can be a useful attention-getting device in many cases, perhaps deterring bad behavior. It may also be useful, once again, as a signal (to oneself, and at times to others) of a problem, and as a source of motivation to address it—albeit often unreliably.

And forgiveness? In the Middle Realm what is needed above all is to mourn and move on (if the damage is serious) or simply to move on if it is not. Apology can be useful as a sign of what we can expect of the offender in the future. But there's a big difference between receiving an apology and extracting one, and putting the offender through a forgiveness ritual is usually counterproductive. Unconditional forgiveness is better, but, once again, it often retains a whiff of moral superiority that is all too common in this realm, as my examples will illustrate.

II. Stoics on the Middle Realm

Seneca's critique of anger sets itself in a long-established Stoic tradition.[7] Although his is the only complete Stoic work we have on the subject, we know that the great Stoic philosopher Chrysippus made anger a centerpiece of his four-volume work on the passions;[8] and there were clearly dozens of other philosophical books on the topic of anger, known to us by title, and in some cases by brief extracts.[9] Indeed, anger seems to have occupied the Stoics more than any other individual passion. They have relatively little to say, for example, about grief, compassion, and even fear; and they are surprisingly, and perhaps not consistently, friendly to a variety of passionate erotic love (carefully cabined, however, so as never to be the basis of anger).[10] The focus on anger is not surprising, given that they describe their societies (not implausibly) as obsessed with slights and insults, boiling over at every imagined dishonor, destructively prone to retribution.

The Stoic critique of anger rests on their sweeping disparagement of the value of "external goods," things not under the control of a person's reason and will. They insist that family and friends, health, bodily integrity, work, and political standing have no intrinsic value; and they do not even possess great instrumental value. Although, other things equal, it is rational to pursue these "goods of fortune," a person's well-being is complete without them: so if they are removed or damaged by chance or another person's bad behavior, one should not be upset. This means that their critique of anger starts so far back that there would appear to be nothing more to say about anger in particular: it's just one of the many ways in which people betray unwise attachments to external things. Since I do not accept this account of value, it might seem that their critique has little to offer to my own account.

The Stoics, however, are flexible persuaders, and they deal with interlocutors who do not share their own extreme position. They like to find ways of appealing to such people, nudging them toward the Stoic conclusion long before the full position is unveiled. Seneca typically writes in quasi-dialogue form, whether in the unanswered fictional letters to Lucilius or in the "dialogues," which all have some definite person (usually real, though used as a fictional character) as their addressee. Although that person says nothing directly, his or her responses are often imagined by Seneca. The addressee of *On Anger* is Seneca's brother Novatus, an average sort of Roman gentleman, who begins the work by thinking anger a very appropriate and useful emotion. Seneca nudges him gently out of that stance, presenting the full Stoic theory only in glimpses, and tangentially, late in the work's third book. So his arguments do not depend very much on the extreme theory of value, and many are of interest to us. Most, furthermore, do not concern intimate relationships, or, indeed, other important components of well-being (according to my account)—so we may focus our attention on the "Middle Realm," while noting that the Stoics do not in fact separate that realm from the intimate realm.

Seneca has several distinct arguments against anger. Anger, he claims, is often focused on petty trivialities. Even when it concerns apparently weightier matters, it is extremely likely to be distorted by excessive concern with status and rank—and also with money, a common sign of status and rank. Far from being helpful in promoting useful conduct, anger is a very unstable and unreliable motivator. Far from being pleasant, anger is extremely unpleasant and a cause of further unpleasantness. Far from being a good deterrent, anger makes people look childish, and childishness does not deter. And far from being lofty, anger is smallminded and base, not worthy of the self-respect of a truly self-respecting person. Let us address each of these in turn.

Seneca gets a foothold with Novatus by pointing to the evident fact that anger often concerns either things in themselves ridiculously trivial, or things that can't possibly involve any wrongdoing. In the second category are frustrations caused by the behavior of inanimate objects, nonhuman animals, small children, forces of nature, or the inadvertent acts of well-intentioned people who seek our good. In none of these cases is anger conceptually appropriate, because the intent to harm is absent (II.26). (Seneca is clearly assuming that the benign people have not been culpably negligent.) And yet, people do get worked up over all of these things. Novatus is expected to grant quickly that such people are foolish. In the first category are all sorts of actions that may involve some wrongdoing, but are so trivial that Novatus will immediately see that it is not worth getting upset about them. They are "empty shadows" that no more make our anger reasonable than a bull is reasonable when he charges at the color red (III.30). Among the trivia are

> A clumsy slave or luke-warm water to drink, the couch in a mess or the table carelessly laid—to be provoked by such things is lunacy. It takes a sickly invalid to get goose-bumps at a light breeze.... Only someone out of shape from overindulgence will get a stitch in his side at the sight of another person's physical effort.... Why should someone's coughing or sneezing... drive you crazy, or a dog who crosses your path, or a servant who carelessly drops your key? Can you expect a man to put up calmly with public abuse, with slanders heaped upon him in the Assembly or the Senate House, if his ears are hurt by the grating of a dragged bench? (II.25)

These vivid examples suggest a personal set of pet peeves and an all-too-lively propensity to irritation: who, for example, could invent that dragged bench?[11] Seneca adds a point he emphasized in Letter 12: anger is often the result of a mistaken imputation of hostile intent. We're inclined to believe people when they tell us we have been insulted or otherwise wronged, or to believe this on slender evidence (II.22). Instead, we should be very skeptical. He adds an interesting point: often people mistake surprising conduct for wrongful conduct (II.31)—presumably because we are creatures of habit, and are jolted by any deviation from routine.

In keeping with this observation, and a thread running throughout Seneca's advice, is the canonical Stoic recommendation of *praemeditatio malorum*: if you keep thinking about all the bad things that can happen, you avoid forming unwise dependencies on things of fortune. If, by contrast (turning to present-day reality) you expect every sales clerk to be intelligent, polite, and helpful, you set yourself up for a life of disappointment.

But Seneca knows that Novatus, while agreeing with Seneca when he makes fun of the hypersensitive and excessively credulous, will be reluctant to agree with him when he urges non-anger in areas that a Roman gentleman prizes greatly: honor, reputation, and rank. Seneca's own real position is that these are not matters that a good person should take very seriously; and in writing to Lucilius he often makes that position clear. But Lucilius, unlike Novatus, is a serious student of Stoic doctrine. By writing *On Anger* as a pseudo-dialogue with Novatus, Seneca commits himself to the more slippery task of arguing against anger in these cases central for a mainstream Roman—without putting the extreme theory of value on the table.

One strategy he uses is the assimilation of insults and reputational damage to cases that Novatus will clearly admit to be either silly or base: thus, when he finally does approach dishonor, abuse, and alienation of affection, he surrounds these cases with some of the trivia that he has mentioned before (rude servants, ill-behaved animals), and he also focuses on money, which is certainly a powerful symbol of status and rank, and yet one that a proud Roman may think unworthy as a reason for intense emotion. By making comedy out of litigation over inheritances and other financial matters (III.33), he strongly suggests that all concern with rank is just this silly. A typical passage begins:

> "How," you ask, "are we to keep in mind, as you urge, the pettiness, the wretchedness, the childishness of what we take to be harm done to us? I would advise nothing more, indeed, than to acquire a lofty mind and to see how base and sordid are all the things for which we bring lawsuits, run around, and lose our

breath. They should not be considered at all by anyone who has ever had a single deep and lofty thought! (III.32)

But Seneca uses, simultaneously, a complementary strategy: he thinks up all the arguments Novatus is likely to make for the utility of anger, and rebuts them one by one. Novatus's first argument—introduced very early in the work and oft repeated—is that anger is a useful, perhaps a necessary motivator of appropriate conduct. Seneca replies, first, by pointing to people who behave in an appropriately manly way but are not angry—hunters, gladiators, dutiful soldiers (I.7, 8, 11)—and, second, by showing that the addition of anger makes behavior less stable and less well calibrated to achieve the desired result. Northern tribes such as the Germani are full of rage, but they are not effective in a prolonged military campaign; far more credit goes to notable Romans (such as Fabius the Delayer) who won precisely by knowing how to withhold their troops strategically. In civic contexts, moreover, anger leads to excess, in punishment (Seneca cites the use of torture and capital punishment)[12] and in personal conduct with others.

Nor is anger pleasant, literary examples to the contrary (II.32): it is like a fever, an illness (I.12), a gathering of wild beasts (II.8); and if once one gives way to it, it will fill up one's whole day with unpleasantness, since there is so much bad behavior at which one could be angry if one were going in for anger (II.9).

Does anger deter bad behavior? Seneca addresses this issue together with the motivation-question, by showing that anger is not very efficacious: the army that is effective as a deterrent force is the army that wins repeated victories, not the army that makes a lot of noise.

Finally, Seneca addresses (repeatedly) the claim that anger is evidence of a lofty or great-souled character (I.20, II.15, III.38), hence a way of avoiding contempt and commanding respect. Actually, he tells Novatus, it is a sign of uncontrol, disease, and empty inflation. Just as it's the out-of-shape or sick body that hurts at the slightest touch, so it is the weak and ailing character that gets upset about everything (I.20). Indeed, the shoe is on the other foot: the really stalwart, lofty, and admirable person is able to endure insults and rise above them, making enemies look petty by overlooking their provocations. Here, right at the end of the work, Seneca finally brings out the stock Stoic hero, Cato, who is of course a generally admired Roman hero as well:

[Cato] was pleading a case when Lentulus, that figure of uncontrollable factiousness (as our fathers recall him), worked up a thick mass of spit and landed it right in the middle of his forehead. Cato wiped off his face, saying, "I will swear to anyone,

Lentulus, that people are wrong to say that you cannot use your mouth." (III.38)

Getting spat on is one of the most humiliating things that could happen to any Roman giving a public speech. Seneca, however, successfully turns the tables on Novatus's expectations by making the spitter, not his target, look disgusting and base. To be able to rise above humiliation with grandeur and even humor—the remark is actually quite funny in Latin, since *os habere* means both "to have a mouth" and "to have proficiency as an orator"—shows much more class than to be baited by rivalry into a low and unworthy display.

As we saw, Seneca depicts himself as having an anger problem that focuses on status and insult. In *On Anger*, he offers a famous description of his own nightly practice of self-examination, revealing in the process the interesting fact that a rejection of self-anger is an integral part of his Stoic self-therapy:

> A person will cease from anger and be more moderate if he knows that every day he has to come before himself as judge. What therefore is more wonderful than this habit of unfolding the entire day! How fine is the sleep that follows this acknowledgment of oneself, how serene, how deep and free, when the mind has been either praised or admonished, and as its own hidden investigator and assessor has gained knowledge of its own character! I avail myself of this power, and plead my cause daily before myself. When the light has been removed from sight, and my wife, long since aware of this habit of mine, has fallen silent, I examine my entire day and measure my deeds and words. I hide nothing from myself, I pass over nothing. For why should I fear anything from my own errors, when I can say, "See that you don't do that again, this time I pardon you." (III.36)

Seneca then offers a representative sample of this self-scrutiny: inappropriately harsh speech to one person, too much sensitivity to the insulting jokes of some others, too much made of the rudeness of a doorman, anger at a host who has given him a bad seat, and indeed at the guest who was given the "good" place; coldness to someone who speaks ill of his talent. In all of this, his stance is to reprove himself, but without self-anger: the self faces the self without fear, with a forward-looking determination to be better prepared the next time. Not even Transition-Anger is present: he is not outraged at his behavior, just patiently resolved to improve.

Seneca's arguments remain to be evaluated. But they clearly make a lot of good points that are independent of the extreme Stoic theory of value. Seneca does not distinguish the Middle Realm from the intimate realm; nor does he securely distinguish it from the political realm, although some remarks about the incompatibility of anger with the rule of law early in the work are an Aeschylean beginning (I.16). But these deficiencies do not remove the value of his arguments. The rejection of Novatus's various pro-anger claims will turn out to be a little one-sided; beyond this, the view leaves no room for a type of Transition-Anger that has a real, albeit limited, role to play. But most of the arguments are quite promising.

Particularly valuable is the work's reminder that the struggle against anger must be fought inside oneself, as well as in the social realm. In that sense, the Middle Realm is at times intimate, since people get angry with themselves over lots of things that do not involve major components of well-being. Perhaps, however, the constant self-scrutiny that Seneca's method demands is too inquisitorial to be entirely ideal from a Transitional viewpoint. I'll argue later that both a sense of humor (self-teasing) and generosity to oneself have an important role to play.

III. Misattribution and Skewed Valuation in Casual Interactions

Let us now assess the Middle Realm ourselves, armed with Seneca's insights, but also with our own analysis—and the experience of life. First, Seneca is absolutely right to say that a lot of people's anger in this realm is the result of mistaken attributions of insult and malice, and that these mistaken attributions, in turn, result from a hypersensitivity often caused by a morbid narcissism. His analogy to bodily fitness seems right: people in good psychic condition don't weigh every minor occurrence as a possible slight: they have more important things to occupy their attention.

He is also right to say that a great deal of anger in this realm is the result of a socially engendered overvaluation of honor, status, and rank. When much is made of what seat at a dinner table each guest has, something is amiss in the culture. What was true of dinner parties in ancient Rome is true now in countless spheres of contemporary life, but perhaps the Internet offers an especially keen example, offering people the possibility of spending their entire day searching for dishonor and insult, anxiously scanning the world for signs of their own ego and its up-ranking or down-ranking. This is a distinct problem from the problem of misattribution, because people sometimes are really down-ranked by others. But the problems are closely related. The more you obsess about rank, the more likely you are to construe some innocent remark as an insult. And rank is likely to assume outsize proportions in the Middle Realm. In the intimate realm we choose people out of love, or family concern. Strangers don't have these appealing properties. Sometimes they seem to be nothing more than a set of tokens of our social reputation or lack of it. So the Middle Realm must above all focus on containing the inflated concern with rank that disfigures so much social interaction. The error of status-focus bulks large, and the payback-error, all by itself, is less frequently the problem—at least when central elements of well-being are not at issue.

Seneca is right, as well, when he points out that a great deal of anger is absurd in two further ways. Some anger attributes malicious intent to things or people who could not possibly have such intent; other cases of anger concern things that are just too trivial to take seriously, although we do. Considering my examples of flying and driving, we can see that both errors abound: for many inconveniences are not wrongdoing at all, but we often believe that they are; and we also ascribe great importance to setbacks that are actually not worth serious attention.

But here we reach a gap in Seneca's analysis. For, although courteous and respectful treatment by strangers is not a major constituent of well-being, it does have enough importance that we are rightly concerned when it is absent. Society goes better when people are polite and helpful, and obey a long list of implicit rules of safety, courtesy, fair play, and reciprocity. Is anger appropriate when these rules are violated? On the one hand, we have Seneca's correct contention that such things are not worth our serious emotional energy, and his ancillary claim that we would fill up our day with unpleasantness if we did get angry every time something like that occurred. On the other hand, we have the need to enforce these rules in some way, and not to let things slide that are damaging to socially useful practices. This is a realm without law, for the most part, so isn't anger a good enforcer?

This is exactly where Transition-Anger comes in handy. Without getting sidetracked emotionally, or only a little, one can have a genuine emotional reaction whose content is "That is outrageous, and it should not happen again." Expressing such an emotion is often useful as a deterrent. One must be careful, however. Sometimes calmly expressing outrage makes things worse. I've discovered that the men who grab your suitcase to put it in the overhead rack really hate it when a woman calmly tells them that this is not a good way to treat another person's suitcase; such a reply does not promote social welfare, but only embroils one in further conversation with these people, which is unpleasant. So I have discovered a way of secretly expressing Transition-Anger without their knowing it: I say, "I'm terribly sorry, that suitcase contains fragile items, and I'd rather handle it myself so that, if anything should happen, I would know that I'm responsible and not you." Or, sometimes, I have a brief moment of real anger, thinking that they ought to be put in their place—but then head quickly for the Transition.

It's good not to congratulate oneself prematurely, however. On my flight home from delivering the Locke Lectures, I was just hoisting my small carry-on (heavy luggage already checked) into the overhead rack, and it was already 90 percent in, when a very large man asked whether he could help me. I said, "No thank you," and was about to thank him for asking—when, and by this time the bag was already in, he grabbed it and shoved it in further. I said, politely, "If you were going to do it anyway, why did you ask?" He said he was a German trauma surgeon and had "lots of experience with patients who . . ."—then he stopped, seeing something in my face, perhaps, that reminded him that I was not his patient. I said, somewhat less politely, that I do not spend hours lifting weights in the gym each day only to be insulted, and I bet I could overhead-press more weight than he could (since, though large, he was not in good shape). Obviously he was the sort of doctor, and surgeons are often of this sort, who has no interest in the individual history of the patient. He must have been thinking of all those faceless women— necks and shoulders merely—who had injured themselves in such activities, very likely without daily weight training. Nonetheless I really was angry, and my response was pretty stupid. I was so mad that I asked the stewardess if she could change my seat, since I thought that flying home from the Locke Lectures I ought to enjoy my flight with no temptations to anger. But then it turned out that he had taken someone else's seat anyway (he was that kind of surgeon), so, as he was replaced by a cheerful and amusing British man, my problem was solved!

Still, such are the obstacles posed by one's own psyche. I continued to seethe, even two weeks later. I found myself imagining little German conversations in which I pretend, ironically, that we simply have a linguistic misunderstanding, and I tell him in perfect German that in English when one says "no" that means "Nein," and if one wants to say "Ja" one says "yes"—thereby insulting him, since his English was actually perfect. Clearly I was still angry, in a way that deserves teasing. But much though I would have enjoyed teasing by a friend, I found that I had no capacity for self-teasing in that instance, and no desire to undertake sober meditative exercises to get rid of my quite ridiculous and disproportionate anger.

And notice this: had I chosen to forgive this rude man unconditionally, my forgiveness would have had, very likely, the moral difficulties I identified in chapter 3: a smug superiority, and a failure to think constructively about the future (an easy failure, when you won't be seeing the person again).

One difficulty of the Middle Realm suggested by this story is that one's sole encounter with a stranger may reveal irritating properties without ever showing other aspects of the person that might be good to focus on if one wants to achieve non-anger. (A surgeon with similarly irritating characteristics who is a leader in my Chicago temple revealed a rich basis for non-anger when he repaired the hand of one of our most talented students.)

What about a performance of anger? Sometimes, when anger is not a real temptation, a performance achieves good results, particularly in our litigious culture. One Saturday my hair stylist, as I was leaning back with my head in the sink for a wash, reached up for the shampoo, opening an ill-organized cabinet out of which various bottles fell, and one—plastic, luckily—hit me on the brow. I was startled but not really hurt or upset. But I thought it was useful to signal to others the significance of this event, since someone else could be seriously hurt in future (if a heavier bottle had fallen, or it had broken). So I gave a display of polite outrage, adding that they really should install a rack in that cabinet to hold the bottles securely. Yes, the hairdresser replied, we've told that to management for weeks. So, I repeated the performance with heightened vigor at the front desk, perceiving that this would help both the employees and the customers, and relying on the usual American fear of a lawsuit. This case seems to me similar to the Utku interpretation of Jesus in the temple: giving the culturally expected performance, in order to produce good results. Let's give Seneca credit again: the further it is from real anger, the easier it is to control and modulate. The performance achieved the result that anger-as-signal-to-others might have achieved, with more reliability. Even a brief moment of real anger could have inflated itself into an attempt to humiliate those people and make them feel awful. A performance aimed at good social outcomes carries no such risk. Transition-Anger, poised in the middle, is another reasonable response, but it is a little riskier than a mere performance, capable of sliding imperceptibly into real anger.[13]

Here's a case where I didn't entirely avoid the risk. At the Frankfurt airport security checkpoint, being selected for an additional body patdown, which was then administered by some unusually rude and ill-trained staff, I decided to speak calmly in my best German and tell them that "Est is wirklich viel besser, höflich zu sein."[14] But when I uttered these words it came out sounding like a parody of German rigidity and obsessiveness, especially as I tried to bite out all the consonants in my jet-lagged state (I had just flown in from India)—and I realized that real anger was in there, since I evidently wanted, at some level, to mock them and put them down.

These stories raise a question: for anger is so much a part of the fabric of social life that responding non-angrily is often itself misconstrued as insult or disrespect. I've found that women are expected to react emotionally, so when they talk calmly and analytically guys get annoyed, and feel that someone is talking down to them (as indeed I probably was talking down to the German agents). We have two questions here: is non-anger therefore ethically problematic? And, can it sometimes make things worse? I think the answer to the first question is no, though one had better be sure that it really is non-anger and not anger with a rational surface; but the answer to the second, unfortunately, is yes. I'm afraid that I have to say that when men get mad because a woman is calm and analytical (particularly, no doubt, when she speaks with an unnatural accent that she could have learned only in Bryn Mawr), that is really their problem, and it is not my responsibility to behave like a child in order to avoid their annoyed response. But sometimes, knowing the likelihood of that response, it could be better to give a performance of annoyance, or some other emotion, in order to humanize the interaction, even if one does not wish to humanize the interaction. I think that this also helps avoid the genuine error of using one's rationality to put them in their place, a temptation from which such encounters are rarely free.

Still, I cannot avoid one more observation. Men in particular think that they have achieved something if they can make a woman mad, particularly if she is calm and intellectual. Often, they use the attempt to make you mad as a way of flirting, no doubt thinking that unlocking the pent-up emotions of such a woman is a sexual victory. (And note that they assume these emotions are pent up in general, not merely unavailable to them!) This exceedingly tedious exercise shows that they have few or no interesting resources for flirting (such as humor or imagination), and it really has the opposite effect from the one intended, boring the woman, who has certainly seen this before, and making them look very silly.

As we know, however, the devil has many guises, and while I have learned to avoid anger in the suitcase-lift scenario, one virtually irresistible lure into anger is behavior in the Middle Realm that makes no sense at all. Of course this realm is filled with irrationality, and its forms are so manifold and so staggering that it is difficult to anticipate them, whereas the behavior of suitcase-lifters is boringly predictable. Internet service agents contradict themselves with stupendous inventiveness; bank officials, besides being barely able to speak English (whether educated in the United States or not), parrot absurd policies that make no sense. Here's one such occasion: I received an email notice of a possible fraudulent charge on my credit card. I called the bank, and, after being on hold for twenty-five minutes, was connected to an agent in the fraud department. The charge, we quickly agreed, was not mine. But it had also not really been charged: the number had evidently been random-dialed, and the party didn't have the other information (expiration date, CVC code), so the charge was declined. Nonetheless, the fraud agent insisted on giving me a new credit card, something that entails horrible time-waste and inconvenience. I resisted: If one number could be random-dialed so could another, so I and the bank were getting no improvement in safety. But, says he, he is required by rule to give a new card whenever there is fraud. Actually, I said in my most legalistic manner, there was no fraud because the charge was declined: at best an attempted fraud. Because I was about to go on a long international trip, and all bookings had been made with the old number, meaning a slew of international phone calls, I dug in and argued, pointing out that (a) his decision was not entailed by the rule he cited, which mentioned fraud and not attempted fraud, and (b) his behavior was bad for business and had no purpose. After over an hour of this, I lost (and slept badly later).

Should one yield immediately to the irrationality of life? The world often poses that question. But the belief that the world ought to be rational, and that simply pointing out that something is irrational will effect change, is a Senecan recipe for constant anger, and for dreams filled with irritating people who ought to be no part of one's inner life.

Sometimes, however, insults in the Middle Realm are not just personal slights: they target group traits that are used to stigmatize and subordinate. At this point they are not just slights, they can under some circumstances constitute assaults on our equal dignity as citizens and on the terms of political cooperation, as in the torts of sexual and racial harassment defined under U.S. Title VII. At this point, insults implicate serious aspects of well-being, since political equality is very important, and some types of denigrating behavior constitute illegal discrimination. So I postpone that type of insult for the next section, noting, however, that we see here a major gap in Seneca's analysis. So convinced was he that insult and degradation are trivial that he did not even think the status of being a slave was something about which one should be upset. While counseling nonviolent and respectful treatment of slaves, he lets the status itself slide, telling the slave that inner freedom is the only thing that counts.[15] That's very likely an inconsistent position anyway: if the status is trivial, why is rude and disrespectful treatment within it a big deal? Inconsistent or not, however, the position is wrong: certain types of insults are politically significant and involve unacceptable discrimination.

Another gap in Seneca's account, and a similar case where the "Middle" shades into the political, is the area of false accusation. Some false statements are mere irritants. Others inflict very substantial reputational damage, which cannot be dismissed as a merely trivial matter. When does a false accusation cross the line, becoming a damage to components of one's well-being that one rightly takes seriously? When it affects employment or career prospects, surely; when it so affects social relationships that the person has difficulty carrying on friendships and work, and even maintaining health, as with much Internet defamation, and much bullying, both on the Internet and elsewhere, that has no truth-value and is thus not exactly defamation. Of course people who attach inordinate importance to status often get terribly upset, and find their work and relationships disrupted, by things that Seneca and I agree to be petty and not worth serious concern. So the challenge is to separate such cases from cases where the damage is related to obstruction of important components of well-being. The law of defamation tries to draw this line, as does the tort of "intentional infliction of emotional distress." One cannot sue if one is made to work in a racially integrated workplace, even if one is genuinely upset, since law takes the position that racial integration is an important public good. When should sincere upset be recognized by law, and when, by contrast, should we just tell the person to grow up? As societies evolve the line shifts, in both directions. Sexual harassment, which once was regarded as falling into the "grow up" category, is now recognized as implicating major elements of equal citizenship and dignity. These complicated issues will be sorted out, as best one can, in section VI.

Seneca has too simple a conception of well-being; he also has a skewed idea of anger's utility. It is implausible to deny that anger ever has a useful deterrent or motivational role. Still, he is right to remind us that it can be slippery and unreliable in that role, and that a carefully controlled performance—or, to supply a concept he doesn't use, a carefully monitored Transition-Anger—would be even more efficacious because more controllable. Even when we consider driving, an area where there is so often bad behavior without law, anger can sometimes deter, but it can also provoke, or contribute to a dangerous escalation, whereas a carefully calibrated expression of outrage may be more effective.

Above all, however, Seneca has the right answer to the perpetual objection that our self-respect requires us to get angry at serious wrongs. The shoe, he rightly says, is on the other foot: it is the person who rises above such wrongs who is a really lofty character. We can recognize that a lot of behavior is subpar, without thinking that we owe it to ourselves to descend to the level of the aggressor or insult-giver. As Hamlet says: there are constant opportunities to react to the bad behavior of others, but why should one do that? Why does the fact that someone has done something outrageous justify my behaving, myself, in an intemperate or aggressive way? "Use them after your own honor and dignity" means, "Don't be the sort of person they are: don't descend into the gutter just because they have done so. Think what sort of person you are, and what your character requires of you. Model good behavior."

But, says our own imaginary interlocutor, angry people often succeed. To this we should reply, "Usually not for long." In politics, the explosive person usually gets into trouble pretty quickly, and sunny calm types such as FDR, Bill Clinton, and Ronald Reagan wear far better. When people given to angry outbursts are found at the top, it is usually not in a democracy, and even then they often get removed pretty quickly: Claudius and Nero had brief reigns, while the calm Augustus and Trajan, not to mention the Stoic philosopher Marcus Aurelius, had longer reigns—and died of natural causes.[16] Even in sports, where athletes are taught to react to insults and slights, deeper inspection shows that angry types usually have a rough road. People value the non-anger of a Paul Konerko, a Jim Thome, or a Brian Urlacher, and they have a hard time with the antics of Ron Artest—who, after undergoing required anger management therapy, reemerged to a successful and far less tumultuous career under the new name of Metta World Peace.[17] And though people applaud the motivational role of self-anger (a constant in Serena Williams's play), they frown on the use of anger to deter or humiliate others (which sometimes marred the play of John McEnroe). Obviously these are not exceptionless rules, especially when you are a tyrant (think of the long-lived Mao), but it is worth contemplating.

Does apology make a difference? Certainly it does going forward, by leading us to expect good things from the apologizer, other things equal. Apology may remove the need for protest, or a performance of anger.

So far, notice, we have been focusing on wrongdoing that does not seriously threaten well-being: thus Seneca's advice is all too easy, since I have constructed the list of cases so as to exclude the grave wrongs that strangers can do to us. My view about these will become clear in section VI, where I shall urge that instead of getting involved in retributive anger we should turn these issues over to the law.

IV. The Middle of the Middle: Colleagues and Associates

We are not finished with non-grave wrongdoing, however. So far I have focused on strangers and on people whom we see only casually and rarely. Life, unfortunately, is much more complicated than that. We work and associate with many people whom we know pretty well. They are not intimates, and we are not in any relationship of deep personal trust with them, but we have other sorts of interdependence and even trust, and we have institutional relations that define norms and expectations. These norms are frequently violated. Sometimes our associates are irritating in chronic ways, and we don't have the option of not associating with them. Indeed, since good comedy is usually based on character, there's more good comedy to be made in what we can call "the middle of the middle"—that is, neither deep intimacy nor casual interactions with strangers—than in the more casual domain, something that good sitcoms have known since the hilarious anger of Gale Gordon as high school principal Osgood Conklin on *Our Miss Brooks*.

The workplace is not very intimate, but in it we pursue some of the most important projects of our lives.[18] So it's an odd place: you don't really have any reason to trust your colleagues with your life, and yet, in a real sense, you have to. That oddness adds to the comedy (and at times the tragedy, but we'll turn to that later).

The comedy of the workplace is an old story. And indeed, although in his serious philosophical works Seneca focuses on the casual—one gets the impression of a very lonely individual with no colleagues around him—his one comic work, a satire written after the death of the emperor Claudius, focuses on characters he knew all too well—the emperor, his freedmen, his lawyers, and other personae of the imperial court. And it shows Seneca as a man who was irritated by many things: by Claudius's boring loquacity, his limp and stammer, his flatulence, and so forth—before we get to the serious damages to public well-being that occupy most of the work.[19]

Colleagues are different from casual associates because we have fewer options of not dealing with them. They are different from intimates in that we don't exactly choose to deal with them, and we may actually not like them. So we need to figure out what to make of our relationship with them in the light of the many occasions of anger that are sure to arise, in a context in which we almost certainly will need to deal with them again. Seneca is right to urge us to avoid the presence of irritating people, and that can be a legitimate factor in the choice of a workplace. (And it is certainly a reason to avoid spending time in that larger workplace the Internet, which is sure to give ample occasions for anger.) But only up to a point, since one can't really police a workplace around one's own taste, or move every time one feels excessively irritated (though some people try this).

I leave for later treatment the really grave damages colleagues inflict on one another: for example, plagiarism, sexual harassment, discrimination, and wrongful termination of employment. These are, rightly, the focus of law. Our focus here is on chronic patterns of behavior that often occasion an angry response, but are not grave well-being damages. What I said before about mistakes concerning insult goes here too: when one works daily with people, not being too thin-skinned is essential, and it's even better to make a habit of construing dubious remarks in a generous light. But there are many things colleagues do that are genuinely problematic: they talk too much, they talk rudely, they try to dominate a joint project, they don't do their share of the work in a joint project, they renege on important commitments, they try to get special treatment that nobody else is getting. These things happen all the time, and as Seneca says: if one did get angry at such things, one would go nuts. Even if one has oneself succeeded in not treating insults to honor and status as serious things (and few have won this battle stably or completely), other people haven't, and one has to deal with their misplaced values and consequent behavior. You have to figure out how to live with such people, so you can't just walk away as in the casual cases. So: is anger a fitting response? Is forgiveness useful? We shall see that here apology, at least, is significant and potentially productive going forward, but it can also be a trap.

Let me study the issue using four real-life examples. Since we're no longer dealing with strangers whom nobody knows, I introduce here a fictional alter ego named Louise, to provide an additional layer of fictionality and a fig leaf of protection for the other people who are represented as fictional characters here.

Case A. Louise is teaching a course with a colleague, of rank and achievement similar to hers—and students have to apply to be admitted. After a while of jointly reviewing the applications, her colleague writes, "I'm happy to leave the decisions to you. I'm too busy at the moment to attend to them."

Case B. Louise is organizing a major conference. A colleague from another department, whom she knows rather well, agrees to give a paper—definitely, unequivocally, in writing (she has just reread it!). Nine months later, with the conference date rapidly approaching, he writes a breezy message saying that he is unable to be there because he will be at a conference in Australia. He gives no sign of seeing any problem with his conduct, and it is too late for Louise to replace his contribution.

Case C. Louise has a colleague who is marvelous in many respects, brilliant, generous, full of good will to others, but also a big baby, who simply talks all the time. He won't stop talking unless he is interrupted. In group discussions he frequently ends up silencing younger faculty, not with the slightest ill will, but just through lack of sensitivity to the effects of his behavior, combined with an obstreperous intemperance of self-expression.

All of these incidents are annoying, and with good reason. We might say, then, that anger would be well-grounded. In the first case, Louise's colleague probably does not intend to be insulting, but by suggesting that his time is worth more than hers, he does insult, and also expresses a kind of grandiosity that is out of place in the academic workplace (ubiquitous though it is there). In the second case, more serious, Louise's other colleague jeopardizes the success of the conference and thus the well-being of all who have been devoting time and energy to it, and he also violates established norms. Either he accepted a later invitation and reneged on a prior commitment because he wanted to go to Australia, or he had a prior commitment in Australia when he accepted hers, and didn't realize it.

His casual treatment of the entire episode, without contrition or apology, indicates that he has no idea of the burden he has inflicted on others, nor of the norms he has violated—although he has surely been around long enough to know them. In the third case, potentially the most serious, a non-malicious person threatens to disrupt an entire community through lack of self-control.

Notice here what apology can offer. In A and B, if the colleague had apologized, the insult would remain, but Louise could have had much more confidence, going forward, that the two men had realized the problem in their conduct and it would not be repeated. (In Case C, she could have no such confidence, because lack of self-control is the problem.) So apology can provide evidence that norms are recognized going forward, and thus a basis for continuing to deal with the person in normal collegial interactions.[20] But, what to do? The cases unfolded in an interesting way.

In the first case, Louise let her colleague know by email that his remark seemed out of place, since she was just as busy as he, and his remark conveyed the suggestion that she was comparatively idle and unproductive; nonetheless, she would be happy to review the applications (which she was, since it took less time than sending them to him and waiting several days for his reply). He did not reply, which was not auspicious. However, having understood for many years that this person, who has many wonderful human as well as intellectual characteristics, is a person of slender self-knowledge who absolutely hates to admit that he is wrong, Louise just decided to let it go. Notice that the decision to let the colleague know about the insult was carefully taken, in order not to have festering irritation affecting future interactions, and in order not to baby him as others at times do, but also as a cue to him that apology would be appropriate, if he wanted to give her a return gesture indicating that he would not say such heedless things again. But when he didn't take the hint, the landscape changed: Louise would have to up the ante, extracting an apology by asking for one, and maybe she would succeed and maybe not. But she would risk poisoning future interactions and creating a climate of tension in the class, which after all was going to take place one way or another. So, Louise just had to consider whether she wanted to continue the close working relationship with that colleague, with all his flaws. If the answer was yes, not extracting an apology seems like the most productive course. People usually don't change in response to a request for apology, so you just have to decide what you are going to do about and with them. But you should remember that you only have to teach with such a person, not live with him.

The second case is actually similar, since both involve people who *hate* to say that they are wrong. Here Louise did try, twice in fact, to explain why the casual blowing off of the conference that she and others had planned struck her as inappropriate, but all she got was a gruff (on email), "I don't have to explain myself to you." At this point, Louise really did have a decision, for she did not have to see that person again or teach with him; but she also thought more and more that he had probably just had a big memory lapse and was ashamed, and worried about aging. Furthermore, she really did want a paper by him. So in the end she decided that to try further to extract an apology was going to doom future interactions. Looking to the general welfare (!), she proposed that he should write the paper anyway, and have someone else deliver it; and she invited him to talk about it over a drink. He accepted. (Louise might not so quickly invite him to a future event, however.)

I think that both of these were pretty good solutions (no doubt influenced by the fact that Louise has been writing a book on anger and its futility). Relationships were preserved, she had a clearer idea what she could and could not expect from these two people, and she had preserved the fruitful intellectual collaboration, and quasi-friendship (real friendship in Case A). Did Louise get angry? Sure, for a short time. In the first case, it probably was Transition-Anger, and nothing more: Louise knows the person well enough not to let him make her really mad (usually). In the second case Louise really was annoyed, but then she headed back from the abyss, and decided that a positive take on the situation would create more welfare for all in the long run. So she had a short spurt of real anger, but then turned to the Transition. After all, when you work with people you buy into who they are. It's foolish to expect to change them, so you just have to figure out how to grapple with reality.

Now for the third. This one is slippery, because the whole group is involved, and different people react in different ways. What does not work: getting visibly angry at the person and treating him rudely. This reaction, natural enough among some colleagues, just creates tension in the whole group. What doesn't work for long is talking to him about it—his behavior is just too much a part of who he is by now, and the whole problem is that he doesn't know how he affects others. What does work, often, is firm and frequent interruption, which he takes very well. But the most creative welfare-enhancing solution of all was devised by an administrator, who changed the person's teaching schedule so that he would finish class some minutes after the lunchtime discussions had already started, and thus arrive late, with the result that he did not get to set the topic, and was therefore much less disruptive. This case shows that forward-looking thinking is everything. What would be accomplished by getting mad at this person? It would be like getting mad at a genius two-year-old. Even Transition-Anger probably is a waste of emotional energy. And it's important that this is a nice and generous genius two-year-old.

Let's briefly contrast another case, Case D, of a genius two-year-old who is not so nice. Unfortunately, the academy is filled with such people. This important scholar was being invited to participate in a panel inaugurating a new research center Louise's university was opening in a developing country. Louise was in charge of planning one of the big opening-event panels, and this person was an important part of the plan, because of the unique value of his work, recognized by a Nobel Prize. Other high-quality participants would probably accept only if his participation was assured. This man engaged in characteristic delay tactics, and then requested first-class transportation, along with business-class transportation for his wife (!), something that is illegal under usual university rules and a sign of infantile narcissism. But Louise knew from bitter experience that it was futile to get upset or even mention these defects to D, so she told university administrators that this is just how he is, and we want him there, so you'd better resign yourself to giving him what he asks. They knew their man, and agreed with Louise. In this instance, anger was not even in the offing, just weary detachment. But there was also no reconciliation or restoration of a working relationship: Louise was thinking, don't do anything with this person if you can possibly avoid it, but if you really have to work with him, treat him like a selfish genius two-year-old. This case shows the limits of non-anger: it doesn't make a good working relationship when people are like this one. (Case C is quite different, and, with the help of non-anger, one may continue to feel much affection for the protagonist.) But at least non-anger makes it possible to get on with an intellectual event. (The difficulty of working with D is so notorious that on the occasion of Louise's one prior cooperation with D, a conference at their own university, their invited plenary speaker, another Nobel Prize winner in D's field, announced to a friend, himself yet another Nobel Prize winner in the same field, that he was on his way to city Z to speak at a conference co-organized by Louise and D. The friend's response was, "That's the most implausible thing I've ever heard." So: non-anger can achieve the implausible!)

In short: more or less everything we said about the casual domain is true in the collegial domain, with even richer occasions for comedy, given the deeper temptations to narcissism that the workplace offers, and perhaps especially the academic workplace. And the idea that one owes it to one's self-respect to get mad is even more pernicious here than it was in casual interactions. In all four of my cases one might have had righteous indignation, and been "justified" after a fashion, but with disruptive consequences all around. The main difference is that in the collegial domain apology can be of real, albeit limited, usefulness—as evidence, going forward, that things will work better in the future, and thus as evidence that pursuing a close collaborative relationship could be fruitful.

But receiving an apology is very different from extracting an apology, which is usually a mistake. If people have the character flaw of not wanting to admit they have made a mistake, a very common flaw, you could joust with them until doomsday, upping the emotional ante, and you would still get nowhere, except into the abyss. Instead of seeing things as all about oneself and one's "due," however, one can simply realize that some people don't like to admit they are wrong, but they have other good characteristics that one can value and even like—and just figure out what to do about working with them henceforth. Others have true infantile narcissism, which comes in many varieties, some more benign than others—and then one must once again figure out what to do about that.

Another thing we learn from these cases is that imagination and seeing the situation from the other person's viewpoint is an essential corrective to the narcissistic focus on one's own insulted need for payback. Extracting an apology would have been a way of (apparently) achieving payback, but it would really not have changed the situation in a useful way. Realizing something about the character and limits of each (that both the first and second have a particularly childish aversion to admitting they were wrong, that the second very likely is annoyed with himself for forgetting something important and doesn't want to admit it, that the third is full of good will but incapable of listening) helped construct a response that was useful. Human relations are full of problems to be solved. It takes empathy to solve them well. And a sense of humor: for it helped to think of these interactions as scripts for an academic sitcom.

Was Louise's non-anger a way of not taking these four people seriously? Yes, if "taking seriously" means not finding what they do funny, or even childish. But why should we define "taking seriously" that way? Louise's attitudes would probably make for bad intimate relationships with all four (although no doubt a strong maternal instinct would be an essential ingredient of any good intimate relationship with colleagues C and D—for someone else!), but that, fortunately, is not what we are contemplating here. Maybe Louise was a bit manipulative in Case B, using the colleague as a means to the success of the conference; and maybe the administrator was manipulative in Case C. But this just goes to show that in non-intimate relations it is not always bad to influence people's behavior for the common good.

V. Gratuitous Gratitude

Although gratitude is in many respects a backward-looking cousin of anger, I argued in chapter 4 that it can be valuable in intimate relationships because it helps constitute the reciprocal good will that such relationships rightly involve. But what about the Middle Realm? If the Stoics are correct that our dealings in this realm are not worthy of serious concern (with exceptions to be considered in the next section), what then of gratitude? Basically, it seems to be inappropriate for similar reasons: just as we shouldn't get angry because of the manifold insults and indignities of air travel, driving, and so many other aspects of daily life, we shouldn't feel gratitude either when other people make these things go well: such an emotion betrays too intense a dependence on external goods. But, as before, we need to observe that gratitude is not exactly symmetrical to anger. First, it involves a wish to do good for someone, which seems less problematic than the wish to do ill, and is accompanied by pleasant feelings, which are not welfare-disruptive, rather than painful feelings, which often are. Second, it does not seem to be infected by magical thinking: the grateful person does not fantasize that giving a benefit to the person who has helped her will change the past. She usually thinks either that it will promote future goods or that it is just a nice thing to do. So the real problem the Stoics raise is that of inappropriate dependency.

But there is a type of gratitude in the Middle Realm that may be free from this problem. This is what I propose to call "gratuitous gratitude." So often one becomes accustomed to the bad things that travel and other daily interactions bring with them. Avoiding anger in the Stoic way typically involves lowering expectations for how these interactions will go, as one practices the usual Stoic *praemeditatio malorum*. Then, when something really nice happens, it is surprising and delightful. A really smart and competent car repairman, a tech support person on the phone at Comcast who actually knows what he or she is doing and is pleasant to talk to; a sales clerk at Walgreens who does not behave as if the very idea of answering a customer's question is an insult; a guy waiting for a weight machine you are using in the gym who does not exhibit steroidal rage and impatience, but actually smiles and jokes, nicely; a teenage girl at the same gym who returns a piece of paper I have dropped with a courteous "Excuse me, ma'am"—all these are windfalls of daily life, surprising because so rare, and therefore occasions for real pleasure. Is it only pleasure, or is the emotion gratitude as well? Often the latter, I believe.

Is the pleasant emotion to that extent inappropriate? Here's how one might argue that it is: You, Louise, have been insulating yourself from anger by expecting the worst, in true Stoic fashion, but you haven't truly stopped caring about these things. Underneath your shield, you really care about politeness and good behavior, you child of the Main Line, and you are only pretending that you do not, in order to avoid being angry all the time. When good behavior arrives as a windfall, the strong emotion you feel betrays the residual attachment to these fragile goods of fortune, and the emotion therefore is a sign that your Stoicizing project is woefully incomplete.

Maybe. But maybe, too, it is perfectly all right to feel sudden pleasure and to think that the person who acted so well deserves a good turn in return (whether mere thanks and a warm smile, or a good review on the Internet). I prefer the more charitable interpretation, since after all, we're talking about pleasure and doing good, which are always in short supply and don't require elaborate justification.

Let's study an example, to make these intuitions more precise. I go to the market on the morning of a big dinner party, to buy fish for an elaborate Indian dish. I am fully expecting that I will be skinning the filets myself, and that it will take me a long time. (The market is not one where extraordinary service can be expected, and I do not expect it.) The man from whom I buy six pounds of salmon filets asks me whether I would like him to skin them and cut them into pieces (because I have mentioned the type of dish I'm making). My eyes widen, and I say yes. Watching his tremendous skill with his superior knives and superior deftness and strength, I feel more and more grateful: he is not only saving me a lot of time, he is doing it much better than I would do it. Part of my emotion is pleasure at his artistry, but part, too, is gratitude for the generosity of his offer and the help it has given me. I would definitely not have felt annoyed had he not made the offer: it was a total windfall. So I don't think I am betraying any residual attachment to external goods in my emotion. But it is a really nice emotion, and I am hoping, in addition to warm thanks, to do him a good turn in some way (though, since he is head of his department, I am not sure what, despite having written down his name, I could possibly do).

In the collegial domain, these cases take a more complex form. Let me give two examples, returning to my alter ego Louise as I narrate them. In the first case, Louise is working on a project that involves giving a series of lectures, and she suddenly receives lengthy and extremely helpful and insightful comments from a member of her profession with whom she has not conversed in years, and who had previously treated her work with contempt. He had heard one of her lectures, and then bothered to go read, with great care, the related parts of her manuscript. She certainly was not awaiting comments from him, and would not have been even slightly irritated if he had not sent any. Indeed, after thirty years she had finally brought herself to a point of non-anger at which his presence in a large auditorium did not have the psychic effect of Seneca's dragged bench—or, at least, only that of a bench dragged a long way away! But nonetheless: she was extremely pleased and grateful, since the comments were really very helpful to her revisions. While it would have been a mistake for her to carry on her career with any reliance on this person, and while it would have been excessive to express her gratitude by inviting him to a dinner party, since she doesn't like him, she felt it was right to feel gratitude, since the comments were extensive and had taken him at least some time to write. (He is a very rapid worker, but even so. . . .) Maybe he did it only out of a rigid deontological standard of hospitality, but so what? It was good.

With the second case, we return to Case D of my earlier discussion, and an update. When this difficult colleague did finally attend the opening in the developing country, he arrived after traveling approximately twenty hours. But instead of being tired and cranky he was a bundle of positive energy. He not only gave a marvelous lecture at the opening, he also rushed out to see the historical sites of the city, returning with passionate enthusiasm and many questions. Louise was grateful for his excellent contribution, and for the additional contribution that his sheer presence gave to the event, since he is truly very distinguished—but also for his love of a country she loves, and for his general quite unexpected good will and positivity.

Colleagues can give pleasant surprises. Since many are children, and many of the problems of working with them derive from that source, it is well to remember that children also delight and please. As in the more casual cases, we could read Louise's reaction critically and uncharitably, saying that her gratitude betrays unwise and inappropriate dependency on two undependable people. But why not just allow her to enjoy the surprise, uncriticized, and feel an emotion wishing them well? So long as she doesn't alter her basic strategy of prudent caution, why can't she simply enjoy the windfall? In short, if generosity to self is a good thing, why not exercise it here?

These two cases are different from the casual cases because they concern important goods to which Louise is rightly attached: her work in the first case, the opening of her university's Center in the second. Given that her emotions are rightly attached to these important goods, someone who unexpectedly promotes those goods elicits a more robust type of gratitude than in my casual cases. It's not just, "*Finally* there is a competent Comcast tech to deal with," it's "This person has seriously advanced an important project." Had the person proven unhelpful or even damaging, Louise should have avoided anger (turning things over to the law if the damage were serious enough). She can certainly get good comments from others, and she did. But in this windfall case, why not feel a limited sort of gratitude, and why not wish that person a limited sort of reciprocal benefit? If he were to send her something for comments, she might even reciprocate, and given that her basic rule is that colleagues take first priority and everyone else is optional, this would be a gratuitous good deed. Once again, it's not as if there's too much pleasure and delight in life. When gratitude comes as a windfall, too much censorious questioning betrays an ungenerous disposition.

There is a further argument in favor of limited gratitude in such cases: the emotion enhances future cooperation. The workplace involves relationships that are limited. They do not involve trust of the deep sort involved in intimate relationships, only a more superficial type of reliance. But they do concern intensely important matters, so it's useful to encourage moral sentiments that make everyone's lives go well.

VI. Well-Being Damage: Turning to the Law

The Middle Realm, as so far analyzed, is fundamentally a comic domain. Comedy so often concerns vices of overinvestment in things that actually have slender importance: vanity, miserliness, obsessive attention to reputation. For the Stoic, the whole of the Middle Realm is comic, because none of the things others do to us is serious. But that is wrong. There is genuine tragedy in this realm, when things that people rightly prize are damaged by non-intimates: life, health, bodily integrity, work and employment, major aspects of one's property, even property that has emotional though not financial value. We should also include here reputational damage serious enough to obstruct work, employment, and friendship; and we should include dignitary damage of a sort that constitutes discrimination violative of political equality. Finally, we include such damages inflicted on people we love, not just on ourselves.

Even here, my analysis does not collapse the Middle Realm into the intimate realm. In the intimate realm, I hold, the relationship itself is of intrinsic value, so the grief, loss, and anxiety that we rightly feel when things go wrong take the other person, and the relationship itself, as their object. In the Middle Realm, we rightly grieve, or feel anxiety, about the well-being damage to self or loved ones, but the stranger who inflicted that damage is, or should be, incidental to our focus. Still, it's right to do something about the damage, and that is where we need the Eumenides.

It's not an accident that these serious well-being damages are the offenses that the law takes seriously. In some cases it took a while (sexual harassment), in some cases the boundary is disputed and differently drawn in different countries (hate speech), and in some it is very squishy and hard to adjudicate (defamation). Still, a central question the law typically asks is about the seriousness of the well-being damage. A "hostile work environment," for example, in the law of sexual harassment, has to be one that rises above casual offense to some serious obstruction. The conduct has to be "severe or pervasive,"[21] "threatening or otherwise deeply disturbing."[22]

We'll discuss the legal/political aspects of some of these cases in chapter 6. But we still have to think about the victim. Here we have many cases of people who have been damaged, often severely, by other people, often with wrongful intent, or at least with negligence. We'll ask later how the status of the victim is appropriately acknowledged by legal institutions. But what is the victim's appropriate emotional reaction? Once again: these cases are unlike those discussed in chapter 4 because no reciprocal relation of trust exists between the parties, and usually no relationship at all—unless it be what Thomas Scanlon calls the "bare moral relationship,"[23] the set of expectations and norms that bind people just because they are human and moral—added to which is often shared membership in a political community. But this is a thin relationship, and in most cases there need be no future connection between the parties, except to the extent that they are joined in a legal proceeding.

Grief is an extremely important and legitimate part of such cases, responding to the significance of the loss that has been inflicted (not the relationship loss, as in intimate cases, but the well-being loss). That is clear. And victims have to deal with that grief, which is often very difficult. But what about anger?

In such cases, anger at the perpetrator is understandable, and it would be surprising if most victims did not have a period of real anger with a desire for the perpetrator to suffer, or to do badly in some way. The first thing we can say, however, is that victims should turn the business of dealing with the perpetrator over to the law, rather than taking matters into their own hands. That is the fundamental shift that Aeschylus shows us, and our next chapter will discuss it further. There is often a residual desire to punish the offender oneself, and law even understands this up to a point. The defense of "reasonable provocation" in the common law of homicide involves the idea that a person who has killed in the "heat of passion" after a "sufficient" or "adequate" provocation—defined in terms of the normative figure of the "reasonable man"—and without sufficient "cooling time," can win a reduction of the level of offense from murder to manslaughter. A provocation defense is mitigation, however, not excuse: the person is still judged severely for not turning things over to the law. But it is interesting that the law shares our idea that anger takes a while to rein in, and may be judged less harshly right after a damage than after a lapse of time.

In most cases, however, the victim does not become a perpetrator, but turns matters over to the law. Even in these cases there is an emotional analogue of the provocation defense. That is, we should not judge people severely if they are very angry at the perpetrator for a short period of time, and if they focus, during that time, on wanting the particular perpetrator who has harmed them to be punished. It's very understandable that the individual face and body of the perpetrator may dominate a victim's thoughts and dreams for a while. If the fixation on the perpetrator becomes an ongoing obsession, however, we would be correct in blaming the person (and urging her to seek treatment for the problem). What would be acceptable would be anger for a brief period, followed by movement toward a Transition in which the victim's focus now becomes social welfare, and how the legal system can promote it. Rather than obsessing about the individual traits of the murderer or rapist or thief, one focuses on the crime in a more general way, and seeks the type of engagement with law that will promote the well-being of other victims or potential victims—just the Transition that Angela made in chapter 2. Often victims focus on the type of crime from which they themselves have suffered, just as people who have been ill seek social welfare through a focus on their own (or their family's) particular disease, and this seems all right if not ideal, just so long as overall social welfare is sufficiently promoted by the collectivity of such efforts.

As we've insisted, victims do need to mourn and to deal with the losses they have experienced. But that need not entail ongoing payback fantasies about the perpetrator. By turning things over to the law, they transform the injury, making it not just about them, but about what makes society go better. Once again, we need to insist that a person's dignity does not require hounding an individual and obsessing angrily about that individual. Letting impartial justice take its course is not a pusillanimous response. How are things improved by adding one excess to another? Obsessive focusing on the future suffering of the perpetrator just implicates me in the perpetrator's hostile and degrading conduct. Why should that conduct have the power to make me turn into a dog? Whether the offender should be made to suffer becomes a purely forward-looking question, which institutions will handle in their way.

What about forgiveness? By the same token, focusing on forgiveness for the particular offender is questionable, because of the way in which it rivets thought to that individual and that past. It's the same question as in chapter 4: if an inner struggle with anger can be won no other way, perhaps this focus on inner forgiveness is appropriate. But we should be skeptical when therapists tell us so, since that is their trade. Perhaps focusing on work, or on constructive political efforts, would be just as good or better. Where grief is concerned, people usually think that prolonged therapy wrestling with sadness is unnecessary—it's necessary only in cases of obsessive pathological mourning. Why should we think differently about anger? In intimate cases the person is deeply entwined in one's life, so a broken relationship, like a death, takes time and effort to heal. But there's no necessity that the interaction with a stranger would have this feature, and one should discourage obsessive focusing by whatever means seem to work.

But doesn't the anger of victims deter? In this sphere we must carefully distinguish this claim from the claim that punishment deters. That claim is plausible, and we shall investigate it in our next chapter. But the first claim is not plausible. Of course if victims never noticed rape or murder there would be no statutes dealing with them, and thus no deterrence. And both victims and others do need to be in a frame of mind to support whatever policies are useful in deterring crime. Sometimes the advocacy of victims is useful in galvanizing the public to take a certain type of offense seriously, as has happened in the case of drunk driving and sexual harassment. But in these cases it is overwhelmingly the magnitude of the *loss* and *suffering* of victims (and their families) that has been socially useful, not their anger. And victim behavior has been overwhelmingly Transitional rather than retributive. So I see no reason why victims and their families should nourish and indulge an otherwise useless and fantasy-ridden anger on the speculation that this emotion would contribute to optimal deterrence.

VII. The Gentle Temper

Seneca's advice is easy to state, difficult to follow—as he himself acknowledges by depicting himself as repeatedly falling into anger, even after years of self-attention. (I've followed his example in this chapter, both in my stories about myself and in my portrayal of my alter ego Louise.) But he reminds us that there is much we can do to insulate ourselves from temptations. He urges Novatus to surround himself with people who are not irritating, and this can at least sometimes be achieved. More generally, one may try to avoid scenarios in which one will be provoked (for example, by not searching one's own name on the Internet all the time, and by not reading reviews of one's own books). Finally, to those of us in the legal profession, he offers chastening advice: avoid lawyers and lawsuits!

And he also offers what is good advice always: cultivate a sense of humor about the vagaries of life. "Anger must be confined in many ways; let many [possible occasions of anger] be converted into play and joking" (III.11.2). (Although Seneca does not say so, teasing by a friend may be the best way to achieve this "conversion.") Conversion typically requires stepping out of one's own immersion in one's ego-injury: "Step a long way back and laugh" (III.37). Aristotle's insight about the "gentle temper" here receives further support. But Seneca also recommends something further, of great importance: an attitude of amused detachment toward ourselves, so that we simply don't take what happens to us as the most world-shaking thing. It probably isn't. To the extent that it is of serious weight, we should turn things over to the Eumenides.

6

The Political Realm

Everyday Justice

The general object which all laws have, or ought to have, in common, is to augment the total happiness of the community; and therefore, in the first place, to exclude, as far as may be, every thing that tends to subtract from that happiness: in other words, to exclude mischief.

But all punishment is mischief: all punishment in itself is evil. . . . If it ought to be at all admitted, it ought only to be admitted in as far as it promises to exclude some greater evil.

—Jeremy Bentham, *The Principles of Morals and Legislation*, ch. XIII

"At this festive season of the year, Mr. Scrooge," said the gentleman, taking up a pen, "it is more than usually desirable that we should make some slight provision for the Poor and destitute, who suffer greatly at the present time. Many thousands are in want of common necessaries; hundreds of thousands are in want of common comforts, sir."

"Are there no prisons?" asked Scrooge.

"Plenty of prisons," said the gentleman, laying down the pen again.

—Charles Dickens, *A Christmas Carol*

I. The Eumenides

Aeschylus depicted the creation of legal and political justice out of archaic attitudes of retributive anger. The Furies, existing only to track down wrongdoers, inflicting pain and ill, become kindly and forward-looking, blessing the land and seeking the well-being of its inhabitants. They also become rational, listening to the voice of persuasion. As guardians of law they continue to discourage lawbreaking by inspiring fear. But they put their anger to sleep (832–33). They focus on preventing wrongdoing rather than on payback. Their prevention strategy includes a capacious plan for social prosperity and welfare, the amelioration of hunger and illness, and the inclusion of all citizens. But it also includes the creation of a system of criminal justice.

My next two chapters investigate the political domain, asking about the consequences of the critique of anger for some aspects of political institutions. Aeschylus gives us suggestive images, not a theory. The fifth-century BCE Athenians who watched his play were passionate about democracy. But in the area that interests us they thought too little about institutional design. There was no public prosecutor, an office that at least promises impartial judgment about which offenses merit prosecution. All prosecutions had to be initiated by a citizen.[1] (There was also no distinction between criminal and civil law.) This system gave rise to many problems, including the likelihood of hostile prosecutions of controversial individuals (such as the prosecution of Socrates, initiated by some of his enemies), the sheer unevenness of prosecution in terms of wealth and status (prosecution takes time, and if you engage a lawyer it takes money), and the non-prosecution of offenses that didn't have a relatively affluent citizen to take them up. Plato's *Euthyphro* depicts this last problem, showing the burden the system imposes on a person of good will. Euthyphro's father has murdered a day laborer, a noncitizen. Nothing at all happens, since the day laborer has no relations to initiate prosecution—until Euthyphro himself decides to prosecute his father on the dead laborer's behalf. As the dialogue makes clear, it is deeply problematic for a son to haul his father into court; and yet it is also problematic for the murder to go unprosecuted. In the absence of public prosecution, such problems must have been ubiquitous.

Worst of all, though, was the encouragement the private-prosecution system gave to the retributive passions. Chapter 5 argued that the desirable course for the victim is to mourn the loss but to disengage from further personal involvement with the perpetrator, letting impartial justice take over. The Athenian system prevents this disengagement, putting the victim in the position of the Furies, obliged to hunt down the particular offender. The system itself seems to fuel ongoing anger and fixation. Thus, although in other respects the classic Athenian system takes the issues dramatized in the *Eumenides* seriously—treating anger as a disease in the political community, and viewing the public task as the healing and reconstruction of diseased interpersonal relations—in this structural respect the system is all too continuous with the revenge morality that preceded it.[2]

No doubt this unsatisfactory feature, together with its prominent role in the trial and death of Socrates (who was prosecuted by a group of personal enemies), helps explain the fascination of many Greek philosophers with the critique of political retributivism and their repeated attempts to replace it with a legal system focused on both reform and deterrence. Indeed, this search probably began with Socrates himself, who seems to have rejected the *lex talionis* ("an eye for an eye") as the basis for dealing with people by whom one has been wronged.[3] Certainly the search assumes prominence in Plato's relatively early *Protagoras*, with its elaborate account of deterrence and reform. In that dialogue, Protagoras announces the following policy:[4]

> One who undertakes to punish rationally does not do so for the sake of the wrongdoing which is now in the past—for what has been done cannot be undone—but for the sake of the future, that the wrongdoing shall not be repeated, either by him or by the others who see him punished.... One punishes for the sake of deterrence. (324A–B)[5]

If it is right to say, with Danielle Allen, that ancient Greek punishment was all along a search for a cure for the disease of anger, then these thinkers are not breaking with the prior tradition, as Allen suggests, but, rather, taking the logical next step—by arguing that the best way of curing the disease of anger in political life is to refuse to base institutional arrangements on it.[6] At any rate the search for a forward-looking and non-vindictive account of punishment, and of criminal justice more generally, did not begin with Jeremy Bentham: it was a major feature of how both Plato and the Stoics approached the topic of wrongdoing—not only as a feature of personal relations but also as a feature of laws and institutions. In this respect they followed the suggestive images created by Aeschylus, urging that that attractive ideal requires rejecting some prominent features of Athenian practice. Still, their positive institutional proposals were both too thin and too bound up with their rejection of democracy to offer us much help.

In this chapter I consider what happens to wrongful acts and the emotions they inspire when they are made the concern of a working system of everyday political justice: what features of such a system best perform the job of taking wrongdoing seriously, without embracing anger? In the next chapter I consider the transition from an era of profound structural injustice to an era in which, it is hoped, these injustices will be transcended. This distinction is not always a sharp one. A transition from pervasive injustice to a more nearly just regime can occur within one basic ongoing constitutional framework, as during the U.S. civil rights movement, a time of significant upheaval involving a major reinterpretation of the Constitution, but not its repudiation. Or it may involve the replacement of one regime by a new regime, as in the case of South Africa, which adopted a new constitution. But the two cases are different more in degree than in kind, and both will be treated as cases of what I shall call "revolutionary justice"—leaving this chapter to deal with wrongful acts against individuals or groups within an ongoing legal framework that is not itself based, at least at the most abstract and general level, upon fundamental injustice.[7]

In both cases I follow the thread of the critique of anger and ask what becomes of that critique in this new context. A long tradition has held that political justice requires angry emotions. Such emotions, it is often claimed, are a necessary feature of our interactions with one another as responsible agents, and they are required to express concern for the dignity and self-respect of the wronged.

What, though, do such claims actually mean? Sometimes they are empirical claims about what is needed to motivate and sustain people as they seek justice. Such claims are interesting, but speculative and difficult to assess in the context of everyday legal transactions, which involve in each case a large number of agents (victims, defendants, lawyers, judges, and many others), and in which different people are no doubt motivated by many different sentiments and combinations of sentiments. Often people don't even know what motivates them. A more tractable question, which will be mine, is, what sentiments are expressed in the structure of the legal institutions themselves, and which ones are desirable from a normative viewpoint? To put this point in a different way: Imagining justice anthropomorphically, should justice get angry at offenders? If not, what attitudes should that mythic figure express?

We must also follow our ancillary concern with forgiveness and apology. What role is there within political justice for public rituals expressing these ideas and sentiments?

Political institutions, I argue, should emulate the Eumenides: they should express forward-looking concern for social welfare and eschew the backward-looking angry attitudes that the trilogy rightly depicts as both nonsensical (spilled blood never comes back again) and normatively pernicious to the state (encouraging payback fantasies that create cycles of private vengeance). Political institutions should not embody incoherent and normatively defective ideas. Nonetheless, as part of their welfare-guarding function they ought to take wrongful acts seriously, seek to prevent them, and attend to them if they occur, in a Eumenidean spirit (which I'll attempt to describe). There are many specific ways in which institutions can guard against the reentry of the Furies, and we can illustrate these, although an exhaustive description is beyond my scope.

Institutions, as Athena emphasized, must be fair and impartial, swayed by favor. At the same time, they should also have kindly intent. Like good parents, partners, and colleagues, they should embody not only a love of justice but also a spirit of generosity that goes beyond strict legalism. Our study of anger and forgiveness in other realms has pre-pared us to think well of generous forward-looking attitudes. Our task in this chapter must be to map out, for this realm, the proper combination of impartial justice, acknowledgment of wrongdoing, and empathetic generosity.

We must remain alert to the issue of trust, important in our analysis of intimate relationships. Intimate relationships, I argued, flourish only when parties are willing to be vulnerable to one another in major ways, not simply *relying* on the other to behave thus and so (which might be compatible with cynicism about the other party's likely conduct), but allowing crucial elements of one another's flourishing to rest in one another's hands. Something similar is true of political communities. A society with decent institutions will not remain stable if citizens sim-ply *rely* on institutions to function in a certain sort of way: for reliance is compatible, once again, with great cynicism toward both institutions and officials. For example, in a very corrupt society citizens often *rely* on the corruption of officials, the rottenness of the justice system, and so forth. In a racist society, minorities *rely* on the dominant group to oppress them. In such cases, reliance produces self-defensive evasion and resistance. If a decent society is to remain stable not just as a grudging *modus vivendi*, but, as John Rawls puts it, stable "for the right reasons," it needs to gen-erate attachments to its principles, and attachment brings vulnerability.[8] This vulnerability would be unendurable without trust. Producing trust must therefore be a continual concern of decent societies.

The type of trust political communities need to cultivate is different from the type that animates intimate relationships, just as the type of love involved is different. But both types of love and trust involve the will-ingness to place important elements of one's own good in the hands of others—in this case the institutions of one's society—rather than engaging in self-protective and evasive action.

Since I shall be defending an approach that is in the most general sense consequentialist or welfarist, I need to say at the outset what I do and do not mean by that. As in my other work on political justice,[9] I hold that a major necessary condition of a minimally just society is that it pro-tect a set of central human opportunities, or "capabilities," up to some appropriate threshold level. These capabilities are plural, and each of them has intrinsic value, apart from other goods that they may produce. A society that neglects them to pursue opulence or growth cannot be min-imally just. Nor can a society justly trade them off against one another, where that means pushing some citizens below the threshold on any one of them. These capabilities include economic goods, but they also include basic rights and liberties, and the notion of human dignity plays a central role in knitting them all together.[10] Although the capabilities are separate, they are also mutually supportive, and to some extent defined with reference to what is feasible as an overall target set of political goods.

My view, then, is neither Benthamite nor similar to most familiar forms of economic Utilitarianism. But it is quite Millian in spirit and it seems not inappropriate to categorize it as, overall, a philosophically informed type of welfarism.[11] It certainly has deontological elements, in the sense that a capability violation is an injustice, whatever wealth or other good it produces; and the protection of each capability is an intrinsic political good. Moreover, the capabilities are a partial political doctrine of (minimal) welfare, not a comprehensive doctrine. The view as a whole, however, seems to me correctly classified as a form of political welfarism that has a richer, more variegated picture of welfare than many of its competitors.

II. False Social Values Again

Like the intimate and Middle realms, the political realm confronts us with a ubiquitous problem of false social values. People will not long support or even comply with a legal regime if they strongly disapprove of its underlying values. Popular support of some type, moreover, is not just a practical limit, but also a constraint on political legitimacy. Any program that cannot be justified to people fails a basic normative test. For example, the "Government House" Utilitarianism favored by Henry Sidgwick, according to which the true principle of political choice is known only to small elite, flouts constraints of transparency and popular consent that seem necessary, in some form, for political legitimacy. But current values are often defective: so what do we need to show about the values we propose?

John Rawls's *Political Liberalism* insists that legitimacy requires showing that the values proposed can become the object of an overlapping consensus among holders of the major reasonable religious and secular doctrines that citizens embrace. He did not insist, however, that the overlapping consensus must be a present reality. More plausibly, he held that one need only show that there is a plausible route to such a consensus over time and through argument.[12] I agree, and I agree further with Rawls in thinking that we must be able to show that the political conception is not a comprehensive doctrine, but shows equal respect to citizens who hold a wide range of reasonable comprehensive doctrines. But I then must face a tough challenge: what precise form of our non-anger doctrine can possibly be "sold" to citizens in a pluralistic society? Right now, it seems, many if not most people in most modern societies have notions of competition, status-seeking, manly honor, and revenge that are likely to make them not just disagree with the ideas about anger and retribution that I have defended, but also deride them as weak and unmanly.

The challenge, I believe, can be met. We may begin by pointing to recent instances in which just such ideas have enjoyed great popular success: the protest movements of Mohandas Gandhi and Martin Luther King, Jr., and the conduct of Nelson Mandela as leader of the new South Africa. All these cases will be examined further in chapter 7. To these we can add the non-angry response of the families of the victims in South Carolina, which I discussed in chapter 3. These cases show us that the critique of anger offered here can be persuasive not only to an audience of intellectuals, whose occupational bias may lead them to disfavor familiar paradigms of "manliness," but also to large masses of people—and often, people who did not accept those ideas prior to the persuasive power of these movements, or didn't think they accepted them. Part of the rapid success of these three leaders, who over relatively short periods of time brought millions of people around to accepting their norms, can be attributed to their ability to tap familiar religious traditions: significant strands or counter-strands of Christianity, Hinduism, and traditional African religion, as well as the entirety of Buddhism. Such religious references helped people feel that at some level they were already committed to the critical ideas: they saw their leaders' persuasion less as alien imposition than as a demand to sort themselves out, getting rid of cultural baggage that clashed with some very deep and previously unexamined commitments.

Thus we should not exaggerate the idea that all of modern culture is against us. If so many people change so rapidly, under the influence of King, Gandhi, and Mandela—or a gripping personal experience—it is evidence that our culture is actually torn about them.[13] People may romanticize the vigilante in fiction, but on the whole they do not want to meet up with him in life, and they are quite happy to admire such fictional types while supporting a legal order based on non-angry talk and argument.[14]

What are the areas in which law needs to resist some strong currents in popular belief? One is in determining where legal intervention is appropriate. As I said, not every common cause of anger involves a serious injury to well-being, but people often think that it does. As Seneca says, they exalt trivialities into major events, and they often become punitive as a result: "road rage" is just one example. In many if not most cultures, insults to honor have been occasions for anger-based violence, and law does not side with the popular view (or once-popular) of such insults. Dueling has long been illegal. Stalking and intimate partner violence are now recognized as a problem worthy of legal intervention. Once again, then, even if popular culture sometimes valorizes "manly" rage, modern democracies generally reject the idea that an insult or other status-injury is an offense justifying violence, no matter how angry it makes people.

In U.S. homicide law, the defense of "reasonable provocation" is a relic of a pre-Eumenidean society: a person who kills out of anger motivated by an "adequate provocation" can sometimes win at least a reduction in level of offense from murder to manslaughter. In the past, anger at offended honor or some other status-injury could rise to the level of an "adequate provocation," especially if the issue were adultery; now it is far more likely that the offense would have to be a real harm in Mill's sense: assault, for example, on oneself or a member of one's family. As I observed in chapter 5, the provocation defense, by (usually) requiring the defendant to show that the retaliatory violence took place without sufficient "cooling time," conforms to my idea that people can be judged less harshly for getting angry inappropriately for a short time, before getting their minds in order and turning to the law. Still, the use of illegal violence against the aggressor is always inexcusable, as the defense concedes—it is mitigation, not excuse—and the defense itself seems to me an unfortunate archaism that creates a loophole for old ideas about insult and status to sneak into the criminal law.[15] In most respects, however, the law has long internalized the critique of anger I make here.[16]

The categorization of offenses, however, is not the only place where false social values threaten the legal order. Far more tenacious and un-Aeschylean are the views many people hold about punishment, once an offender is indicted and convicted. Here retributive ideas continue to dominate, although they have been criticized for over two thousand years, and the critique is well understood. Despite all the arguments of Socrates, Plato, and Bentham, not to mention Gandhi, King, and Mandela, many people still favor punishments that fit a retributive model, according to which the "doer must suffer," and there must be "payback." Even if they also favor deterrence, they tend to think that only retributive punishments, inflicting pain for pain, could possibly deter. Other ideas of punishment are repeatedly derided as soft and unmanly, and politicians lose elections for not being sufficiently "tough on crime," a phrase that means "harsh," "inflicting retributive suffering" (whether it deters or not).[17] If one thinks, as I do, that the appropriate response to injury is forward-looking and welfarist, incorporating, in addition, ideas of generosity and reintegration, one will have to contend with a large amount of opposing popular sentiment, and this itself is likely to imperil the practical success of a proposal in my spirit, even if not its theoretical justification (since one might be able to show a path by which people might arrive at an overlapping consensus over time on this question, even if they are far from there right now).

Nonetheless, even on this issue the practical task is not hopeless, and the sheer failure of harsh forms of incarceration to deter has gradually led to the substitution of the phrase "smart on crime" (meaning doing what can be shown to deter) for the phrase "tough on crime"—responding to public sentiments.[18] People on the whole want what helps discourage crime, and they understand that punishment is ultimately about protecting important human goods.

The issue of harsh punishment is so vast that one cannot hope to treat it exhaustively here. But a persuasive account of how to confront wrongdoing in the spirit of non-anger can go a good way toward removing the objection. One may note, before beginning, that conventional ideas of punishment already incorporate certain ideas of non-anger, such as the rejection of humiliation and cruelty in punishing. The U.S. Constitution's ban on "cruel and unusual punishments" has proven difficult to interpret, and has never been taken to apply to the average type of U.S. incarceration; but the presence of the phrase in the Constitution certainly shows that even the eighteenth-century framers saw moral limits to the punitive role of the state. Let us, then, simply turn to the constructive theoretical task.

III. Wrongful Acts and the Rule of Law: Retributivist and Reformist Challenges

How, then, should the state deal with wrongful acts and the anger they engender? My account suggests that law must take harms very seriously if they involve significant damage to well-being (not just status). But of course law could take harm seriously without taking wrongdoing seriously, if it refused to make any distinction between accidents and damages from natural events, on the one hand, and intentional wrongdoing, on the other. Such a legal system could still show compassion for victims, compensating them and trying to protect them from such damages going forward, but it would not even get close to expressing anger, since it would not even contain the concept of a wrongful injury.

Such a legal system, however, would be crude and inefficient in protecting citizens going forward, since protecting people from earthquakes, floods, and other natural events requires utterly different strategies from those required to protect them against wrongful damage by others. Moreover, it would lack something that victims seem right to demand: the public acknowledgment that the conduct was wrongful, not simply unfortunate. If the system treats a murderer like a tiger who just happened to tear into a victim, it will not only fail to prevent such abuses in the future, since human beings and tigers are deterred by different strategies, it will also shortchange the victim, and all of us, since it fails to acknowledge the importance of the human values that law protects. To that extent, institutions need to look back, in order to move forward. Even if the healing of diseased social relations is the primary task, the restoration needs to take place on the terrain of acknowledgment.[19]

Why is acknowledgment so important? Many things can be said here, but I think the most important one is forward-looking: public acknowledgment of wrongdoing is necessary in order to preserve and strengthen trust, or to restore it. To the extent that bonds of trust have been violated or, even, have broken down utterly, restoring them requires a shared understanding of what is wrongful and what is not.[20] Even in a well-functioning community, trust in the justice of political institutions would erode if those institutions did not take wrongs seriously and acknowledge that importance in some public fashion. The social contract is about protecting human life and other human goods, and the state must announce that life and other elements of human well-being are important.

So institutions should not treat murder as like being mauled by a tiger. They should express clearly the thought "X did this, and it was wrong." On the other hand, if my account is correct, they must not at this point fall into either of the two traps that anger sets for the unwary. On the one hand, they should not suppose that proportional suffering rights wrongs. This archaic and powerful thought grips most of us; but it is a form of magical metaphysics that does not stand the light of reason. It is therefore normatively defective, since we want ourselves, and our laws, to make sense. Murder is not undone by any amount of suffering on the part of the perpetrator, nor is any other crime. We feel that somehow a "balance" has been restored, the doer has suffered—and all the things people say at this point, suggesting that tormenting Y makes X's suffering less, or rescinds the damage done. But law is irrational if it behaves as if law could fix the past. The popularity and the deep human roots of these thoughts should not make us ignore their incoherence.[21] As Plato says: the person who punishes rationally does not punish for the sake of a past injustice, but rather for the sake of the future.

Law must also not make the error of seeing the crime as simply a "down-ranking" or humiliation of X that can be fixed by humiliating Y in turn and putting Y down below X. That makes sense conceptually, but is normatively problematic. Law should not collude in the status-obsession that disfigures so many societies, but should insist on the equal human dignity of all. (Human equality and dignity, as I have already said, are a special status, inherent in and more fully defined by all the protected capabilities; they are not a matter of relative ranking.)

So what can the law say? It can say, first, that O committed a wrongful act and the wrong is serious. If someone wants to call this a retributive element in the law, that's fine with me, but most familiar forms of retributivism say a lot more than this—and Bentham's Utilitarian account of punishment, too, says this. If law is both rational and focused on the right things—on well-being rather than status—it will, having made that statement, then focus above all on the future, choosing strategies that promote both incapacitation and specific and general deterrence. In the process, law may certainly express Transition-Anger, saying that wrongdoing is an outrage and that something should be done about it. Transition-Anger, indeed is simply an emotional combination of the two claims I have just imagined the law making: that wrongdoing is seriously bad and that we need to think well, going forward, about how to deal with it.

At this point, a rational lawgiver will reject the entire way in which the debate over the management of wrongdoing is typically cast, as a debate about the "justification of punishment." In fact I am inclined to think that the rational course is to refuse for several decades to use the word "punishment" at all, since it narrows the mind, making one think that the only proper way to deal with wrongdoing is through some type of "mischief," as Bentham puts it, inflicted on the wrongdoer. The question before us is how to deal with the whole problem of wrongful acts, not how to punish people who have already committed one. Punishment, if we end up using it, ought to compete for our attention with other strategies for addressing the problem of crime, and thus the debate about the "justification of punishment" really ought to be about how it measures up to other strategies a society can use *ex ante* (and to some extent *ex post*) to reduce crime. Even the most nuanced retributivism errs at this point, focusing on what this offender "deserves" rather than on the larger issue of human well-being and how to protect it, which surely ought to interest retributivists as well as Utilitarians.

We can certainly think about *ex post* punishment as a deterrent (both specific and general), and thus as one way of protecting important human goods. Perhaps many offenders can be reformed, although not by prisons as America knows them. But we must also consider the much larger issue of deterrence *ex ante*. As Bentham emphasized, preventing wrongful acts is a complicated task. We need to consider it in the broadest possible way, asking how nutrition, social welfare, education, employment, and a variety of constructive policies may contribute. He argued that the focus on punishment *ex post* is quite inefficient if what one really wants is less offending: often the same result can be attained "as effectually at a cheaper rate: by instruction, for instance, as well as by terror: by informing the understanding, as well as by exercising an immediate influence on the will."[22] Punishment *ex post* is a fallback mechanism, in using which we acknowledge some degree of failure in our *ex ante* strategies.

At any rate, one must study the entire question. Bentham had a lot to say about the larger issue in other writings, many of which remain unpublished (and are being gradually released by the Bentham Project). His magnum opus was never finished. In *Principles of Morals and Legislation*, he focuses instead on the narrower task of reconstructing "punishment" in a Utilitarian spirit. But we should agree with him: the failure of most societies to consider "punishment" in the context of a larger inquiry into prevention is a grotesque failure.

We do not always err in this way. Let us consider elevators. A traveler to a distant country finds that elevators are very unreliable. They are often badly constructed and maintained, and they break down often. There are no laws about elevators, no mandatory inspections, no licensing or certification. Never mind, her hosts inform her: we don't spend money on such things, but we do spend a great deal of money tracking down the offenders, and we give them long prison sentences at state expense, to show them what we think their bad behavior deserves. Our traveler would be justified in thinking this a very odd and irrational society, and one that, at some level, did not take the whole issue of human safety seriously. (One could say the same for earthquakes, fires, etc.) But that in some sense non-serious way, I suggest, is how most societies treat most crimes. This neglect is even stranger in that criminals, unlike elevators, are equal citizens, among those whose welfare society is committed to protect and advance.

Why has the debate about crime become narrowed in this way? One possibility is that the "justification of punishment" is an appealing topic for philosophers and one that philosophical skills seem well suited to address, whereas the larger problem of crime clearly requires a multidisciplinary inquiry and is extraordinarily difficult in any case. But such problems do not make societies treat elevators, building construction in flood and earthquake zones, etc., in the thoughtless *ex post* way I have imagined.

A second explanation for the narrowing of debate is that welfarist deterrence theorists have also narrowed their focus: in order to reply to retributivists, many of them, unlike Bentham, also focus on punishment to the neglect of other welfarist strategies.

A third possible explanation is that people think *ex ante* welfare strategies will cost too much money, and they have forgotten that incarceration is extremely expensive. The cost of incarceration in the United States varies, but for federal prisoners it is around $30,000 per year, and for state prisoners it can be far higher (over $40,000 per year in California). For New York City, according to a recent study, the figure is over $60,000, but if one factors in the total cost of incarceration (including salaries and benefits for guards, maintenance of buildings, etc.) the cost to the city is a staggering $167,731 per inmate.[23] The United States has 5 percent of the world's population, but 25 percent of its prison inmates. One estimate is that the total cost to taxpayers is $63.4 billion per year.[24] (As the prison population ages, costs are going way up, due to the high cost of medical care.) Of course we have a hard time comparing these costs with the costs of education, employment opportunities, etc., but at least we can understand how they compare to the costs of parole and community service, given a lot of the prison population is in prison for nonviolent offenses (such as drug offenses) that would have been handled that way prior to "three strikes" and "tough on crime," and are handled that way in many countries.

Given that these costs are easy to discover, and yet the obsession with incarceration continues, I think we may also at least entertain a further explanation: that retributivism, with its deep roots in popular sentiment, has so shaped the debate that backward-looking considerations about "desert" have simply silenced concern for welfare. This doesn't happen so much with elevators and buildings, since members of the dominant group live in buildings and use elevators. It does happen with violent crime. Perhaps we do not actually love all of our fellow citizens or want them all to flourish; and academic philosophers, like many other Americans, are inclined to think that the people who commit crimes are distant from "us." Or perhaps we suppose that there is a class of people (surely not "us") who are hardwired for violence and predation and can be deterred only through fear of unpleasant punishment. The fact that "we" do not think this about the development of "our" own children shows that the ideas that underlie the demand for harsh punishments need to be critically scrutinized.

One thing that we do know about crime: early intervention in childhood education diminishes the likelihood that these children will become criminals—if the program is of the right sort. The pathbreaking work of James Heckman, for which he won the Nobel Prize in Economics in 2000, involves longitudinal studies of a group of preschool projects that involved not just classroom education but also nutrition and work with families.[25] Results many years later are excellent, in terms of both employment and law-abidingness. The fact that no society has taken these results fully to heart is discouraging, suggesting that with all the knowledge we possess, people still prefer to address crime through the incoherent and inefficient ideas of anger. There are signs that this inefficient mentality is shifting in the United States, with interest in preschool on the rise not only in New York, but in many other parts of the country. On the whole, however, Heckman's cogent analysis has fallen on deaf ears.

Why is this so? Racism is surely one reason in the United States: if you already view a group with fear and disgust, you are likely not to choose the measures that demonstrably improve the lives of this group, even (sometimes) when they may improve your own as well. The fact that the larger inquiry Bentham rightly recommends is too rarely the focus of public attention betrays the strong grip of intuitive ideas of payback, but it also betrays the subterranean influence of stigma, disgust, and fear toward minorities. The idea that all problems of wrongdoing are best addressed, and rather easily addressed, by simply incarcerating more people in harsh and degrading conditions has thus become a very common and intuitively appealing idea—witness Illinois senator Mark Kirk's recent statement that gang violence should be addressed by locking up all eighteen thousand members of Chicago's leading gangs. Such an idea at least contains the thought of incapacitation, not just the retributive idea, so it at least has some relation to human welfare. But it gets its traction through retribution, the idea of "throwing the book" at people, etc. And: this idea that cannot stand the light of reason, as Kirk himself promptly realized.[26] Incarceration on the U.S. scale is a quick and inefficient "fix" for a very complicated set of social problems, and as such it does not work. I think the only reason it can have even been supposed to be an acceptable primary strategy to address crime involves racial stigma, conscious or unconscious.

It is difficult to unravel the tangled skein of emotions involved in the demand for more and more incarceration. Fear is surely one motivator, and disgust-based racism another. But anger is also a powerful force: because these minorities harm us, making our lives insecure (people think), we ought to punish them for the discomfort they cause. Thus the zealous focus on victimless crimes such as drug offenses is surely motivated partly by disgust, but is probably abetted by a general desire to punish people who are seen as inflicting discomfort and insecurity. In the next chapter, my study of Alan Paton's *Cry, the Beloved Country* will study this nexus of emotions further.

In addition to bracketing "punishment," welfare-oriented legal thinkers would do well to put the term "criminal justice system" in scare quotes for a while, to remind ourselves that what we usually call by that name is a tiny sliver of a set of institutions that ought to be promoting social justice for all, including those who may at some point become or have already become criminals.[27]

So far as traditional "punishment" goes, the forward-looking legal system may continue to use incarceration, which incapacitates offenders, and which may contribute to deterrence, but it must look hard at the evidence that incarceration simply breeds hardened criminals with nothing positive to live for—thus undermining specific deterrence and reform, and perhaps general deterrence, given the influence of such hardened offenders in their communities. This inquiry must take seriously the experience of nations that use prisons far less. Certainly we have no reason to suppose that there is any special deterrent value to be reaped from unsanitary, violent, and humiliating conditions, which are well known to breed hopelessness, a sense that crime is the only future, and a very basic collapse of agency, while they also undermine family and community (in that way further undermining general deterrence). Furthermore, since part of the larger task is rebuilding or supporting relations of political trust, the state must consider how trust and mutual respect among citizens are affected by its willingness to use punishments that offend dignity (even if they aren't found to violate the Eighth Amendment).

Thus the stock debate about the "justification of punishment" seems both too narrow and too crude: too narrow because it conceives of all our dealings with wrongdoing, including its deterrence, as forms of payback *ex post*, rather than seriously examining the many other possibilities; too crude because what typically goes by the name of punishment gets traction because it seems to people like a form of payback, and payback ideas prevent the serious consideration of treatment that might actually better promote general welfare and bonds of trust among citizens.

We must, however, pause at this point: for I have simply assumed, on the basis of my prior arguments, that the right approach is forward-looking, rejecting the "blame game,"[28] and I have not fully confronted the strongest retributivist arguments. I have argued against anger, holding that it is either irrational (in the grip of a fantasy of payback) or unduly focused on relative status. But retributivist arguments do not always endorse anger or build their proposals on a validation of anger's cognitive content. (Nor, indeed, do they always propose extremely harsh forms of punishment.) So I need to say more at this point about how my argument so far relates to the subtler forms of retributivism. Because there is a vast literature on this topic and this is not a book about punishment, I must be highly selective, omitting many worthy contributions to the debate and treating others with compression; I do not hope to satisfy all readers.[29]

My argument so far is sufficient to disable any form of retributivism that relies on the *lex talionis*, that is, any idea that a wrongful act is somehow balanced out or paid back by similar suffering. As I've said, this fantasy of payback is simply not rational. Moreover, in daily life we agree. We never think that the right response to having your wallet stolen is to steal someone else's wallet, or that the right response to a rape would be to arrange for the rapist to get raped. What good would that do? The fact that the U.S. prison system operates on the basis of a related fantasy (where rape and humiliating conditions satisfy the payback wishes of victims) does not make it any more rational. The wrongful act has been done and cannot be undone; it is mere magical thinking involving a strange metaphysics of cosmic balance to suppose that the past is balanced out by a gruesome suffering in the future.

But there are two more sophisticated forms of retributivism still to consider. First is the famous view of Herbert Morris.[30] The second is the abstract retributivism of Michael Moore.[31] Both appear not to rely on the type of "magical thinking" that I have criticized. However, I shall argue that both ultimately do rely on it, as well as having other problems.

According to Morris, society is held together by a system of benefits and burdens. Criminal offenders defect from that system, refusing to bear their share of the burdens, and/or seizing benefits to which they are not entitled. A system of punishment corrects this imbalance, by inflicting proportional disabilities on the offender. Because he has claimed more liberty than he has a right to, his own liberty will be proportionally constricted, etc. Morris goes on to argue that persons have a right to be punished, because that way of treating them—by contrast to a regime that infantilizes them and treats them simply as ill—treats them with respect, as rational agents.

Let me begin by enumerating points of agreement with Morris. A system of law should recognize a wrongful act as a wrongful act. It should not refuse to distinguish between wrongful acts and mere accidents or cases of diminished responsibility. Moreover, I am prepared to agree with some aspects of the basic picture of society and of crime from which he starts, although I am dubious whether the idea of taking undue liberty is the best way of capturing what is distinctively wrong about rape, homicide, etc. The idea is so abstract that we lose the sense that law is about protecting important, and distinct, aspects of human lives.[32] That emphasis on human flourishing is important, because if that's what we are doing—not primarily preserving an abstract structure—then it appears that we should choose a solution that actually does promote human flourishing, and this surely pushes us in a welfarist direction. The social contract is *about* and *for* something; it's not an agreement for agreement's sake.

But even if we grant Morris his basic picture, according to which the criminal has taken someone else's space or freedom, we now have the question why the right response to that is a proportional diminution of the criminal's freedom. Surely on Morris's own account what is important is the protection of a system of equal liberty and a fair regime of opportunity. So shouldn't the question be, what treatment of the criminal is most likely to promote and sustain that fair and balanced system? There seems no reason to suppose that proportional payback is the most effective response in terms of what really matters. And why would Morris urge us to select a system that does not protect human liberty and opportunity as well as some other imaginable system?

It is at this point that Morris's view begins to collapse into a version of the *lex talionis*, I believe. Although Morris's idea of payback is far more subtle and symbolic than the standard one, it still gets its grip through a payback fantasy. For it is only the intuition that proportional payback makes sense that enables him to bypass the question of its value as a way of preserving the social contract and, more important, the human well-being that the contract is really about. Let us think back to chapter 4: a marriage is a kind of contract. Sometimes one party violates that contract, seizing "an undue liberty." Payback fantasies suggest that it is fitting that this person's liberty be proportionally diminished (as by a punitive divorce settlement). That seems to be in keeping with Morris's picture. And yet, if what really matters is the happiness of human beings, which is what the marriage contract is all about, then it is not at all obvious that punitive litigation is the appropriate strategy. Even if what is important is the preservation of an ideal and equal system of abstract liberties for all, we need to ask whether punitive payback at divorce time does that, including children in our calculus. The fact that Morris does not feel the need to justify his choice of penal (or litigation-related) suffering as a response to the problem of crime shows, I believe, that he is riding on the back of powerful intuitions about payback and proportionality that are a form of magical thinking and not a particularly good way of promoting the social goals that he actually has. Moreover, his view seems to commit him to neglecting the fact that many criminals begin life in the harshest of circumstances, a fact that any attempt at shoring up the social contract ought to regard as highly salient.

Another problematic aspect of Morris's view is its underlying picture of human beings. Apparently people are all eager to steal, rape, and kill; that's what they would do with a "greater liberty," and those "liberties" are seen (by Morris apparently, and by most people, in his view) as positive advantages.[33] This seems humanly odd (and out of step, I would add, with the very subtle understanding of human emotions shown in other essays by Morris). And certainly it is not the message that we want the legal system of a decent society to communicate about people. We should not send the message "that th[e] actions [of rapists and murderers] . . . are . . . inherently desirable and rational, and that we object to them only because, if performed by everyone, they would be collectively harmful."

We may add that even in terms of his own views, Morris's focus on punishment is one-sided. He utterly ignores the victim, whose rights have been breached, because he is thinking only about inflicting harm on the perpetrator and not on issues of rectification or restoration. Moreover, any sensible focus on victims would also demand general forward-looking thinking about deterrence, which punishment may serve better or worse, but we have been given no reason to think that proportional punishment serves this interest well. The social contract, in short, is about human welfare, and that ought to be the main concern for anyone with Morris's views. That it is not betrays, it seems, the deep grip of intuitions about payback on his thinking.

Things initially seem otherwise with the extremely abstract retributivism advocated by Michael Moore. Moore carefully distinguishes his view from a view built upon angry emotions. He also distinguishes it from all versions of the *lex talionis*. In his view, retributivism is just the view that moral desert is both necessary and sufficient for punishment, where punishment is not understood in terms of welfare or consequences. Because the view is so spare and so unconnected to any type of consequence, it is difficult to justify, and Moore grants this. Nonetheless, he argues, it could be justified in two ways: either by showing that it follows from an appealing set of general principles, or by showing that it best accounts for our particular judgments. He takes Morris to have pursued the first course; he will pursue the second.

At this point, Moore falls back on the standard examples of emotionally satisfying payback that we can all summon up. Front and center is an example of the execution of a murderer who has committed revolting and horrible crimes. A friend of the victim's exults and feels the execution is exactly right, despite the presence of anti-death-penalty protesters.[34] To me this is quite unsatisfactory. Nobody could doubt that retribution is very popular and conforms to many deep-seated intuitions. But we need something more, some overall account of why those intuitions rather than others that conflict with them should be taken to be reliable. As chapter 2 already showed, even the iconic "manly man" often eschews retribution in favor of welfare. And we all have powerful intuitions that go in the direction of Dr. King, as well as (no doubt) conflicting retributivist intuitions. So it seems to me that the case must be made in some more systematic and principled way. Even more problematic is the fact that Moore relies on this example in a way that rides on a newspaper description laden with gruesome rhetoric, which, by his own account, is one of many "examples . . . used [by this journalist] to get the blood to the eyes of readers."[35] Surely to the extent that we want to rely on intuitions—and I agree with Rawls in thinking that we rely on these only as part of an overall network of principles, theories, and judgments—the judgments on which we rely ought to be "considered judgments," that is, judgments that are the fruit of some testing and reflection, not the ones that are maximally designed to bypass reflection. Moore denies that his theory is emotion-based, but what he means by that is that it is not an expressive theory that justifies punishment by its ability to vent emotions. That's true. But at the level of justification, the view does appear to be emotion-based, and based on just those emotions that we are subjecting to critical scrutiny.

Indeed I think Moore's theory may also be inconsistent. He announces that his form of retributivism does not rely on the *lex talionis*. But then he uses in justification intuitions that probably rely on exactly that. At least he has not attempted to show that there is a class of reliable intuitions supporting his theory that do not at some level rely on the *lex talionis*, or what I have called "magical thinking."

As to Moore's abstract contention that wrongdoing is sufficient for punishment,[36] don't we have to ask, "Why?" And doesn't he owe us something in return? He tries to avoid the "why" question, appealing to the intrinsic appeal of his view, but it does appear that we can't do away with that question altogether. When a child does wrong, we don't just punish away without thinking of consequences. Indeed we typically think of consequences above all: we want a child who will become a moral and rational adult, and we choose strategies reasonably aimed at that end. We seek out expert theories, and try to figure out what treatment best produces good results. If some type of punishment is shown to be useful, we might choose that. But we do it because it is a good route to our goal. A parent who sent a child to her room "because she deserves it," and who had nothing more to say about whether this was a good way to produce adult virtue, would not be my favorite type of parent. The revolution in the punishment of children that has taken place since the time of Dr. Spock is built on clinical and empirical data: harsh treatment does not work. If parents did not care about what works, but simply thought wrongdoing sufficient for punishment, they would not care about the data, and change would not have occurred. Does Moore think that parents are wrong to care about what works? (Of course I think that even if harsh punishments did work one should not use them, but at least at that point we would have a real debate.)

Moore will certainly reject this example, on the grounds that children are not fully rational, and therefore not fully responsible moral agents. I doubt this, particularly when we think about older children and young adults who are our children. And I have already argued in chapter 4 that retribution is a bad way to deal with adults who are our children. But let us in fairness to Moore think instead about friends one of whom has wronged the other, but who remain in an ongoing relationship. (And remember that Moore thinks moral desert sufficient for retribution.) Surely, as I've argued in chapter 4, piling on punishment just on grounds of desert is not an unproblematic or obvious strategy. It seems to me that anyone who deals with such a situation merely in terms of backward-looking blame, without focusing a major part of her attention on the future, is likely to lead a lonely and unhappy life. In human relations generally, we are always wrong to neglect the future; it is the only thing we can change, and it is in effect the only life we have.

On the whole, I greatly prefer Morris's overall approach to justification. Although I do not think it succeeds in this particular instance, it is at least built upon principles for which he offers appealing arguments. Moore's bare retributivism seems to latch onto some powerful emotions, but those emotions are precisely the ones whose rationality and usefulness we are calling into question.

It is instructive to ponder two more nuanced interventions in the retributivism debate that one might dub "borderline retributivism": those of R. A. Duff and Dan Markel.[37] The "core retributivist thought," according to Duff, is that "what gives criminal punishment its meaning and the core of its normative justification is its relationship, not to any contingent future benefits that it might bring, but to the past crime for which it is imposed" (3). In terms of my argument, this is a bad starting point, both because it focuses on punishment to the exclusion of other strategies for addressing crime and because it refuses to focus at all on the future. Nonetheless, as Duff elaborates the nature of the backward focus he has in mind, the proposal has attractive features: the core idea is that of a "calling to account," and its significance is political, expressing core political values. All this I can agree with, and I have already said that it is important to focus on the past to just this extent: it is right and important that the truth about the past be publicly acknowledged. Capabilities are intrinsic goods, so a society that aims to protect them for all should take note of violations: an intrinsic damage to social welfare has occurred. But for the most part the reasons for such a focus will be forward-looking: we are trying to build a society in which capabilities are protected, so we need to note the problems in our way. Moreover, I've argued that a decent society needs to engender bonds of trust and related moral sentiments among citizens, and citizens will not trust political institutions if they feel that political principles are just words on paper, proclaiming the importance of certain capabilities while in practice their violation is taken lightly.

In the article in question, Duff does not say why this "calling to account" is socially important. But in his earlier book *Punishment, Communication, and Community*, Duff says something very like what I have just said: If law is to mean what it says, "it is committed to censuring those who engage in such conduct."[38] To remain silent would be to go back on its commitment to its own values. Duff does not explicitly allude to trust here, but it is surely part of the picture. (But if that is so, then the proposal is inconsistent, to the extent that it officially denies forward orientation but justifies itself in terms of such forward-looking elements.) Duff also seems right to insist that, while the civil law is focused on damages, the criminal law is focused on wrongdoing. I agree. And I also welcome Duff's insistence that the criminal law should not view itself as the agent of the moral law: such moralistic views are not appropriate to law in a pluralistic liberal society (14). However, all these promising moves appear to be undermined when Duff abruptly shifts course, stating that the "core retributivist thought" is that "the guilty deserve to suffer (something), and that a proper aim for the criminal law is to subject them to that suffering" (16). Here he appears to embrace the moralism he has previously rejected, and he endorses a different view of the core of retributivism from the one with which he began (and a view that is much more familiar and less "borderline"). Still, the process of "calling to account," as Duff describes it, is actually quite forward-looking and reform-oriented, no matter what he says: "By imposing a burdensome punishment, we hope to make it harder for the offender to ignore the message, to keep his attention focused on what he has done, and to provide a structure within which he can face up to his wrongdoing and on what he must do to avoid its repetition" (17). In an important footnote (45 p.n. 21), he insists again that the purpose of punishment is "to affect his future conduct."

On balance, then, Duff's proposal has promising elements, but in its attempt to set itself squarely in the retributivist tradition it sells those elements short.

Markel has basically the view embodied in that last extract from Duff: the retributivism he favors is a "confrontation" with the offender. It should focus on communication and not on suffering, its aim should be to affect future conduct, and its focus should be the wrongful act of a person, rather than the person him- or herself. Like Duff, he emphasizes that this conception of punishment is political, and not part of a comprehensive ethical or metaphysical doctrine. He therefore explicitly gives up all views that rest on notions of metaphysical balance or cosmic fittingness. He nonetheless insists that punishment must be "proportional" to the severity of the offense, apparently because he believes that only that carefully calibrated severity accurately communicates the perceived magnitude of the offense.

It seems to me that Markel has more or less abandoned retributivism, in favor of a forward-looking theory that focuses on the reform of the offender.[39] If that is his goal, he certainly ought to be more interested in the empirics than he seems to be. Does punishment actually produce acknowledgment and reform, or does it more often produce hardened offenders? How might a system that is still a type of punishment really contrive to communicate a message that would be useful to reform? (This is Braithwaite's question, and I think Markel really ought to become a Braithwaitean.) Are there not lots of other variables that are pertinent to whether an offender repeats the offense—such as skills training, employment opportunities, and education? At one point Markel does note that subsidized drug and alcohol treatment, and skills training, might reduce crime (59), but he says that the difference between these programs and punishment is that they ought to be open to all people, not only those who have offended (59). It's not at all clear, though, that punishment of the traditional sort is the only program particularly suited to criminal offenders that we could devise. (Perhaps criminal offenders need specific types of counseling and therapy, as Braithwaite plausibly argues.) Nor is it clear why the fact that a certain sort of program is good for everyone is taken to show that it is not the best way of addressing criminal offenders. So Markel is just guessing when he asserts that the most effective way of reforming offenders is through punishments calibrated to exhibit "proportional severity." It seems implausible to me—although it would certainly be an improvement if punishments really did this, rather than exhibiting over-the-top severity for such victimless crimes as drug offenses.

What is especially interesting about these two proposals, which present themselves as nuanced forms of retributivism, is the inexorable pull of the future. Rather than engage in the type of cosmic balance thinking I have rejected, these two theorists turn to communication and reform— all the while maintaining that they are still in the retributivist camp.

Much the same can be said of the family of views dubbed "expressive retributivism"—of which Duff, indeed, is standardly classified as a leading exemplar, although, because of the complexity of his view, I have given it separate treatment. These views combine the claim that certain crimes are serious wrongs that ought to be publicly acknowledged as such with the claim, so to speak, that "talk is cheap"—that only hard treatment properly expresses society's extremely negative evaluation of these crimes and, by the same token, the value society attaches to human life and safety.[40] Now I have already agreed with the first claim, and my own Millian form of consequentialism can admit it, whereas other types of welfarism might not. But surely the first claim cannot be meant as purely backward-looking: these are things that society commits itself to protecting in an ongoing way. To say, "This thing that occurred is very bad" has a point beyond cheap talk only to the extent that it reinforces commitment and determination to protect human life and safety going forward. So, the claim may be partly retrospective, but it is at least partly prospective.

But then the claim that only hard treatment properly expresses the severity of society's negative judgment needs prospective empirical evaluation. Very likely just letting violent offenders go free is not a good strategy for protecting human life; we can all agree on that. But surely using the methods that empirical study shows to be best at protecting human life would be the best way for society to show that it takes the problem of crime seriously. It's just not serious to indulge in fantasies of proportion-ality: indeed that seems to me a lot of "cheap talk." Instead, let's really study the problem and see what works. And of course, back to our ear-lier point, this means thinking not just about the deterrent effect of pun-ishment *ex post*; it also means spending money on education, nutrition, and other *ex ante* strategies. The idea that many people are hardwired to offend and are deterred only by fear of something extremely unpleasant is common, but utterly implausible. Only serious social investment really shows that a society takes crime seriously—seriously enough not just to throw people into brutal and degrading conditions, but seriously enough to spend money where it will really do good going forward. We might call this the expressive theory of social welfare spending.[41]

Indeed, one of the best accounts of the expressive theory (which does not present itself as a form of retributivism), namely Jean Hampton's "The Moral Education Theory of Punishment," insists that the promo-tion of social welfare is a substantial part of what justifies punishment. She then adds that an important part of its function is the way in which it can "teach both wrongdoers and the public at large the moral reasons for *choosing* not to perform an offense."[42] She thus combines my emphasis on public acknowledgment with an interest in reforming offenders going forward. She appears to be open to empirical evidence concerning how those goals might best be pursued.[43]

Public expression of political values is particularly important when those values have not been generally acknowledged. Thus, in cases ranging from sexual harassment in the workplace to fraud in banking, the greater the disregard and arrogance the conduct exhibits, the more important it becomes to make a public statement affirming the fact that we take this conduct to be very wrongful. In such contexts attaching an unpleasant penalty to the conduct may well be essential for both specific and, especially, for general deterrence. The idea of "teaching someone a lesson" gets real traction in such cases, and is a reasonable prospect. More important, the penalty educates the society about the conduct, which they might unreflectively have approved. However, one should not assume even in such cases that people are eager to commit bad acts the minute they get a chance, and are deterred only through fear. In the case of sexual harassment, education and public discussion have done a great deal to make the harmfulness of this conduct evident. To pursue penalties without also pursuing such education would be as foolish as to punish elevator builders who cause harm, while neglecting to regulate elevators *ex ante*.

Let us now turn to the other side of the "punishment" debate. Socrates insisted that the state must never do wrong. Do we have an account of why punishments, even those that are both humane and forward-looking, are not wrongs inflicted on people? It's clearly not enough to say, "Well, X asked for it," since we have rejected the payback idea. And it is also not enough to say, "Social welfare requires that we use X for our own ends," since we have said that the rule of law requires equal respect for human dignity, and using someone as a mere means runs afoul of that idea. Reformists will surely press these objections.

Some of the familiar swipes against consequentialist theories of punishment (it can justify harsh or degrading punishments, or punishments of the innocent) disappear once we point out that the type of consequentialism I defend includes the protection of dignity and non-humiliation as among the most fundamental "consequences," since these embody entitlements of citizens based on justice.[44] They are thus among the central components of the consequences to be promoted; so too are political affiliations expressive of (political) trust and equal respect.[45] Bentham had a hard time with these questions, though he struggled valiantly to show that public utility was not promoted by harsh punishments, or punishments of the innocent. My view (rather like Mill's, I think) makes this a nonissue from the start. The feeling that Utilitarian views make too little room for the acknowledgment of wrongdoing is also removed by my account, in which the acknowledgment of culpability is central (though I don't say "desert," because it remains an open question exactly what treatment is the appropriate response to culpability).

Is truthful acknowledgment valuable intrinsically, or only instrumentally? A view of my type could go either way. I am inclined to think that the most important issues are instrumental. A system in which truth is an important value promotes the protection of important human entitlements better than one that does not care so much about truth—above all because truth in these matters protects well-being and promotes trust, both between citizens and between citizens and the government. Because trust is a central issue in revolutionary justice, and pertinent to the role of truth commissions, I shall say no more about it here, but take it up again in chapter 7.

My account of social welfare, then, requires any governmental use of coercion to satisfy very demanding constraints: it must be compatible with equal dignity and non-humiliation, it must be accompanied by public acknowledgment of the seriousness of wrongdoing, and it must be justified to the person involved as only one part of a much more comprehensive project in which we reasonably aim to promote social welfare. Often the aim of reform will help us to justify the use of coercion. But it is permissible, too, to say to the offender, "We are removing your liberty for a time for the sake of the public welfare, promoting good for the society of which you are a part." It seems to me that, if incarceration really were humane and respectful, not disgusting, violent, and an offense to basic dignity, there would be no more difficulty justifying it than there would be in justifying fines or community service—nor, indeed, more than in justifying taxation, or military conscription, which are unpleasant costs paid by many for the sake of the welfare of all. Anti-Utilitarians typically do not hold that taxation uses people as mere means to social welfare, unless they espouse an extreme form of libertarianism that is uncommon. A decent society is entitled to use coercion to get people to make needed contributions to the general well-being. And we can certainly say that the reason we have chosen you for this particular lot, incarceration (rather than, say, for a fine), is that you have been convicted of a dangerous type of wrongdoing.[46] If this is retributivism, make the most of it. But of course the state's interest here is in incapacitation and deterrence, not in some alleged cosmic suitability of incarceration as proportional payback for certain offenses. It never says that we are making you pay, or that you are getting what you deserve, or that your suffering balances or is proportional to or atones for the harm you did. These assertions, which my state eschews, are rightly regarded as essential characteristics of even a non-vindictive retributivism.[47] We may, on the other hand, say that one reason we assign a given punishment is to make a statement of commitment to our fundamental political principles, which is at the same time an acknowledgment of the importance of the equal dignity of all citizens. Such statements would be cheap talk if punishing were all we were doing about the problems of crime; but the nation I imagine will be pursuing a wide range of intelligent strategies.

IV. Non-Anger and the Criminal Law

By the time we reach crime and the criminal justice system, we have already missed the most significant opportunities for social improvement. The criminal law system, and "punishment," are a fallback mechanism, in turning to which we admit a degree of failure in other strategies for prevention and deterrence. It's only if we convince ourselves that certain people or groups are hardwired to be and do evil that we can feel comfortable about turning to the criminal law for help with a social problem. In chapter 7, indeed, we shall see that even people who seem as evil as can be, for example the Afrikaners who administered the evil system of apartheid, do contain the capacity for good, and if they are approached in that spirit, rather than sternly held to account, they may become cooperative and productive citizens. Our discomfort, indeed, should infuse our thought about the criminal law.

Beyond this point, I must become vulnerable to the same criticism that one might level at Bentham's *Principles*: for, instead of taking on the whole job of thinking about crime prevention through all the devices available to government (including education, nutrition, social security, non-discrimination, and much more), I shall simply talk about a few aspects of the system of "criminal justice" as it currently exists. (Notice, too, that I do not even talk about the implications of my idea for civil law—not because there are none, but because my legal knowledge in that area is insufficient.) The full inquiry that is needed is vast, multidisciplinary, and contextual. My account points to the need for that larger inquiry; but it also has implications for existing institutions in one narrow area of the subject. These implications are heterogeneous, and only a few issues will be treated here, to give a representative sense of what the theory might offer.

IV.1. The Role of the Victim in Criminal Trials:
       Victim Impact Statements

In contemporary trials, anger at criminals has led to the demand for an organized institutional vent for that resentment. As section V will discuss, criminal law provides, at the sentencing phase, an institutionalized opportunity for a sympathetic consideration of the convicted criminal's entire life, which may possibly lead to mitigation. But why, then, if sympathy has its day in court (it is said), should resentment not have equal time?[48] Many victims and victims' advocates maintain that it should, arguing that victims themselves, or, more often, their families, have a right to appear and to describe the toll the crime has taken on them. Usually this sort of request is made in homicide cases, presumably because when the victim is still there, testimony about the toll taken by the act can often be admitted at trial somehow or other. So what is at issue is admitting testimony that seems unrelated to the actual crime and its actual victim, on the grounds that friends and family suffer too and should be able to influence the sentencing process. Since the testimony amounts to a venting of anger, it is not surprising that I am troubled by such proposals. The idea of bringing the Furies into the courtroom in an unregenerate form is precisely what the entire spirit of my Eumenidean proposal has set itself against: the Furies, in entering the state, should be transformed into forward-looking goddesses who think about the welfare of the community as a whole.

We might say, too, that this procedure is all too like the Athenian custom of private prosecution, in which the voices of the victims take the place of an impartial legal institution. Here they do not displace law, but they certainly deflect it.

Notice that everything relevant to convicting the offender has already been presented at trial. Assuming O is convicted, the wrongful act has been acknowledged. Moreover, in setting levels of offense, the effects of a type of wrongful act on the victim and on the rest of the community have already been considered, so the victim impact statement is redundant insofar as it is relevant, and simply serves to whip up retributive emotion. As for deterrence and general welfare, it is not at all clear how victim impact statements bear on that goal, nor is that what victims are seeking. Their goal is to express anger and to secure a heavier retributive punishment for the offender. So their demand has all the problems that we have already found with retributive accounts, and it has the ongoing irrationality of anger: expressing anger in public and getting a heavier sentence for the offender does nothing to bring the dead person back or to create a better future for this family. Indeed, by prolonging entanglement with the criminal justice system and encouraging fixation, it often makes the future worse.

We may now introduce two additional problems. The first is that murder victims don't all have grieving families. Like Euthyphro's father's servant, they may lack people to take their part. So what victims' families are asking is an opportunity to influence the sentence of offender O, in a way that those of offenders P and Q are not influenced, just because they are there and are angry. This does not seem like a very persuasive reason: the crime is what it is, and similar crimes should be treated similarly. A solitary person whom nobody loves is worthy of the same concern as a beloved patriarch or matriarch. The second problem is that empirical evidence shows that juries are more likely to bond with people who are more like them. In a preponderance of cases, victims' families will seem more like them than the defendant will, and this extra presence on the scene will impede them from listening attentively to the defendant.[49]

A sensible policy would be to address concerns of victims going forward insofar as these are genuinely practical concerns. Where a crime has removed a major source of income or domestic labor, the family should be compensated, for example. But victim impact statements are typically not forward-looking requests for compensation, which would typically be made in a civil suit. They are typically retributive denunciations, aimed at getting a harsher criminal sentence for the wrongdoer, and it is this aspect that should be rejected.

What about the effect of punishment on families of the criminal?[50] As with crime itself, so here: the broad social welfare implications of every practice must be considered. When thinking about whether incarceration is a suitable punishment, we should think about its influence on families and communities, particularly when a large proportion of men in certain subgroups end up being incarcerated and thus removed from productive community life. Incarceration for nonviolent offenses (such as drug offenses) is problematic for many reasons, but one of these is surely the impact upon the community as a whole.

In chapter 2 I considered the objection that the anger of victims is a valuable deterrent to crime. In the context of the criminal trial, that claim seems particularly flimsy. Will people really be deterred by thinking of the (usually unknown) probability that some family members will come to court and testify? (Maybe they will just be incentivized to kill the whole family!) There appears to be no good data on perpetrators' knowledge of the family circumstances of their victims, or of their knowledge of whether a given jurisdiction allows victim impact statements. It seems likely that most perpetrators don't have any idea about these things. The loss and grief of victims can be highly effective in lobbying for better laws (for example, against child sexual abuse or drunken driving). But that is quite a different claim from the claim that victim anger in the penalty phase of a trial deters.

The best that can be said about victim impact statements is that in some cases they help victims move forward by satisfying their desire to tell their story. Well, fine, we should be all in favor of narration if it helps and does no harm. But we must remember that victims have been raised on narratives of payback, and, more recently, have been led to expect that they will not achieve "closure" without a narrative that (typically) denounces the defendant and attempts to secure a harsher sentence.[51] We should not support victims in sating their desire for payback, with all its problems for fairness to the defendant. Perhaps we should subsidize a type of trauma counseling for victims based on confronting what has happened to them and telling their stories to a group. Such therapies are well known in the treatment of PTSD and rape trauma. But those therapies do not consist in encouraging the victim in payback thoughts, nor do they occur in a setting where those payback thoughts have real-life consequences for someone who has been tried and convicted already. To be sure, the satisfaction of expressing payback wishes is a real satisfaction, but a wise society will not build criminal law policy on what economist John Harsanyi has called "sadistic and malicious preferences."[52]

But, it will be said, victims need to be heard—and to be heard not just by a therapist, but by the criminal who wronged them, and in a public setting. Just as in intimate relations even people who do not wish for payback still want the party who wronged them to *hear* and *understand*, so too with victims of crime. Their sense of their equal dignity in society, and their trust in social institutions, may even depend upon this sense of responsiveness. If victim narratives are too prejudicial to include prior to sentencing, as I believe they are, we might then cautiously consider an institutional setting for victim narratives after sentencing. Such narratives are likely to remain mostly retributive in content; but they will not be able to undermine the legal process.[53]

Notice, however, that the hypothetical victim is imagined as demanding two very different things. One demand is simply to be heard and understood by the wrongdoer. That demand can be satisfied by my post-sentencing proposal. The other demand that is usually mixed in with this is the demand to express retributive denunciations—and usually the whole point of this demand is to influence the judge and jury. To the extent that the second demand is the primary one, as I believe it usually is, victims will not be interested in my post-sentencing proposal.

One very remarkable instance of victim confrontation occurred in Charleston, South Carolina, when admitted killer Dylann Roof appeared, at his pretrial bail hearing, before representatives of the nine people he has admitted to killing in an attempt to start a "race war." Analyzing the victim statements in chapter 3, I argued that they express unconditional forgiveness in an unusually pure form, with no assertion of superiority and no hint of payback wishes. Such statements, surprising because they are so unusual, could certainly put a new face on the whole question of victim impact statements, if a substantial proportion of Americans came to share the very rigorous view of unconditional love, untainted by rancor, that the Charleston church communicated to its members.

IV.2. Dignity and Shame

One of the more unpleasant effects of unfettered anger is its tendency to inflict shame or "down-ranking" on others. Anger often, though not always, focuses obsessively on status or down-ranking, and its wish is to reverse positions, pushing the offender down below the previously down-ranked self. As I've said, this is the one way in which anger makes good sense: humiliating the offender really does remove the wrong, if the wrong is seen as a pure status-injury. Nonetheless, I also said that it makes a very unpleasant and normatively substandard kind of sense. Certainly in public life we do not want to encourage obsession with relative status, especially when it leads to practices of humiliation.

If public principles eschew down-ranking, it follows that punishments, to the extent that we rely on them, should eschew humiliation. Obviously a good society that wishes to avoid humiliating people should begin in childhood, with policies for housing, schools, and so forth. Criminal punishment, as before, comes too late. But to the extent that it is used, society must not simply mouth the slogan, "No cruel and unusual punishment," but must really try to make punishment non-humiliating. Alternative sanctions such as community service are useful here, but prisons themselves can be something other than a constant source of humiliation and shame, as cross-national comparisons show. European prisons, by and large, are much more dignified places than U.S. prisons (apart from white-collar prisons). If the United States were not determined to incarcerate on flimsy grounds, thus incarcerating a huge number of people, it would have a much easier time providing decent conditions.

Can incarceration ever be respectful of dignity? It's hard to say, given the distance between current practices and really respectful practices. But here are some of the things prisoners have a right to, which go toward making prison non-humiliating. Even in the United States, they have rights to clean facilities and decent plumbing. They typically have rights to some forms of personal property (photos, mementos). Importantly, they have the right to get married, even when serving life terms.[54] Some judges would like to see prisoners' personal privacy and modesty protected better than currently.[55] In Europe, prisoners typically retain their basic civil rights, including the right to vote and welfare rights. Many are also permitted to work outside the prison and to visit their families. Such practices need to be studied to see whether they remove the idea that temporary incapacitation entails a loss of basic human dignity.[56]

Nor should society accept the invitation to reintroduce punishments explicitly based upon public humiliation—once very common in history, where the penal tattoo or brand and the scarlet letter are famous.[57] Sometimes these contemporary shame punishments are offered as alternatives to incarceration, in which case they are just different forms of humiliation, and perhaps a tiny bit more attractive, given the current conditions in prisons, at least in the United States. But typically they are proposed as alternatives to fines and community service for lighter offenses, on the grounds that they better express society's desire to down-rank the offender. Community service, by contrast, it is alleged, gives people something good to do and can create personal pride and confidence—which Dan Kahan, the main theorist of shame penalties, finds incompatible with the expression of society's core moral values.[58] So let's consider shame penalties as alternatives to community service, since that is Kahan's focus.

The deliberate infliction of stigma (in the form of signs, placards, etc.) upon people who commit (typically) nonviolent offenses such as solicitation, public urination, or drunk driving is objectionable for a number of reasons.[59] First, it assails dignity in a very painful way, and a way that is unacceptable on grounds of basic justice even if it is not felt as painful. My type of welfarism, as I've emphasized, makes the protection of dignity and the social conditions of self-respect an intrinsic value, thus entailing that we reject state-administered degradation of citizens even were it to be very effective in deterring crime. (As we shall see, it is not.)

Second, punishments based upon shaming issue an invitation, in effect, to mob vindictiveness: the sign or placard is ordered by the court, but the punishers are the mass of citizens, who jeer and inflict shame;

thus these punishments gratify the wish of the majority to down-rank and stigmatize certain unpopular types of people. It is normatively problematic for a society based on an idea of impartiality and the rule of law to turn punishment over to such biased and un-lawlike forces.

Third, as we might expect, and as history shows,[60] such tendencies quickly get out of hand, migrating from truly harmful acts to mere unpopular ways of being: thus, in many times and places, religious and sexual minorities have been targeted for stigma and branding.[61] Giving the mob the ability to confer a "spoiled identity" is an open invitation to a type of bullying that is all too common. This migratory tendency also indicates that shame-based penalties will not really deter crime, since they will not (or not primarily) target real criminals. And they send a signal to society at large that stigmatized identities, rather than serious crimes, are salient targets of the criminal justice system.

Fourth, shame-based penalties encourage retaliatory anger. One of the problems the Eumenides had to deal with was the unending nature of anger, which keeps cycling back again in a new generation. So with stigma and shaming: James Gilligan's excellent empirical study of violence shows that such punishments actually increase violence in society, by increasing the tendency of criminals to self-define as outlaws and to bond with other outlaws to retaliate against society. They are therefore extremely bad deterrents.[62]

Finally, such penalties lead to what criminal law theorist Stephen Schulhofer, and others, call "net-widening": that is, to simply increasing the amount of punishment in society. Because they appear less harsh than incarceration, they are often substituted for either outright release or parole, thus simply increasing the amount of "hard treatment" in society.[63] We have reason to think that this net-widening, which is very expensive, is bad for the deterrence of really serious crimes.

Three of my five arguments against penalties based on shaming are empirical, supporting the contention that they are not good deterrents. (The third argument pertains to both specific and general deterrence, the fourth and fifth primarily to specific deterrence.) Only the first and second, being normative in character, leave open the question, "Shouldn't we do this if and because it works?" In fact all societies eschew certain forms of "cruel and unusual punishment," and practices such as slavery, on grounds independent of their efficiency. My form of welfarism has no trouble concurring with them. Still, it is helpful to point out that such punishments, on a variety of grounds, actually appear to be quite inefficient.

But, as I said in chapter 2, some status injuries are in a special category, because they involve the denial of people's equal dignity. Discrimination on the basis of race, sex, or disability; sexual harassment in the workplace;

certain types of bullying or threatening hate speech: all are humiliating practices of a special kind, and one that a society committed to equality before the law needs to take very seriously. Making such practices illegal is usually justified by a forward-looking welfarist argument anyway, since it is plausibly believed that such actions are highly deterrable. So we do not need to urge a change in common patterns of public argument. Even additional penalties for hate crimes standardly receive a deterrent justification.[64]

A society pursuing overall welfare will have to weigh the speech issue with great caution, since ambitious hate speech laws of a type known in Europe (including laws against "group libel") may not prove welfare-enhancing, for the reasons given by Mill in *On Liberty*. They are also highly prone to being hijacked by majorities for the humiliation of minorities: blasphemy laws in nations as different as Britain and India criminalize offense to the majority religion (or, the majority is in the strongest position to demand enforcement of a general law) in ways that prove over time extremely punitive to minority speech and to internal religious criticism.[65] But narrower laws focusing on bullying and threats targeted at an individual seem to lack this problem. Reforming Internet anonymity so that defamed individuals can successfully sue under existing laws seems an urgent priority.[66]

In short: my strictures against status-obsession do not mean that there is no way in which political principles should attend to status. The competitive search for *relative* status and rank is what I have been targeting. Our equal dignity as human beings and citizens is a special status, rightly given constitutional protection. This gives non-discrimination laws, prohibitions on sexual harassment, and, I personally would add, affirmative action policies, a prominent role to play. (Thus affirmative action would not be acceptable as mere identity politics or assertion of relative group status: it must be defended in terms of equality.)

IV.3. Confrontation and Reintegration

When a child commits a bad act, a good family will convey to the child a clear message about the unacceptability of the act, but in a spirit of love and generosity, encouraging the child to separate the child's basic ongoing self from the wrongful act and to think of him- or herself as capable of good in the future. It helps if parents model the virtues themselves, and their delicate combination of confrontation and reintegration is made more effective by the child's own love and emulation.

Influential Australian criminologist John Braithwaite argues that many crimes, especially involving youthful offenders, are best addressed in precisely this way, through community conferencing in a supportive quasi-parental spirit. Braithwaite's approach is complex, involving an elaborate theory of community social control, public shaming, and punishment administered by the community rather than (at least in the first instance) impartial agencies of government.[67] I think some aspects of his vision are extremely attractive and others less so. What I shall now do, consequently, is to describe a "Braithwaitean core," a proposal for reintegrative conferencing that includes central features of his idea; I shall then examine this promising idea in a critical spirit. Finally, I shall mention other aspects of the surrounding Braithwaite theory of crime that seem separable from the attractive core, and not so attractive in their own right.[68]

Braithwaite's basic idea is that what offenders—especially young offenders—need, if they are to change their ways (and if others are to be deterred) is a clear moral message about the wrongfulness of their act, combined with an avenue to reintegration with the society they have offended. His approach is in a general way Utilitarian: his goal is ultimately to deter crime, and he commends his reintegrative method as more effective than other approaches.[69] Most impersonal criminal punishments, he argues, alienate offenders, particularly young and malleable offenders, causing them to identify with criminal subcultures and to become hardened in their ways. This result is especially likely to occur when the criminal justice system conveys a message of stigmatization or humiliation, treating the offender as low, lacking in dignity, and not worth caring much about. This happens all too often. Braithwaite believes that it is endemic to large impersonal institutions to behave in this disrespectful and stigmatizing way.[70]

On the other hand, most reform efforts, he holds, do not successfully imprint on the young offender the moral message that crime is not acceptable to the community. They rely on rational persuasion, whereas Braithwaite holds that a community, like a family, works best when it inspires strong emotions toward the moral norms of the community. He calls his key emotion "shame," meaning by this a painful emotion that acknowledges having failed to meet some community ideal or norm.

Just as a good family (in his view) emphasizes, through love and respect, that the child is separate from the child's offense, so too a successful intervention with juvenile offenders must separate offender from crime. Braithwaite believes that the best way to get the right features is to deinstitutionalize and personalize dealings with offenders, by setting up community conferences, in which, in effect, the community itself is the criminal justice system, and, if all goes well, the young offender never falls into the hands of the formal system. These conferences—which he and his colleagues have tried out and then studied in Wagga Wagga, Australia, and Auckland, New Zealand—are used only for predatory crimes, thus avoiding the obvious problem that communities like to tyrannize over people's liberty in intrusive ways, even when there is no victim. Most systems of punishment, in his view, brutalize the conscience; this system, by contrast, aims to awaken conscience, by making clear to the offender the cost of the act to the community and the strong disapproval of the community. Throughout, respect is shown to the offender, who is treated as someone who has the potential to do good. Braithwaite is emphatic on this point, sharply distinguishing his approach from other proposals for shame-based penalties that focus on stigmatization or humiliation.[71]

What actually happens? Typically the conference includes the victim or victims, who can make clear to the offender the costs of the act.[72] A faceless person becomes "a vulnerable elderly woman who did without something significant because of the loss of the money."[73] But it also includes relatives, teachers, and other community figures whom the young person admires or loves, so that a structure of familial emulation is built into the entire situation.[74] Moreover, even when the victim does not directly touch the emotions of the offender, who may have developed a capacity to avoid feeling responsibility, the victim is very likely to touch the relatives and friends, and their distress, in turn, may get through to the offender, even when the victim has not.[75] The coordinator keeps things forward-looking and positive. Thus, when a mother at one point says, "He used to be a good boy until then," the coordinator immediately steps in, saying, "And he still is a good boy. No one here thinks we're dealing with a bad kid. He's a good kid who made a mistake and I hope he knows now that that's what we all think of him."[76] The crime is constructed as the bad act of a good person. At the same time, any bad circumstances in the offender's life are brought to light, in a way that awakens sympathy.

Who and what does the coordinator represent? This, Braithwaite says, is complicated and challenging. For the coordinator must identify him- or herself with offenders, victims, families—but also with "suprapersonal values enshrined in the law."[77] A tall order indeed. Above all, the coordinator must convey the idea that this conference is about reintegration, not about the "mischief" standardly associated with the idea of punishment. And the process is patient: Braithwaite describes one case in which eight successive conferences are used to reach a repeat offender.

How is reintegration achieved?[78] The idea is for all alike, offender, victim, and friends, to acknowledge a split between act and person, and to express closeness and inclusion toward the person, while casting stern disapproval upon the act. "Rituals of reintegration" are devised by the coordinator, drawing on his or her knowledge of the community. Apology figures here as a ritual gesture through which the offender splits him- or herself into two, dissociating self from offense and supporting society's rule.[79] But apology is carefully structured so that it does not involve abasement, but positively reinforces self-respect. And what is hoped for is that the distance that crime has created between the various parties will be closed, creating "opportunities . . . for perpetrators and victims to show (unexpected) generosity toward each other."[80]

This method has obvious appeal, in terms of our ideas of the "Transition" and of a forward-looking focus on welfare. It really is Transition punishment: non-angry, generous in spirit, yet insistent about the wrongfulness of wrongful acts. If skillfully conducted, it seems likely to be very fruitful, as indeed the experimental evidence suggests. Surely a trained coordinator will be better at working with offenders in a forward-looking way than prosecutors and judges. And Braithwaite is no doubt correct that all too often the official criminal justice system alienates and stigmatizes.

On the other hand, in terms of our Eumenidean idea of turning anger over to impartial agencies of justice, the proposal has questionable features. Braithwaite is well aware that conferences may seem to flout ideas of procedural justice and due process. For this reason, if the offender denies the charges, he or she is then transferred into the normal justice system. He or she does not have to plead guilty.[81] There are also obvious worries about anger, shame, and humiliation emerging within the conference setting itself, despite the best efforts of the coordinator. Braithwaite knows this too, but replies that victims are really much less angry and vengeful than one might expect, once they are in a room with a real person whose story they hear.[82] Nor is he oblivious to the danger that his type of shame, which is based on emulation, will slide over into ostracism and stigmatization, and he proposes to head this off through a variety of "rituals of inclusion." As for the idea that community norms may themselves include stigmatization of subgroups, he proposes to head this off by focusing only on predatory offenses about which there is a high level of consensus across groups. And as for inevitable power imbalances in the conference setting itself (often tracking asymmetries of race and class in the outside world), these are held at bay through the careful construction of the conference and especially the vigilance of the coordinator.

What should we say about these proposals? One obvious difficulty is that Braithwaite is comparing an idealized and carefully controlled version of his own process with the daily run-of-the-mill work of the criminal justice system. If his system were practiced widely, across a diverse country, how many coordinators would really perform the difficult task he assigns to them, and what would the average look like? As with all discretionary systems, we need to look at the rule, not the ideal. Run in a routinized or inattentive way, conferences would lack the procedural safeguards of the criminal justice system while lacking, as well, the impressive virtues of the Braithwaitean system.

I think that Braithwaite is right about the need to supplement formal justice with something intimate, insistently forward-looking, focused on awakening and not brutalizing conscience, and that interventions of his sort can have unexpected power because they communicate love, generosity, and respect, virtues hard to find in the juvenile justice system. Whenever we can feel confident that the coordinators have the requisite expertise and judgment, this is indeed a promising supplement to formal approaches, and certainly to be preferred to the intensely retributive attitudes that usually animate society's dealings with youthful offenders.

Indeed, we do not need to wait for a crime to occur in order to use some Braithwaitean techniques. The principal of a high school for troubled teens in Chicago who had been expelled from other public schools used a related type of conferencing, run by a team of psychiatric social workers, to get these kids, possibly bound for crime, to think about themselves in a different way. When I visited this program, the coordinators of the group therapy emphasized that the main thing they took themselves to be contributing was not any particular method or expertise, it was just listening to the kids and taking them seriously, which other adults in their world usually didn't (although they got the families involved whenever they could). I think wherever we can inject into the system this virtue of personal care and listening, this should certainly be attempted, and group therapy of the sort these social workers conducted at Morton Alternative can be tried out much more pervasively in the school and in the juvenile justice system.

However—and here is where I would separate my view from Braithwaite's larger theory as set out in his book—the right way to use these alternative techniques is as a delegation from the impartial justice system, a way it has found of pursuing some of its goals, especially with juveniles. There is absolutely no reason to accept an overall theory that the community is the locus of justice, or to hold, as Braithwaite seems to, that the primary agent of justice always ought to be the community first, and the legal system only second. It's like privatizing anything else: government may choose to do so if there is reason to believe the private system will work better than the usual public approach, but the alternative must remain transparent to public critique, accountable to voters, and subject to procedural constraints of basic justice. Such an approach would also reassure victims that their concerns were taken seriously: Braithwaite has difficulty responding to feminist critics who complain that informal conferences "privatize" domestic violence and sexual assault in a bad way, treating these victims as of lesser dignity under the law.[83]

It seems to me, too, that Braithwaite should be clearer about the emotions that he is attempting to inspire in the young offender. "Shame" is usually understood as an emotion that involves a feeling of pervasive inadequacy, keyed to an enduring trait, not a single act.[84] Thus, it is a misleading name for an emotion that involves, centrally, the separation of act from offender. I would say that "regret" and "agent-regret" (see chapter 4) are good terms for a negative emotion directed at the act, and both are compatible with, at the same time, emulation of good models and good paths in life. Emulation is very different from shame as typically conceived. Braithwaite seems to have begun with a rather humiliation-based picture of punishing: the chapter on Japan in his book shows him approving of a system that involves harsh interrogations and lots of confessing and lowering; it is only later that he shifts to the much more attractive picture that animates his empirical work. But the concepts are never sufficiently clarified. So I think that Braithwaite's proposal, while totally different from the proposals for shame-based penalties that I have already rejected, which involve humiliation as his does not, still leaves itself open to misunderstanding on this point.

Braithwaite's specific proposal is tailored to the needs of the juvenile justice system. But there are many ways in which a Transition mentality can generate a critique of backward-looking practices in the criminal law. In many ways, the current system is not forward-looking at all, but insists on tying offenders to their prior bad act. Three-strikes laws, sentencing based on "criminal history" and "career criminal" categorizations are just some of the practices that a rational society will study empirically in a forward-looking spirit, asking whether they promote social welfare. It seems likely that at least some of them will fail to pass the test: they are popular because of the payback mentality.

V. Mercy: Linking the Ex Post to the Ex Ante

Throughout my discussion of the *ex post* punishment perspective, I have emphasized the immense importance of *ex ante* thinking. If societies protected human welfare better, there would no doubt still be crime, but there would be less of it. Education, employment, nutrition, and housing do make a difference. Now, in concluding this discussion of punishment, I want to suggest that an attitude much praised by the Stoics makes a valuable contribution, linking our ongoing interest in sympathetic imagining to a normative account of the good judge (or juror).

According to the Greco-Roman conception, mercy (Greek *epieikeia*, Latin *clementia*) is an attribute of the good judge, in deciding how to respond to wrongful acts.[85] Seneca defines it as "an inclination of the mind toward leniency in exacting punishment." Mercy, then, is not the same thing as compassion (Lat. *misericordia*, Ital. *pietà*, Gk. *eleos* and *oiktos*). Mercy is a mental inclination but not necessarily an emotion; compassion is an emotional reaction to the plight of another person. Mercy recognizes that the person is at fault: it belongs, so to speak, at the penalty phase of a trial, after conviction. Compassion, by contrast, need have nothing at all to do with fault: indeed, as typically understood, it recognizes a large role for uncontrolled events in getting people into the bad situation that inspires the painful emotion: its content involves the thought that the person is either wholly or partly blameless.[86] And yet there is a link between the two attitudes: for mercy, as the Stoics define it, recognizes that the person's bad behavior is in part the outgrowth of substandard prior conditions, for which they are not to blame.

I am speaking only of the Greco-Roman conception of mercy, not of a very different conception that one also finds in the history of Western legal thought, which I shall call the "monarchical" conception.[87] The monarchical conception, which we find, for example, in Portia's famous speech about mercy in Shakespeare's *The Merchant of Venice*, holds that mercy is the free gift of a divine God or ruler, permanently situated above the erring mortal. It presupposes hierarchy, and it suggests that mercy's source is perfect or flawless. The monarch can bestow mercy not because of a recognition of common humanity, but because of a secure knowledge of permanent difference and superiority. Nor does monarchical mercy require any effort of sympathy or imagination: for all are alike low, base, and sinful, so imagining the heart of another will show us no particular reasons for mitigation and would thus be a waste of time. It is notorious that Portia makes absolutely no effort to imagine what a Jew in Venice might feel, what experiences of stigma and hatred might have led to his obdurate insistence on his bond.

The monarchical conception of mercy has a close relationship to the religious ideas of forgiveness we have scrutinized critically in chapter 3. Greco-Roman mercy, by contrast, is not monarchical, but egalitarian: it says that we are all in this together, we understand human life because we are in its midst and burdened by its difficulties, though some are more burdened than others. Nobody is secure, and the judge no more than the offender. This conception has its own long tradition. And it certainly plays a role in Shakespeare, whose *Measure for Measure* is far more Senecan than monarchical.

Senecan (or more generally Greco-Roman) mercy begins from a simple insight: there are many obstacles to acting well. Thus, when people do bad things, it is sometimes fully their own fault, but often we want to say that they have been tripped up by unusual circumstances and pressures. Circumstances, and not innate evil propensities, are at the origins of a lot of the crime we see. Thus, close inspection of circumstances often leads to a generous spirit of mitigation in assigning a sentence. Typically such considerations figure at the penalty phase of a trial, but they can inform criminal justice thinking more generally (as they do, for example, in Braithwaite's approach to juvenile justice).

In a sense, the merciful judge looks backward. But at the same time, while acknowledging the fact of wrongdoing, and thus expressing society's commitment to core values, the judge also looks forward to a world of reintegration. The general spirit is that of Transition-Anger: there is outrage at the wrong done, but a generous spirit takes the place of the merely punitive spirit. In addition to the usual concern about specific and general deterrence, and sometimes incapacitation, this judge also asks about how, in a world of human frailty, we may all be able to live together as well as possible. This concern may sometimes take the form of specific mercy to a specific defendant. But, given that this judge tries to understand the background conditions that are implicated in crime, his or her concern should also lead onward to a more general consideration of what may be done *ex ante* to prevent future cases. The *ex post* attitude leads to a rededication to the *ex ante* perspective. Sympathetic appreciation of the defendant's circumstances may not, and should not, lead to mitigation in every specific case. (Obviously much depends on the baseline from which a downward departure is contemplated, as well as on empirical facts about deterrence.) But it does something better: it reminds us that we share a common humanity, which can be damaged by conditions that are in our power to change. All too often, retributive harshness is nourished by demonizing the defendant, and telling stories, usually false, about how this person is utterly different from the "good" members of the community. And this mindset gets in the way of good social thinking.

Since, like Bentham, we are for a time confining our observations to the sphere of "criminal justice," we can imagine many ways for a Transition mentality to work in that sphere. Such a welfare-focused system will almost certainly avoid mandatory minimum sentencing and harsh punishment for victimless crimes. It will also, where possible, use Braithwaitean techniques, particularly when dealing with juvenile offenders. With adults, the merciful judge may imagine alternative avenues within the justice system that lead to sentences involving therapy (drug and alcohol treatment, domestic violence and anger management programs) rather than to incarceration and brutalization. And at the sentencing phase, courts can encourage the victim to narrate any unusual obstacles to good action that his or her life story affords, although, as I've said, this should not lead to mitigation in each and every case.[88] What, in general, society ought to express is this: the crime is outrageous, but we can see the offender, with sympathy, as someone who is more and better than the crime, capable of good in future, and we can adjust sentencing in the light of that thought. Meanwhile, we redouble our dedication to creating more propitious conditions for all.

I have emphasized the role that helplessness plays in retribution: retributive wishes are often a displacement from underlying powerlessness, giving the illusion that one can do something about one's bad situation. We might, then, speculate that people, and institutions, become more capable of mercy to the extent that they are more confident about their stability and power. Such a connection, in fact, was persuasively made by Nietzsche.[89] Nietzsche, like Seneca (by whom he is much influenced), argues that the revenge-based morality that he sees in Christianity is connected psychologically to a sense of weakness and impotence. He traces the way in which this sense of impotence leads to delight in fantasized projects of retribution, often by God in the afterlife. Retribution, he argues, is not likely to be a characteristic preoccupation of a strong person or community. Indeed, in a strong person or community, the interest in retribution will gradually overcome itself in the direction of mercy. He focuses, as do I, on the "criminal justice system":

> As its power increases, a community ceases to take the individual's transgressions so seriously, because they can no longer be considered as dangerous and destructive to the whole as they were formerly.... As the power and self-confidence of a community increase, the penal law always becomes more moderate; every weakening or imperiling of the former brings with it a restoration of the harsher forms of the latter. The "creditor" always becomes more humane to the extent that he has grown richer; finally, how much injury he can endure without suffering from it becomes the actual measure of his wealth. It is not unthinkable that a society might attain such a consciousness of power that it could allow itself the noblest luxury possible to it—letting those who harm it go unpunished.... The justice which began with "everything is dischargeable, everything must be discharged," ends by winking and letting those incapable of discharging their debt go free: it ends, as does every good thing on earth, by overcoming itself. This self-overcoming of justice: one knows the beautiful name it has given itself—mercy; it goes without saying that mercy remains the privilege of the most powerful man, or better—his beyond the law.[90]

The idea that the ability to forgo retribution is a mark of both personal and societal strength is a persistent leitmotif of the present book.

What is the relationship between Senecan mercy and forgiveness? If we confine ourselves to the central case of transactional forgiveness, mercy and forgiveness at first blush seem rather close. For don't both involve the suspension or waiving of angry feelings in the light of a person's remorse? Yes and no. Mercy insists on truth, so it never wipes away or "forgets" a wrongful act, as forgiveness does in some accounts. That is one very significant difference. But there are two others, of even greater importance. Mercy doesn't need to be preceded by anger at all: it can and often does express a pure form of Transition-Anger, simply acknowledging the wrongful act, but in a forward-looking and generous spirit. To put this point in a different way, forgiveness is all about how we deal with the past. Senecan mercy is from the beginning about the future: it looks ahead to reintegration. If anger is briefly on the scene, mercy turns quickly to the Transition. And, finally, the third difference, transactional forgiveness requires apology. Mercy just gets on with things, looking to the next day. The past is past, now see that you don't do this again—and also, let's see how our society can solve the problem better than it has. It lies close, then, to the sort of unconditional forgiveness or, better, unconditional love that some of our dissident religious texts embody and that our examples of revolutionary justice will embody. It refuses to play the "blame game" or to create a hierarchy of good (victim) and bad (offender). For that reason it does not put offenders in an abased or humiliated position. Instead, the idea is that we are all in this together, and we had better try to live together as well as we can.

As we'll see in chapter 7, this forward-looking spirit produces an approach to revolutionary justice that is very different from a forgiveness-based approach. The contrast between the two will be better understood when we reach that case.

My focus has been the institutions of the "criminal justice system," not the emotions of actors within it. By now, however, we see that many roles within the system have discretion built into them, and to that extent require people who can inhabit those emotional roles well. People cannot be good judges or jurors if they are robotic or unresponsive. However, it is also crucial that they do not let their emotions wash all over the place—that they inhabit the carefully demarcated emotional roles that a decent system constructs for them.[91] They need, then, both developed emotional capacities and considerable self-restraint. This latter virtue is especially important given the siren song of anger that is so alluring in many societies.

The Eumenides will not be satisfied, and they should not be. For they asked for "something that has no traffic with evil success," by which they meant success through payback. "Let there blow no wind that wrecks the trees" can be understood to mean, let us bring up citizens with good nutrition, good housing, good education, good health care, early and late.[92] "Let no barren deadly sickness creep and kill." No modern society has heeded these words (nor, of course, did that of ancient Athens, a slave society that allowed great inequalities to persist even between citizens, while waging brutal wars of conquest in the vicinity). We are stuck with the mechanisms of incarceration and "punishment" as we know them because we have failed at these other tasks. If we did our job well, these institutions would probably still exist, but they would have much less to do.

Recall Ebenezer Scrooge: Approached for a donation to give food to the hungry at Christmas, he asks with surprise whether the prisons, the treadmill, and the workhouses have ceased their useful operations. Modern societies, and perhaps the United States more than others, are like Scrooge—imagining that default institutions, on which no society should rely for justice, are a permanent fixture of the way things must be. The debate about the "justification of punishment" ought to be like a debate with Scrooge about the "justification of the workhouse"—a debate in which, in order to make a place for the workhouse, he would have to convince us that everything possible had been done to prevent hunger and misery first. "Punishment as opposed to what?" should always be our question, and the "what" should be not some tepid alternative such as therapy inside disgusting prisons, but a thorough transformation of the way we look at poverty and inequality, particularly in dealing with our youngest citizens. Nonetheless, we are very far from that goal, and for the time being, tepid proposals, some of which I have defended here, are the only ones that seem likely to win a hearing.

7

The Political Realm

Revolutionary Justice

> But when I say we should not resent, I do not say that we should acquiesce.
>
> —Mohandas Gandhi, regulations for the Satyagraha Ashram
> in Gujarat, 1915[1]

I. Noble Anger?

But isn't anger noble, when society is corrupt and brutal? When people are kept down, they all too often learn to acquiesce in their "fate." They form "adaptive preferences," defining their lot as acceptable and acquiescence as fitting. But if they acquiesce, change is unlikely. Awakening people to the injustice of society's treatment of them is a necessary first step toward social progress. And don't we expect that awakening to produce justified anger? If people believe they are being wrongfully abused and don't get angry, isn't there something wrong in their thinking somewhere? Don't they, for example, seem to have too low an opinion of their dignity and rights?

Anger seems to have three valuable roles. First, it is seen as a valuable signal that the oppressed recognize the wrong done to them. It also seems to be a necessary motivation for them to protest and struggle against injustice and to communicate to the wider world the nature of their grievances. Finally, anger seems, quite simply, to be justified: outrage at terrible wrongs is right, and anger thus expresses something true.

When the basic legal structure of society is sound, people can turn to the law for redress; the Eumenides recommend this course. But sometimes the legal structure is itself unjust and corrupt. What people need to do is not just to secure justice for this or that particular wrong, but, ultimately, to change the legal order. That task is different from the task of preserving daily justice, albeit continuous with it. It appears to require anger, even if daily justice does not.

On the other hand, if we examine successful struggles for revolutionary justice over the past hundred years, we see immediately that three of the most prominent—and stably successful—were conducted with a profound commitment to non-anger, though definitely not in a spirit of acquiescence. Gandhi's noncooperation campaign against the British raj, the U.S. civil rights movement, and South Africa's struggle to overcome the apartheid system were all highly successful, and all repudiated anger as a matter of both theory and practice. To the extent that any of them admitted anger as acceptable, it was either our borderline species of "Transition-Anger," a sense of outrage without any wish for ill to befall the offender, or else a brief episode of real anger, but leading quickly to the Transition. Mohandas Gandhi, utterly repudiating anger, and apparently successful in not feeling it, showed the world that non-anger was a posture not of weakness and servility but of strength and dignity. He expressed outrage, but always in a forward-looking and non-angry spirit. Martin Luther King, Jr., followed Gandhi, espousing both non-anger (or at least a quick Transition to non-anger) and nonviolence. It appears that King, less saintly than Gandhi, both experienced anger (or at least expressed it in speeches) and encouraged it to a degree in his audience— but always with a quick move to the Transition, and with a strict emphasis on nonviolence—although he granted that violence in self-defense could be morally justified. Nelson Mandela urged the African National Congress to drop nonviolent tactics when they were not working and to use violence in a limited strategic way; but he never ceased to look at any situation he was in, even the worst, in a generous forward-looking spirit. Though a man evidently prone to anger, he was also impressively capable of moving rapidly beyond it, through an unusual freedom from status-anxiety and an equally remarkable generosity. Studying this record will help us to see why the idea of "noble anger" as signal, motivator, and justified expression is a false guide in revolutionary situations, and why a generous, even overgenerous, frame of mind is both more appropriate and more effective.

A subtheme in this chapter will be the role of forgiveness in such situations. As before, I shall argue that forgiveness of the conditional, transactional sort is not the only alternative to anger; an unconditional generosity is both more useful and, at least in many cases, morally more defensible because less tainted by the payback mentality.

Finally, we must focus a lot of our attention on the issue of trust, as a necessary part of the stability, hence the legitimacy, of any society. In situations of profound oppression and systematic injustice, trust is non-existent. It is very easy for the oppressed to believe that trust is impossible, and that they can win their struggle only by dominating in their turn, or perhaps by establishing a grudging *modus vivendi* in which each side defends itself from incursions by the other. Such an uneasy and trustless compromise is not likely to be stable. The three revolutionary movements this chapter studies all understood, therefore, that the creation of political trust is a very important part of their job. I shall argue that, whatever the appeal of revolutionary anger may be for many revolutionaries, strategies based upon non-anger and generosity prove their worth in this essential area, making it possible for formerly hostile groups to have confidence, going forward, in political institutions and principles.

I begin with a case (in historical fiction) where individuals have no secure path forward. Injustice is ubiquitous, political mobilization is only nascent, and institutions are deeply corrupt. Here, just where we might have thought that anger shows a way forward, a future-directed non-angry perspective commends itself as far more productive—and as amply expressive of the equal human dignity of the oppressed. Next I analyze the theory of non-anger behind the movements of Gandhi and King.[2] I find in their work an appealing picture of revolutionary non-anger, and some good rebuttals of objections to non-anger, but nonetheless there are some crucial gaps in their argument against anger. To fill those gaps I turn to the career of Nelson Mandela.[3] Though informed by theory, Mandela did not produce deeply theorized writings. His whole approach, however—as recorded by others and in two volumes of autobiography—gives a compelling account of the reasons supporting the choice of non-anger in the struggle for justice. In the light of the critique of anger, I then turn to the role that forgiveness might play in revolutionary movements, and conclude with some remarks about truth and reconciliation commissions.

II. A Transition Story: Paton's Cry, the Beloved Country

Alan Paton's 1948 novel *Cry, the Beloved Country* is the outcry of a passionate and immersed protester.[4] Paton was a liberal juvenile justice reformer who later formed an illegal racially integrated political party. A primary purpose of his novel, written and published abroad, was to make the world aware of race relations in South Africa and their devastating toll on the nation.

On its face, the novel is an intimate personal tragedy. Two fathers lose their sons. One, James Jarvis, is rich and white. The other, Stephen Kumalo, is poor and black. One is the father of a murder victim, the other the father of his killer. Absalom Kumalo, who killed Jarvis's son Arthur during a burglary, is technically guilty under the felony murder rule, but, firing wildly in panic without intent to harm, he is far less morally guilty than the two older and more hardened companions whose pliant henchman he was.[5] (They are acquitted through clever legal maneuvers, even though one of them intentionally assaulted Jarvis's servant Mpiring with a clear intent to cause grievous bodily harm.) The reader feels that Absalom is never taken seriously as a person, in a thoroughly racist system of criminal justice; and his plea for mercy, which clearly has merit, falls on deaf ears.

Awaiting his only son's execution, father and Anglican priest Stephen Kumalo has, in consequence, valid grounds for anger against white society. On his side, James Jarvis has reasons for extreme anger against the killers, and perhaps, too, against a family who let their son move to Johannesburg with no supervision and without sufficiently preparing him for the lure of crime and bad companions. " 'I hope to God they get them. And string 'em all up,' " says Jarvis's friend Harrison (182).

On the other hand, why has Absalom Kumalo left his home? The novel from the beginning draws attention to the lack of livelihood in Ndotsheni, as erosion dries up the river valley and causes everything to wither. Jarvis and other rich whites who live in the area are aware of the problem and its causes, and yet have done nothing to address it. Why did Absalom fall into crime? Much blame no doubt attaches to a racist society that has not educated him or provided him with employment opportunities. That is what Arthur Jarvis was writing, in an unfinished manuscript found in his study by his grieving father. Absalom does encounter some good treatment: a reformist corrections officer modeled on Paton himself, who in real life created a pioneering juvenile corrections facility that was all too successful for white prejudices and was therefore quickly dismantled by the government. But Absalom also encounters incentives to crime in the form of his hardened criminal cousin, and his sheer fear of the city and his reasonable mistrust of law make him a submissive accomplice. He would not have had a gun at all but for the fact that he is afraid of the city, and decides that he needs to learn to defend himself.

Early in the novel, then, we see that payback, in the form of "string 'em all up," will do no good at all. South Africa is a society in the grip of terrible fears and hatreds, which feed off one another. Fear of the black majority drives white society to escalating strategies of punitiveness and enforced separateness. (As the novel was being published, the Nationalists, architects of apartheid, were just winning their first electoral victory.) The law is an expression of that fear, and its retributive zeal simply expresses the desire of the surrounding society to keep fear at bay through increasingly harsh treatment. On the side of the black majority, there is also tremendous fear: fear of the dangers of the city, fear of the hatred and punitiveness of whites, fear of a closed future, fear of the law itself. Although whites say they favor deterrence, they do not take reasonable strategies toward that goal, which would involve education, rural development, and job opportunities. Instead, their strategy is simply to pile on the punishment, exacting retribution for the fear and discomfort they feel, as if the very existence of the black majority were a wrongful act directed at them. Black crime, meanwhile, is a desperate, fear-inspired survival strategy, not an expression of hate, but the desire for payback is brewing. The most likely future would appear to be one of retributive violence on both sides and bloody civil war.

The fathers, like their communities, are apparently launched on a collision course of obduracy, fear, and hate that would (the novel shows) not only prove counterproductive but would utterly fail to address the real social problems that need to be resolved if a nation is to prosper. The failure to think productively is above all a failure of the white minority. "We do not know, we do not know. We shall live from day to day, and put more locks on the doors, and get a fine fierce dog when the fine fierce bitch next door has pups, and hold on to our handbags more tenaciously.... And our lives will shrink.... And the conscience shall be thrust down: the light of life shall not be extinguished, but be put under a bushel, to be preserved for a generation that will live by it again, in some day not yet come" (111).

Written in the mode of prophetic poetry, Paton's novel is above all a parable of a nation. It calls calling South Africa to a painful reckoning and, eventually, gestures toward a distant future of hope. The intimate story of the two fathers unfolds against a background of social voices that speak, but refuse to listen, that opine, but refuse to think. To them, Paton addresses the urgent call for acknowledgment and genuine thought from which his title derives:

> Cry, the beloved country, for the unborn child that is the inheritor of our fear. Let him not love the earth too deeply. Let him not laugh too gladly when the water runs through his fingers, nor stand too silent when the setting sun makes red the veld with fire. Let him not be too moved when the birds of his land are singing, nor give too much of his heart to a mountain or a valley. For fear will rob him of all if he gives too much. (111)

This agonized voice speaks from afar, yet with intense love for the near. Its message is that the fear and hate of the white minority are killing a beautiful country—and it really does not matter whether the unborn child is imagined as black or white, for all are alike going down a path of doom.

The story of Stephen Kumalo and James Jarvis, both searingly particular and allegorically political, is the novel's prophecy of hope. Defenders of anger would say that both fathers ought to be angry, for both have been grievously wronged. Doesn't their self-respect require not being meek and gentle with the adversary?

We learn early on, however, that neither man is prone to anger or to fruitless thoughts of payback. Stephen Kumalo has interpreted the job of a Christian priest to require forgoing anger—so that when he finds himself yielding to anger against his brother John, who saves his own son through a tricky legal defense but abandons Absalom, he criticizes himself relentlessly. As for Jarvis, as he reads his son's manuscripts he finds himself wishing that Arthur had not gone downstairs to investigate the noise (of the break-in). "But these thoughts were unprofitable; it was not his habit to dwell on what might have been but what could never be" (186). Both, then, are ripe for the Transition, and it is a Transition story that Paton wants to set before us as his prophecy of hope—scattering clues on the way: the generosity of a white motorist, who defies the police to help blacks during a bus boycott (81–82), the productive experiment of that white corrections officer, the generous philosophy of the urban black minister Msimangu, "Msimangu who had no hate for any man" (311), whose simple, "It would be my joy to help you," lifts Kumalo's depression (116).

The Transition begins in solitary meditation, as Jarvis sits for hours alone in his son's study, reading his son's manuscript entitled "Private Essay on the Evolution of a South African," and reading, too, the speeches of Abraham Lincoln that were Arthur's inspiration. The Second Inaugural, in particular, rivets him. Paton does not quote the speech; he relies on readers to know that it contains a recipe for binding the wounds of a nation "with malice toward none, with charity for all." (The novel was written in the United States.) Shortly thereafter, by sheer chance, Jarvis meets Stephen Kumalo: staying at the home of his daughter-in-law, he opens the door when Kumalo comes to inquire about a neighbor's daughter who has been a servant there. Gradually, Jarvis, puzzled by Kumalo's consternation and grief, becomes aware of Kumalo's identity. "I understand what I did not understand," he says. "There is no anger in me" (214). From that moment on, the fathers are joined in an uneasy but profound relationship; neither offers any apology, neither asks for or grants forgiveness. (Indeed the Anglican bishop who urges Stephen Kumalo to undergo penance and seek forgiveness by leaving his community is shown to be obtuse and unhelpful.) They simply understand one another and share one another's grief. And on the day when Stephen Kumalo climbs the mountain to be alone as his son is executed far away, Jarvis, passing him on the path, understands that, too.

A primary agent in the Transition is a small child—and this, too, is Paton's allegorical intention, indicating that a mental disposition free from rancor must guide policy. Jarvis's grandson, whose "brightness" reminds everyone of his dead father, visits Stephen Kumalo while out riding. He asks to be taught words of Xhosa—but when he asks for a glass of milk, he learns that there is no milk in Ndotsheni, because of the failed harvest and the dire effect on cattle, and that many children are dying because they do not have milk (270). Not long after this, milk, "in shining cans," arrives at Kumalo's door—with a message that it is for the children of the town. Jarvis's emissary, delighted by his mission, drives away in high good spirits. And Stephen Kumalo "laughed . . . that a grown man should play in such fashion, and he laughed again that Kuluse's child might live, and he laughed again at the thought of the stern silent man at High Place. He turned into the house sore with laughing, and his wife watched him with wondering eyes." Both fathers have started looking to the future rather than the past.

The new future flows from that beginning: Jarvis hires a young, scientifically trained black engineer to come to Ndotsheni and make a plan for the rescue of its agriculture. With the cooperation of Stephen Kumalo and the tribal chief, they persuade the people to adopt new methods of farming. The black engineer is already the product of a new type of interracial cooperation: for he credits his "love for truth" to a white professor, who also taught him that "we do not work for men, that we work for the land and its people" (303). A nascent freedom fighter, he brings the singing of "Nkosi Sikelel' iAfrica" to the village. But he listens, too, to Stephen Kumalo: "[H]ate no man, and desire power over no man. . . . For there is enough hating in our land already" (303). Instead of hatred, Ndotsheni gets hard work, rational planning, and hope.

As the two fathers turn aside from anger to imagine, with generosity, a future of interracial cooperation and constructive work, they create, outside the corrupt legal order, a vision or allegory of a new legal and political order, one committed to justice, but generous and forward-looking in spirit, and grounded in historical, scientific, and economic truth. As the novel ends, hope is real, but its time has not yet come:

> The great valley of the Umzimkulu is still in darkness, but the light will come there. Ndotsheni is still in darkness, but the light will come there also. For it is the dawn that has come, as it has come for a thousand centuries, never failing. But when that dawn will come, of our emancipation, from the fear of bondage and the bondage of fear, why that is a secret. (312)

III. Revolutionary Non-Anger: Theory and Practice

The revolutionary non-anger of Mohandas Gandhi and Martin Luther King, Jr., is proposed not as a distant hope but as an immediate task, to be embraced here and now in the confrontation with injustice. It involves, ultimately, a set of psychological and behavioral practices that need to be both accepted and deeply internalized by the movement's members. But because it is not personal psychotherapy, but, instead, a form of mass cultivation, it needs to be accompanied by an explicit theory, so that everyone in the movement can be aware of their aim and teach both attitudes and practices to new recruits. This is our good fortune: both Gandhi and King have left us a copious body of theory describing, and justifying, the emotional and behavioral aspects of non-anger. And Mandela has left us a remarkable set of more informal observations from which a compelling argument for non-anger may be extracted. I shall argue that Gandhi and King leave a gap in the argument, which they fill with resonant religious imagery that inspired many followers, but that does not answer all our philosophical questions. Mandela fills that gap.[6]

First we must ask: non-anger, or nonviolence? The two are often held together, and many people who revere Gandhi and King believe that nonviolence is the primary concept, non-anger a supererogatory ideal. They feel that people can be held accountable for actions, but surely not for their emotional states, and it is too much to demand of people that they modify their inner states. Gandhi and King do not agree: they hold that a revolutionary movement will only be able to achieve a reliable commitment to nonviolence through a mental revolution in which people look at their goals and at their oppressors with new eyes, in a spirit of love and generosity. They believe that this revolution is possible through training and solidarity—although King makes important concessions to human frailty. And they also hold that in the end, in the creation of a new political world, non-anger is the main thing, since we must be able to work together in that generous and non-resentful spirit long after the occasion for violence has passed. Nonviolence could be merely negative: we refrain from something. It is only through the inner transformation involved in replacing resentment by love and generosity that nonviolence can ever become creative. I agree with this emphasis, and with the idea that this way of relating to others can be taught and learned, and that creating a public emotional climate is not unrealistic idealism. I shall also, however, agree with King that we must build in some concessions to the angry tendency in people—so long as it is stably channeled toward the Transition.

But I have also insisted that non-anger does not entail nonviolence. Gandhi did not agree. It seems likely that he embraced a metaphysical view of the person according to which a correct inner disposition entailed nonviolent behavior, and in which violence required an incorrect inner disposition.[7] (His speculations on meat-eating and violence in the *Autobiography* are just one sign of this idea.) As Richard Sorabji shows, Gandhi did make a few exceptions, primarily in connection with killing dangerous animals: but the constraint was always that physical violence is admissible only when it is for the good of the recipient. This constraint is almost never satisfied in human relations.[8] We should not reject Gandhi's views simply because they have their roots in metaphysical views about the body that are not widely shared and that seem superstitious to many of us. But we must ask whether Gandhi is persuasive when he holds that a person of a generous and loving spirit will never endorse or participate in violence.

He is not persuasive. Gandhi's views about war are not sensible. His idea that the best way, and a fully adequate way, to approach Hitler was through nonviolence and love was simply absurd, and would have been profoundly damaging had anyone taken it seriously. He made two grave errors. First, he equated a violent response to Hitler with "Hitlerism," saying that "Hitlerism will never be defeated by counter-Hitlerism" (G 337). This is simply unconvincing: self-defense is not morally equivalent to aggression, nor is the defense of decent political institutions equivalent to their subversion. Second, he also held that Hitler would respond to a nonviolent and loving overture: "Human nature in its essence is one and therefore unfailingly responds to the advances of love" (G 340).[9] Responding to an imagined objector who says that all nonviolence would accomplish is to offer Hitler an easy victory, Gandhi interestingly backs off from this preposterous empirical prediction, and simply concludes that in any case Europe, behaving nonviolently, would be morally superior, "And in the end I expect it is the moral worth that will count. All else is dross" (G 338). It is fortunate indeed that Nehru, who had observed German fascism in action while accompanying his wife to a sanatorium in Switzerland, had no interest in Gandhi's proposal, and neither, of course, did the British, who were still there. Gandhi's even uglier proposal not to resist the Japanese if they invaded India requires no comment.

So Gandhi did not show that non-anger entails nonviolence. Mandela, as we shall see, has the right idea, thinking of nonviolence and negotiation as preferred strategies, but strategies to be abandoned if over a long period of time they don't work. King, a more faithful Gandhian, is often understood to have had an unequivocal commitment to nonviolence. But in fact, King is with Mandela more than with Gandhi. He often acknowledges that there is a morally legitimate role for violence—self-defense being the general rubric he uses (K 32, 57). He does not oppose all wars, nor even all personal defensive violence. He does, however, argue that in the particular situation of the freedom movement, leaving a loophole for the appeal to self-defense would be too dangerous, giving lots of opportunities for self-serving blurring of boundaries and, ultimately, strengthening resentment's hand. If people can easily appeal to self-defense in justification of vengeful acts, they will be less likely to make the inner transformation he requires of them. Nor would such a movement, unpredictable and prone to outbursts, attain the coherence and stability King saw as necessary to win the respect of the majority and achieve the movement's social goals.

In what follows I shall draw heavily on Gandhi's eloquent writings but shall pursue the Mandela line (at times that of King as well), treating nonviolence as instrumental and strategic, non-anger (and its positive correlate, loving generosity) as the main thing, and as having both strategic and intrinsic political significance.

Philosophers and non-philosophers alike have seen anger as appropriate in situations of oppression, and as linked to the vindication of self-respect. It is, then, not surprising that non-anger should have struck many onlookers as strange, unmanly, even revolting. Webb Miller, the UPI correspondent who reported the nonviolent protest action at the Dharasana Salt Works in 1930 (under the leadership of the poet Sarojini Naidu, since Gandhi was in jail), observed scores of marchers getting beaten down by the police, and reacted with perplexity, as he records in a later memoir:

> Not one of the marchers even raised an arm to fend off the blows. They went down like tenpins. From where I stood I heard the sickening whacks of the clubs on unprotected skulls.... At times the spectacle of unresisting men being methodically bashed into a bloody pulp sickened me so much that I had to turn away. The western mind finds it difficult to grasp the idea of nonresistance. I felt an indefinable sense of helpless rage and loathing, almost as much against the men who were submitting unresistingly to being beaten as against the police wielding the clubs, and this despite the fact that when I came to India I sympathized with the Gandhi cause. (G 250–51)

The marchers were not simply acquiescing. They continue to march, and they chanted the slogan "Long live the revolution." And yet, as Miller says: there is something in the mind, and not only the Western mind, that resists accepting this way of reacting to brutal behavior. (Interestingly, the police treated Ms. Naidu with the utmost respect, and when she asked them not to lay a hand on her they did not even touch her. Would the men's commitment to nonviolence have held up had they assaulted her as well?) What do Gandhi and King have to say to people who think anger the right response to oppressive behavior, and the only response consistent with self-respect?

First, they point out that the stance they recommend is anything but passive. Gandhi soon rejected "passive resistance" as a misleading English rendering of his ideas. As Dennis Dalton documents in his important philosophical study, starting already in 1907 Gandhi repudiated the term "passive resistance," insisting that "passive resistance" could be weak and inactive, whereas his idea was one of active protest; he eventually chose *satyagraha*, "truth force," as a superior term.[10] Both he and King continually insist that what they recommend is a posture of thought and conduct that is highly active, even "dynamically aggressive" (K 7), in that it involves resistance to unjust conditions and protest against them. "But when I say we should not resent, I do not say that we should acquiesce," says Gandhi (G 138). For King, similarly: "I have not said to my people 'Get rid of your discontent.' Rather, I have tried to say that this normal and healthy discontent can be channeled into the creative outlet of non-violent direct action" (K 291). Both men hold, as I do, that anger is inherently wedded to a payback mentality: Gandhi says that resenting means wishing some harm to the opponent (even if only through divine agency) (G 138); King speaks of a "strike-back" mentality (K 32). That is what they want to get rid of, and we shall soon see with what they replace it.

Moreover, the new attitude is not just internally active, it issues in concrete actions with one's body, actions that require considerable courage (K 7). King calls this "direct action": action in which, after "self-purification" (i.e., rejection of anger), one's own body is used to make the case (K 290–91). This action is a forceful and uncompromising demand for freedom (292). The protester acts by marching, by breaking an unjust law in a deliberate demand for justice, by refusing to cooperate with unjust authority. The goal? In King's case, to force negotiation and move toward legal and social change (291, 294). For Gandhi it is no less than to overthrow a wrongful government and to "compel its submission to the people's will" (G 193, 195). The idea of acquiescence in brutality is presumably what revolted Webb Miller, but he misunderstood: there is no acquiescence, but a courageous struggle for a radical end.[11] (The Attenborough movie, in which the Webb Miller role is played by Martin Sheen, depicts Miller as understanding exactly what he is seeing, and reporting to the world that the dignity of Indians carried the day over the hapless brutality of the British. Certainly, whatever the real Miller felt, his dispatches did show people what was really happening.)

What is the new attitude with which they propose to replace anger? King, interestingly, allows some scope for real anger, holding that demonstrations and marches are a way of channeling repressed emotions that might otherwise lead to violence (297).[12] He even appears to grant that anger may play a valuable part in motivating some people to get involved. Nonetheless, even when there is real anger, it must soon lead to a focus on the future, with hope and with faith in the possibility of justice (K 52). Meanwhile, anger toward opponents is to be "purified" through a set of disciplined practices, and ultimately transformed into a mental attitude that carefully separates the deed from the doer, criticizing and repudiating the bad deed, but not imputing unalterable evil to people (K 61, GAut 242). (Notice the striking resemblance to Braithwaite's conferences with juvenile offenders.) Deeds may be denounced: people always deserve respect and sympathy. After all, the ultimate goal is "to create a world where men and women can live together" (K 61), and that goal needs the participation of all.

Above all, then, one should not wish to humiliate opponents in any way, or wish them ill (K 7, G 315), but instead should seek to win their friendship and cooperation (K 7). Gandhi remarks that early in his career he already felt the inappropriateness of the second stanza in "God Save the Queen," which asks God to "Scatter her enemies / And make them fall, / Confound their politics, / Frustrate their knavish tricks" (G 152). How can we assume that these opponents are "knavish"? he asks. Surely the believer in non-anger should not encourage such attitudes. The opponent is a person who has made a mistake, but we hope he can be won over by friendship and generosity.[13] This attitude can be called love, so long as we understand that Gandhi and King refer to an attitude that is not soft and sentimental, but tough and uncompromising in its demand for justice. It is an attitude of respect and active concern, one that seeks a common good in which all are included.[14]

An important insight of Gandhi (present in Paton's novel) is that anger is frequently rooted in fear. In Nehru's shrewd diagnosis, Gandhi's greatest gift to his followers was a new freedom from the "all-pervading fear" that British rule had inspired in Indians. That "black pall of fear was lifted from the people's shoulders"—how? Nehru suggests that this massive "psychological change" (which he compares to a successful psychoanalysis) had its source in Gandhi's ability to show an exit route from the reign of terror, and to inspire people, simultaneously, with a sense of their own worth and the worth of their actions. This made possible a form of protest that was calm, dignified, and strategic, rather than furtive, desperate, and prone to retributive violence.[15]

The ultimate goal of the protester must be a beautiful future in which all have a share: "the creation of the beloved community" (K 7). King's famous "Dream" speech, which I have discussed as an example of the Transition, is also a sentiment map that turns the critical and once-angry protester toward a future of enormous beauty, and one that is shown as possible and shortly available, by being rooted in concrete features of the real American landscape, all of which are now seen as sites of freedom.[16] Belief in the possibility of such a future plays no small part in the Transition. King was really outstanding here, and Gandhi somewhat less so: because of his asceticism he kept portraying the future as one of impoverished rural simplicity, which was not very inspiring to most people, and was quite unrealistic in thinking about how to build a successful nation. King's prophetic description of the future, furthermore, repositions opponents as potential partners in building the beautiful future: so then the question naturally becomes, how can we secure their cooperation? How can we get them on our side, joining with us? King doesn't just tell people they ought to try to cooperate, he encourages a cooperative frame of mind by depicting a compelling goal that needs the cooperation of all. Gandhi's strategy is a little different, in that he wants the British simply to leave India, not to help build it. They had tried to "build" long enough, and not well. But he encourages the thought that a free nation can be constructed, not through hatred and bloodshed, but by negotiation. The British don't have to be seen as fellow citizens, but they do have to be seen as reasonable people who will ultimately do the right thing and depart, remaining peaceful Commonwealth partners.

I have linked some anger to excessive preoccupation with status. One very significant aspect of Gandhi's movement was its renunciation of artificial distinctions of status through a detailed and comprehensive sympathy. The powerful must live the simple lifestyle of the powerless, thus beginning to forge a nation in which all can see their fate in the lives of all. Lawyers washed pots, upper-caste people cleaned latrines, breaking down lines of both caste and gender. As so often in our inquiries, non-anger is in this way linked to practices that support empathetic participation in the lives of others. This was also a prominent feature of King's movement, in which blacks and whites associated together in defiance of law, and in which white supporters were constantly urged to imagine the indignities and hardships of a black person's life.

In trying to respond to likely criticisms of the Gandhi/King idea, we must confront the objection that it imposes on people an inhuman set of demands. We have begun to reply by showing that, and how, they made it possible for people to accept and internalize non-angry practices. But this worry is certainly heightened by Gandhi's views about emotional and sexual detachment. Gandhi was close to being a thoroughgoing Stoic. He repeatedly asserted that one cannot pursue *satyagraha* or non-angry resistance adequately without conducting a struggle against all the passions, prominently including erotic desire and emotion. Nor did he cultivate the type of personal love and friendship that would naturally give rise to deep grief and fear. If he is correct in insisting that Stoic detachment is necessary for non-anger, that would give us reason to think it an unworkable and also an unattractive goal.

First of all, we must ask whether Gandhi was making an instrumental claim (emotional and passional detachment is instrumentally necessary for successful *satyagraha*) or offering a stipulative definition (*satyagraha* consists in nonviolent and non-angry resistance carried out with a commitment to emotional and passional detachment). The answer is unclear. For himself, Gandhi most likely meant the latter, given the evidence of his systematic self-discipline. For his movement, however, he does not appear to endorse even the limited instrumental claims, since he made no attempt to convince Nehru and other key leaders to renounce particular love and other forms of strong passion.[17] Perhaps his idea was simply that the *leader* of a successful nonviolent resistance movement must (whether instrumentally or conceptually) pursue Stoic detachment. Even this, however, might worry a modern reader: if the path of non-anger demands an implausible and in some ways unappealing detachment of its leaders, how attractive can it be, as a path to justice?

We can begin by looking at history, where the examples of King and Mandela (indeed also Nehru) seem to refute Gandhi's theory. All three had lives of passionate devotion to individuals, and none renounced sexuality. Certainly King's love affairs compromised the success of his movement by putting him into the power of J. Edgar Hoover. But that just shows that leaders had better obey social norms, or conceal their actions well if they don't.

The case of Mandela tells us something further and different, which he repeatedly discusses: that the leader of a movement may encounter great obstacles to the successful pursuit of love and family life. The long hours away from home in the early days and the long years of imprisonment later on made successful marriage impossible and successful fatherhood problematic. But the evidence (his prison letters to Winnie, for example) suggests that love was still an energizing force in his political life, nor does anything in his writings indicate that he would have been a better leader had he pursued detachment rather than love and family care. One can say much the same of Nehru.

Moreover, if people sometimes like to be inspired by a leader like Gandhi, who seems to be apart from the common human lot, they also, and probably more often where politics is concerned, respond to a leader who is demonstrably human in need and vulnerability, albeit more self-controlled than many other leaders. Nehru, like Mandela, took great care in his *Autobiography* to emphasize his own vulnerable human side, including his passionate love of his wife and his grief at her death.[18] George Orwell speaks for many people when he concludes that "Saints should always be judged guilty until they are proved innocent"—a judgment that he applies to Gandhi with complicated results.[19]

Psychologist Erik Erikson goes one step further, in his insightful book on Gandhi: he treats Gandhi's attitude to human love in general, sexuality in particular, as one of self-anger, indeed of violence. Addressing the dead leader directly, he says, "You should stop terrorizing yourself, and approach your own body with nonviolence."[20] He then contrasts psychoanalysis, a nonviolent art of self-change through truth, with Gandhi's punitive attitudes. There is much in Gandhi's biography to recommend Erikson's view that self-anger is continually expressed in his attitude to his own body. The genesis of his idea that all sexual desire is destructive was, by his own account, a very specific experience. As a young married teenager, he was making love with his wife at the very moment when his father died. His father had long been ill, and he felt it was his duty to sit with him. Nonetheless, he allowed himself to be distracted by the lure of desire, and went to his wife even though his father's state appeared dire. As a result he was not there at the moment of death. "It is a blot I have never been able to efface or forget. . . . It took me long to get free from the shackles of lust, and I had to pass through many ordeals before I could overcome it" (GAut 27). Erikson's idea that self-anger is exacting a payback is extremely cogent, and of course even Gandhi's retrospective narrative portrays his behavior in the most pejorative light. If we accept Erikson's claim, we have a further reason not to hold that non-anger entails Gandhian renunciation: renunciation in this case, and perhaps in others, is itself an expression of anger. George Orwell agrees, saying of Gandhi: "If one could follow it to its psychological roots, one would, I believe, find that the main motive for 'non-attachment' is a desire to escape from the pain of living, and above all from love, which, sexual or non-sexual, is hard work."[21]

So, non-anger not only does not demand an inhuman sort of renunciation, it is incompatible with (at least this form of) it. In that important respect, King, Nehru, and Mandela were more successful practitioners of non-anger than Gandhi, though all of them found it difficult to be adequate partners and parents, given the all-consuming demands of a political vocation.[22] One may grieve and love intensely while avoiding anger's specific errors.

We now have a picture of non-angry revolutionary action, and we have some persuasive answers to some of the most powerful objections that have been raised against it. We also have an appealing picture of the non-angry revolutionary: dignified, courageous, and proud, but not emotionless or inhumanly detached. But perhaps we do not yet have enough to answer the normative question with which we began. If we have shown that non-anger is acceptable, we have not conclusively shown that it is preferable when oppression is bad. What is really wrong with anger, even if another attractive way of conducting a revolution can be found?

In response to this imagined challenge, Gandhi and King repeatedly turn to religious metaphysics, giving us accounts of divine love.[23] Such metaphysical accounts were and are deeply appealing to those who hold one of the religious views in question, but they seem insufficient to answer our philosophical questions, and insufficient, too, to persuade citizens in a pluralistic society. In Mandela we get something more.

IV. Mandela's Strange Generosity

In Mandela's writings we find not a systematic theory of non-anger, but a self-aware human being of remarkable insight. I shall construct his responses into a quasi-theory, and I shall note the likely influence of Stoic theories on his personal development. But it is important to observe that in so doing I add nothing: I just point to the structures already latent in his thought and conduct.

I have argued that anger leads down two paths, each of which has an unattractive error built into it. Either anger's wish for ill to befall the wrongdoer is pointless, since payback does no good for the important elements of human flourishing that have been damaged, or it remains focused on relative status, in which case it may possibly succeed in its aim (relative abasement), but the aim itself is singularly unworthy. I shall now argue that Mandela instinctively comes to the same conclusion, in a way shaped by his long period of self-examination, which included daily introspective meditation (LW 200–212), during twenty-seven years in prison, a time that he says was extremely productive in meditating about anger.

What did Mandela realize, in those long hours of what he calls "conversations with myself," alluding to the *Meditations* of Marcus Aurelius, a text that was almost certainly brought to Robben Island by Ahmed Kathrada, and read by other prisoners?[24] First, he recognizes that obsession with status is unworthy, and thus refuses to go down that road. (Perhaps his royal origins helped him, relieving anxiety.) He never fussed about whether a particular role or activity would be "beneath" him. Through introspection, he pruned from his responses any hint of status-anxiety, even when it would have been defensible and natural. Thus, when a new prisoner on Robben Island was asked to clean the toilet bucket for another prisoner who had had to leave for Cape Town at 5:00 a.m., before buckets could be emptied, the new man objected, saying that he would never empty the bucket of another man. Mandela intervened. "So then I cleaned it for him because it meant nothing for me; I cleaned my bucket every day and I had no problem, you see, in cleaning the bucket of another" (C 149; the transcript reports that Mandela chuckled telling this story). Later on, he showed none of the reluctance about the Afrikaans language that bitter and angry black revolutionaries often evinced. So far was he from thinking it beneath him to speak Afrikaans that he took a course in the language while in prison and took advantage of every opportunity to converse in Afrikaans, for example with the warders (Inv 28)—having no sense that this was giving them a status victory, and thinking only of future utility and present respect. He repeatedly told his fellow prisoners that it was important to learn Afrikaans and Afrikaner history, in order to understand how their opponents think: for the time for negotiation would come sooner or later.[25] Writing to Winnie from prison in 1975, he says that most people focus wrongly on status: instead, they should focus on their own inner development (C vii).

Mandela knew, however, that most people did worry a lot about status. Leadership, for him, meant patiently training your capacities as an athlete trains, and one capacity he constantly trained was the ability to understand how other people think (Inv 138). He therefore understood that to disarm resistance you needed to disarm anxiety first, and that this would never be accomplished by expressions of anger or bitterness, but only by courtesy and respect for the other's dignity. The key to good relations with warders—often burdened by class anxiety—was "respect, ordinary respect" (Inv 28). When his lawyer arrived on Robben Island during Mandela's first year there, Mandela made a point of introducing the attorney to the warders, saying, "George, I'm sorry, I have not introduced you to my guard of honor." He then introduced each warder by name. The attorney remembers that "The guards were so stunned that they actually behaved like a guard of honor, each respectfully shaking my hand" (Inv 29–30). He was told by one warder that the warders don't even like to talk to one another because they "*hate* their status" (219). Mandela's reaction was to get to know the man's story: he was brought up in an orphanage, and never knew his parents. Mandela concludes, "The fact that they had no parents, no parental love, and his bitterness, to me was due to that. And I respected the chap very much because he was a self-made chap, yes. And he was independent and he was studying" (219).

So the status path of anger was not only a path that Mandela carefully eschewed, but also one that he understood with empathy and thus deftly undermined.

As for the wish for payback, Mandela understood it very well, and felt it in his own life. He recalls incidents that made him extremely angry.

"This injustice rankled," he says of an early incident at Fort Hare school (LW 62). Moreover, anger was not just a constant possibility, it was at one time a crucial motivation for deciding on a political career:

> I had no epiphany, no singular revelation, no moment of truth, but a steady accumulation of a thousand slights, a thousand indignities and a thousand unremembered moments produced in me an anger, a rebelliousness, a desire to fight the system that imprisoned my people. There was no particular day on which I said, Henceforth I will devote myself to the liberation of my people; instead, I simply found myself doing so, and could not do otherwise. (LW 109)

But he recognized, he tells us, that payback simply doesn't get you anywhere. Anger is human, and we can see why wrongdoing might produce it—but if we ponder the sheer futility of the payback wish, and if we actually want good for ourselves and others, we quickly discover that non-anger and a generous disposition are far more useful.

As he tells his own story, the early roots of these attitudes were taught to him in tribal meetings, where the regent listened calmly to each person's opinion, and respect was shown to each (LW 25). Stories of heroes of former times stressed their "generosity and humility" (LW 26). Whether this is strictly veridical or a reconstruction of African traditions suited to the present and future is of course unclear; what is important is the message for the living.[26]

Mandela was no saint, and his tendency to anger was a constant problem with which he wrestled. As he records, much of his introspective meditation in prison focused on his tendency to anger in the form of a payback wish. Thus on one occasion he concluded that he had spoken too sharply to one of the warders, and he apologizes (C 219). The deliberate choice to frame his conversations as analogous to Marcus Aurelius's *Meditations* shows a determined self-watchfulness, which may have been directly modeled on Stoic sources, although his ideas also have deep connections with the African concept of *ubuntu*.[27] (By contrast, he never reports trying to get rid of disappointment and grief, and indeed he always acknowledges such experiences forthrightly, although he also emphasizes that it is important not to lose hope.) Repeatedly he draws attention to the importance of systematic self-inspection. In a letter to Winnie, then in prison, from his own prison in 1975, he writes (encouraging her to adopt this same meditative discipline): "The cell is an ideal place to learn to know yourself, to search realistically and regularly the process of your own mind and feelings" (C vii).

Notice that even in the early experiences of anger that Mandela identifies as formative, the forward-looking predominates. He wants to change the system and to liberate his people, not to inflict pain or bad conditions on others. So his early anger, while it seems to be genuine anger and not Transition-Anger, still heads very rapidly toward the Transition. And even that anger was carefully pruned away through prison meditations.

In general: Mandela never seems to have had the thought that making white South Africans suffer or inflicting on them any form of payback would be of the slightest interest. As he saw it, the goal is to change the system; but that would very likely require the cooperation of whites, and would at the very least be unstable and continually threatened without white support. Albie Sachs, an important (white) member of the freedom movement, and later one of the founding justices of the South African Constitutional Court, says that they always felt that they were struggling for the positive goal of political equality, a goal that in principle included all.[28]

Non-retributive attitudes, in Mandela's view, are particularly crucial for the person who is the fiduciary of a nation. A responsible leader has to be a pragmatist, and anger is incompatible with forward-looking pragmatism. It simply gets in the way. A good leader must move to the Transition as rapidly as possible, and perhaps for much of his life just stay there, expressing and even feeling Transition-Anger and disappointment, but leaving genuine anger behind.

A good summary of Mandela's approach can be found in a little parable he told to his interviewer Richard Stengel, as one he had previously used with his followers:

> I told the incident . . . of an argument between the sun and the wind, that the sun said, "I'm stronger than you are" and the wind says, "No, I'm stronger than you are." And they decided, therefore, to test their strength with a traveller . . . who was wearing a blanket. And they agreed that the one who would succeed in getting the traveller to get rid of his blanket would be the stronger. So the wind started. It started *blowing* and the *harder* it blew, the *tighter* the traveller pulled the blanket around his body. And the wind blew and blew but it could not get him to discard the blanket. And, as I said, the *harder* the wind blew, the *tighter* the visitor tried to hold the blanket around his body. And the wind eventually gave up. Then the sun started with its rays, very mild, and they increased in strength and as they increased . . . the traveller felt that the blanket was unnecessary because the blanket is for warmth. And so he decided to relax it, to loosen it, but the rays of the sun became stronger and stronger and eventually he threw it away. So by a gentle method it was possible to get the traveller to discard his blanket. And this is the parable that through

> peace you will be able to convert, you see, the most determined
> people . . . and that is the method we should follow. (C 237–38)

Significantly, Mandela frames the entire question in forward-looking pragmatic terms, as a question of getting the other party to do what you want. He then shows that this task is much more feasible if you can get the other party to work with you rather than against you. Progress is impeded by the other party's defensiveness and anxious self-protection. Anger, consequently, does nothing to move matters forward: it just increases the other party's anxiety and self-defensiveness. A gentle and cheerful approach, by contrast, can gradually weaken defenses until the whole idea of self-defense is given up.

Mandela, of course, was neither naïve nor so ideological as to refuse reality: thus we would never find him proposing to drop armed resistance to Hitler or to try converting him by charm. His parable is offered in a particular context, that of the ending of a sometimes violent liberation struggle, with people on the other side many of whom are genuine patriots, wishing the future good of the nation. He insisted from the start of his career that nonviolence should be used only strategically. Still, behind the strategic resort to violence was always a view of people that was Transitional, focused not on payback but on the creation of a shared future.

So Mandela has a reply ready for the imaginary opponent who says that the oppositional payback mentality is appropriate and a fine alternative to non-anger. It is that payback just doesn't do any good. That way of approaching his opponents would have set back the cause for which he was fighting. He readily accepts the criticism that his way of seeing opponents is only one option, not dictated by morality: so he advances a weaker claim than I do. His reply is that his way works:

STENGEL: People say, "Nelson Mandela's great problem is that he's too willing to see the good in other people." How do you respond to that?
MANDELA: Well, that's what many people say. That has been said right from my adolescence and I don't know. . . . There may be an element of truth in that. But when you are a public figure you have to accept the integrity of other people until there is evidence to the contrary. And when you have no evidence to the contrary, and people do things which appear to be good, what reason have you got to suspect them? To say that they are doing good because they have got an ulterior motive? It is until that evidence comes out that you then either deal with that point, with that instance of infidelity, and forget about it. Because that's how you can get on in life with people. You have to recognize that people

are produced by the mud in the society in which you live and that therefore they are human beings. They have got good points, they have got weak points. Your duty is to work with human beings as human beings, not because you think they are angels. And therefore, once you know that this man has got this virtue and he has got this weakness you work with them and you accommodate that weakness and you try and help him to overcome that weakness. I don't want to be frightened by the fact that a person has made certain mistakes and he has got human frailties. I can't allow myself to be influenced by that. And that is why many people criticize me.... So it's a criticism I have to put up with and I've tried to adjust to, because whether it is so or not, it is something which I think is profitable.... And one has made a great deal of progress in developing personal relationships because you [make] the basic assumption ... that those you deal with are men of integrity. I believe in that. (C 262–63)

To Mandela, the angry and resentful approach is simply not appropriate to a leader, because a leader's role is to get things done, and the generous and cooperative approach is the one that works.

He made the case this way to his allies and followers too. When a group of prisoners from the Black Consciousness group arrived on Robben Island determined to show resistance by rage and angry attacks on the guards, he gradually and patiently prevailed on them to see that militancy can also be expressed, and more productively, by non-angry strategies.[29] Much later, in the first days of the nation, after the murder of black leader Chris Hani by a white man, there was a real danger that the payback mentality would derail unity. Mandela went on television expressing deep grief but appealing for calm in a paternal way, so that people felt, "If the father himself was not baying for revenge, then what right had anybody else to seek it?" (Inv 119). He then tried to redirect emotions by pointing out that the murderer was a foreigner[30] and that an Afrikaner woman had acted heroically, writing down the hit man's license plate and thus enabling the police to track him down. He said, "This is a watershed moment for all of us.... Our decisions and actions will determine whether we use our pain, our grief, and our outrage to move forward to what is the only lasting solution for our country, an elected government of the people ... by remaining a disciplined force for peace" (Inv 120). No more moving example of the Transition could be found, since Mandela had loved Hani like a son and was evidently experiencing profound grief at his death.

We are now ready to examine three examples of the non-angry attitude at work, seeing how unexpected Mandela's generous spirit was, and what remarkable forms of cooperation it made possible: his dealings with white security forces, including a 1985 discussion with Kobie Coetsee, minister of Justice and Corrections, and subsequent treatment of white security forces after his release; his persuasions over the two-part national anthem; and his sponsorship of the Springboks, South Africa's rugby team. All took place against the background of a firm conviction that the appropriate goal was the building of trust and confidence in the united nation, with two groups "marching together into the future" (LW 744).

IV.1. Kobie Coetsee, Trust, and Security

The transition from armed resistance to negotiation had to begin somewhere, and the way in which it was initiated, the signals that were sent, would greatly influence the prospects of the new nation. The issue of creating trust was critical. As Mandela was, seemingly, on his way to release (which took place in a complex series of transitional moves), he was at one point in a prison hospital for his recurrent lung infection. It was at this time that a very important political figure, Kobie Coetsee, the nation's minister of Justice and Corrections, arranged to pay a call on him. A lot hung on the outcome of this meeting: for had Mandela shown himself an angry revolutionary, that would have retarded his release, or perhaps made it simply impossible. The meeting might have been extremely fraught: for police and security forces had been responsible for atrocities, and Coetsee was by no means innocent. Still, Mandela was master of the situation. Despite being in pajamas in a hospital room, Mandela was the perfect host. He greeted Coetsee—who was almost a foot shorter—with regal graciousness and warmth, and the two men quickly established a relaxed rapport.[31] They could talk with humor and gentleness, and they easily listened to one another. Mandela's years of self-training to understand the history, concerns, and emotions of Afrikaners began to bear fruit that day.

Nor was his rapprochement with Coetsee an isolated incident. In 1994, on the day of his inauguration of the nation's first democratically elected president, during the parade itself Mandela made a point of showing respect and inclusion to the white security forces. Looking back in 2013, an Afrikaner who was then a young recruit described watching Mandela unexpectedly walk up to one of his officers. Mandela looked the officer straight in the eye, and said, "You have become our peace. You are our peace." Expecting some sort of hostility or coldness, the officer was amazed and disarmed; he began to weep, and his men around him joined in. Years later, at the time of Mandela's death, the former policeman remembers this incident as one that created a revolution in his own thinking about the future of the nation.[32] He had been brought up like all young Afrikaners on the story of the ANC as evil and destructive. What he saw that day was utterly different, inspiring feelings of trust and friendship rather than fear and resentment.

Both of these incidents show Mandela winning over forces that were and are of the utmost importance for public trust. He understood that anger breeds mistrust, and only respect and friendship sustain it.

IV.2. The Two-Part Anthem

South Africa's national anthem today is a composite of two anthems with very different histories. "Nkosi Sikelel' iAfrica" ("God Bless Africa"), and "Die Stem" ("The Call"). The former is itself a hybrid, in that its lyrics employ three major African languages: Xhosa, Zulu, and Sesotho. The anthem, written in 1897, became a freedom song of the anti-apartheid movement. "Die Stem," written in 1918, was the national anthem of apartheid South Africa (sharing the stage with "God Save the Queen" until 1957). The current hybrid begins with "Nkosi," then shifts to the first verse of "Die Stem" in Afrikaans, but ends with a further verse of that anthem with new lyrics written in English: "Sound the call to come together / And united we shall stand, / Let us live and strive for freedom / In South Africa our land." The two anthems were sung separately side by side at Mandela's inauguration in 1994, and it was this hybrid that the Springboks learned to sing, as we shall see; the merged version took over in 1997.

Anthems have deep emotional resonances, and these two had come to define utterly clashing goals and sentiments. Black Africans learned to hate "Die Stem" in no less visceral a way than a Jew would detest "Deutschland über Alles." White South Africans, for the most part, detested and feared "Nkosi," the anthem of protest. But things were not so simple: for "Nkosi" was sung and endorsed by liberal whites; and many whites all along had reservations about "Die Stem," which of course had anti-English resonances left over from the Boer War, and some of its verses praised the specific achievements of Boer trekkers. In such a situation, what should a new united nation do? One course might be to junk them both, and write something new. This course, however, would have forfeited the powerful motivational power for potential good that resided in people's emotional connections to these songs, which speak of noble abstract goals of peace, prosperity, and freedom, meanwhile alluding to beautiful features of landscape, which all can love. For related reasons, despite her utter repudiation of Nazi ideology, Germany has not removed "Deutschland über Alles," reasoning that its Haydn melody and many of its lyrics are free from taint: instead, the unobjectionable third verse ("Einigkeit und Recht und Freiheit") has taken the place of the three-verse anthem.[33]

Most ANC leaders wanted simply to get rid of "Die Stem" and to replace it with "Nkosi." Indeed the executive had decided to do so while Mandela was out of the room on an international call. He protested, asking them to reconsider their decision. "This song that you treat so easily holds the emotions of many people who you don't represent yet. With the stroke of a pen, you would take a decision to destroy the very—the only— basis that we are building upon reconciliation" (Inv 147, cf. LW 747). It was a large demand: each group had to learn to see the world, in effect, through the eyes of the other.

The next step was to get each group to sing the anthem it associated with the other. Although this is as yet an incomplete work, since at times people sing only the part they know or like best, decisive progress was made with Mandela's next stratagem.

IV.3. The Rugby Team

Because the events surrounding the 1995 Rugby World Cup have been ably narrated by John Carlin in his book *Invictus*, and much more briefly depicted in the 2009 Clint Eastwood movie of the same name, they are familiar to many, and Morgan Freeman's portrayal of Mandela has powerfully conveyed the generous, self-contained, and joyful spirit of the leader.[34] Here is a sketch of what happened: Mandela was aware that sports, because of the deep patriotic emotions they can arouse, were a powerful avenue of potential reconciliation and unity for the nation. But sports had heretofore been separated along racial lines like everything else. Rugby was a white man's sport, and black Africans scorned and resented it. White fans and players were quite likely, on their side, to view black Africans with suspicion.

Through patient interaction with the coach and players of the national rugby team, the Springboks, Mandela—who by then was president— changed all that. First, he made a profound personal impression on the players, creating trust, hope, and friendship. He forged a particularly strong bond with the team's coach, Morné du Plessis, and with its captain, François Pienaar. He then prevailed on the team to sing both halves of the national anthem with passion, publicly, thus creating a paradigm for white fans to follow. At the same time, he set up training sessions where members of the team taught the game to scores of young black kids, and the children "reveal[ed] to their flabbergasted elders that big Boers could be friends too" (Inv 196). After these successes, he became the team's most enthusiastic cheerleader, spurring them on to victory in the World Cup. If it was a performance, it was one that convinced everyone of its emotional warmth and genuineness—and, most probably, it was genuine. Insofar as will and plan were involved, it was a will to believe and care. Mandela was not cold, but jovial and relaxed, full of warmth and humor (Inv 185). Above all, Mandela's conduct was utterly free of resentment or racial division: the team were simply "my boys" (Inv 194), and his parental embrace of his former adversaries made no allusion to the past. Feeling comfortable with him, and accepting his affection, the team members became, gradually, zealous fans of the new united South Africa.

The 1995 World Cup final, in which South Africa defeated New Zealand, proved a crucial emotional event for the nation, allowing South Africans of all backgrounds to come together in a celebration of national identity. When Mandela appeared wearing the number 6 jersey of François Pienaar, the mostly white crowd erupted in cheers, chanting Mandela's name.[35] Pienaar, describing the occasion shortly after Mandela's death, finds the transformation incredible. He also remarks on Mandela's humility and sincere love of the team: when he tried to tell Mandela that he, Mandela, had done a great thing for South Africa, the leader would have none of it: he said, "I want to thank *you* for what *you* have done for South Africa." Eighteen years later, the eyes of the large, powerful athlete were filled with tears.[36]

Anyone who ponders this story must marvel at Mandela's good luck: for if his support had energized the team, it certainly was not sufficient for victory over a stronger and more talented team. So his judgment in allowing weighty emotional matters to rest to some degree on the outcome of the match can be questioned. His antecedent achievement in forging a unified public cannot.

It was crucial that Mandela embraced rugby not coldly and politically, but as a real sports fan and former athlete (he was a good amateur boxer). Sports fans everywhere could see that he understood the power of sports personally, from within. At his death on December 5, 2013, in addition to the expected tributes, came warm tributes from the world of sports. The ESPN website quoted him as saying, "Sport has the power to change the world. . . . It has the power to inspire. It has the power to unite people in a way that little else does. It speaks to youth in a language they understand. Sport can create hope where once there was only despair. It is more powerful than government in breaking racial barriers." Major sports figures from Muhammad Ali to FIFA president Sepp Blatter paid tribute to his embrace of sports in the cause of freedom.[37]

These incidents all show that generosity and forgetfulness of past wrongs—in the spirit of the father of the Prodigal Son—have enormous creative power. Mandela does not claim that anger is never justified, and thus he makes a weaker claim than I do. He claims, and shows in his conduct, that anger is politically futile and generosity productive. If he had put whites on guard, taking away their anthem, treating the rugby players as racist bigots and oppressors, he could claim historical justification for that sort of payback. Who could fault the ANC for refusing to sing the anthem of the oppressor? But resentment would have undermined their cause. Anger's payback mentality would have been a pointless and childish type of self-indulgence when the future of a nation was at stake.

Couldn't all this have been achieved by a performance of non-anger and generosity, rather than the real thing? Or: does this show the superiority of non-anger, or only of a non-angry style of conduct? Mandela certainly thought these two things could not be separated. Indeed he repeatedly credits his years in prison with giving him time to introspect and discipline his entire personality.[38] His strong attachment to the William Ernest Henley poem "Invictus" (a work much influenced by Stoic ideas) is just one expression of an intense commitment to being "captain of my soul." He was already inclined toward the Transition, but he needed to discipline urges toward anger, and he said he thought this internal discipline was necessary.

Can we really imagine otherwise? Could a consummate hypocrite fool so many people and for so long? At any rate, even if such a thing were possible (and I certainly don't oppose performance, when the only alternative is bad thought and perhaps action), the important thing is that it would be a performance of a psychology that my argument, following Mandela, has shown to be superior in a revolutionary context, as in other contexts. As Gandhi repeatedly insisted, the soul of a person who has not undertaken an inner transformation is not free; being in thrall to anger is a normatively unstable and undesirable state, even if by some miracle for a time it produces no differences in outward conduct.[39]

Our three thinkers, then, clearly show us the strategic superiority of non-anger: for it wins world respect and friendship, and it also eventually can win over the adversaries, enlisting their cooperation in nation-building. Their arguments do not prove that anger is not instrumentally useful as signal and motivation—up to a point. (Indeed King strongly suggests this.) There may be some cases in which the main problem to be addressed is public passivity—and then, a limited use of anger as motivation may be quite useful, as it almost certainly was as Britain geared up to resist Hitler. But our three cases show that, strategically, the Transition is crucial, making it possible to move into the future with trust and cooperation.[40] I have also argued (going beyond Mandela's explicit statements, and agreeing with King and Gandhi) that the Transition is also morally superior: the path, or paths, of anger go wrong, either by exalting status to a value more important than it is, or by holding, falsely, that payback achieves something, atoning for the damages of injustice.

The inner world is morally and politically valuable, even when (rarely) it makes no difference to external choice and action.[41]

In all three of my cases, non-anger was practiced by a group that a dominant group had previously derided and demonized as subhuman animals. Angry words and conduct would have nourished baneful stereotypes, and thus non-anger was commended by prudent thought of what the situation required. Does this show that anger is an acceptable strategy for groups who have never been so demonized (white European males, say)? I see no reason to think this. Should people feel licensed to be irrational just because nobody has accused them of being so? Mandela offers reasons for non-anger that do not depend on the contingencies of oppression. If some people accepted his lead only because they feared fueling ignoble stereotypes, they were right for the wrong reasons.

Nation-building requires a great deal more than non-anger. It requires good economic thinking, an effective education system, efficient public health services, and much more. The task undertaken by James Jarvis in Ndotsheni needs to be undertaken on a national scale, and that process remains incomplete in both India and South Africa. Nation-building also requires careful thought about how to structure legal institutions so that they correct power imbalances. Generosity does not reform the corrupt justice system that executed Absalom Kumalo. But non-anger infuses these deliberations with a productive spirit, and the impressive achievements of the South African Constitutional Court owe much to its beginnings.

V. No Future without Forgiveness?

The spirit of the new South Africa, then, was the spirit of James Jarvis and Stephen Kumalo: one of forward-looking and generous friendship. It involved, however, another famous element: the Truth and Reconciliation Commission, which by now has become a model for dozens of similar commissions in other countries. Its story has been told by one of its chief architects, Archbishop Desmond Tutu, in his influential book *No Future without Forgiveness*.[42] Because Tutu frames the work of the commission in terms of Christian ideas of confession, contrition, and forgiveness, we must ask whether these ideas fit what the commission actually did, and whether, if so, it contravened the generous spirit of Mandela.

The topic of truth and reconciliation commissions has by now generated a vast literature, and I do not intend to survey it.[43] Instead, I offer some general directions for thought that emerge from the cases I have considered. Each situation calls for sensitive contextual thinking, and I believe that no blanket prescription would be appropriate, given the diversity of histories and cultures, except at the most abstract level.

My argument so far suggests that two things are necessary in a revolutionary transition: acknowledgment of wrongdoing and its seriousness, and a forward-looking effort of reconciliation. A further helpful element suggested by prior chapters (and by the practice of Mandela) is the cultivation of empathy, the ability to see how the world looks from the other party's perspective.[44] The apparatus of abasement, confession, contrition, and eventual forgiveness, by contrast, often impedes reconciliation by producing humiliation rather than mutual respect, and it frequently acts as a covert form of punishment, discharging a hidden (or, often, not so hidden) resentment.

Acknowledgment of the truth of what happened is essential, because one cannot go forward into a regime of justice, establishing trust, without insisting on the seriousness of the human interests that were damaged in the prior time: that insistence is a way of dignifying those interests and committing the nation to not repeating the wrongs. It gives weight and reality to fundamental political principles. Thus both Gandhi and King were unsparing in their truthful description of the wrongs of the raj and of white racism; although no formal inquiry took place, they made sure that truth was out there for all to see. In the case of King, formal judicial proceedings against the wrongdoers accompanied and continued the narratives of wrongdoing produced by King and other civil rights leaders.

Trials are the normal means of establishing a public truth. In a nation with a legal system that commands public trust, they are, as Aeschylus saw, a preferable means. By allowing trials to go ahead, and by insisting that they be fairly conducted, a working democracy takes its stand against continued injustice. In the case of Gandhi, what was needed was a new constitutional order following the departure of the British. Because they were gone, they could not be tried, but they were certainly tried in the court of public opinion, and had long since been convicted. Gandhi's canny relationship with international journalism was his way of conducting a truth commission, and it proved remarkably effective.

Where truth has been for the most part concealed, one can see that trust is severely threatened, even after a prolonged effort at reconciliation. Northern Ireland has made great strides toward reconciliation, both between Ulster's Protestants and Catholics and between both and Britain. The Queen's willingness to visit Belfast wearing green in 2013, and, later, to shake the hands of both Gerry Adams and former terrorist Martin McGuinness, all gave reconciliation a large boost. I happened to be on the first British Airways flight from London to Belfast in June 2013, and the joyful spirit, as we were greeted planeside by green cupcakes, was a heartening sign. And yet, by the spring of 2014 the ongoing debate about the "secret" transcripts of interviews with former IRA members being held at Boston College had led to the (brief) arrest of Gerry Adams in connection apropos of the 1972 abduction, execution, and secret burial of Jean McConville. This episode shows the fragility of the future, when truth about the past has been deliberately concealed (and yet is on record in an archive that people can't see).[45] In conversation with a leader of an NGO dedicated to the peace process,[46] I have heard that many people just won't trust Gerry Adams because it is thought that a lot of his real conduct has been concealed. (Interestingly McGuinness is thought more trustworthy by some on the grounds that the truth of his murderous activities is known.) Whether Northern Ireland could have had or can still have a truth and reconciliation commission is beyond me to judge. What is evident is that the absence of truth jeopardizes reconciliation, even after forty years.

Returning now to the three leaders we have been considering, all of whom promoted the emergence of truth in their own different ways: the question of reconciliation also took different forms in the three cases. King, like Lincoln, had to "bind up the nation's wounds," and he did so with his prophetic vision of a transfigured America in which freedom and equality would produce genuine brotherhood. From that time onward, reconciliation was promoted by energetic use of the existing legal system, as well as through social and educational strategies. The effort of reconciliation is ongoing, since race-based abuses in police practice and in the criminal justice system more generally must be corrected if trust is to be established. Terrible events around the nation in 2015, at least many showing extremely bad behavior by police to African-Americans, have at least made the nation take notice and make some efforts at both truth and reconciliation. Achievements are likely to be piecemeal, gradual, and regionally specific, but one can at least hope that determination to achieve justice will make progress. Especially heartening has been the use of King's methods of nonviolent protest in many of the affected cities. Although no doubt in many cases the protests were not free from retributive anger, they typically at least expressed Dr. King's spirit and emulated his firm and uncompromising demand for justice.

Gandhi's challenge was different. Since the British were, eventually, gone, reconciliation became an issue of foreign policy, and the nation's careful policy of nonalignment during the early years of the republic buttressed independence and promoted respect for sovereignty, without rancor or hostility. Meanwhile, Gandhi's movement, self-consciously based upon Indian rather than British symbols and phrases, helped provide the new and highly diverse nation with a common language of nationhood that has lasted against all odds, producing a stable democracy, albeit one with ongoing tensions and profound economic and religious problems. (Needless to say, producing India's democracy was the job of many, and both Jawaharlal Nehru and constitutional lawyer B. R. Ambedkar, both of whom disagreed with Gandhi on some important matters, played central roles. Gandhi was an inspirational leader rather than a legal or institutional thinker, and these other minds made a crucial contribution.)

The South African case had unique complexity. For there was in a sense a working legal system, but it had been captured by white supremacy, and it therefore did not command public trust. The new nation required, and received, a new constitution. But it also needed a mechanism by which to acknowledge the wrongs of the past, restoring public trust in government and creating a shared public sense of right and wrong. In short, it had aspects of the U.S. and aspects of the Indian experience.

Could those who committed crimes be tried by some ad hoc tribunal, as at Nuremberg? Tutu and other leading South Africans posed this question. They quickly rejected that alternative. First, in the circumstances, they worried that a lengthy series of trials would deepen the rift between white and black, intensifying black resentment and white fear. Trials would prove a mechanism of ongoing revenge, and would undermine agreement on and good will toward the new constitution.[47] Second, trials would be very expensive, and waste the scarce resources of the state. Third, they would likely result in less truth, because the accused would have access to high-powered lawyers, who would instruct them to admit nothing.[48]

On the other hand, an immediate general amnesty would also undermine public trust going forward, because it would fail to say that outrageous deeds had occurred, which seemed necessary for future trust in the nation and the constitution.[49] Tutu suggests that this silence would revictimize the victims, by failing to acknowledge their suffering.[50]

Accordingly, leaders converged on a process then innovative, though since much imitated: the Truth and Reconciliation Commission. In effect, the structure of this Commission is that of what I have called Transition-Anger: a statement of outrage, followed by generous forward-looking thoughts.

The idea of the TRC was that people would be summoned to testify, and the reward for acknowledgment would be amnesty. As Tutu makes clear, this combination was very controversial: for many thought acknowledgment no use without punishment. And many doubted that truth would emerge, even in the absence of punishment. But, given the presence of so many victims as witnesses, there was a strong incentive for perpetrators not to contest the truth, given the fact that the usual most powerful incentive, fear of punishment, was lacking. And even the incentive of social standing was ambivalent, since in the new nation it was already clear that one could no longer take pride in claiming that wrong was right or in other ways resisting the demand for acknowledgment. Moreover, the Commission made a point of investigating wrongdoing by ANC members and other revolutionaries, as well as whites: it was in this way that the actions of Winnie Mandela came to light. This even-handedness helped in no small measure to inspire trust.

I have said that Mandela was careful to show respect for his former oppressors and never to humiliate them. Did the Commission follow his lead, or did it humiliate? This is a very difficult and, to some degree, an individual question. But the procedures were dignified, and showed respect; and the future amnesty, a palpable presence throughout, assured those who testified that they would subsequently be received as equal citizens in a new nation, rather than being stigmatized as criminals. Telling what one has done need not humiliate, if it is framed as a precondition for a future of trust and equal respect. Perhaps the most troubling feature of the testimony is that it often involved telling not only what one had done oneself but also what friends and associates had done. That sort of "ratting" can be seen as deeply humiliating and emasculating.[51] On the other hand, given the amnesty, to tell was not to deliver one's buddies to a despised and stigmatized fate, but simply to state a fact, which would be followed by a future of equal respect. So in principle, if not always in practice, it seems to me that the design of the Commission was shrewd, emphasizing exactly the two things that the welfare of the new nation required: truth about the past, creating public trust and respect for right and wrong;[52] and reconciliation, in the form of the amnesty, which provided a new start.

This is the picture one gets if one reads Tutu's detailed narrative of what the Commission actually did. But his framing of it in at least some of his subsequent speeches, from which he quotes in the book's conclusion, is a different matter. For here he introduces the full transactional version of the Christian account of confession, contrition, apology, and conditional forgiveness that I have said we should regard with skepticism, as punitive and often a covert form of anger. It is significant that those close to Mandela regard this sort of confessional language with skepticism as well.[53] According to Tutu, reconciliation is part of a divinely ordained cosmic process that moves human beings gradually toward unity in Christ. This is essentially an extra-human process, "the process at the heart of the universe."[54] Individual human beings can either join in or obstruct. In order to join in, they have to "walk the path of confession, forgiveness, and reconciliation."[55] This path requires of wrongdoers that they confess the truth, apologize, express "remorse, or at least some contrition and sorrow," and "ask for forgiveness."[56] When these conditions have been met, wronged parties should let go of their resentful feelings. Tutu adds that they may occasionally be able to forgive without the confession, but that in this case the "root of the breach" will not be exposed, and the whole process may remain incomplete. So it is incumbent upon the wrongdoer to initiate the process by exposing himself, confessing, assuming "a fair measure of humility,"[57] and asking contritely for forgiveness. The victim then ought to accept the apology with an "act of faith"—which Jesus tells us to repeat as many times as the wrongdoer offers a confession.[58] He continues with much more about Christ's forgiveness and the metaphysical teleology it suggests to him.

Here we see the transactional and conditional strand of the Christian picture: not the behavior of the father of the prodigal son, but the behavior of penitent and confessor. Clearly Tutu believes deeply in these religious concepts and believes that they are what make the process of reconciliation work. More recently, he has spoken of the roots of these ideas in his own experience of anger at seeing his father abuse his mother.[59] Such concepts clearly are meaningful to many. On the other hand, if we try to imagine the conversation of Mandela with the rugby team in these terms, its limits become clear. The demand to repent would have been like a gust of that cold wind in his parable, and would surely have intensified resistance. Mandela had no taste for this type of religious teleology, nor for the extraction of apology and remorse from others. He believed that only open-hearted generosity enabled him and the team to move forward to mutual respect and friendship. Indeed, the prominent role of lightheartedness, kindliness, and humor in his dealings with all former oppressors was remarkable. Nor does Tutu misrepresent him: he describes Mandela as "a man regal in dignity, bubbling over with magnanimity and a desire to dedicate himself to the reconciliation of those whom apartheid and the injustice and pain of racism had alienated from one another."[60]

So Tutu has painted his own picture, and it is significantly different, as he himself shows, from the process that Mandela enacted, and different, too, from the process that, by his own account, the Commission enacted. Not surprisingly, given the modern hold of Christian ideas, Mandela's legacy is often described in Tutu's terms, as one of forgiveness. But in reading his published writings I find no use of that word or those ideas. Nor does Albie Sachs recall any such use of the ideas of confession and forgiveness by Mandela: he says that these ideas were utterly alien to his movement. At one point in the recent Mandela film, when Mandela appears on national television as violence impends, he is made to say, "I have forgiven them, and you too should forgive them." Sachs tells me that this is utterly made up. Mandela said no such thing, but the screenwriters must have thought their audience could relate to it.[61]

Of course the Commission was not a process that could be described as lighthearted, or "bubbling over with magnanimity." It was solemn and in many ways tragic, as so many told their stories of loss and harm, and so many told of their own bad acts. And yet, at least as described, the process was respectful, not demanding humility, and certainly not humiliation, and as protecting the dignity of the wrongdoers as potential equal citizens in the nation of the future. Nobody was asked to apologize as a condition of amnesty, and the statement of truth was not framed as a confession to an authoritative confessor, but instead as a straight retelling of what occurred. Nobody is asked to show contrition, or to promise not to do it again—a promise that, by the abasement it would enact, would surely prove counterproductive. If you really want someone to cooperate with you as an equal, the worst place to begin is by treating him as a likely criminal. So the promise not to offend would be, as I've said, "One thought too many," branding the person as a suspect type.

A nation that moves forward needs both trust and mutual respect. It seems that truth is very important for trust, but it also seems that a certain way of positioning the truth jeopardizes respect, hence reconciliation. By offering amnesty, South Africa wisely took the process out of the retributivist framework that it might so easily have inhabited, facilitating attitudes of trust and emotions of national solidarity. Tutu's reinterpretation, however, sneaks a subtle variety of retributivism back in, in the form of a confessorial enactment of humility and superiority. Instead of his title, *No Future Without Forgiveness*, we might well propose, "No Future Without Generosity and Reason."[62]

Significantly, Tutu himself has had second thoughts. In his recent *The Book of Forgiving*, coauthored with his daughter Mpho Tutu, he develops a picture of forgiveness that is both secular and unconditional.[63] In fact the Tutus speak quite critically of the conditional, transactional model of forgiveness, which they call "the most familiar pattern of forgiveness" (20). It is like a gift "with strings attached," they say. They only briefly state my objection that conditional forgiveness can be a covert form of payback (20, see also "mutual resentment," 21); instead, they emphasize the point that conditional forgiveness keeps one tied to the wrongdoer and dependent on that other person's conduct (21). Still, the model they themselves now prefer is totally unconditional. Since their book focuses on personal relations and on solitary work with and on oneself, I have discussed their proposals in chapter 4; but clearly they intend the proposal for the political sphere as well. In that sphere, although most of their spiritual exercises would have no place, the basic idea does have a place, and it is much more consistent with the TRC than the conditional picture that Tutu previously endorsed.

A nation torn by horrible acts may find itself unable to move forward. Angry feelings may have such a deep grip on people's minds that they cannot be changed to forward-looking projects and feelings. Chapter 4 argued that in the personal case there is sometimes a limited role for backward-looking forgiveness rituals, if they do prove the way to get people off the hook of the past, especially when no other approach has proven successful. This individual point has relevance to the political realm as well, since individuals damaged by other individuals and unable to let go of their anger may find a type of forgiveness ritual valuable—as in the well-known case of Eric Lomax, the "railway man," who achieved reconciliation with the Japanese officer who had tortured him, after many years of being unable to move on in life.[64] Similar individual cases are known in South Africa.[65] Surely any interaction that helps people let go of overwhelming anger and bitterness should be favored, whether it meets the constraints of a philosophical norm or not.

Following the sketchy lead of the Tutus' new book, we can now make a similar point about nations. There is evidence that in the scarred society of Rwanda, forgiveness rituals have had a good effect. Such efforts are encouraged by the nation and implemented in a range of ways, but one such project is run by an NGO called AMI, which counsels small groups of Hutus and Tutsis over many months, culminating in a formal request for forgiveness and a grant of forgiveness—typically solemnized by a gift of food from perpetrator to victim and a shared song and dance celebration.[66] Forgiveness rituals are clearly no substitute for a formal process such as that of the TRC, which creates public trust and confers public amnesty. And as the Tutus argue, unconditional forgiveness is in many ways preferable to conditional forgiveness. But forgiveness rituals, even when in some ways conditional, may be a useful supplement to more formal procedures, allowing the past to be discharged in an effective way, for people who might have resisted all urging toward generous love and forward-looking rationality. In South Africa too, where people need to live with neighbors who have done bad things, an approach based upon personal forgiveness, but elevated to a public plane, sometimes has merit, forging human connection between formerly alienated individuals.[67]

Nonetheless, such backward-looking rituals can easily be hijacked by the spirit of revenge, and the conditional form of forgiveness can become, itself, a form of revenge. As Pumla Gobodo-Madikizela says of her complicated reaction to imprisoned police chief Eugene de Kock, whom she interviewed for forty-six hours over a three-month period: "[T]he victim becomes the gatekeeper to what the outcast desires—readmission into the human community.... In this sense, then, forgiveness is a kind of revenge.... I sometimes sensed this feeling of triumph myself while visiting de Kock. I felt a sense of power over him as a person who needed my understanding."[68]

So the errors embedded in anger need to be pondered at all times, and techniques of non-anger need to be assiduously cultivated. Let me end this chapter, then, with just one more Mandela story, which shows him renouncing both the status error and the payback error. Mandela is talking here about an interaction with a white Afrikaner warder who watched him while he was in the transitional prison, Viktor Vorster, prior to his official release. The question was how the dishes would get done, a question in many households all over the world:

> I took it upon myself to break the tension and a possible resentment on his part that he has to serve a prisoner by cooking and then washing dishes, and I offered to wash dishes and he refused.... He says that this is his work. I said, "No, we must share it." Although he insisted, and he was genuine, but I *forced* him, literally forced him, to allow me to do the dishes, and we established a *very* good relationship.... A *really* nice chap, Warder Swart, a *very* good friend of mine.

It would have been so easy to see the situation as one of status-inversion: the dominating Afrikaner is doing dishes for the once-despised ANC leader. It would also have been so easy to see it in terms of payback: the warder is getting a humiliation he deserves because of his complicity in oppression. Significantly, Mandela doesn't go down either of these doomed paths, even briefly. He asks only, how shall I produce cooperation and friendship?

This remarkable capacity for generosity and reciprocity was Mandela's genius—the fruit, as he tells us, of years of critical self-examination on Robben Island. It's a difficult goal, but it is that goal that I am recommending, for both individuals and institutions. Even when there is no charismatic leader to show the way forward, and anger appears to be the only recourse for people who want to protect important human goods, it is a bad strategy and a fatally flawed response. Anger is a prominent part of most people's lives. I've argued that, although it has limited value as a signal and a motivator, anger lacks most of the virtues often claimed for it, and has both normative and practical problems all its own, in both personal and political relations.

We might sum it all up in the words of one of Mandela's most worthy successors (albeit an educator, not a power in national politics), Jonathan Jansen, the first non-white rector of the University of the Free State,

Blomfontein, right in the heart of Afrikaner society. In 2009, Jansen said this to the graduating class: "I urge you, in a country where there's still a lot of rage, never respond by rage, respond through reason, and you will have gotten not just a degree, but an education."

That, in all our lives, would be a revolutionary transformation indeed.

8

Conclusion

The Eyes of the World

During the darkest days of World War II, Gandhi said, "We must look the world in the face with calm and clear eyes even though the eyes of the world are bloodshot today."[1] That's basically the message of the *Eumenides*: the world has been propelled, to a large extent, by rage and retribution, but let us create something better, in ourselves and in our political culture. Let's not be the way the world is right now.

A likely response to Gandhi's call, and to this book, is to say, "How on earth can that be?" Or: "That's too hard. We're in and of the world." Or: "We're only human." But that's not an adequate reply. Lots of things are done badly most of the time, and we don't stop trying to do them better, even when it's very difficult. We do not think that the prevalence of cancer gives us reasons not to devote massive efforts to cancer research. We do not think that the fact that producing a well-functioning economy is a task both difficult and elusive gives us reasons not to work at the task as hard as we possibly can. And, as William Harriss points out in the conclusion to his remarkable study of Greek and Roman anger, apropos of the objection that anger is difficult to manage: we do not think that the fact even the best historians inevitably make some mistakes means that they should not strive extremely hard to avoid making them.[2]

We typically do not treat our own lives with the concessive casualness this objection displays. We think it makes sense to work hard getting between twelve and twenty years of full-time education, in order to develop our skills and our knowledge. When we become parents, we typically insist that our children work hard in school even when they don't want to. And most of us think that it makes sense to work extremely hard at eating well and achieving fitness through exercise, even though we often don't do what we think we should. If we continue to smoke, we usually don't console ourselves by saying, "It's too hard, I'm only human." Instead, we probably think that we should try harder.

Anger is hard. But so are many other things in life. Why do contemporary Americans tend to think that health, and learning, and fitness deserve tough personal effort, and anger does not? Why do we think that medical and economic research deserve our public political effort, and that the social disease of anger does not?

Here are three likely reasons. One is that Americans may believe the tendency to anger is hardwired in human nature. To a large extent, this book has tried to show, that belief is inflated. Anger may have evolutionary roots, but its centrality in society is far more a construction of cultural norms and personal cultivation or lack thereof. Let's grant that there is some truth to the belief in inherited roots: still, what is inherited is a tendency, not its inevitable outward expression in action. We work hard to correct many tendencies or propensities that are hardwired in human nature, from myopia to memory lapses. As with diet and exercise: we do not have to believe that we will ultimately free ourselves from all illicit cravings in order to embark on a program of self-cultivation. Who knows? Maybe non-anger will make our lives go so much better that we will not even miss the strife-torn days of our past, any more than we always retain an acute craving for French fries and donuts. And even if we continue to experience anger, we need not make public policy based on its misleading normative promptings.

A second reason for our cultural reluctance to pursue non-anger may be that we believe that it entails an inhuman, extreme, and unloving type of detachment. Gandhi's example is surely not reassuring in this regard, nor is that of the Stoics.[3] But I have made it very clear that the pursuit of non-anger does not entail this unattractive goal. It allows us to maintain deep loves, friendships, and other commitments (for example, to causes and projects), and to maintain the vulnerability to grief and fear that such loves entail. Nor do we need to be harsh with ourselves when we fail, as we often do. Gandhi was harsh, but this harshness, I have argued, was not an entailment of non-anger, it was actually a type of self-anger, although he apparently did not recognize this.

The largest reason why we typically do not embrace the pursuit of non-anger, both personal and social, is that, despite the fact that modern cultures are deeply torn on this question, many people in modern American society continue to think anger is good, powerful, and manly. They encourage it in their children (especially boys), and they indulge it in both self and others. They encourage legal policies based upon its alleged goodness. The Greeks and Romans, by contrast, did not encourage anger. Although they still got angry a lot, and although they differed about whether anger should be wholly removed or just greatly restrained, for the most part they saw anger as disease and as weakness, and they viewed the angry person as infantile (or, in their terms, feminine), rather than powerful (and, in their terms, male).[4] Getting to that insight is half the battle. Self-cultivation is hard, but it is impossible if one never gets started.

If this book achieves anything, I hope it achieves that sort of square-one reorientation, getting its readers to see clearly the irrationality and stupidity of anger. Whether readers take the next step is up to them. As chapter 5 makes clear, I don't always take my own medicine, succumbing to the lure of thinking that the world of airlines, banks, and Internet repair people ought to be rational, and yielding to anger when (predictably) the real world does not meet that expectation. It's hard not to be stupid.

Even if people don't work hard on, or even perhaps embark on, personal self-cultivation, however, it seems simply inexcusable to tolerate and even encourage political and legal institutions that embrace and valorize the stupidity of the retributive spirit. Our institutions should model our best selves, not our worst. They should exemplify adulthood, even if we are often children.[5] Even if every single person continues to nourish personally a degree of irrational retributivism, we should not tolerate stupidity in systems of law and justice. Instead, we might treat the problem of crime the way people usually treat the challenge of building the economy: as a highly difficult, multifaceted intellectual and practical problem that requires expert *ex ante* strategies with many parts, as well as some related *ex post* strategies linked rationally to a valuable goal. All too often, instead, we dream that the world of a modern society is like a shootout on the (fantasy of the) old frontier, which was not like that at all, really, and, insofar as it was occasionally like that, was not such a great place to be.

Furthermore, when there is great injustice, we should not use that fact as an excuse for childish and undisciplined behavior. Injustice should be greeted with protest and careful, courageous strategic action. But the end goal must remain always in view: as King said so simply: "A world where men and women can live together." Building such a world takes intelligence, control, and a spirit of generosity. That spirit has many names: Greek *philophrosunē*, Roman *humanitas*, biblical *agapē*, African *ubuntu*[6]—a patient and forbearing disposition to see and seek the good rather than to harp obsessively on the bad.

I hesitate to end with a slogan that surely betrays my age: but, after so many centuries of folly orchestrated by the retributive spirit, it finally does seem time to "give peace a chance."

Appendix A: Emotions and *Upheavals of Thought*

The analysis of anger and forgiveness in the present book can be fully grasped without studying the emotion theory I developed in *Upheavals of Thought*. Nonetheless, for a deeper understanding of the theoretical background, some readers may be interested in a brief summary of its main contentions.

In the earlier chapters of *Upheavals*, I defend a conception of emotions according to which they all involve intentional thought or perception directed at an object (as perceived or imagined by the person who has the emotion) and some type of evaluative appraisal of that object made from the agent's own personal viewpoint. This appraisal ascribes importance to the object in terms of the agent's scheme of goals and ends. Thus, we do not grieve for every death in the world, but only for deaths of people who appear to us to be important in our lives; we fear not all possible bad events, but only those that seem to pose some serious threat to our projects; and so on. These appraisals need not involve full-fledged beliefs, although they often do; indeed, they need not involve language or even complexity. Most animals make at least some appraisals of objects, from the point of view of their sense of their well-being, and have emotions in consequence. All that is required is that they see the object (a bit of food, say) as good from the point of view of the creature's own pursuits and goals. Similarly, very young human infants, not yet capable of language, are still capable of many emotions, because they have an inchoate sense of their own good and ill, and of the way in which objects and events contribute to that good or ill.

Some emotions are "situational," fixed on a particular set of circumstances; others are "background," meaning that they are ongoing in the fabric of life (for example a fear of death that most people carry around with them), but can also become more concrete focused on a particular event (a particular threat to the person's life). Background emotions are sometimes consciously experienced, but not always. The fear of death often motivates behavior without being an object of conscious awareness.

In the balance of the book's first chapter, I then investigate the role of non-cognitive elements (feelings, bodily states) in emotions. I argue that, although some such elements are present in most of our emotional experience, and although, indeed, all human and animal emotions are embodied in some way, these non-cognitive elements do not have the constancy and regular association with the emotion type in question that would be required if we were to include them in the definition of an emotion of a particular type. Even with an emotion as simple as fear, which is indeed frequently associated with something like shivering or trembling, there are numerous counterexamples—including the fear of death. Most of us have that fear most of the time, in a way that has psychological reality and motivational power, but (usually) we are not consciously aware of shivering or shaking. In this case, then, there is not only no single feeling, but, sometimes, no conscious feeling at all. With other more complex emotions—for example, grief and compassion—there are usually feelings of some sort involved (again, not always), but it is not easy even to begin to identify, in a general way, the bodily feelings that would belong to those emotions. And often, even when we think we have identified such elements (grief feels like a pain in the stomach, say), we find, on closer inspection, that one may continue to have grief over time while these bodily manifestations change, often greatly. (A grieving person may sometimes feel achy, sometimes exhausted, sometimes endowed with extra energy—and yet it would be wrong to say that she is not still grieving.) Compassion does not have any close association with a particular feel. Love is accompanied by bewilderingly many different feelings—but also, at times, no marked feeling at all. (A parent's love for her child may persist without being linked to any particular feeling.)

We can still insist that emotions often feel visceral and profoundly agitating (not the non-conscious ones, however). What we should not do is to associate a given emotion type with any one particular sort of feeling state. Furthermore, we should understand correctly what the agitation is. What feels wrenching and visceral about emotions is often not independent of their cognitive dimension. The death of a loved individual is unlike a stomach virus because it violently tears the fabric of attachment, hope, and expectation that we have built up around that person.

What is true of feelings appears to be true, as well, of physical states. Although we are learning more about the brain and its role in emotions of many kinds, and although we should certainly learn as much as we can, we do not yet have an account of any particular emotion, not even the relatively simple emotion of fear, that identifies it with changes of a particular sort in a particular area of the brain. Studying the work of Joseph Le Doux, I conclude (agreeing with him) that we have reason to think that fear has precursors or common concomitants in a particular area of the brain, but that this does not entail that, once fear is learned, there could be no case of the emotion that was not accompanied by changes in that part of the brain. Once again, the case of the fear of death is instructive.

I do not rely on this relatively controversial aspect of my theory anywhere in the present book, although it still seems to me to be correct and important. I do not think that it is even that controversial if all my qualifications are taken duly into account.

Next, investigating the emotions of nonhuman animals in chapter 2, I argue that we should not understand the cognitive content of emotions to involve, in every case, anything like the acceptance of a linguistically formulable proposition. Many emotions, both nonhuman and human, involve only an evaluatively laden sort of seeing-as, where a creature sees an object as salient for its well-being. Where humans are concerned, such simpler emotions are particularly common in prelinguistic infants, but they can persist in adulthood as well, as many infantile emotions do. Moreover, even with complex emotions that have something like a propositional structure, it would be wrong to think that this structure always takes a linguistic form or could be formulated in language without awkward translation. Thinking about emotion in music (which I study in chapter 5) informs us that language is not the only symbolic structure capable of rich emotional expressiveness, and there is no reason to think that the linguistic formulation of an emotion is always primary.

Chapter 3 then turns to the role of society and social norms in constructing an emotional repertory. The cognitive content of emotions is shaped in many ways by specific social norms and specific societal circumstances. These give instructions for the manifestation of an emotion, but they also more deeply shape the appraisals that make up an emotion, and may create specific types of emotion that are unique to a given society. General shared features of human life also exert a major influence, but even those shared circumstances (mortality, bodily illness) are differently shaped in different societies. Sometimes divergent social norms shape only people's views about the proper objects of a given emotion (what it is appropriate to fear, or grieve for). But sometimes, in addition, they shape the emotional taxonomy itself, producing subtly different forms of anger, grief, and fear. Thus, applying that account to the present case, anger is in a way a cultural universal, since in all societies people react to wrongful damages and wish for payback; but specific forms of anger are strongly shaped by social norms regarding what an insult is, what honor is, what manliness is, and so forth.

I then study (in chapter 4) the developmental character of human emotions. Our earliest emotional experiences precede the acquisition of language and even the secure individuation of objects. Moreover, causal thinking of the type involved in anger, though earlier than many have thought, still takes time to develop. Such facts color not only the emotional life of infancy but also a person's later history. Archaic patterns often persist into adult life, underneath the often sophisticated structure of adult love and grief. (This part of *Upheavals* parallels the account of human development in chapter 7 of my *Political Emotions*, which, however, goes beyond it in many respects, discussing the role of love in overcoming infantile anxiety and guilt.)

An issue of particular delicacy is the difficulty of distinguishing between "background emotions" that persist through situations of many types, and moods. Moods (as I understand them) are objectless states, lacking the intentionality of full-fledged emotions. An objectless sadness, a global fearfulness, a chronic irritability, an endogenous state of depression, all are moods. However, given the imperfection of our self-knowledge, it is very difficult to distinguish these from emotions whose object is either highly general or unknown to the person. Take depression. Some depressions may have purely chemical causes, and no object. But sometimes people are depressed about their lives and prospects in a very general way. Their depression has an object, albeit a highly general one. Or they may be depressed about some crisis or loss in early life and are not fully aware of this. In such cases therapeutic work is frequently needed to uncover the roots of the depression, determining whether it has an object, and, if so, what. The same thing is true with fear.

What about anger? People who are chronically irritable often are really angry at something or someone, but just can't uncover the roots of their emotional state. Or their anger may have a highly general object: a universe that they perceive as unfair to them, or just a set of life-prospects in which they are never treated with the respect that is their due. As we've had reason to see, such irritability may be connected to a sense of helplessness: people can feel extremely vulnerable and in consequence feel that the "slings and arrows of outrageous fortune" are wrongly directed at them. Is there any irritability that is purely endogenous and lacking intentionality? Certain physical states (for example, premenstrual tension, in at least some women's experience) often do appear to predispose a person to annoyance or anger; but perhaps they do so through creating a feeling of powerlessness or weakness or unattractiveness that then predisposes the person to think the world, or the people in her life, are against her in some way, rather than through direct endogenous causation. The entire question is difficult, and badly understood.

The existence of such difficult borderline cases, however, does not call an intentionalist account of emotions into question. Any category-demarcation is likely to yield unclear cases, since the world is not preordered for the convenience of philosophers.

Appendix B: Anger and Blame

If anger has been too little analyzed in the recent philosophical literature, this may be in part because the focus of discussion has been elsewhere. The analysis of "blame" has moved to center stage, inspiring work of high quality and diverse viewpoints. Even though, as the editors of a fine recent anthology on the topic hold, "work on blame is still in its infancy,"[1] there is enough philosophically valuable work that any project like mine needs to pause and situate itself in relation to this burgeoning literature.

The form of this literature is a familiar one in philosophical analysis. Candidate definitions are proposed and debated, against an implicit background assumption that a unitary account is the right goal. Although some participants in the debate emphasize the flexibility of their accounts, and the way in which they can allegedly accommodate different types of blame, there is little or no skepticism about unity, at least at a general level.

Some concepts, perhaps most concepts, are well illuminated in this way, provided that the unitary account is flexible enough to cover disparate instances of the phenomenon in question. There are, however, other concepts that are so deeply ambiguous at their core that the single term conceals more than it reveals. In an influential essay on the idea of privacy, Judith Jarvis Thomson made a very strong case against the search for a unitary account of that term.[2] The values of informational secrecy, personal autonomy, seclusion, and perhaps yet others that are standardly picked out under that rubric are so heterogeneous in nature and function that it is more misleading than useful to treat privacy as a single notion for which we need simply to search for the best single account. I have followed Thomson, arguing that the public/private antithesis is so profoundly multiple that using these terms without immediate disambiguation misleads political and legal analysis.[3] Some so-called "privacy interests" are interests in shielding personal information from prying eyes. Others involve a desire for seclusion or solitude. But still others have nothing to do with either secrecy or solitude, and have to do, instead, with personal control or autonomy. Contraception, for example, is misleadingly protected under "privacy" rights, because what is really at stake is the decisional autonomy to use contraception—whether it is used in seclusion or publicly (Bill Baird, plaintiff in one important case,[4] gave contraceptives to young women at a public event), and whether or not its use is a secret. The use of the word "privacy" misleads judges, at times, into thinking that the acts that are protected are only those in a privileged and secluded place (e.g., the marital home), or acts that are characterized by intimate association. Thus there is a tendency to think that sexual autonomy gets special protection when it comes into play in a place of privileged seclusion, though why this should be so is never argued: the unitary term substitutes for argument. Things would have been much clearer had different words been used—"rights of informational secrecy," "decisional autonomy-rights," "rights of seclusion"—which would of course not prevent people from asking what relationships might obtain among the phenomena those different words introduce.

Let's assume for the sake of argument that Thomson and I are correct: the term "privacy" is not useful, since it conceals differences that are at least as significant as any common ground among the different notions that it standardly introduces. Now the question is, is "blame" more like "privacy," or more like the many other notions that do seem to be illuminated, up to a certain point anyway, by a unitary analysis?[5] The former, I believe; but argument is needed, given that many excellent people hold the latter as a working assumption.

We should begin by reviewing the main candidates for a unitary account that have been offered.

One common account of blame is *judgmental*: to blame someone is to judge that the person acted wrongly (or morally wrongly, if moral blame is the focus).[6] (Sometimes this is called a "judgment of blameworthiness," but let us eschew that circular term.) Some versions specify the nature of the judgment more narrowly: it is a negative judgment pertaining to the moral virtues; or a judgment of ill will. To this account a variety of objections have been raised, all involving the idea that it does not capture the human depth or force of blame.

At the other end of the spectrum, so to speak, is an account that makes blame not psychological at all, but a type of action: to blame is to punish, or sanction in some other way. Such accounts, it is claimed, cannot do justice to hidden or unexpressed blame, or, indeed, to blame where the person is not in a position to act against the aggressor.

Strawson's very influential account, further developed by Wallace, defines blame in terms of the "reactive attitudes": to blame is to experience resentment and other such attitudes, which involve at least some renunciation of good will and at least some "modification . . . of the general demand that another should, if possible, be spared suffering."[7] (To the extent that Strawson and Wallace fail to analyze these emotions, their view is actually a family of views, depending on whether one would adopt a non-cognitive account of anger or some variety of cognitive account. In the latter case the reactive attitudes account would overlap partly, though not totally, with the judgmental account.) Critics object, however, that one can blame someone without hostile or punitive emotions.

George Sher concludes that the element that has to be added to the judgment of wrongdoing in order to get blame is a backward-looking desire that the person not have so acted.[8] This account, he argues, is broad enough to cover both wrongdoing by people we know and wrongdoing by strangers. It can be objected, however, that Sher's account fails to cover a case where a loved one (say, an erring child) has done wrong; the parent both believes he has done wrong and wishes he hadn't, but may have an attitude more akin to grief and compassion than to blame.

Thomas Scanlon's influential account insists, like Sher's, that blame does not require punitive attitudes, but does go beyond a judgment of wrongdoing. Instead, Scanlon argues, blame is best understood in terms of a modification in the relationship between wrongdoer and wronged. Friendship-defining intentions are reciprocal, and so the recognition that the other party has acted with ill will leads the wronged party to withdraw good will.[9] This account is obviously rich and significant; but it has encountered a number of objections. Those who like the Strawsonian account feel that it does not do justice to the intensity and heat of blame.[10] Sher believes that it cannot do justice to the blame of strangers—although Scanlon has anticipated this objection, insisting that a bare moral relationship connects us to all moral agents. Finally, Angela Smith argues that it cannot handle the mother/criminal son example any better than Sher's account: for the mother may indeed modify her attitudes, intentions, and expectations toward the son, but she might do so by showing extra love and affection. Surely it would be strange to think of this modification as a way of blaming him.

Finally, Angela Smith suggests that the most inclusive account of blame, and one that really gets at the common link among all the cases of genuine blame, is one that invokes the idea of protest (in addition to the judgment of wrongdoing). Smith builds on Scanlon, saying that blame requires, and is constituted by, both a judgment of wrongdoing and a particular sort of modification of attitudes, namely one that is a protest against "the moral claim implicit in [the wrongdoer's] conduct, where such protest implicitly seeks some kind of moral acknowledgment on the part of the blameworthy agent and/or on the part of others in the moral community."[11]

Smith's account is in many ways attractive, but it appears to purchase inclusiveness at the price of vagueness: for (in addition to the circularity involved in the term "blameworthy person"), the definition pushes off much of the indeterminacy of blame itself onto the equally indeterminate notion of protest. Is protest an action? A set of reactive emotions? What does it add to the modification of relationships, or what particular type of modification does it introduce? Smith makes it clear that it introduces an idea of weight or seriousness (since she gives an example of a person who acts wrongly in a silly way, and she thinks he acted wrongly, but can't blame him because it is just too silly). She also suggests that protest is closely linked to apology and forgiveness, and perhaps she thinks of it as including a demand for apology, but this remains inchoate, and I suspect that if she did make this a necessary condition of blame, the account would lose the virtue of inclusiveness.

What should we make of all this? We have certainly learned a lot about different types and instances of blame from these accounts. What remains to be clarified is whether they possess the sort of unity that would make us conclude that one account is right and the others wrong, or whether we should, instead, conclude that they are descriptions of different phenomena somewhat misleadingly grouped under a single rubric. Is there a shared core running through all the cases? Insofar as there is, it is well expressed by Smith as the idea that blame is "a response to a person on the basis of some wrongful, objectionable, or untoward conduct on her part."[12]

It seems to me that in some cases (let's call them Cases A), a judgment of wrongfulness is all that there is: the response is just that. The word "blame" includes such cases, and such cases are important to my account, which insists on accountability but urges non-anger. The term "blame" also includes cases (Cases B) in which there is a judgment accompanied by anger; and, if one holds a non-cognitive account of anger, it may even include cases in which there is anger but no judgment. These too are genuine cases of "blame." It seems right to point out that Cases B are not like Cases A, but not right to say that the word "blame" is incorrectly applied to Cases A. At least it seems natural to use the term of cases in the A range. Some further cases to which the word is plausibly and correctly applied, Cases C, are Scanlon/ Smith cases, in which there may be no hostile emotion, but, instead, modifications of relationship. I see no reason to think that the only sort that is correctly called "blame" is the sort in which there is a protest (though I feel I don't understand that notion very well). Scanlon's type of case, in which a judgment of wrongdoing is simply accompanied by distancing, seems perfectly recognizable as a case to which the term is rightly applied, although Smith is right to point out that it is different in interesting ways from her central cases. Finally, we have a group of Cases, Cases D (Sher cases), in which what is added to the judgment is a retrospective wish rather than any sort of forward-looking modification. While it is certainly important to say that many cases of blame are not like this, being prospective rather than retrospective, is the word "blame" inaptly used of such cases? This seems unclear. Possibly Smith's case of the loving and indulgent mother is a borderline case, even for the very most inclusive use of the term. She does judge that her son acted wrongfully, so her case is at least a case of type A. I think what Smith is getting at is that her emotional attitudes are so positive and so out of kilter with the judgment of wrongdoing that it's possible she is simply mouthing the judgment and doesn't really believe it. If that is her attitude, she does not blame him. But if she really truly judges that he acted wrongfully, but loves him more than ever, why isn't that a case rightly called "blame"? We should not grant as a matter of conceptual analysis that people cannot combine a judgment of accountability with love and generosity: indeed that combination, which interests me greatly, seems common, though certainly not common enough.

In short, while it is very useful to distinguish these different cases, and while we surely learn a lot from the distinctions that these fine philosophers have introduced, human reactions come in many types, and the word "blame" is very imprecise. Maybe it's not quite as duplicitous as "privacy," which covers things that have no common thread at all. But it's pretty empty and uninformative.

As far as my project goes, it seems important to remember that there can be cases of blame (A, C, and D) that do not involve anger and its hostile payback wishes. Indeed I make much of these possibilities. This important set of possibilities can be discerned in the literature on blame, but we learn about it more in spite of the literature than because of it. Insofar as all these fine philosophers are pursuing a single essence, they appear to be pursuing a will-o'-the-wisp.

Appendix C: Anger and Its Species

My strategy in this book is to work with a generic notion of anger, to define it as a genus, and to introduce pertinent variations through description of cases. In one case ("Transition-Anger") I introduce a technical term to characterize a borderline species that lacks one prominent feature of the genus (the payback wish). This strategy follows that of Aristotle, and especially clearly that of the Greek and Roman Stoics; numerous later thinkers, including Butler and Smith, follow the same strategy.

The Stoics were obsessed with definitions in the emotional realm, and they have left us lists upon lists of definitions of the major emotion-types and their more concrete species.[1] (These categories are rendered into Latin by Cicero in the *Tusculan Disputations*, with some alterations necessitated by linguistic and cultural differences.)

As I have mentioned in the text, the Stoics categorize anger (*orgē* is their generic term, as it is Aristotle's) as among those emotions that are defined by a favorable attitude toward a future good. That is because they place the payback wish in a central position. Their generic definition refers to the wish for payback, but also to the belief that one has been wronged; so it is in essence like Aristotle's, with the reference to "down-ranking" replaced (correctly) by a more general reference to wrongfulness.[2]

In some recent philosophical discussions, one encounters a different approach, usually without explicit defense. People suggest (although they don't really argue) that there are a number of different things, "anger," "resentment," "indignation," and others, which are not related as species of a genus. What is this all about, and what significance does it have for my project?

Three different issues deserve attention. First, many people hold that there are emotions in the area of anger that are specifically moral, which have a moral judgment as part of their content, and that these are worth being treated as separate emotions, rather than as types of anger. "Resentment" and "indignation" are the ones usually singled out in this way. I have argued that the generic emotion, anger, does contain a judgment of wrongfulness. So the question for me, then, is whether "resentment" contains a particular type of judgment of wrongfulness, namely, a moral type? I think our linguistic intuitions just do not support that claim. When a person describes her emotion as resentment, that typically would suggest that she believes it has some grounds. But must those always be moral grounds? If a person is insulted in a typical down-ranking way, she might well say, "I resent that." If a school rejects one's child as an applicant, the aggrieved parent, believing that the school was both careless and mistaken, might say that she resents the way the school acted—without even raising the question whether a moral principle was involved. "Indignation" is similarly slippery. I can be "indignant" about insults to status and rank, about nonmoral affronts of many kinds. So, although many cases of resentment and indignation are surely moral, I don't think they all are. We can do better, I think, by focusing on the generic term with its implied judgment of wrongfulness, and then getting clear, in each case, about what type of judgment it is.[3]

In other words, I don't omit morally grounded anger, I just prefer to use the generic term "anger," and then to characterize the case by further description, rather than by trying to make the imprecise terms of daily language do that for me.

A second issue that is often raised, implicitly or explicitly, is whether there are species of anger that do not involve a payback wish. I have dealt with that question at length in chapter 2, arguing that there is such a borderline case, although it is rarer than we often like to think. I introduce the technical term "Transition-Anger" for this case, defining it as anger, or quasi-anger, that lacks the payback wish. The ordinary word "indignation," as I note there, often characterizes an attitude that lacks a payback wish, but by no means always. So I prefer the technical term.

Third, we must ask whether there are types of anger that are wholly without a judgment of wrongfulness. I think one reason why people like to focus on the terms "resentment" and "indignation" is that they want to emphasize the presence of a judgment of wrongfulness, and they are not convinced that anger by itself entails this. I've already discussed this question, but let me do so a little further. When anger bursts out suddenly, it may appear to onlookers to be without a judgment. But of course many cognitive attitudes that are based on habit and on deeply internalized patterns of thinking erupt suddenly, without the implication that there is no judgment involved. Every time we walk, we rely on a whole host of beliefs about the world that we do not pause to inspect consciously: that objects are solid, that things obey the laws of gravity, etc. The absence of conscious focus does not entail that we are not using beliefs. In my view, anger is often like these cases: its patterns can be laid down in childhood, and these habitual patterns may guide behavior, on many occasions, without conscious focus. I have suggested, consistently with that view, that anger always contains a cognitive appraisal, even if stored deeply in the psyche and not fully formulated. It may certainly be true that in the cases we call "resentment" there is apt to be a conscious focus on the wrongfulness, but of course that is true of all sorts of cases in which we use the term "anger."

What about the anger of young infants? With many emotions, as I discussed in Appendix A, there will be varieties that rest upon "seeing-as" and not full-fledged judgment. Thus the fear of many animals is probably best described as nonjudgmental, and that of very young infants as well. Anger seems more complicated, since it requires causal thinking. If infants bawl in rage, with no sense of wrongful injury at all, that might be metaphorically described as anger, but it really lacks something that infants acquire soon enough—by the age of one, it now appears—namely the idea that some type of wrong is being done. Paul Bloom's research has shown that very young infants have incipient judgments of fairness, right, and wrong.[4] As soon as those thoughts are present, even in an inchoate form, we have, I believe, full-fledged anger. Before that, we have something that may be on the border of anger but is not yet anger. I'm inclined to think that many fewer animals have full-fledged anger than have fear, simply because anger requires more complicated cognitions.

We can certainly debate these boundaries, and we should. What is pertinent to my enterprise here, though, is that there is a phenomenon that we typically use the word "anger" to describe, which does involve some type of thought of wrongfulness, however inchoate, however inarticulate.

What about "irritation"? This is an interesting case, because it refers to phenomena of two distinct sorts, which are difficult to distinguish for the reasons given in Appendix A. On the one hand, the term "irritation" may mark a case of genuine anger in which the consequences for well-being are not thought to be terribly severe. But "irritation" may also designate a persistent mood that does not rest on a judgment of wrongfulness, and indeed that may altogether lack an intentional object. We would call the person in such a state "irritable," but we might call the state one of "irritation," just as we would use the term "depression" for a mood of a different sort. As I argued in Appendix A, only a prolonged inspection of a particular case can inform us whether there is an intentional object or not. "Annoyance" seems ambiguous in a similar way, though perhaps it is more likely to denote a mild state of anger that has an intentional object.[5]

Two other terms, "rage" and "fury," clearly characterize cases of anger, usually indicating that the anger has either unusual intensity or unusual suddenness, or both. There is no reason to think that the terms designate a phenomenon without cognition, and in fact the desire for payback often fuels anger of this intense sort. (One *locus classicus* is Aeneas' slaying of Turnus at the end of the *Aeneid, furiis accensus*.)

I conclude that it is best to operate, as I have, with generic term "anger," defining its species by description of specific cases and types of case. A rare exception, the borderline phenomenon that I call Transition-Anger, is best designated by a technical term, since the natural-language terms are used imprecisely with regard to the key issue at stake.

Notes

FRONTMATTER

1. My translation. *Preumenōs*, the word I translate as "with a gentle-temper," is from the same word-family as the adjective *praos* and the noun *praotēs*, Aristotle's terms for gentleness of temper in the quote below and elsewhere. (The word is usually translated "mildness," but that suggests context-neutral lack of affect, whereas Aristotle is talking about a way of treating people that aims at situational appropriateness, and is not incompatible with strong affect.)

CHAPTER 1

1. Aeschylus, *Eumenides*, translation and commentary by Hugh Lloyd-Jones (Englewood Cliffs: Prentice-Hall, 1970), 76.
2. Translations mine, with influence from Lattimore. Remarkably, she pauses long enough to mention that she knows what Gorgons look like, since she has seen them in a painting by Phineas.
3. He mentions various cruel punishments that are associated in Greek lore with Persian despotism.
4. On the various species of the genus anger, see Appendix C.
5. Wild dogs feed their puppies by chewing and swallowing the kill, then vomiting it up again in a more digestible form.

6. I write this after many hours of unfortunately close observation of wild dogs in Botswana. Strictly speaking, "African wild dogs" are not actual dogs, if we mean members of the genus *Canis*: their biological name is *Lycaon pictus*; they are thus canids but not canines.

7. See Allen (2000) and Allen (1999).

8. See Gewirtz (1988). Gewirtz rightly emphasizes that Athena has already gone ahead without them. The question is not whether the law courts will exist: they do exist. The only question is whether they will join or oppose.

9. I typically follow Lloyd-Jones's excellent and very faithful translations, unless I want to bring out a point by greater literalness.

10. She exempts foreign war, which they are permitted to encourage.

11. See note 1 above. The term surely suggests that they have put their anger to one side, although it doesn't clearly connote complete renunciation of anger.

12. Of course "Eumenides" is, in real Greek life, a cautious euphemism as used by citizens of these goddesses, but Aeschylus is doing something else with it. The ex-Furies are explicitly called *metoikoi*, resident aliens, and the group of escorts is said by Athena to be composed of those who guard her shrine—thus priestesses of the cult of Athena Polias.

13. For the general shift in attitudes to punishment that occurred in the fifth century, see Harriss (2001). This important and remarkable study provides an extremely convincing argument that the Greeks and Romans came to criticize the spirit of payback, and anger seen as involving it. Harriss documents the shift in speaking of punishment from the *timor-* word-family, denoting payback, to the *kolazein* family, denoting punishment without implication of payback. The shift Harriss documents, as he emphasizes on p. 26 and elsewhere, involves non-intellectuals as well as intellectuals, although intellectuals play a prominent role.

14. In this regard, the opera is the exact inversion of Mozart's *Le Nozze di Figaro*, in which every phrase, even those of the "bad" characters, is illuminated by love. Strauss wrote his own *Figaro*—in *Der Rosenkavalier*.

15. *Suggnōmē:* sometimes this is translated "forgiveness," but it just means "thinking-with," i.e., participatory understanding, and its connection to forgiveness is added by modern theorists and translators. See below note 29, and further in chapter 3. Aristotle's position is not mine, because he still recommends revenge in some cases, particularly in connection with family bonds.

16. For the place of the *Eumenides* in the evolving Greek critique of anger, see Harriss (2001, 162).

17. As Harriss argues, this position becomes gradually more common in Greece and Rome.

18. See also Konstan (2010), to be discussed further in chapter 3.

19. See Griswold (2007, xxiii). Griswold does not unequivocally endorse this development. His first-rate, subtle, and carefully argued book is an indispensable starting point for any further work on these questions, especially work like mine, which disagrees with some of his main contentions.

20. Murray (2010). The book itself is actually a great deal better than its title, and, not coincidentally, has nothing to do with forgiveness: the author's generous and nonjudgmental attitude toward her parents is evident throughout. She does not even contemplate forgiving them, because she simply loves them.

21. Murphy (2003, viii).

22. See chapter 7.

23. Griswold's book is the best example, in its detail and thoroughness, and it gives a balanced discussion of many other people's views and a full bibliography.

24. Leading examples are Murphy (2003) and Miller (2006).

25. See Murphy (2003, ix and 19).

26. See Griswold (2007) and Konstan (2010). Konstan refers to this form of forgiveness as capturing "the strict or ample sense of the English word" (57), and as forgiveness "in the full sense of the word" (57).

27. From the *Dies Irae*, incorporated in the Requiem Mass: *Liber scriptus proferetur, in quo totum continetur, unde mundus iudicetur* (A written book will be brought forth, in which everything is contained from which the world will be judged). For full text, see appendix to chapter 3.

28. The hymn continues: *Oro supplex et acclinis, cor contritum quasi cinis: gere curam mei finis* (I implore, bent down, a suppliant, my heart as contrite as ashes, show concern for my end).

29. *Suggnōmē*, often wrongly associated with forgiveness (above n. 15), and even translated that way: see the Oxford translation of Aristotle, *Nicomachean Ethics* IV.5, 1126a1–3. Griswold's discussion of the Greeks also goes too far at times in this direction: see p. 4 and note 5. I used the term "forgiveness" loosely in part of my discussion of Aristotle's *Rhetoric* in Nussbaum (1999a, 161), and hereby withdraw that sentence! An important point made by Konstan (2010) is that *suggnōmē*, unlike forgiveness, often involves denial or diminution of responsibility: see pp. 28–33, and the similar point made about Latin *ignoscere*, p. 55.

30. I agree here with Konstan (2010) and Konstan (2012, 22). The impressive emotion study of Robert Kaster comes to the same conclusion: see Kaster (2005, 80–81). Another interesting contrast is that between transactional forgiveness and ancient supplication: see Naiden (2006), discussed in Konstan (2010, 13).

31. As we'll see in chapter 3, this tendency even influences translation: the Greek term *charizesthai*, which means simply "to be gracious to," often gets translated "to forgive" in the New Testament, where, however, a very different word, *aphiesthai*, is the canonical term for forgiveness.

32. Tutu (1999).

33. Segal (1970). Segal, a Classics professor, was an expert on ancient comedy, known for *Roman Laughter: The Comedy of Plautus* (1968) and *The Death of Comedy* (2001).

34. Here I shall be agreeing with Griswold, who distinguishes political apology from forgiveness.

CHAPTER 2

1. Strawson (1968). Strawson does not say that resentment is an emotion, and he does not identify it as a type of anger—although he does treat it as something one can "feel." He just is not interested in the emotions as a philosophical category. R. Jay Wallace, summarizing Strawson's views, does, however, treat the "reactive attitudes" as emotions: "On P. F. Strawson's view, emotions such as guilt, resentment, and indignation—what Strawson calls the reactive attitudes—provide the key to understanding moral responsibility and its conditions." See Wallace (1994, 18). I think Wallace is right about Strawson, but this interpretive issue plays no role in my own argument. On my view about the relationship between resentment and anger, see Appendix C.

2. See for example Hieronymi (2001).

3. See Allen (2000; 1999).

4. See Vlastos (1991).

5. Butler (1827).

6. See Santideva (1995, 45–62).

7. Strawson (1968). Strawson does mention items, including resentment, indignation, gratitude, and "moral disapprobation" (87 and elsewhere). He does not define them or investigate their internal structure, however.

8. Wallace (1994).

9. Thus a valuable recent discussion of therapy in prisons, linking that question to discussions of blame and responsibility, speaks of a long list of "hostile, negative attitudes and emotions that are typical human responses to blameworthiness: . . . for instance, hatred, anger, resentment, indignation, disgust, disapproval, contempt and scorn" (Lacey and Pickard [2013, 3]). Hieronymi (2001), similarly, emphasizes the importance of studying specific emotions before approaching the topic of forgiveness, but she really does not do this: she does not dissect different elements in anger or differentiate it from other "reactive attitudes."

10. Especially Lazarus (1991), Averill (1982), and Tavris (1982); see below.

11. For a short summary of the overall view of emotions for which I have argued in earlier work, see Appendix A.

12. I introduce this term in Nussbaum (2001).

13. See Batson (2011); Smith (1982), discussing an earthquake in China and the reaction of a "man of humanity" in Europe. I discuss this issue in Nussbaum (2013, chs. 6, 9, 10).

14. Lazarus (1991).

15. Meaning that they are token-identical to neurochemical changes in the brain.

16. On all these claims, see Nussbaum (2001, chs. 1, 2); on the role of feelings, see also Nussbaum (2004b).

17. Aristotle's project is to show orators what anger's distinctive content is, in order to help them learn how to produce it or to take it away. Thus his whole procedure assumes that anger is in large part constituted by cognitive appraisals; the orator does not light a fire in people's hearts.

18. Here I am following later versions of Aristotle's definition, which substitute wrongful injury for down-ranking, which I consider too narrow: see below.

19. The grasp may be rudimentary: Paul Bloom's research shows that babies as young as one year old have an inchoate sense of fair play and an inchoate approval of retribution. See Bloom (2013), and Appendix C.

20. Lazarus (1991, 219).

21. Arnim (1964, III.478). Compare Lazarus (1991, 224).

22. It does appear to be a male phenomenon, at least in this study. Or perhaps women who reacted angrily did not kick or rock the machine enough to topple it. Or perhaps they did not want to ruin their shoes and other clothing.

23. Tavris (1982, 164, cf. 72). See also Averill (1982, 166).

24. Butler (1827).

25. And if we accept psychoanalytic ideas of infantile omnipotence of the type expressed in Freud's "His Majesty the Baby," we can go further: the infant expects to be waited on and to be the center of the world, and considers all deviations from that state of affairs to be wrongful damage. In other words, the real and full existence of other people, with lives of their own and not just slaves of the baby, is itself a wrongful damage—a terrible problem in human development.

26. See Appendix C.

27. *De Ira* I.2. Unfortunately this part of the work has a gap, which editors fill up from quotations of the work in later Christian authors. It appears that Seneca is mentioning a number of common philosophical definitions, rather than giving his own.

28. Arnim (1964, III.397): in Greek, *ēdikēkenai dokountos*, in Latin *qui videatur laesisse iniuria*. On this shift, see also Harriss (2001, 61).

29. Lecture by Rashida Manjoo, UN Special Rapporteur on Violence Against Women, University of Chicago Law School, May 14, 2013.

30. See Hossain (2013).

31. See for example Tavris (1982, 72 and 94).

32. Lazarus (1991, 221). See Tavris (1982, 152–53).

33. See also Lazarus (1991, 225), who argues that this goal is essential to differentiate anger from anxiety.

34. On different accounts of compassion in the tradition, see Nussbaum (2001, ch. 6).

35. I heard this interview on the news while in a gym away from home and cannot document it. But it happened. Jordan, Sr., was murdered in 1993. A suspect, Daniel Andre Green, was convicted in 1996 and given a life sentence. (A jury opted not to assign the death penalty. A second suspect, Larry Demery, agreed to a plea deal in exchange for testimony implicating Green. Demery will be eligible for parole in 2016.) In April 2015 Green requested a new trial, claiming that false evidence was presented during the original trial. An FBI audit found that the State Bureau of Investigation erred in a total of 190 cases in handling blood evidence, including this case.

36. See the similar critique of payback in Brooks (2012).

37. On this see Mackie (1982). Mackie agrees with my claim that payback thinking makes no sense, calling this the "paradox of retribution." Bloom's research (2013) with young infants purports to show that the idea of fair play is present in infants under the age of one, but what it really shows is that such infants like seeing someone get a painful punishment when they have done something unfair (for example, taken something from someone else): so it shows the deep-rootedness of payback pain-for-pain ideas, as well as those of fair play.

38. See Vermeule (2011), a Darwinian account of our interest in certain story patterns.

39. Compare Mackie (1982, 5): "It should be clear beyond all question that the past wrong act, just because it is past, cannot be annulled.... The punishment may trample on the criminal, but it does not do away with the crime."

40. See the similar analysis in Murphy (1988, ch. 1) and in Murphy's other writings on this topic.

41. Hampton and Murphy (1988, 54–59).

42. See Averill (1982, 177), reporting a survey in which subjects were asked about their motives in becoming angry. The two most common were "To assert your authority" and "To get back at, or gain revenge on, the instigator."

43. For my own view about the concept of dignity and its political role, see Nussbaum (2008), summarized in Nussbaum (2010a).

44. When the Stoics said that animals are not rational, their opponents pointed to an ingenious dog allegedly belonging to Chrysippus, who came to a three-fork crossing, following a rabbit. He sniffed down the first path; no scent. He sniffed down the second; no scent. Without sniffing further, he galloped off down the third path—thus showing, they said, that he had mastered the disjunctive syllogism.

Angela might be like that dog—but as I've imagined here she is not quite as smart, since she goes part of the way down the second path before turning back.

45. On the cultural construction of the idea of closure, and its subsequent psychic reality, see Bandes (forthcoming).

46. I borrow this characterization from Harsanyi (1982).

47. I am not claiming that retributivism is all about status. As will be clear in chapter 6, I believe that retributivism suffers from the second, not the first, problem. But the correct alternative, here too, is a focus on future welfare.

48. Butler insists that anger "ought never to be made use of, but only in order to produce some greater good."

49. By which I mean rational and constructive.

50. See the longer analysis of it in Nussbaum (2013). The text of the speech can be found online at http://www.americanrhetoric.com/speeches/mlkihaveadream.htm.

51. Throughout the speech King keeps on returning to the injustices that African-Americans have suffered, but he does not indulge in payback thinking. He keeps looking forward.

52. In the larger plot of the series, McCord really is a welfarist, enduring personal ignominy to prevent revelations that he thinks will ignite a war between the United States and the Apaches.

53. Butler (1827, Sermon VIII).

54. See Bloom (2013).

55. See Hampton and Murphy (1988, 58).

56. I owe these examples to Charles Larmore and Paul Guyer.

57. See Seneca, *De Ira*, particularly I.12.

58. Bishop Butler sees anger's role as in large part motivational: see Butler (1827, Sermon VIII). He argues that compassion by itself would render the "execution of justice exceedingly difficult and uneasy."

59. See Smith (1982, 35).

60. I owe this point to Saul Levmore.

61. See Butler (1827, Sermon VIII): "Since perfect goodness in the Deity is the principle, from whence the universe was brought into being, and by which it is preserved; and since general benevolence is the great law of the whole moral creation; it is a question which immediately occurs, 'Why had man implanted in him a principle, which appears the direct contrary to benevolence?'"

62. See Santideva (1995).

63. I.48–49 = II.650–51.

64. See Harriss (2001, 31, ch. 16).

65. Lactantius, *De Ira Dei*, chs. 4 through 8. As we'll see, Lactantius has some more interesting things to say later in the treatise.

66. See also Harriss (2001, ch. 16) on struggles to reconcile biblical texts with Greco-Roman norms.

67. See the excellent discussion in Halbertal and Margalit (1992, ch. 1).

68. Lactantius, *De Ira Dei*, ch. 16.

69. See Harriss (2001, 393 and notes). Harriss also shows that Paul's statements on anger are not wholly consistent: sometimes he blames all anger, sometimes he permits some anger but urges that it be brief.

70. Briggs (1970). See my detailed discussion in Nussbaum (2001, ch. 3).

71. Briggs (1970, 330–31).

72. October 13, 1988; the question was asked by Bernard Shaw.

73. See Kindlon and Thompson (1999).

74. See Condry and Condry (1976). There are a lot of other interesting contrasts. In the experiment, the baby was the same baby, but was just differently labeled.

75. See Levmore and Nussbaum (2014).

76. See Harriss (2001, ch. 11).

77. Typical is Cicero, *Ad Quintum Fratrem* I.1.37–40, discussed in Harriss (2001, 204–5): Cicero tells his brother Quintus, then governor of a province in Asia, that his reputation for effective leadership is undermined by his evident propensity to anger, and Cicero urges him to work on himself, concluding that angry outbursts are "not only inconsistent with literary culture and *humanitas*, they are also inimical to the dignity of imperial office."

78. See Kindlon and Thompson (1999).

79. Again: by the bare term "anger" I mean garden-variety anger, not the special case of Transition-Anger.

80. I owe the question to Katerina Linos.

81. See my lengthy analysis of disgust in Nussbaum (2004a, ch. 2), with references to the psychological and philosophical literature; see also the update in Nussbaum (2010b).

82. Hence the long-standing confusion, in the law of sexual orientation, between discrimination on the basis of an act and discrimination on the basis of orientation.

83. Thus Dante's distinction between Hell and Purgatory seems somewhat arbitrary: if people are located in the former by a single act, in the latter by an enduring trait, the single act somehow becomes definitive of the person, once it becomes the basis for their eternal punishment.

84. The best treatment of contempt in the recent philosophical literature is Mason (2003).

85. Mason (2003, 241).

86. This is the central issue in Mason's fine article. Mason argues that it is justified, when contempt is properly focused on a legitimate ideal and gets things right about the person's blameworthy failure to exhibit the ideal trait.

87. For a longer discussion of envy, see Nussbaum (2013, ch. 11). A very fine analysis is in Rawls (1971, 530–34).

88. See Lazarus (1991, 254).

89. Miceli and Castelfranchi (2007).

90. Proust's novel is one classic development of that idea.

91. He analyzes anger and "being calmed down" in the *Rhetoric* II.2–3, and discusses the virtuous disposition in this area in the *Nicomachean Ethics* IV.5. The two accounts are never connected by him, but they are consistent.

92. Smith (1982, 34).

93. The Oxford translation uses "good-tempered" for the adjective and "good temper" for the noun, which is not terrible, but it seems too general, since it does not suggest a particular relation to anger.

94. The Oxford translation says "tends to forgive" for *suggnōmonikos*. But in fact there is no warrant for this: the word literally means "thinking with" and designates sympathetic understanding. See chapter 1, notes 15 and 29.

95. Konstan (2010) emphasizes that this is often the case with *suggnōmē*.

96. Of course I think all anger is inappropriate, but Aristotle does not.

97. See Marcus Aurelius, whose first lesson in avoiding anger is not to be "a fan of the Greens or Blues at the races or the light-armed or heavy-armed gladiators at the circus."

98. See Winnicott (2005).

CHAPTER 3

1. Griswold (2007, 149–50). This is not the entirety of Griswold's account, since he has a lot to say about what the forgiver should do. Konstan's account (2010) is basically the same.

2. Indeed, it is often suggested that forgiveness is incomplete without these transactional elements: thus Konstan (2010, 21 and *passim*); similarly Bash (2007), who summarizes his argument by saying that "the idea of unconditional forgiveness is difficult to defend from a pragmatic, practical, and philosophical point of view" (78), and who takes pains to show that the early Christian tradition contains the full-fledged transactional account. It will become clear that on this point I agree with Bash, and disagree with Konstan: the early tradition surely does contain this concept; however (here disagreeing with Bash), it also prominently contains ideas of unconditional forgiveness and unconditional love, and I disagree with Bash about the normative evaluation of these alternatives.

3. I shall, however, aim at greater historical detail and precision, which I think Nietzsche's general goals require.

4. I import this image of unreflective conformity from Mahler, to be discussed later in this chapter. He saw conventional Christian behavior as like the aimless and unalert swooping of the fish to whom St. Anthony preaches, appropriately represented by swooping phrases on the E-flat clarinet, whose entrance is marked "mit Humor." (The St. Anthony song in *Des Knaben Wunderhorn* was composed around the same time as the St. Anthony material in the third movement of the Second Symphony, to which I allude here: and see the detailed analysis in Nussbaum [2001, ch. 14].

5. Foucault (1975).

6. Foucault has a European audience. He is not talking about the degrading physical cruelty of actual imprisonment in the United States; he is talking about the intrusiveness and manipulativeness characteristic of programs of prison supervision and reform, with Jeremy Bentham's Panopticon prison/workhouse a leading case study.

7. God's anger often needs to be allayed by penitence, or sacrifice. In Isaiah 43:25–26, sins are apparently remitted because of an apology and an attitude of mindfulness. Similarly in Hosea 12, the prophet calls on Israel to repent, and in chapter 14, he urges a specific form of atonement, which, he imagines, will be followed by forgiveness. There are many such examples.

8. An excellent discussion of both biblical and Talmudic sources is Morgan (2011).

9. Although obviously enough Reform and Conservative Jews do not accept many aspects of this codified account—at least not its complete list of the commandments for violation of which *teshuvah* is required—there is continuous adherence, on the whole, to the overall conception of the *teshuvah* process as mapped out in the tradition. Thus Peli (2004) notes in his introduction that leading Reform rabbi Arnold Jacob Wolf praises the centrality and importance of the thought of Soloveitchik on this topic (p. 7). Soloveitchik (1903–1993), a highly influential Orthodox rabbi and professor, follows faithfully the accounts of Maimonides (twelfth century) and Yonah of Gerona (thirteenth century). (Soloveitchik's oral discourses were originally given in Yiddish but later written down in Hebrew by Peli; the English translation was done by Peli and a large group of advisors.)

10. 1138–204, often referred to as the Rambam.

11. Yonah, d. 1263, was an influential Catalonian rabbi, a first cousin of the more famous Nachmanides. The story goes that Yonah was initially a bitter opponent of Maimonides and instigated the public burning of his work by Christian authorities in Paris in 1233. He later admitted error and undertook a pilgrimage to Maimonides's grave in Palestine. However, he never got further than Toledo, where he taught for the rest of his life. However, his teachings were consistently reverential toward Maimonides. For Maimonides, I have consulted two English translations available online, one by Immanuel O'Levy (1993), and one by Rabbi Yaakov Feldman (2010). For Yonah, I use the bilingual text with translation by Shraga Silverstein (1967).

12. Soloveitchik, cited above; Deborah E. Lipstadt, contribution to Wiesenthal (1997, 193–96). Lipstadt was the defendant in a famous Holocaust denial libel trial; sued by David Irving, she won on grounds of justification.

13. See Maimonides, ch. 1.1.

14. There is an interesting dispute in the tradition about whether one ought to confess and repent for sins that one has already confessed the previous year. Yonah's view is that one should not, both because it could distract from a focus on this year's sins and because to confess again shows a lack of trust in God's forgiveness: see Yonah (1967, 379–83). The sinner should nonetheless offer a general confession of sin that in principle covers former as well as current transgressions. But Maimonides holds that one should confess former as well as current sins, to keep them before one's eyes (2.8). There is also discussion of how many times one must confess on Yom Kippur. Maimonides mentions that one ought to confess before eating the large pre-fast meal, even though one is about to spend an entire day confessing repeatedly—because one might choke on the meal and die, and thus never get to the main confession (Maimonides, 2.6).

15. Maimonides, 1.4.

16. Soloveitchik emphasizes a traditional distinction between *kapparah* (acquittal) and *taharah* (purification): for the former, remorse is sufficient; for the latter, a revolutionary change of life and thinking is required. See Peli (2004, 49–66).

17. Maimonides, 1.5. By contrast, if the offense is only against God, one should not publicize one's repentance.

18. Ch. 2.2. (I've replaced the translator's "to never do" by "never to do.")

19. Ch. 2.4. Cf. Yonah (1967, 31).

20. Ch. 3.4: he connects the *shofar* particularly with charitable deeds and asserts that Jews are more charitable in the period between Rosh Hashanah and Yom Kippur than at other times.

21. Maimonides, 2.1.

22. Maimonides, 2.1.

23. Yonah (1967, 92).

24. Yonah (1967, 39).

25. Yonah (1967, 59).

26. Maimonides, 2.10. See Yonah (1967, 377).

27. For the dead, the transgressor brings ten men to the grave and makes a confession; if money is owed he pays the inheritors. But if he doesn't know them, he leaves the money with the court and makes confession there.

28. Compare John 7:53–8.11, where the woman taken in adultery is apparently offered a conditional forgiveness: "Go, and sin no more."

29. See the detailed philological discussion of the Greek text in Bash (2007, 80–87). As a Christian theologian, however, he may be imputing too much unity and

consistency to these early texts: John practiced baptism before Jesus died, and may have had no clear idea that a further necessary condition remained to be supplied.

30. John does not require sacrifices or offerings, presumably thinking that the ritual of repentance takes the place of this Jewish ritual of atonement: see Bash (2007, 81–82), emphasizing again that repentance, while necessary for forgiveness, is not sufficient.

31. Thus, the Book of Common Prayer asks the parents and godparents (or any old enough to speak for themselves): "Do you renounce Satan and all the spiritual forces of wickedness that rebel against God?" Answer: "I renounce them." Question: "Do you renounce the evil powers of this world which corrupt and destroy the creatures of God?" Answer: "I renounce them." Question: "Do you renounce all sinful desires that draw you from the love of God?" Answer: "I renounce them." And the ritual continues with much about accepting Jesus as one's savior and trusting and obeying him.

32. See appendix to this chapter for the full text of the hymn. It remains in the Tridentine Mass today, and is still a respected text, although, with other depictions of suffering in Hell, it has been de-emphasized.

33. This work predates Tertullian's split from mainstream Christianity and his espousal of the Montanist heresy (around 207).

34. See Hanna (1911).

35. Hanna (1911).

36. See also Konstan (2010, ch. 4).

37. Naturally, as with any generalization about Jewish norms, this one has putative exceptions. The prohibition *lo tachmod*, "Thou shalt not covet" appears to focus on attitudes, not acts, although there is much debate about this.

38. Strictly speaking one should not say "quasi," since, following the Greek and Roman Stoics, this tradition thinks of inner movements as fully acts. The Stoic rationale is that they involve "assent" to an "appearance" to which, in principle if not in fact, one might always refuse assent. Cicero even called the external action a mere "afterbirth," the core of the act being this inner performance of assent.

39. See Tertullian, *On Penitence*, section 3, in William Le Saint's translation, *Tertullian: Treatises on Penance* (Westminster, MD: Newman Press, 1959). For the Latin text, see the edition by Pierre de Labriolle (Paris: Alphonse Picard, 1906). Tertullian lived from around 160 to 225 CE; *De Paenitentia* is probably a relatively early work, from a period prior to Tertullian's break with the established Church (in the direction of greater Puritanism, as a Montanist heretic).

40. Brion and Harcourt (2012); an English version by Bernard Harcourt will soon be published.

41. But see Brion and Harcourt (2012, 104–8).

42. Brion and Harcourt (2012, 124–60).

43. Thus, unabsolved sexual sin, when heterosexual, puts one in the circle of Hell in which we find Paulo and Francesca, and when homosexual, in the much lower circle of the "violent against nature"; characteristic but absolved lustfulness, whether same-sex or opposite-sex, puts one in a relatively cheerful circle of Purgatory in which one encounters all the famous poets, learning chastity through long penance.

44. And the occasion is all too often turned into a type of prurient control over young "transgressors."

45. For some very different studies coming to this conclusion, see Boyarin (1995); Kugel (1999); Schofer (2010).
46. *De Paenitentia*, section 9. Since the term is Greek, it is clearly already in use before Tertullian (the first major Christian thinker to write in Latin), but he is credited with codifying it into a set of practices supervised by religious authorities.
47. Nietzsche (1989).
48. See also Daniel 9:9.
49. This passage is not in the best manuscripts, so it may not be contemporaneous with the rest of the text. There is also the problem that ignorance mitigates culpability, so it is not terribly clear whether Jesus is offering forgiveness in the usual sense.
50. See above n. 31.
51. The difficult phrase "give place to anger" seems to mean clearing the way for God's promised vengeance.
52. For extensive extracts from the statements, see Stewart and Pérez-Peña (2015) and Nahorniak (2015).
53. Its aftermath has certainly been Transitional, in the debates over the removal of the Confederate flag from the state capitol, and the somewhat surprisingly lopsided votes that led, on July 9, to the final passage of a law ordering its removal.
54. See for example Matthew 19:19, 22:39; Mark 12:31, John 13:34, 15:12.
55. A salient example is Ephesians 4:30–32, where *charizesthai* just means "be gracious," "be generous," and does not entail a reference to antecedent anger—and yet it is translated "forgive" in all translations I have been able to find. The standard word for forgiveness, *aphiēmi*, is not found anywhere in the context. On mistranslations of biblical texts concerning forgiveness, see also Konstan (2010, 99). Konstan's entire chapter 4 is a valuable treatment of the biblical material, both Hebrew and Greek.
56. My own translation; the precise distinction intended between *thumos* and *orgē* is not entirely clear.
57. I have modified the King James Version, substituting "wrongs you" for "trespasses against you," and removing the gratuitous verbal additions in verse 4.
58. Luke 15:12–34, King James Version, with two alterations: I have put "and before you" in verse 21 as in verse 18, since the Greek is exactly the same; for no particular reason the translator has put "and in thy sight" the second time. Both are fine translations; the point is that the two statements ought to be exactly the same. The second change is more important: In verse 20, *esplanchnisthē* is translated "and had compassion," which is too flat and weak for this rare word, and also inaccurately implies that the father was aware of the son as suffering, or in a bad way.
59. The metaphor is from sacrifice, where the entrails of the victim are removed and devoured. See LSJ, s.v. *splanchneuō*. Such is the prestige of the King James Version that the nineteenth-century lexicographers also list a metaphorical meaning "Have compassion," for which they attest only this passage—one reason why one should always look beyond the lexicon. In the New Testament, the word does occur a few more times, but not enough that we should think that the reference to "guts" has been lost and it has become a dead metaphor.
60. On the classical antecedents of this generous spirit, see Harriss's discussion (2001) of the ideal of *philophrosunē*, p. 149, and of Roman *humanitas*, p. 205.
61. I have analyzed the symphony in detail in Nussbaum (2001, ch. 14).

62. Mahler, program for the Dresden 1901 performance; quoted in De La Grange (1973, 785–86), with a more literal rendering of the second paragraph substituted for his.

63. De La Grange (1973, 786).

64. Wagner (1850).

65. Mahler frequently characterized musical creativity as feminine in its emotionality and receptivity (see Nussbaum 2001).

66. See my discussion of *geschlagen* as both "heartbeat" and "downbeat" in Nussbaum (2001).

67. Strictly speaking, the father is never angry with the son at all, so far as the story tells us.

68. See Nussbaum (2001) for a more detailed argument on this point.

69. An interesting case in point is Britten's *War Requiem*, in which greed, anger, and destructive resentment certainly make their appearance—but then are sur-mounted, in settings of texts by Wilfred Owen that contrast the unconditional love of Jesus with the practices of the organized Church. More generally, it is interesting that music expressing (officially) a longing for revenge often expresses this-worldly joy instead. Thus the "revenge duet" in Verdi's *Rigoletto*, "Si, ven-detta," is actually full of joyful energy. When my daughter was three, it was her favorite piece of music on account of its joyfulness, and of course she had no idea what it was supposed to be "saying." A search for real musical revenge would take us quickly to the realm of stifling and oppressive music, as with my com-ments about Strauss's *Elektra* in chapter 1.

70. Thus Schoenberg could not permit Moses to sing, in his opera *Moses und Aron*: the religious attitude must be expressed in speech, leaving operatic music to Aaron and his followers.

71. Perhaps these examples just go to show that Mozart and Verdi were joyous and generous souls, who wrote Requiem masses out of cultural convention, rather than because of any profound spiritual affinity—as indeed is often said about the Verdi work. But the inner connection of music with love seems to me to lie deeper, and it is difficult indeed to think whom one would commission to compose a Requiem in the spirit of the analysis of divine anger I have presented. Of course a composer can ventriloquize the mentality I have described without writing an entire work in its spirit (as Wagner superbly ventriloquizes loveless narcissism in the music of Alberich and Hagen, though the work as a whole is supremely concerned with loving generosity). But an entire Mass? Wouldn't this be like an entire *Ring* sung by Alberich and Hagen? I have suggested that *Elektra* is like that, but it is a short work designed to be almost unendurable, and it is an outlier in Strauss's output.

72. In what follows, I am indebted to Halbertal (forthcoming), so far published only in Hebrew, but an English translation was made for the author by Joel Linsider, and sent to me for reference. A short version was published in *Jewish Review of Books*, Fall 2011.

73. See Halbertal (forthcoming).

74. Griswold (2007, 12–17).

75. Epictetus, *Encheiridion*, ch. 48.

CHAPTER 4

1. All translations are mine. I discuss the play in detail in Nussbaum (1994b, ch. 12)

2. Again, we can note that the Greeks and Romans typically do not hold this view. Indeed they are inclined to think that even should some people think anger

attractive in the outer world, they will quickly grant that it is destructive in the family. See Harriss (2001, 29), discussing Cicero, *Tusculan Disputations* 4.54. Cicero addresses the Peripatetics, who defend a moderate anger (rather than, as Cicero prefers, its complete elimination): "This warrior irascibility of yours, when it has come back home, what is it like with your wife, children, and slaves? Do you think that it's useful there too?"

3. See Hieronymi (2001).

4. The case of anger between siblings is fascinating, but my account can easily be extrapolated to fit it. Anger at strangers who damage one of our loved ones will be discussed in the next chapter.

5. See Sherman (1989, ch. 4 and 118–56).

6. Baier died in New Zealand in November 2012, at the age of eighty-three. Apart from her many other accomplishments, she was the first woman in almost a hundred years to be President of the Eastern Division of the American Philosophical Association (in 1990, and preceded only by Mary Whiton Calkins in 1918), and the first woman ever to give the Carus Lectures in that same association.

7. See Baier (1995), "Trust and Anti-Trust" and other essays. For two other good philosophical accounts, see Hawley (2012) and O'Neill (2002).

8. Thus I agree in part and disagree in part with Hardin (2006). Hardin holds that trust is "cognitive," meaning that it involves beliefs. Since he does not tell the reader whether he thinks that emotions are partly cognitive, it is not possible to tell whether he would agree with my claim that trust involves the sort of cognitive appraisal that frequently plays a constituent role in an emotion. He then says that because trust is cognitive it is not possible to decide to trust—thereby bypassing a large philosophical debate about whether one can decide to believe something, and simply failing to consider the sort of willingness to be vulnerable that is in part a life-choice.

9. See Lerner (1985), to be discussed in what follows.

10. Butler (1827, Sermon 9).

11. Williams, "Persons, Character, and Morality," in Williams (1982, 1–19). In its original context the phrase refers to the moral reasoning of a man who saves his wife in a lifeboat situation, not with the thought that it is his wife, but rather, "that it was his wife and that in situations of this kind it is permissible to save one's wife" (18). My use of the phrase is thus quite different and does not require the repudiation of impartial morality. Its link with Williams is that both of us oppose a spirit of moral discipline and strict moral scrutiny that he associates with Kant and I with one strand in Judeo-Christian ethics.

12. See Baier (1995), "Trust and Anti-Trust."

13. Dickens (2004, ch. 4). Note, too, the terrible view of animals that this comparison betrays.

14. Orwell (1952).

15. Trollope (2014, ch. 3); see my analysis in "The Stain of Illegitimacy," in Nussbaum and LaCroix (2013).

16. Dr. Thorne's fellow heretics, in the nineteenth-century British novel, are, significantly, usually either female (Peggotty, Betsey Trotwood) or true social outsiders (Mr. Dick).

17. I say this in order to include children of divorced parents who divide their time between them.

18. Or other caregivers, of course. This chapter focuses on the familiar nuclear family, but the analysis applies to any intimate group that focuses on the child's well-being.

19. See Baier (1995) again.

20. Baier (1995).

21. See Plato, *Symposium*, where, however, it is only pretty low and unimaginative people who try to make themselves immortal by having children, rather than, say, by writing books or participating in politics.

22. It's not surprising that the two brothers are not just contrasting individuals but contrasting types of American Jews. The Swede's name says it all: athletic, tall, reserved, he's the successful assimilated WASP-Jew (he even marries a former Miss New Jersey, after all, although she is a Catholic, not a WASP), whereas Jerry is closer to the urban Jewish norms Roth depicts obsessively.

23. There is one flaw in this interpretation of Swede Levov. As Zuckerman invents the past, one time, asked by the prepubescent daughter to kiss her on the lips, he briefly, but passionately, complies. One could then read Merry's later problems as imputable to him—although prior to that time she already has the stutter, the hatred of her mother, and the signs of obsessive-compulsive disorder, that form her later trajectory. I actually think the kiss a literary error of Roth's—or at least of Zuckerman's—since the character depicted throughout the novel would not do that, however Oedipal such relationships often are. Zuckerman, childless, sex-obsessed, has reconstructed history after his own fashion. But then, as Zuckerman says, "getting people right is not what living is all about anyway. It's getting them wrong that is living, getting them wrong and wrong and wrong and then, on careful reconsideration, getting them wrong again" (35).

24. Lerner (1985, 69–70).

25. Lerner (1985, 76).

26. Lerner (1985, 77).

27. Lerner (1985, 79).

28. See also Tavris (1982), who emphasizes this point throughout.

29. I omit here the violent and terrible things children more rarely do to their parents, on which see Condry and Miles (forthcoming), and Condry (2007).

30. Murray (2010, ch. 1).

31. Returning us to the issue raised in chapter 2, this case of grief does appear to involve a wish to change the past, and to have at least an element of magical thinking, and she lets go of that.

32. For one typical contrasting Stoic example, in which a refusal of anger is part of a global program of emotional detachment, see Juvenal x.357–62, discussed in Harriss (2001, 226 and n. 99).

33. Really, any sort of intimate adult partnership, but I will use marriage as a shorthand.

34. Not of course a blanket permission, as has often been believed.

35. On the ambiguities of Tess's rape/seduction by Alec, and the larger issues of shame and purity, see Baron (2012, 126–49). A related case is Mrs. Gaskell's *Ruth* (original edition 1853), in which Ruth, seduced at a very young age, then lives "blamelessly" for many years, and is admired by all for her character and values; but the revelation of her long-ago "sin" makes her an outcast.

36. See also Tavris (1982, ch. 8), "The Marital Onion," which contains many examples of a similar type.

37. I owe this point to Sharon Krause. On the futility of the "blame game," I have learned from Iris Marion Young's marvelous posthumous book, *Responsibility for Justice* (2011). As the author of a foreword to that book, I expressed some skepticism about Young's repudiation of retrospective analysis, but I am now totally on her side.

38. Hieronymi (2001).
39. I am grateful to Emily Buss for suggesting this example.
40. The play is "Mojada," by Luis Alfaro.
41. See Martin (2010).
42. Some representative titles would include Robert D. Enright, *Forgiveness Is a Choice: A Step-by-Step Process for Resolving Anger and Restoring Hope* (Washington, DC: APA LifeTools, 2001); Beverly Flanigan, *Forgiving the Unforgivable: Overcoming the Bitter Legacy of Intimate Wounds* (New York: Wiley Publishing, 1992); and Michael E. McCullough, Steven J. Sandage, and Everett L. Worthington, Jr., *To Forgive Is Human: How to Put Your Past in the Past* (Downers Grove, IL: InterVarsity Press, 1997).
43. See Tavris (1982).
44. EN IX, and see Cooper (1981).
45. See Nussbaum (2004a, ch. 4).
46. See Herbert Morris's sensitive observations on this issue in Morris (1976, ch. 2).
47. See Nussbaum (2004a, ch. 4), and Nussbaum (2001, ch. 4).
48. See Sherman (2011).
49. On all this, see Nussbaum (2001, ch. 4).
50. Morris (1976), especially ch. 3.
51. Morris (1976, 96–103). The longer discussion explores this picture in a detailed and attractive way.
52. Williams (1985) makes a number of distinct arguments against Kant, and I am developing only one prominent strand. He and I have a related disagreement about the role of shame, which I shall not investigate here.
53. As a graduate student I observed with interest the fact that German scholars reconstructing the chronology of Aristotle's writings typically reasoned that he would not have made sharp criticisms of his teacher Plato during Plato's lifetime, while Anglo-American scholars, and my thesis advisor G. E. L. Owen in particular, reasoned that Aristotle would have become able to see the truth in Plato's doctrines only after Plato's death.
54. Nietzsche (1989, II).
55. See Croke (2014).
56. See Halberstadt (2014), an article ranging widely over recent research on animal emotions.
57. In Nussbaum (1986, chs. 2 and 3); "Flawed Crystals: James's *The Golden Bowl* and Literature as Moral Philosophy," in Nussbaum (1990); Nussbaum (2000a); and Nussbaum (2013, ch. 10).
58. Williams, "Ethical Consistency," in Williams (1973, 166–86). Compare Nussbaum (1986, ch. 2).
59. Meaning that I follow the spirit of his critique of Utilitarianism, although he did not apply it directly to the case of moral dilemmas: see "A Critique of Utilitarianism," in Smart and Williams (1973, 77–150).
60. To recant properly I must be more precise. In "Ethical Consistency," Williams uses the word "regret," not "remorse." (In *Moral Luck* [1982], in a different context, he coins the term "agent regret," to which I'll return.) In *The Fragility of Goodness* (1986) I said that the agent's emotion should include the thought "that this is an act deeply repellent to him and to his character," and that for this reason "regret" is too weak a term. "His emotion, moreover, will not be simply regret, which could be felt and expressed by an uninvolved spectator and does not imply that he himself has acted badly. It will be an emotion more like remorse, closely bound

up with the wrong that he has as an agent, however reluctantly, done." In *Love's Knowledge* (1990) I went further, in writing about James's *The Golden Bowl* (1904). There I spoke of the proper emotion as "guilt," and suggested that the pervasive nature of these conflicts, particularly in the family, was a secular analogue of the biblical notion of original sin. I did not define guilt, and I'm really not sure whether I meant it as self-anger, including a wish for self-punishment. In the case of two conflicts late in the novel, I did observe that to respond with that emotion would be poisonous to the future of a loving and trusting relationship—so love, I said, required of Maggie Verver and of her husband a morally imperfect response. In those cases, at least, I was thinking of the proper emotion as painful self-castigation. These two cases, however, were not standard moral dilemmas, since the genesis of both dilemmas involved serious moral error, not forced on anyone by circumstances. So what I said about those cases, while certainly inconsistent with what I have said earlier in this chapter about the proper response to a betrayal, has no clear implications for the case of involuntary dilemma we are considering here. Finally, in my more recent paper on cost-benefit analysis, I used the word "guilt" a couple of times, but in the sense of accountability, and a duty to make reparations; I did not imply that the emotion ought to be self-punitive anger.

61. See Walzer (1973).
62. In short, Nussbaum (1986) and (2000a) both have the right idea, but (1990) wandered into error.

CHAPTER 5

1. Seneca, *Moral Epistles* 12.1–3, my translations from the Oxford Classical Text. The term is *deliciolum tuum*, literally, "little delight," which signifies considerable intimacy. (Robin Campbell's Penguin version says "your pet playmate.")
2. Seneca lived from c. 4 BCE to 65 CE. The *Moral Epistles* were very likely published in 63–64, and composed shortly before. Seneca does represent himself in the letters as in ill health, whether hypochondriacally, or really, or just for philosophical effect. Since he dies from politically commanded suicide shortly thereafter, after joining a conspiracy to overthrow Nero, it is difficult to assess the state of his health, apart from noting that Greek philosophers typically enjoyed long lives, in that salubrious climate. Ages at death: Socrates 70 (murdered), Isocrates 107, Plato 80, Aristotle (who had a bad stomach) 61, Zeno the Stoic 72, Cleanthes (a boxer and the second head of the Stoa) 100, Chrysippus 73, and Cicero 63 (murdered). When I delivered the Locke Lectures in 2014, I had just turned 67.
3. Lucilius is a fiction loosely based on a real Roman *eques*, but it's important to see that the collection uses both self and other as philosophical exempla, and should not be read as straight biography or autobiography. See Griffin's definitive *Seneca: A Philosopher in Politics* (1976). The collection is arranged with a fictive idea of philosophical progress, so the early letters represent Lucilius as less wholeheartedly Stoic than do the later letters.
4. I'm boringly explicit about this because I've been misunderstood before. I did the same thing in Nussbaum (2001), which opens with an account of my grief at the time of my mother's death. As with Seneca's readers, so with mine: this was widely understood as intimate autobiography, by people who had no reason to know whether any of it was at all true, apart from the obvious fact that I did have a mother. As it happens, such is the poverty of my imagination, the anecdotes in this chapter (like a fair amount of *Upheavals*) are all based on things that happened,

and anyone planning to grab my suitcase had better beware. But it really doesn't matter: my purpose, like his, is to remind readers of the sort of thing that provokes everyday anger, and to get them thinking about their own examples.

5. Seneca, *De Ira* III.38.

6. The Greeks made a big mistake here, since they had no public prosecutor. The bereaved individual would have to bring the prosecution. We shall see why this is a bad idea in chapter 6.

7. In what follows I typically cite the Procope (1995) translation, though I make occasional alterations for greater literalness.

8. Chrysippus died around 207 BCE, thus more than two hundred years before Seneca's birth.

9. See Fillion-Lahille (1984). Not all the works were Stoic: we possess fragments of Philodemus's (Epicurean) *On Anger*. Seneca himself knows a work on anger by the middle Stoic Posidonius, as well as (no doubt) Chrysippus's work.

10. See Nussbaum, "Erōs and Ethical Norms: Philosophers Respond to a Cultural Dilemma," in Nussbaum and Sihvola (2002, 55–94). The love in question is imagined as that of an older male for a younger male who does not feel erotic love in return, in keeping with well-established norms of Greek courtship. *Erōs* is defined by Zeno the Stoic as "an attempt to form a relationship of friendly love, inspired by the beauty of young men in their prime." In *Tusculan Disputations*, Cicero makes fun of them, suggesting that they make this exception to their rule about avoiding strong passions only because of pervasive Greek homoeroticism, but Craig Williams's magisterial *Roman Homosexuality* (1999) shows convincingly that Roman norms were very similar. And though Cicero never seems to have had a sexual relationship with a man, his best friend Atticus was well known for this practice.

11. Again, though, that isn't to say that it could not be fictional—or borrowed from some other author whose pet peeve it was.

12. Seneca does not oppose capital punishment on principle; he merely suggests that it is often misapplied because of emotion.

13. See also Harriss (2001, 415) on ancient examples of simulated anger.

14. "It's really a lot better to be courteous."

15. See Letter 47.

16. Trajan and Marcus both ruled for nineteen years and died of illness; Augustus ruled for forty-one years.

17. World Peace (now retired from the NBA and playing in Italy), who credits his psychiatrist with his share in the Lakers' NBA championship, crusades for the Mental Health in Schools Act; he also records bedtime stories for children and works with PETA against animal abuse. A related "track" away from anger is prominent in the career of ex-Bears wide receiver Brandon Marshall, who now crusades energetically for the Borderline Personality Disorder Foundation. His earlier angry phase included several suspensions for rampages of various sorts, and culminated in the famous brawl in 2004, during which he assaulted several fans as well as players. He was also convicted of domestic violence in 2007 and suspended again. In October 2015 Marshall, now playing for the New York Jets, admitted on national TV that he had quarreled angrily with a teammate after a bad loss. But, he said, "we talked it out and we love each other."

18. Those of us, that is, who are lucky enough to have work that is meaningful and rewarding.

19. Seneca, translated in Nussbaum (2010c).

20. See Martin (2010).

21. *Harris v. Forklift Systems, Inc.,* 114 S. Ct. 367 (1993).
22. *Baskerville v. Culligan,* 50 F. 3d 428 (1995), where the opinion by Judge Richard Posner holds that the offensive incidents were silly and just not concentrated or grave enough to constitute sexual harassment.
23. Scanlon (2013); see Appendix B.

CHAPTER 6

1. See the outstanding discussion in Allen (2000; 1999).
2. Allen gives an excellent account of anger as disease, but she then offers a defense, to me unconvincing, of the structure of Athenian prosecution as a good way of addressing the problem of deformed social relations.
3. See "Socrates' Rejection of Retaliation," in Vlastos (1991, 179–99). His primary sources are early dialogues of Plato, particularly the *Crito.*
4. Although it is Protagoras and not Socrates who says this, he is presented as a sympathetic figure, and it is likely that Plato endorses this statement.
5. Trans. Vlastos (1991).
6. See Allen (1999).
7. Of course this is a matter of constitutional interpretation, where both civil rights and the rights of women and gays and lesbians are concerned. And there are many matters in which it could be argued that the U.S. Constitution still admits fundamental injustice (in the socioeconomic realm). But one could also argue, with Franklin Delano Roosevelt, that core commitments of the nation entail the recognition of social and economic entitlements.
8. See Nussbaum (2013).
9. For example Nussbaum (2000b; 2006; 2010a).
10. For caveats about the role of the notion of dignity, which, in my view, cannot be defined apart from a range of other notions and principles, see Nussbaum (2010a).
11. Certainly it is so understood by Amartya Sen, who orients his version of the "capabilities approach" with reference to Mill, and who has gone to some pains to argue that consequentialism can accommodate rights as intrinsic goods (see Sen 1982). One way in which my normative political view differs from other forms of consequentialism is in its limits: for I introduce the capabilities approach only as a basis for political principles in a pluralistic society, not as a comprehensive doctrine of the good or flourishing life, whereas most consequentialists portray their views as comprehensive doctrines. That difference, however, plays no role in the arguments to come.
12. Rawls (1986), "The Idea of an Overlapping Consensus." On Rawls's notion, see my introduction in Comim and Nussbaum (2014).
13. See Levmore and Nussbaum (2014), Introduction.
14. An especially fascinating reflection on these complexities is Wallace Stegner's novel *Angle of Repose* (1971), an account of a woman from the talkative East who falls in love with and marries a strong, silent man at home in the (nineteenth-century) West: see the reflections on the connections between this tragic story and American law in retired judge Howard Matz's paper in the Levmore-Nussbaum (2014) collection. See also, in the same collection, Saul Levmore, "Snitching, Whistleblowing, and 'Barn Burning': Loyalty in Law, Literature, and Sports," a reading of Faulkner's story and of the "unmanly" figure of the "snitch" in American law and literature, and Nussbaum, "Jewish Men, Jewish

Lawyers: Roth's 'Eli, the Fanatic' and the Question of Jewish Masculinity in American Law," arguing that (as Roth's Tzuref insists) law is quintessentially Jewish, meaning based upon talk rather than "manly" self-assertion and on compassion rather than outraged honor.

15. On some of the changes over time, away from status offense (particularly male honor) to real injury, see Kahan and Nussbaum (1996).

16. William Ian Miller has argued that even in early "honor" cultures, retributive competition over status was socially disciplined in such a way that it led to the bargaining table. See Miller (1990).

17. See the excellent sociolinguistic study by Coyle (2013, ch. 3).

18. See Coyle (2013, ch. 3).

19. See Allen (1999) and Walker (2006).

20. See Walker (2006).

21. See Mackie (1982).

22. Bentham (1948, 177).

23. Santora (2013).

24. CBS News (2012).

25. I provide a summary of Heckman's results and a bibliography of some of his most important contributions in the appendix to Nussbaum (2010a).

26. For the initial statement, see Zorn (2013); for the concession, Huffington Post (2013).

27. See Coyle (2013) generally for the importance of our terminology in shaping thought.

28. See Young (2011).

29. Of the many well-done overviews of the topic, one that covers the terrain especially well is Tasioulas (2010, 680–91). It will be evident that I don't agree with everything in this piece, but its clarity is admirable.

30. See Morris (1968).

31. Moore (1995).

32. A related point is made by Duff: Morris's view treats crimes such as rape and murder as acts that would not be wrong but for the existence of the criminal law: see Duff (2001, 22).

33. See Jean Hampton, in Hampton and Murphy (1988), who calls the position "strange—even repulsive" (115), and she reports that her coauthor Murphy calls it "creepy" (116).

34. Moore (1995, 98–99).

35. Moore (1995, 98).

36. Note that he holds that moral desert is sufficient for punishment, hence that nonlegal as well as legal wrongdoing warrants retribution.

37. Duff (2011) and Markel (2011). Both authors have published copiously on this question, but these recent articles provide succinct summaries of their positions. Markel was murdered outside of his Florida home in July 2014. His death remains a mystery.

38. Duff (2001, 28).

39. In this respect his view closely resembles Hampton's: see below.

40. I owe the phrase "talk is cheap" to my colleague Richard McAdams. Prominent examples of such views, apart from Duff's, include Bennett (2001); Hampton (1984); and Primoratz (1989). For a critique of such views, see Boonin (2008).

41. I owe this phrase, too, to Richard McAdams. Duff recognizes that it is so far an open question what conduct on the part of the state communicates censure, and

it doesn't automatically follow that "hard treatment" does so best. He justifies a focus on *ex post* hard treatment by a picture according to which punishment is a "secular penance." But apart from the question whether incarceration is reasonably seen in these quasi-religious terms, we need to ask why it isn't best to intervene before the sinner sins, rather than to wait for sin and then impose penance.

42. Hampton (1984, 213). She adds that whereas retributivism "understands punishment as performing the rather metaphysical task of 'negating the wrong' and 'reasserting the right,'" punishment aims at a 'concrete moral *goal*," which includes benefiting both criminals and society. And she argues plausibly that this approach honors the need of victims to have their wrongs acknowledged.

43. In Hampton and Murphy (1988), published several years later, Hampton explores sympathetically, and appears to endorse, a different position, a form of retributivism. She explores two distinct ways of understanding "the retributive idea." One, which understands punishment as "vindicating value through protection," appears similar to the view she has previously endorsed, and is hard to understand as a form of retributivism, since it is an expressive statement with a forward-looking goal. The other idea, which clearly is a form of retributivism, is that of punishment as a "defeat" of the wrongdoer by the victim. Now if the thought were put in general terms, viz., society is stating that wrongdoing is unacceptable and will be inhibited, it would be a form of her earlier educational/expressive position. But she appears to understand it, instead, in personal terms: a particular victim defeats a particular wrongdoer by ensuring the punishment of the latter. Besides being an inaccurate way to think about criminal punishment (surely the state, not the victim, punishes), it seems to raise all the problems of the *lex talionis*: for how, exactly, does the infliction of pain on an individual constitute a victory for someone who has suffered rape or some other crime? By the bare assertion of the victim's worth? But then it collapses into the first (expressive, general) construal. But if Hampton really means to say that the dignity of V rises as the pain of O intensifies, this does seem to be a form of the *lex talionis*, and subject to my critique. Hampton's chapter is exploratory, and she never announces commitment to either form of the idea, nor does she repudiate her earlier view.

44. On the fact that consequentialism can accommodate the importance of rights as part of the consequence set, see Sen (1982); see also Nussbaum (2010a).

45. See Nussbaum (2010a).

46. Some reformists would urge avoidance of the term "wrongdoing," as too closely linked with the demonization of offenders. I disagree. Coyle certainly shows how the term "evil" functions to demonize offenders and to deflect attention away from non-punitive strategies for crime prevention (Coyle 2013, ch. 5); but the term "wrongdoing" seems to me not to have the overcharged valence of "evil." It pertains to an act, not the entirety of the person, and it simply signals what is true: that we ought to distinguish between the intentional acts of human beings and the depredations of wild animals or the accidents of nature. However, my intuitions are not those of Mackie (1982), who holds that "calling for a hostile response" is part of the concept of "wrongdoing." To the extent that one agrees with Mackie's linguistic intuitions, which I believe to be unusual, one should become skeptical of the term. Will Jefferson has informed me that "Nonviolent Communication,"

an approach to conflict resolution started by Marshall Rosenberg in the 1960s, and now used throughout the world on many types of issues, holds that moral language must be eliminated from our thinking, and that this is necessary in order to remove anger. I am not convinced. But the position is subtle and deserves more extensive consideration than I can give it here. Jefferson's D. Phil. thesis will be a significant contribution on this question.

47. See Brooks (2012, ch. 1).
48. See Gewirtz (1998).
49. Bandes (1997). See also, more recently, Bandes (2016).
50. I owe this question to Jeff McMahan.
51. See Bandes (2016) on the socially constructed idea of closure and its relatively recent origin.
52. Harsanyi (1982), arguing that these preferences ought to be excluded from the social choice function. The point is as old as Utilitarianism: Mill's *The Subjection of Women* does not consider the pain of men at having their unjustified privileges abridged as a cost weighing against women's equality. It's not that these costs get outweighed by the benefits; they are simply not considered at all, as in Harsanyi's proposal.
53. I owe this suggestion to Mary Anne Case.
54. *Turner v. Safley*, 482 U.S. 78 (1987), holding that prisoners serving life terms without the possibility of parole nonetheless have a constitutional right to get married, even though they very likely will never consummate the marriage. Marriage, the Court held, has expressive and religious meanings.
55. See Judge Posner's dissenting opinion in *Johnson v. Phelan*, 65 F. 3d 144, in which a male prisoner complained that the practice of having female guards observe him as he showered and used the toilet violated his sense of Christian modesty. Posner commented that some judges "view prisoners as members of a different species, indeed as a type of vermin, devoid of human dignity and entitled to no respect.... I do not myself consider the 1.5 million inmates of American prisons and jails in that light."
56. One valuable study that ought to be made available in English translation is Archimandritou (2000). A detailed summary of the book's contents was given to me orally by the author.
57. See my extensive treatment of this question in Nussbaum (2004a).
58. See Kahan (1996) and my critique in Nussbaum (2004a).
59. These five arguments are elaborated in Nussbaum (2004a).
60. See many references to studies of shame penalties in Nussbaum (2004a).
61. See Posner (2000). His argument and other related historical arguments are considered in detail in Nussbaum (2004a).
62. Gilligan (1997).
63. See Schulhofer (1995).
64. See Nussbaum (2004a).
65. For a good, albeit brief, discussion of this point, see McConnell (2012). And see Nussbaum (2014b).
66. See Levmore and Nussbaum (2010).
67. The theory is given in Braithwaite (1989); the practical implementation, with a thinner theoretical frame, in Braithwaite and Mugford (1994). For an overall assessment of a wide variety of practices of "restorative justice," see Braithwaite (2002).

68. To a large extent, the part with which I agree is the account of the approach in the later article; the earlier book contains a lot of material that is not necessary for the practice as described, and less appealing.

69. See Braithwaite (1989, 81).

70. In Braithwaite (2002), however, Braithwaite clarifies that we should distinguish between restorative processes (dialogue, conferencing) and restorative values (reform, reintegration). A restorative process might impose punitive and retributive sanctions; a process that fails to include all the community members who should in principle be included can still advance restorative goals.

71. See Braithwaite (1989), and also my correspondence with Braithwaite about Dan Kahan's proposals, cited in Nussbaum (2004a, ch. 5).

72. Braithwaite and Mugford (1994, 144).

73. Braithwaite and Mugford (1994, 144).

74. Braithwaite and Mugford (1994, 142).

75. Braithwaite and Mugford (1994, 144).

76. Braithwaite and Mugford (1994, 145).

77. Braithwaite and Mugford (1994, 147).

78. See the fuller discussion of the efficacy of all known programs of this type in Braithwaite (1989, ch. 3).

79. Braithwaite and Mugford (1994, 150).

80. Braithwaite and Mugford (1994, 152).

81. Braithwaite and Mugford (1994, 159–60).

82. Braithwaite and Mugford (1994, 144, 149).

83. See Braithwaite (2002, 152), where Braithwaite describes this as "[t]he most forceful critique of restorative justice."

84. See Nussbaum (2004a, ch. 4).

85. See my treatment of the issue in "Equity and Mercy," in Nussbaum (1999a); and for a new translation of *De Clementia* and *De Ira* by Robert Kaster, see Kaster (2010).

86. See Nussbaum (2001, chs. 6–8).

87. I did not understand this distinction in my earlier writing on mercy. I discuss it more fully in Nussbaum (forthcoming a).

88. On *Woodson v. North Carolina* (1976) and sympathy at the penalty phase of a capital case, see Nussbaum (1993).

89. For the influence of Stoicism on Nietzsche's moral psychology, see Nussbaum (1994a).

90. Nietzsche (1989, II.10).

91. See Nussbaum (1996).

92. Such concerns are not alien to ancient traditions, as Aristotle's *Politics*, with its extensive discussions of communal meals and clean water, makes clear. And consider this wonderful edict of the ancient Indian emperor Ashoka (3rd century BCE):

> On the roads I have had banyan trees planted, which will give shade to beasts and men. I have had mango groves planted and I have had wells dug and rest houses built every nine miles. . . . And I have had many watering places made everywhere for the use of beasts and men. But this benefit is important, and indeed the world has enjoyed attention in many ways from former kings as well [as] from me. But I have done these things in order that my people might conform to *Dhamma*.

CHAPTER 7

1. Reproduced in Jack (1956, 136).

2. When not otherwise stated, my sources are, for Gandhi, Jack (1956); for King, Washington (1986). I refer to these sources with G and K, and with page numbers given in parentheses in the text. Occasionally I shall also refer to Gandhi (1983), cited as GAut.

3. For a valuable collection of interviews, letters, and other writings, see Mandela (2010, 253) (hereafter C). The extract is from lengthy tape-recorded conversations with author Richard Stengel in the early 1990s, while the two men were working together to edit *Long Walk to Freedom* into book form. The title is a reference to the *Meditations* of Marcus Aurelius, emperor and Stoic philosopher, whose reflections have in Greek the title "To Himself." Other sources for Mandela that I shall frequently cite are his autobiography, Mandela (1994) (hereafter LW), and Carlin (2008) (hereafter Inv).

4. The ideas in this section are treated at greater length in Nussbaum (forthcoming b).

5. The felony murder rule is still in force in South Africa. Paton seems unclear about this, since at one point he has the judge say that if Absalom really had no intent to kill, "then the court must find that the accused did not commit murder" (Paton 1987, 235).

6. Sorabji (2012) gives a far more detailed reconstruction of Gandhi's attitudes and practices than I shall attempt here. I focus on the issue of non-anger, and, within this, on the common ground between Gandhi and King.

7. However, Gandhi did think that violence was a constant possibility among his followers, see Sorabji (2012, 122), and it took tremendous preparation to hold a nonviolent protest. He also weeded out followers likely to get angry under attack (122).

8. See Sorabji (2012, 88–92). Human self-defense is not an exception, but there are a few cases where he did hold that violence is less bad than the alternative.

9. Elsewhere, Gandhi also holds that hearts are changed by courageous self-sacrifice: see Sorabji (2012, 83).

10. Dalton (2012, 12–16). As Dalton shows, Gandhi was also concerned not to use an English term for his idea; he even ran a contest for the Indian-language renaming of the central concept, insisting that it was "shameful" to permit the struggle to be known only by an English name.

11. Compare ancient discussions of anger in armies: both Philodemus and Seneca emphasize that the type of discipline successful military strategies require is incompatible with a dominant role for personal anger: see Harriss (2001, 103).

12. Gandhi got angry at times, and criticized himself for this: see Sorabji (2012, 200).

13. See Dalton (2012, 16 and 96).

14. See also Dalton (2012, ch. 1). It is interesting to compare the "agonistic humanism" advocated by Honig (2013); although Honig makes no commitment to non-anger, she repudiates a politics based on grief and mourning and suggests an emphasis on solidarity and hope.

15. Nehru (1989, 274–75). See Dalton (2012, 66–67 and 168–69). Nehru does not mention the connection between fear and violence, but this connection is surely salient for Gandhi.

16. See the analysis of this speech in Nussbaum (2013, ch. 9).

17. He did attempt to impose this demand on his children, unsuccessfully; he was a very judgmental and punitive father, evincing to Harilal attitudes that seem pretty close to anger.

18. Nehru (1939). Nehru's first sentence: "An only son of prosperous parents is apt to be spoilt, especially in India." From that point on, the work makes a point of gentle self-mockery, as well as admission of longing and loneliness. On his release from prison, Mandela "wanted first of all to tell the people that I was not a messiah, but an ordinary man who had become a leader because of extraordinary circumstances" (LW 676).

19. Orwell (1949).

20. Erikson (1993, 248).

21. Orwell (1949).

22. See Nehru's moving meditation on his deficiencies as a husband in Nehru (1989, ch. 2), in a section entitled "The Problem of Human Relationships."

23. As Sorabji (2012, 32–42) shows, Gandhi's attitude owes a good deal to Christian asceticism, sometimes filtered through Tolstoy.

24. See Schalkwyk (2014, 58–59). Schalkwyk argues that Mandela followed Stoic detachment too far, to include a detachment from all emotions. I find his argument unconvincing. (He argues, for example, that Mandela's stunned silence on learning of his son Thembi's death is an example of Stoic non-grief, as if all genuinely grieving people would speak eloquently.)

25. Ahmed Kathrada, a close friend and fellow prisoner, interviewed in CNN's "Nelson Mandela," December 2013.

26. Another early incident he pointedly narrates illustrates the role of charm in race relations. Traveling to Johannesburg in his early twenties with his friend the Regent's son Justice, he was given a ride by a white attorney, who arranged for his elderly mother to drive them. She was at first uncomfortable being in the company of two young black men, particularly since Justice showed no inhibitions about whites. She watched him carefully. But gradually Justice's humor and charm got through to her, so that eventually she would even laugh at his jokes. Disarming anxiety with charm and humor was a strategy Mandela would use to good effect throughout his career.

27. Schalkwyk (2014, 60).

28. Personal conversations, 2013 and 2014.

29. See Schalkwyk (2014, 55–56), drawing on the memoirs of Mac Maharaj.

30. Janusz Walus was a Polish immigrant who was attempting to curry favor with right-wing Afrikaners.

31. Carlin narrates this incident based on Coetsee's memoirs.

32. CNN, "Nelson Mandela," December 2013.

33. In English, the current anthem goes: "Unity and justice and freedom for the German fatherland! Let us all strive for this, in a brotherly way, with heart and hand. Unity and justice and freedom are the guarantors of happiness. Bloom in the gleam of this happiness, bloom, German fatherland."

34. Justice Albie Sachs, recently retired from the South African Constitutional Court, and a freedom fighter who helped the ANC during the years of struggle, knows Mandela well and reported in conversation (2013) that Freeman's portrayal was utterly uncanny in its likeness.

35. Film clips of this moment can easily be seen, and are prominent in CNN's documentary "Nelson Mandela."

36. CNN, "Nelson Mandela."

37. See ESPN (2013).
38. For example, in CNN, "Nelson Mandela": asked about the disadvantages of imprisonment, he replies, characteristically, by emphasizing its advantages.
39. See Dalton (2012, 24 and 138, with references).
40. If it were not a distraction from my focus on recent events, I would also be prepared to argue that the American Revolution was an example of non-anger, though of course not nonviolence. It was accompanied by careful and articulate reasoning, and its objective was not to punish the British for their injustices, but simply to achieve an independent future. Because of these features, it had the strategic advantages of non-anger in winning friendship for the new nation.
41. See Murdoch (1970).
42. Tutu (1999).
43. One excellent survey is Hayner (2001).
44. See the very interesting development of this theme apropos of transitional justice in Eisikovits (2009).
45. See Bennhold (2014).
46. In Oxford, May 2014, name confidential.
47. See Tutu (1999, 22), citing a statement by Justice Mahomed.
48. Tutu (1999, 23). There were some trials in egregious cases: Eugene de Kock, former head of covert operations of the South African police, a squad that hunted down and killed anti-apartheid activists, was tried and convicted in 1996 and sentenced to 212 years in prison. For a remarkable set of interviews with him, see Gobodo-Madikizela (2003).
49. Tutu (1999, 28–29).
50. Tutu (1999, 29–31).
51. See Levmore (2014). Levmore argues, however, that cultural strictures against "ratting" as unmanly often disserve the public interest.
52. See Walker (2006).
53. Personal communication with Albie Sachs.
54. Tutu (1999, 267).
55. Tutu (1999, 269).
56. Tutu (1999, 271).
57. Tutu (1999).
58. Tutu (1999, 273).
59. Tutu (2014).
60. Tutu (2014, 39).
61. In a 1999 speech, on leaving the office of president, Mandela does say, "South Africans must recall the terrible past so that we can deal with it, forgiving where forgiveness is necessary but never forgetting." Albie Sachs comments (email, May 18, 2014) that by this point in his career he did allow the word on occasion, since audiences expected it, but that it did not mean buying into the transactional picture. "All it shows ... is that he was not hard, relentless, and unforgiving. Everybody knows that. And in any event, the emphasis of the statement at that stage was not so much on the forgiving part as on the not forgetting." And the evidence of thousands of pages of his published interviews and writings is that forgiveness is just not the way he himself chose to frame the issue: "The journey was not to forgiveness, it was to Freedom." Sachs also notes that some ANC members, e.g., Oliver Tambo and Albert Luthuli, were deeply religious and used Christian terminology, and yet they too focused on freedom as goal. Liberation was liberation of all, white and black.

62. A range of such commissions might be assessed with this idea in mind.
63. Tutu and Tutu (2014).
64. Lomax (2008).
65. See Fairbanks (2014), describing how former police minister Adriaan Vlok undertook a pilgrimage through South Africa washing the feet of those he had injured.
66. See Dominus (2014). The story includes samples from an exhibit of photographs of victim/perpetrator pairs.
67. See Gobodo-Madikizela (2003).
68. Gobodo-Madikizela (2003, 117).

CHAPTER 8

1. Nehru (1989, 38). The speech, which Nehru reported, was made in 1942.
2. Harriss (2001, 412).
3. On Gandhi's failure of love, see Orwell (1949).
4. See Harriss (2001, *passim*).
5. Compare John Rawls's idea, at the very end of *A Theory of Justice* (1971), that the institutions of a just society are a model of "purity of heart," an attitude that we can enter at any time, though often we do not.
6. These ideas are clearly present in Indian traditions, but I've had difficulty finding a single word, no doubt on account of linguistic ignorance. The same goes for the many other cultures that I have not investigated at all.

APPENDIX B

1. Coates and Tognazzini (2013, 3 and n. 2).
2. Thomson (1975). Not coincidentally, Thomson's own influential analysis of the abortion right does not make use of the notion of privacy, preferring an analysis in terms of equality, stressing that women are unequally made to bear the burden of supporting fetal life: see Thomson (1972, 47ff).
3. Nussbaum (2002b). See Nussbaum (2003) for a shortened version. See also Nussbaum (2010b, ch. 6).
4. *Eisenstadt v. Baird*, 405 U.S. 438 (1972).
5. "Virtue Ethics" seems to me like "privacy," albeit with a very thin common ground uniting its different species: see Nussbaum (1999b).
6. See Coates and Tognazzini (2013, 8–10); a central case is Glover (1970).
7. Strawson (1968, 93).
8. Sher (2006), and see his (2013), esp. 65, summarizing his critique of other approaches; see also Smith (2013, 35).
9. Scanlon (2013).
10. Wallace (2011) and Wolf (2011).
11. Smith (2013).
12. Smith (2013, 29).

APPENDIX C

1. These lists are reproduced in Arnim (1964, secs. 377–442). Arnim cites a variety of ancient sources in both Greek and Latin, but I shall focus on the apparently canonical lists reproduced in the first-century BCE grammarian Andronicus of Rhodes.

2. The Stoics also enumerate and define some species of anger. Thus, *thumos* is defined as "incipient *orgē*," *cholos* as "*orgē* that swells up," *pikria* as "*orgē* that breaks out on the spot like a torrent," *mēnis* as "*orgē* kept in storage for a long time," *kotos* as "*orgē* that watches for the right time to take revenge" (Von Arnim III.397). Those are the species mentioned by Andronicus. I'm not sure how useful those definitions are, since some of the terms are literary (and indeed many centuries removed from the making of the list) and others in more common use. Nor is it clear that the definition captures the usage. For example, since the paradigm of *mēnis* (a poetic term) is surely the anger of Achilles in the *Iliad*, does the definition really capture it? Maybe and maybe not. Equally important, is that the meaning of the word *mēnis*, or does it just happen to be the case that Achilles's anger lasts for a long time? One would be hard put to make the case either way. Again, *thumos* is a term more often used in a variety of classical authors, but a central reference point for the much later scholar would surely be Plato's *Republic*. However, the definition given seems quite off-kilter as a definition of what Plato is talking about there. From now on, then, I'll ignore these subsidiary definitions.

3. Strawson suggests another sort of distinction: "resentment" is first-personal, and "indignation" is the attitude of an observer, or "vicarious": see Strawson (1968, 84–87). This doesn't seem to be generally true: I can resent an insult to someone else (provided it is someone whose well-being I care about, which, I argue, is always the case when one feels emotion for another); and I can be indignant about a wrong done to me.

4. Bloom (2013).

5. See Harriss (2001, 63 and 117) on *chalepainein* and debates about whether this milder state is to be extirpated.

Bibliography

Adler, Matthew D., and Eric A. Posner, eds. (2000). *Cost-Benefit Analysis: Legal, Economic, and Philosophical Perspectives*. Chicago: University of Chicago Press.

Allen, Danielle (1999). "Democratic Dis-ease: Of Anger and the Troubling Nature of Punishment." In *The Passions of Law*. Ed. S. Bandes. New York: NYU Press, 191–214.

———. (2000). *The World of Prometheus*. Princeton, NJ: Princeton University Press.

Archimandritou, Maria (2000). *The Open Prison* (published in modern Greek as *He Anoikte Ektish Tes Poines*). Athens: Hellenika Grammata.

Arnim, Hans Friedrich August von, ed. (1964). *Stoicorum Veterum Fragmenta*. Stuttgart: Teubner. Original edition 1903.

Averill, James (1982). *Anger and Aggression*. New York: Springer Verlag.

Baier, Annette (1995). *Moral Prejudices*. Cambridge, MA: Harvard University Press.

Bandes, Susan (1997). "Empathy, Narrative, and Victim Impact Statements." *University of Chicago Law Review* 63: 361–412.

———, ed. (1999). *The Passions of Law*. New York: NYU Press.

———. (2016). "Share Your Grief but Not Your Anger: Victims and the Expression of Emotion in Criminal Justice." In *Emotional Expression: Philosophical, Psychological and Legal Perspectives*. Ed. J. Smith and C. Abell. Cambridge: Cambridge University Press, forthcoming.

Baron, Marcia (2012). "Rape, Seduction, Purity, and Shame in *Tess of the d'Urbervilles*." In *Subversion and Sympathy: Gender, Law, and the British Novel*. Ed. Martha C. Nussbaum and Alison L. Lacroix. New York: Oxford University Press, 126–49.

Bash, Anthony (2007). *Forgiveness in Christian Ethics*. New York: Cambridge University Press.

Batson, C. Daniel (2011). *Altruism in Humans*. New York: Oxford University Press.

Bennett, Christopher (2001). *The Apology Ritual: A Philosophical Theory of Punishment*. Cambridge: Cambridge University Press.

Bennhold, Katrin (2014). "Northern Ireland Police Sue for Boston College Interviews." *New York Times*: May 22.

Bentham, Jeremy (1948). *An Introduction to the Principles of Morals and Legislation*. New York: Hafner Press. Original edition 1789.

Bloom, Paul (2013). *Just Babies: The Origins of Good and Evil*. New York: Crown.

Boonin, David (2008). *The Problem of Punishment*. New York: Cambridge University Press.

Boyarin, Daniel (1995). *Carnal Israel: Reading Sex in Talmudic Cultures*. Berkeley: University of California Press.

Braithwaite, John (1989). *Crime, Shame, and Reintegration*. Cambridge: Cambridge University Press.

———. (2002). *Restorative Justice and Responsive Regulation*. New York: Oxford University Press.

Braithwaite, John, and Stephen Mugford (1994). "Conditions of Successful Reintegration Ceremonies: Dealing with Juvenile Offenders." *British Journal of Criminology* 34: 139–71.

Briggs, Jean L. (1970). *Never in Anger: Portrait of an Eskimo Family*. Cambridge, MA: Harvard University Press.

Brion, Fabienne, and Bernard Harcourt, eds. (2012). *Mal faire, dire vrai*. Chicago: University of Chicago Press; Louvain: Presses Universitaires de Louvain.

Brooks, Thom (2012). *Punishment*. New York: Routledge.

Butler, Joseph (1827). *Fifteen Sermons Preached at the Rolls Chapel*. Cambridge: Hilliard and Brown. Online edition: http://anglicanhistory.org/butler/rolls/.

Carlin, John (2008). *Invictus: Nelson Mandela and the Game That Made a Nation*. New York: Penguin. Previously published as *Playing the Enemy*.

Caston, Ruth Rothaus, ed. (forthcoming). Festschrift for David Konstan. New York: Oxford University Press.

CBS News (2012). "The Cost of a Nation of Incarceration." April 23.

Coates, D. Justin, and Neil A. Tognazzini, eds. (2013). *Blame: Its Nature and Norms*. New York: Oxford University Press.

Comim, Flavio, and Martha Nussbaum, eds. (2014). *Capabilities, Gender, Justice*. Cambridge: Cambridge University Press.

Condry, John, and Sandra Condry (1976). "Sex Differences: A Study of the Eye of the Beholder." *Child Development* 27: 812–19.

Condry, Rachel (2007). *Families Shamed: The Consequences of Crime for Relatives of Serious Offenders*. New York: Routledge.

Condry, Rachel, and Caroline Miles (2014). "Adolescent to Parent Violence: Framing and Mapping a Hidden Problem." *Criminology and Criminal Justice*, Sage, online.

Cooper, John (1981). "Aristotle on Friendship." In *Essays on Aristotle's Ethics*. Ed. Amélie Oksenberg Rorty. Berkeley: University of California Press, 301–40.

Coyle, Michael J. (2013). *Talking Criminal Justice: Language and the Just Society*. Abingdon, UK: Routledge.

Croke, Vicki (2014). *Elephant Company*. New York: Random House.

Dalton, Dennis (2012). *Mahatma Gandhi: Nonviolent Power in Action*. New York: Columbia University Press. Expanded edition.

De La Grange, Henri Louis (1973). *Mahler*. Vol. 1. New York: Doubleday.

Dickens, Charles (2004). *David Copperfield*. London: Penguin. Original edition 1850.

Dominus, Susan (2014). "Portraits of Reconciliation." *New York Times Magazine*: April 6. Online edition.

Duff, R. Antony (2001). *Punishment, Communication, and Community*. Oxford: Oxford University Press.

———. (2011). "Retrieving Retributivism." In *Retributivism: Essays on Theory and Policy*. Ed. Mark D. White. New York: Oxford University Press, 3–24.

Eisikovits, Nir (2009). *Sympathizing with the Enemy: Reconciliation, Transitional Justice, Negotiation*. Dordrecht: Republic of Letters.

Erikson, Erik (1993). *Gandhi's Truth: On the Origins of Militant Nonviolence*. New York: W. W. Norton. Original edition 1970.

ESPN (2013). "Sports World Mourns Nelson Mandela." December 5. Online edition.

Fairbanks, Eve (2014). "'I Have Sinned Against the Lord and Against You! Will You Forgive Me?'" *New Republic*: June 18.

Fillion-Lahille, Janine (1984). *Le "De Ira" de Sénèque et la philosophie stocienne des passions*. Paris: Klincksieck.

Foucault, Michel (1975). *Discipline and Punish: The Birth of the Prison*. Trans. Alan Sheridan. New York: Vintage Books. Original French edition 1975. 2nd edition 1995.

Gandhi, Mohandas K. (1983). *Autobiography: The Story of My Experiments with Truth*. New York: Dover Press.

———. (1997). *Hind Swaraj and Other Writings*. Ed. Anthony J. Parel. Cambridge: Cambridge University Press.

Gaskell, Elizabeth (1998). *Ruth*. London: Penguin. Original edition 1853.

Gewirtz, Paul (1988). "Aeschylus' Law." *Harvard Law Review* 101: 1043–55.

———. (1998). "Victims and Voyeurs at the Criminal Trial." In *Low's Stories: Narrative and Rhetoric in the Law*. Ed. Paul Gewirtz and Peter Brooks. New Haven: Yale University Press, 135–61.

Gewirtz, Paul, and Peter Brooks, eds. (1998). *Low's Stories: Narrative and Rhetoric in the Law*. New Haven: Yale University Press.

Gilligan, James (1997). *Violence: Reflections on a National Epidemic*. New York: Vintage Books.

Glover, Jonathan (1970). *Responsibility*. London: Routledge.

Gobodo-Madikizela, Pumla (2003). *A Human Being Died That Night*. Cape Town: David Philip Publishers.

Griffin, Miriam (1976). *Seneca: A Philosopher in Politics*. Oxford: Clarendon Press.

Griswold, Charles L. (2007). *Forgiveness: A Philosophical Exploration*. Cambridge: Cambridge University Press.

Griswold, Charles L., and David Konstan, eds. (2011). *Ancient Forgiveness: Classical, Judaic, and Christian*. Cambridge: Cambridge University Press.

Halberstadt, Alex (2014). "Zoo Animals and Their Discontents." *New York Times Magazine*: July 3.

Halbertal, Moshe (forthcoming). "At the Threshold of Forgiveness: On Law and Narrative in the Talmud." Trans. Joel Linsider. Shorter version published in *Jewish Review of Books* (2011).

Halbertal, Moshe, and Avishai Margalit (1992). *Idolatry*. Cambridge, MA: Harvard University Press.

Hampton, Jean (1984). "The Moral Education Theory of Punishment." *Philosophy and Public Affairs* 13: 208–38.

Hampton, Jean, and Jeffrie G. Murphy (1988). *Forgiveness and Mercy*. New York: Cambridge University Press.

Hanna, E. (1911). "The Sacrament of Penance." *The Catholic Encyclopedia*. New York: Robert Appleton Company. Online version.

Hardin, Russell (2006). *Trust*. Cambridge: Polity Press.

Harriss, William V. (2001). *Restraining Rage: The Ideology of Anger Control in Classical Antiquity.* Cambridge, MA: Harvard University Press.

Harsanyi, John (1982). "Morality and the Theory of Rational Behavior." In *Utilitarianism and Beyond.* Ed. Amartya Sen and Bernard Williams. Cambridge: Cambridge University Press, 39–62.

Hawley, Katherine (2012). *Trust: A Very Short Introduction.* Oxford: Clarendon Press.

Hayner, Priscilla B. (2001). *Unspeakable Truths: Transitional Justice and the Challenge of Truth Commissions.* Foreword by Kofi Annan. New York: Routledge. Updated edition 2011.

Hieronymi, Pamela (2001). "Articulating an Uncompromising Forgiveness." *Philosophy and Phenomenological Research* 62: 539–55.

Honig, Bonnie (2013). *Antigone Interrupted.* New York: Cambridge University Press.

Hossain, Anushay (2013). "Femicide in Italy: Domestic Violence Still Persists Despite New Laws." *Forbes* World Views: August 26.

Huffington Post (2013). "Sen. Mark Kirk Retreats on Mass Gang Arrest Plan, Concedes Idea Is 'Not All That Practical.'" July 20.

Jack, Homer A., ed. (1956). *The Gandhi Reader: A Sourcebook of His Life and Writings.* Bloomington: Indiana University Press.

Kahan, Dan (1996). "What Do Alternative Sanctions Mean?" *University of Chicago Law Review* 63: 591–653.

Kahan, Dan, and Martha C. Nussbaum (1996). "Two Concepts of Emotion in the Criminal Law." *Columbia Law Review* 96: 269–374.

Kaster, Robert (2005). *Emotion, Restraint, and Community in Ancient Rome.* New York: Oxford University Press.

———. (2010). Translation of Seneca's *De Clementia* and *De Ira.* In *Seneca: Anger, Mercy, Revenge.* Chicago: University of Chicago Press. Containing translations by Robert Kaster and Martha Nussbaum. 2010.

Kathrada, Ahmed (2013). Interview in "Nelson Mandela." CNN, December.

Kindlon, Dan, and Michael Thompson (1999). *Raising Cain: Protecting the Emotional Life of Boys.* New York: Ballantine Books.

Konstan, David (2010). *Before Forgiveness: The Origins of a Moral Idea.* New York: Cambridge University Press.

———. (2012). "Assuaging Rage." In *Ancient Forgiveness: Classic, Judaic, and Christian.* Ed. Charles L. Griswold and David Konstan. New York: Cambridge University Press, 17–30.

Kugel, James L. (1999). *Traditions of the Bible: A Guide to the Bible as It Was at the Start of the Common Era.* Cambridge, MA: Harvard University Press.

Lacey, Nicola, and Hanna Pickard (2013). "From the Consulting Room to the Court Room? Taking the Clinical Model of Responsibility without Blame into the Legal Realm." *Oxford Journal of Legal Studies* 33: 1–29.

Lazarus, Richard (1991). *Emotion and Adaptation.* New York: Oxford University Press.

Lerner, Harriet (1985). *The Dance of Anger: A Woman's Guide to Changing the Patterns of Intimate Relationships.* New York: Harper and Row.

Levmore, Saul (2014). "Snitching, Whistleblowing, and 'Barn Burning': Loyalty in Law, Literature, and Sports." In *American Guy: Masculinity in American Law and Literature.* Ed. Saul Levmore and Martha Nussbaum. New York: Oxford University Press, 213–24.

Levmore, Saul, and Martha Nussbaum, eds. (2010). *The Offensive Internet: Speech, Privacy, and Reputation.* Cambridge, MA: Harvard University Press.

———, eds. (2014). *American Guy: Masculinity in American Law and Literature.* New York: Oxford University Press.

Lomax, Eric (2008). *The Railway Man: A POW's Searing Account of War, Brutality and Forgiveness*. New York: W. W. Norton. Original publication 1995.

Mackie, J. L. (1982). "Morality and the Retributive Emotions." *Criminal Justice Ethics* 1: 3–10.

Maimonides (1993). *Hilchot Teshuvah* (The Laws of Repentance). Trans. Immanuel O'Levy. Online edition: http://www.panix.com/~jjbaker/rambam.html.

———. (2010). *Hilchot Teshuvah* (The Rules of Repentance). Trans. Rabbi Yaakov Feldman. Online edition: http://www.scribd.com/doc/28390008/Maimondes-Hilchot-Teshuva-The-Rules-of-Repentance.

Mandela, Nelson (1994). *Long Walk to Freedom*. London: Little, Brown.

———. (2010). *Conversations with Myself*. Foreword by Barack Obama. New York: Farrar, Straus and Giroux.

Markel, Dan (2011). "What Might Retributive Justice Be? An Argument for the Confrontational Conception of Retributivism." In *Retributivism: Essays on Theory and Policy*. Ed. Mark D. White. New York: Oxford University Press, 49–72.

Martin, Adrienne (2010). "Owning Up and Lowering Down: The Power of Apology." *Journal of Philosophy* 107: 534–53.

Mason, Michelle (2003). "Contempt as a Moral Attitude." *Ethics* 113: 234–72.

McConnell, Michael W. (2012). "You Can't Say That." *New York Times*: June 22. Online edition.

Miceli, Maria, and Cristiano Castelfranchi (2007). "The Envious Mind." *Cognition and Emotion* 21: 449–79.

Mill, John Stuart (1988). *The Subjection of Women*. Ed. Susan Moller Okin. Indianapolis: Hackett. Original edition 1869.

Miller, William I. (1990). *Bloodtaking and Peacemaking: Feud, Law, and Society in Saga Iceland*. Chicago: University of Chicago Press.

———. (2006). *An Eye for an Eye*. New York: Cambridge University Press.

Moore, Michael S. (1995). "The Moral Worth of Retribution." In *Punishment and Rehabilitation*. Ed. Jeffrie Murphy. Belmont, CA: Wadsworth, 94–130.

Morgan, Michael (2011). "Mercy, Repentance, and Forgiveness in Ancient Judaism." In *Ancient Forgiveness: Classical, Judaic, and Christian*. Ed. Charles Griswold and David Konstan. Cambridge: Cambridge University Press, 137–57.

Morris, Herbert (1968). "Persons and Punishment." *Monist* 52. Reprinted in *Punishment and Rehabilitation*. Ed. Jeffrie Murphy. Belmont, CA: Wadsworth, 1995, 74–93.

———. (1976). *On Guilt and Innocence: Essays in Legal Philosophy and Moral Psychology*. Berkeley: University of California Press.

Murdoch, Iris (1970). *The Sovereignty of Good*. London: Routledge.

Murphy, Jeffrie (1988). "Forgiveness and Resentment." In Jeffrie Murphy and Jean Hampton, *Forgiveness and Mercy*. New York: Cambridge University Press, chapter 1.

———, comp. (1995). *Punishment and Rehabilitation*. Belmont, CA: Wadsworth.

———. (2003). *Getting Even: Forgiveness and Its Limits*. New York: Oxford University Press.

Murray, Liz (2010). *Breaking Night: A Memoir of Forgiveness, Survival, and My Journey from Homeless to Harvard*. New York: Hyperion.

Nahorniak, Mary (2015). "Families to Roof: May God 'Have Mercy on Your Soul.'" *USA Today*: June 19. Online edition.

Naiden, F. S. (2006). *Ancient Supplication*. Oxford: Oxford University Press.

Nehru, Jawaharlal (1939). *Autobiography*. Oxford: Oxford University Press.

———. (1989). *The Discovery of India*. Delhi: Oxford University Press. Original edition 1946.

Nietzsche, Friedrich Wilhelm (1989). *On the Genealogy of Morals*. Trans. Walter Kaufmann and R. J. Hollingdale. New York: Vintage Books. Original edition 1887.

Nussbaum, Martha (1986). *The Fragility of Goodness: Luck, Ethics, and Greek Tragedy.* New York: Cambridge University Press.

———. (1990). *Love's Knowledge: Essays on Philosophy and Literature.* New York: Oxford University Press.

———. (1993). "Equity and Mercy." *Philosophy and Public Affairs* 22, no. 2: 83–125.

———. (1994a). "Pity and Mercy: Nietzsche's Stoicism." In *Nietzsche, Genealogy, Morality: Essays on Nietzsche's "Genealogy of Morals."* Ed. Richard Schacht. Berkeley: University of California Press, 139–67.

———. (1994b). *The Therapy of Desire: Theory and Practice in Hellenistic Ethics.* Princeton, NJ: Princeton University Press.

———. (1996). *Poetic Justice: The Literary Imagination and Public Life.* Boston: Beacon Press.

———. (1999a). *Sex and Social Justice.* New York: Oxford University Press.

———. (1999b). "Virtue Ethics: A Misleading Category?" *Journal of Ethics* 3: 163–201.

———. (2000a). "The Costs of Tragedy: Some Moral Limits of Cost-Benefit Analysis." *Journal of Legal Studies* 29: 1005–36.

———. (2000b). *Women and Human Development.* New York: Cambridge University Press.

———. (2001). *Upheavals of Thought: The Intelligence of Emotions.* New York: Cambridge University Press.

———. (2002a). "Erōs and Ethical Norms: Philosophers Respond to a Cultural Dilemma." In *The Sleep of Reason: Erotic Experience and Sexual Ethics in Ancient Greece and Rome.* Ed. Martha Nussbaum and Juha Sihvola. Chicago: University of Chicago Press, 55–94.

———. (2002b). "Sex Equality, Liberty, and Privacy: A Comparative Approach to the Feminist Critique." In *India's Living Constitution: Ideas, Practices, Controversies.* Ed. E. Sridharan, Z. Hasan, and R. Sudarshan. New Delhi: Permanent Black, 242–83.

———. (2003). "What's Privacy Got to Do with It? A Comparative Approach to the Feminist Critique." In *Women and the United States Constitution: History, Interpretation, Practice.* Ed. Sibyl A. Scharzenbach and Patricia Smith. New York: Columbia University Press, 153–75.

———. (2004a). *Hiding from Humanity: Disgust, Shame, and the Law.* Princeton, NJ: Princeton University Press.

———. (2004b). "Précis" and "Responses." In book symposium on Nussbaum, *Upheavals of Thought. Philosophy and Phenomenological Research* 68 (2004): 443–49, 473–86.

———. (2006). *Frontiers of Justice.* Cambridge, MA: Harvard University Press.

———. (2008). "Human Dignity and Political Entitlements." In Adam Schulman et al., *Human Dignity and Bioethics: Essays Commissioned by the President's Council on Bioethics.* Washington, DC: President's Council on Bioethics, 351–80.

———. (2010a). *Creating Capabilities: The Human Development Approach.* Cambridge, MA: Harvard University Press.

———. (2010b). *From Disgust to Humanity: Sexual Orientation and Constitutional Law.* New York: Oxford University Press.

———. (2010c). Translation, introduction, and notes to Seneca's *Apocolocyntosis.* In *Seneca: Anger, Mercy, Revenge.* Chicago: University of Chicago Press. Containing translations by Robert Kaster and Martha Nussbaum. 2010.

———. (2013). *Political Emotions: Why Love Matters for Justice.* Cambridge, MA: Harvard University Press.

———. (2014a). "Jewish Men, Jewish Lawyers: Roth's 'Eli, the Fanatic' and the Question of Jewish Masculinity in American Law." In *American Guy: Masculinity in American Law and Literature.* Ed. Saul Levmore and Martha Nussbaum. New York: Oxford University Press, 165–200.

———. (2014b). "Law for Bad Behaviour." *Indian Express*: February 22. Online edition.

———. (forthcoming a). "'If You Could See This Heart': Mozart's Mercy." Forthcoming in a festschrift for David Konstan. Ed. Ruth Rothaus Caston. New York: Oxford University Press.

———. (forthcoming b). "Reconciliation without Justice: Paton's *Cry, the Beloved Country*." Presented at the conference "Crime in Law and Literature," University of Chicago Law School, February 7–8, 2014, and forthcoming in the conference volume.

Nussbaum, Martha, and Alison L. LaCroix, eds. (2013). *Subversion and Sympathy: Gender, Law, and the British Novel*. New York: Oxford University Press.

Nussbaum, Martha, and Juha Sihvola, eds. (2002). *The Sleep of Reason: Erotic Experience and Sexual Ethics in Ancient Greece and Rome*. Chicago: University of Chicago Press.

O'Neill, Onora (2002). *A Question of Trust: The BBC Reith Lectures 2002*. Cambridge: Cambridge University Press.

Orwell, George (1949). "Reflections on Gandhi." *Partisan Review*, January, 85–92.

———. (1952). "Such, Such Were the Joys." Originally published in the *Partisan Review*, September–October.

Paton, Alan (1987). *Cry, the Beloved Country*. New York: Scribner. Original edition 1948.

Peli, Pinchas, ed. (2004). *On Repentance: The Thought and Oral Discourses of Rabbi Joseph Dov Soloveitchik*. New York: Rowman and Littlefield. Original publication 1984.

Posner, Eric A. (2000). *Law and Social Norms*. Cambridge, MA: Harvard University Press.

Primoratz, Igor (1989). "Punishment as Language." *Philosophy* 64: 187–205.

Procope, John, trans. (1995). *Seneca: Moral and Political Essays*. Cambridge: Cambridge University Press.

Rawls, John (1971). *A Theory of Justice*. Cambridge, MA: Harvard University Press.

———. (1986). *Political Liberalism*. New York: Columbia University Press. Expanded paper edition.

Rorty, Amélie Oksenberg, ed. (1981). *Essays on Aristotle's Ethics*. Berkeley: University of California Press.

Santideva (1995). *The Bodhicaryavatara*. Trans. Kate Crosby and Andrew Skilton. Oxford: Oxford University Press. Original Sanskrit verse written c. AD 700.

Santora, Marc (2013). "City's Annual Cost per Inmate Is $168,000, Study Finds." *New York Times*: August 23.

Scanlon, T. M. (2013). "Interpreting Blame." In *Blame: Its Nature and Norms*. Ed. D. Justin Coates and Neal A. Tognazzini. New York: Oxford University Press, 84–99.

Schacht, Richard, ed. (1994). *Nietzsche, Genealogy, Morality: Essays on Nietzsche's "Genealogy of Morals."* Berkeley: University of California Press.

Schalkwyk, David (2014). "Mandela, the Emotions, and the Lesson of Prison." In *The Cambridge Companion to Nelson Mandela*. Ed. Rita Barnard. New York: Cambridge University Press, 50–69.

Schofer, Jonathan (2010). *Confronting Vulnerability: The Body and the Divine in Rabbinic Ethics*. Chicago: University of Chicago Press.

Schulhofer, Stephen J. (1995). "The Trouble with Trials; the Trouble with Us." *Yale Law Journal* 105: 825–55.

Schwarzenbach, Sibyl A., and Patricia Smith, eds. (2003). *Women and the United States Constitution: History, Interpretation, Practice*. New York: Columbia University Press.

Segal, Erich (1968). *Roman Laughter: The Comedy of Plautus*. Cambridge, MA: Harvard University Press.

———. (1970). *Love Story*. New York: Harper & Row.

———. (2001). *The Death of Comedy*. Cambridge, MA: Harvard University Press.

Sen, Amartya (1982). "Rights and Agency." *Philosophy and Public Affairs* 11: 3–39.

Sen, Amartya, and Bernard Williams, eds. (1982). *Utilitarianism and Beyond*. Cambridge: Cambridge University Press.

Sher, George (2006). *In Praise of Blame*. Oxford: Oxford University Press.

———. (2013). "Wrongdoing and Relationships: The Problem of the Stranger." In *Blame: Its Nature and Norms*. Ed. D. Justin Coates and Neal A. Tognazzini. New York: Oxford University Press, 49–65.

Sherman, Nancy (1989). *The Fabric of Character: Aristotle's Theory of Virtue*. Oxford: Clarendon Press.

———. (2011). *The Untold War*. New York: W. W. Norton.

Skorupski, John, ed. (2010). *Routledge Companion to Ethics*. New York: Routledge.

Smart, J. J. C., and Bernard Williams (1973). *Utilitarianism: For and Against*. Cambridge: Cambridge University Press.

Smith, Adam (1982). *The Theory of Moral Sentiments*. Ed. D. D. Raphael and A. L. Macfie. Indianapolis: Liberty Classics. Original edition 1759.

Smith, Angela M. (2013). "Moral Blame and Moral Protest." In *Blame: Its Nature and Norms*. Ed. D. Justin Coates and Neal A. Tognazzini. New York: Oxford University Press, 27–48.

Sorabji, Richard (2012). *Gandhi and the Stoics*. Chicago: University of Chicago Press.

Sridharan, Z., Z. Hasan, and R. Sudarshan, eds. (2002). *India's Living Constitution: Ideas, Practices, Controversies*. New Delhi: Permanent Black.

Stegner, Wallace (1971). *Angle of Repose*. New York: Penguin.

Stewart, Nikita, and Richard Pérez-Peña (2015). "In Charleston, Raw Emotion, at Hearing for Suspect in Church Shooting." *New York Times*: June 19. Online edition.

Strawson, Peter F. (1968). "Freedom and Resentment." In *Studies in the Philosophy of Thought and Action*. Oxford: Oxford University Press, 71–96. Originally published in *Proceedings of the British Academy* 48 (1962): 1–25.

Tasioulas, John (2010). "Justice and Punishment." *Routledge Companion to Ethics*. Ed. John Skorupski. New York: Routledge, 680–91.

Tavris, Carol (1982). *Anger: The Misunderstood Emotion*. New York: Simon and Schuster.

Thomson, Judith Jarvis (1972). "A Defense of Abortion." *Philosophy and Public Affairs* 1: 47.

———. (1975). "The Right to Privacy." *Philosophy and Public Affairs* 4: 295–314.

Trollope, Anthony (2014). *Doctor Thorne*. Oxford: Oxford University Press. Original edition 1858.

Tutu, Desmond M. (1999). *No Future without Forgiveness*. New York: Doubleday.

———. (2014). "'I Am Sorry'—the Three Hardest Words to Say." *Guardian*: March 22.

Tutu, Desmond M., and Mpho A. Tutu (2014). *The Book of Forgiving: The Fourfold Path for Healing Ourselves and Our World*. New York: HarperOne.

Vermeule, Blakey (2011). *Why Do We Care about Literary Characters?* Baltimore: Johns Hopkins University Press.

Vlastos, Gregory (1991). *Socrates: Ironist and Moral Philosopher*. New York: Cambridge University Press.

Wagner, Richard (1850). "Jewishness in Music." *Das Judentum in der Musik*. Amazon: Amazon Digital Services, 2012. Kindle edition.

Waldron, Jeremy (2012). *The Harm in Hate Speech*. Cambridge, MA: Harvard University Press.

Walker, Margaret Urban (2006). *Moral Repair: Reconstructing Moral Relations after Wrongdoing*. Cambridge: Cambridge University Press.

Wallace, R. Jay (1994). *Responsibility and the Moral Sentiments*. Cambridge, MA: Harvard University Press.

———. (2011). "Dispassionate Opprobrium: On Blame and the Reactive Sentiments." In *Reasons and Recognition: Essays on the Philosophy of T. M. Scanlon.* Ed. R. J. Wallace, Rahul Kumar, and Samuel Freeman. New York: Oxford University Press, 348–72.

Wallace, R. J., Rahul Kumar, and Samuel Freeman, eds. (2011). *Reasons and Recognition: Essays on the Philosophy of T. M. Scanlon.* New York: Oxford University Press.

Walzer, Michael (1973). "Political Action: The Problem of Dirty Hands." *Philosophy and Public Affairs* 2: 160–80.

Washington, James M., ed. (1986). *A Testament of Hope: The Essential Writings and Speeches of Martin Luther King, Jr.* New York: HarperCollins.

White, Mark D., ed. (2011). *Retributivism: Essays on Theory and Policy.* New York: Oxford University Press.

Wiesenthal, Simon (1997). *The Sunflower: On the Possibilities and Limits of Forgiveness.* New York: Schocken Books.

Williams, Bernard (1973). *Problems of the Self.* Cambridge: Cambridge University Press.

———. (1982). *Moral Luck: Philosophical Papers, 1973–1980.* Cambridge: Cambridge University Press.

———. (1985). *Ethics and the Limits of Philosophy.* Cambridge, MA: Harvard University Press.

Williams, Craig (1999). *Roman Homosexuality.* New York: Oxford University Press. 2nd edition with preface by Martha Nussbaum, 2010.

Winnicott, D. W. (2005). *Playing and Reality.* New York: Routledge. Original publication 1971.

Wolf, Susan (2011). "Blame, Italian Style." In *Reasons and Recognition: Essays on the Philosophy of T. M. Scanlon.* Ed. R. J. Wallace, Rahul Kumar, and Samuel Freeman. New York: Oxford University Press, 332–47.

Yonah, Rabbeinu of Gerona (1967). *The Gates of Repentance: Sha'arei Teshuvah.* Trans. Shraga Silverstein. New York: Feldheim Publishers.

Young, Iris Marion (2011). *Responsibility for Justice.* New York: Oxford University Press.

Zorn, Eric (2013). "There's a Core of Substance in Kirk's 'Empty, Simplistic' Crime-Fighting Proposal." *Chicago Tribune*: May 31.

Index

accountability 3–4, 13, 34–5, 118
Aeschylus
  and the rule of law 1–4, 147,
    165, 169
  Eumenides 2–4, 3n12, 9–10, 135,
    169–172, 199, 209, 247
  Furies 1–4, 6, 47, 169–72, 194
  Oresteia 1–5
Allen, Danielle 171
Anaximander 24–5
anger
  and down-ranking 19–21, 25–7,
    51, 197
  and eudaimonism 16, 19–20
  and evolution 24, 29, 34, 36, 39, 55–6
  and irritation or
    annoyance 263–4
  and payback wishes 6, 11, 15,
    21–6, 50. *See also* cosmic
    balance, ideas of
  Butler on the normative
    value of 34
  and perceived wrongs 17–20
  and rage or fury 264
  and resentment 262
  and solidarity 34
  and status injury 20–21, 25–6
  as deterrent 6, 39, 43, 141, 143,
    146, 153
  as motivation 38–9, 43
  as signal 37–8
  at inanimate objects 18–9
  at oneself. *See* guilt
  between parents and chil-
    dren. *See* relationships,
    intimate
  caused by vicarious ego
    investment 101
  content of 17–8, 22–3
  definition of 15–8
  distinguished from the
    Transition. *See*
    Transition, the
  focus of 17

anger (*Cont.*)
 in infants 263
 in sports and politics 53–4
 "noble" 211–12
 "sudden". *See* Butler, Joseph
 target of 17
 transition anger as borderline
   species of. *See*
   Transition Anger
 well-grounded 35, 49, 52, 97
apology
 and protest 259
 as a sign for the future 124,
   141, 154
 between colleagues 156–60
 in transactional forgiveness
   10–3, 63–5, 86–8, 92,
   105–6, 117–8, 209
 to God 60n7, 68, 71–2
 political 13, 202–3, 216, 241–2
Aristotle
 and gentle temper 4, 54–5
 and playfulness 54–5, 101–2,
   107, 116
 on anger 5, 15–21, 28, 35–6, 53,
   93, 261
 on hatred 50

Baier, Annette 94, 99
Batson, Daniel 22
Bentham, Jeremy
 and ex-ante strategies for
   preventing wrongdoing
   179–80, 182
 forward-looking account of law
   171, 179–80
 his utilitarianism 174
Bible, the
 Hebrew 60n7, 75
 New Testament
   against anger 42
   transactional forgiveness in
     66–7, 76–8

unconditional forgiveness
   in 75–8
unconditional love in
   12n31, 78–81
blame
 accounts of 257–9
 and anger 47, 117–120,
   187, 258–60
 and disgust 49
Bloom, Paul 34, 263
Braithwaite, John
 and impartial justice 204
 and the Transition 203, 205
 and shame 201–2, 205
 compared to regret 205
 concerns about his view 203–5
 his core ideas 201–2
Briggs, Jean 43
Buddhism 14, 40, 175
 Santideva 15n6, 40n62
Butler, Joseph (Bishop Butler)
 on anger 14, 15, 19, 22, 95
   the value of 34–5, 37, 40
 on forgiveness 11
 on responding to
   wrongdoing 30
 on the narcissism of
   resentment 12

Capabilities Approach, the
   173–4, 178, 188. *See also*
   welfarism
Catholic Encyclopedia, the 74
Christian thought. *See also*
   Dies Irae; God; Jesus;
   Lactantius; love, unconditional; Tertullian
 and confession 70
 and penance 68–9
 and retribution 72–3
 and the *Dies Irae* 67–8. *See also*
   Dies Irae
 and the inner realm 70–1, 73

and unconditional love. *See* love,
    unconditional
compared to Jewish
    tradition 66–71
God in
    anger of 41–3
    as a model of interpersonal
        relationships 72–3
    as represented in Mahler. *See*
        Mahler, Gustav
    as represented in the
        Gospels 78–81
    compared to Jewish
        thought 69–74
    transactional forgiveness of
        11, 67–9, 76–8
    the harshness of forgiveness
        of 73–5
    unconditional forgiveness
        of 75–7
    unconditional love of. *See*
        love, unconditional
    Protestantism 69
    the Gospels. *See* Bible, the
Chrysippus 18, 28n44, 142, 142n8
colleagues. *See* workplace, the
compassion
    as a positive motive 120, 131–3
    compared to mercy 206
    compassionate hope and the
        Transition 31, 36
    distinguished from feeling 252
    in Adam Smith 16, 18–9
    in the legal system 177, 256
    nature of 22–4, 22n34
confession
    and exomologésis 72
    as condition of
        forgiveness 10–12
    in Christian tradition 68–74, 76
    in Jewish tradition 62–3, 65,
        68, 86. *See also* Jewish
        thought

in Desmond Tutu's vision 59,
    237–8, 241–3
consequentialism. *See* welfarism
contempt 50–1
cosmic balance, ideas of 5, 24–5,
    74, 178, 184, 190
criminal justice system. *See*
    law and criminal
    justice system
criminals
    anger directed at 194–5
    as a despised subgroup 49–50
    equal dignity of 180, 182
    families of 195

Dante Alighieri 23, 50n83, 71n43
Dickens, Charles 98, 169, 210
Dies Irae
    on forgiveness 67–8
    translation of 89–90
dignity. *See* human dignity, equal
discrimination 28–9, 49n82, 152,
    164, 199–200
disgust 48–50, 52, 55, 181–2
down-ranking
    and discrimination 28–9
    and culture 19–20, 140, 147
    and status-injury 20–1
    and the law 178, 197
    and voluntariness 21
    as the focus of anger 21, 25–7, 51
    in Aristotle 5, 15, 17, 19–20
    the normative problem with
        focusing on 15, 28,
        49, 54, 93
Duff, R. A. 188–90

Eliot, George 119–20
emotions. *See also* eudaimonism
    and feelings 252–3
    and the body 252
    analysis of 16–7, 19–20, 251–2
    compared to moods 254

emotions (*Cont.*)
    content of 253
    development of 254
    in *Upheavals of Thought* 251–5
    negative. *See* anger; contempt;
        envy; hate; jealousy;
        resentment
    situational 252
    social influences on 253–4
envy 51–2
equality. *See* human dignity, equal
Erikson, Erik 225
eudaimonism 16, 19–20, 25
Eumenides. *See* Aeschylus

Fairbairn, W. R. D. 129–30
family. *See* relationships, intimate
forgiveness
    as inquisitorial and normatively
        problematic 10–2, 73–4,
        76–7, 96–7, 106, 206
    as virtue 9, 63, 88–9
    compared to the Transition
        76–8, 118
    Griswold's treatment of. *See*
        Griswold, Charles
    in Christian thought. *See*
        Christian thought
    in Jewish thought. *See* Jewish
        thought
    its absence in Greco-Roman eth-
        ics 9, 11, 209
    its cultural popularity 10
    transactional 10–12, 33, 58–60,
        66, 74, 89
    unconditional 12, 75–8, 81, 86–7,
        96, 106, 125
Foucault, Michel 59, 70

Gandhi, Mohandas
    and acknowledgment of wrongs 238
    and non-anger 8, 175, 212, 218,
        222, 236, 247
    compared to King, Mandela and
        Nehru 218–9, 224–5
    his non-attachment 223–5
        as self-anger 225
    his rejection of status 223
    his remarks on Hitler and
        Japan 219
    his thesis of nonviolence
        39, 218–9
    on the future 223
    the non-passive element in his
        theory 211, 221–2
gender 43–6, 92, 119, 121–3, 254.
        See also manliness
genealogical explanations 58–9
generosity
    between persons 12–3, 65, 106,
        121, 130. *See also* love,
        unconditional
    in institutions 172–3, 200, 203
    in revolutionary justice 212–2,
        217–8, 222, 226–32,
        235–7, 243
gentle temper, 3–4, 11, 52–6,
        67–8, 167–8
God. *See also* Christian thought;
        Jewish thought
    anger of 40–2
    as modeling parent-child
        relationships 98
    emotions of 42
    inhabiting payback wishes 208, 214
Gospels, the. *See* Bible, the
gratitude
    and Stoicism 46
    as a reactive attitude 46–7
    gratuitous 160–4
    in intimate relationships 113–4
    in the Middle Realm 161–4
grief
    and vulnerability 105
    compared to anger 17–18, 23,
        37–8, 47–8, 102

in intimate relationships 4, 7–8,
    23, 92, 94–6, 102–3, 126–7
in marital breakups 122–3
Griswold, Charles 57–8, 60,
    64, 88–9
guilt. *See also* remorse;
    retributivism
and creativity 131
and moral development 129–32
and moral dilemmas 134–5
and moral motivation 131–2, 134
and self-forgiveness 132–3
and the public sphere 133
and the Transition 129
as confining and
    restrictive 130–1
as deterrent 133–5
compared to positive
    reinforcement 132
compared to remorse
    134–5, 134n
Christian roots 132
distinguished from shame 128
nature of 128–9
parallels with self-other
    relations 129
well-grounded 131

Halbertal, Moshe 87
Hampton, Jean 26, 35, 191
Harriss, William 4n16, 247
hatred 50
Heckman, James 181
Hegel, G. W. F. 134–5
helplessness
    and anger 5, 29, 45, 47–8, 54–5,
        94–5, 208
    and women 45, 122–3
    in love and intimacy 94–5, 104,
        116, 122
    in parents-children
        relationships 100–5
Hinduism 14, 40, 175

honor cultures 19–20. *See also*
    down-ranking
human dignity, equal
    anger as allegedly necessary for
        the protection of 8, 47,
        91, 211
    as a central concern for institu-
        tions 27, 182, 196
    distinguished from relative
        status 27–8, 173
    in institutional response to
        wrongdoing 152–3,
        166, 172–3, 183, 192–3,
        196–200, 204
    in revolutionary justice 213,
        227, 242–3
humor
    as alternative to anger 102,
        154–5, 160, 167–8
    in Seneca 145–6
    Mandela's 227n26, 235, 232, 242

incarceration. *See* law and
    criminal justice system;
    punishment
institutions, political. *See also*
    law and criminal
    justice system
    as not motivated by retributiv-
        ist sentiments 3, 42, 166,
        171–2, 178, 249
    as modeling our best selves
        249, 249n5
    equal human dignity as a con-
        cern for 27, 182, 196
    in revolutionary justice 213, 219,
        237, 245
    mercy in. *See* mercy
    their responsibility to respond
        to wrongdoing 1, 27,
        166, 196
    trust in 173, 177–8, 188, 196, 239
    vulnerability in relation to 173

Jansen, Jonathan 245–6
jealousy 51–52. *See also* envy
Jesus. *See also* Bible, the;
        Christian thought; love,
        unconditional
    and anger and transactional
        forgiveness 42–4, 72, 76
    and the inner realm 70
    and unconditional
        forgiveness 75–7
    and unconditional love 78–81
Jewish thought. *See also* Bible,
        the; God; Maimonides;
        Soloveitchick; *Talmud,*
        the; Yonah of Gerona
    God in 11, 61–5, 73–4
    Teshuva
        and the political 64–5
        as transactional
            forgiveness 64–5
        dissident voices about 85–8
        human-God 60–3
        human-human 63–6
Joyce, James 67, 71, 89
justice, impartial. *See* human dig-
        nity, equal; institutions,
        political; law and crimi-
        nal justice system
justice, revolutionary. *See also*
        Gandhi, Mohandas;
        King, Martin Luther Jr.;
        Mandela, Nelson
    anger as awakening to 211–2
    and non-anger 8, 212, 225
    forward-looking spirit in 209
    unconditional forgiveness and
        love in 209
    violence in 218–20

Kahan, Dan 198
King, Martin Luther Jr.
    and acknowledgment of
        wrongs 238

    and divine love 226
    and down-ranking 28–9
    and non-passivity 221–2, 238
    and nonviolence 39, 212, 218–19
    and personal attachments 224
    and the Transition 31–33, 36,
        38–9, 135–6
    on anger and non-anger 8, 118,
        175, 212, 218, 221–2, 236
    on cooperation 223, 249
    on violence 219–20
    on retributivism
    on the future 222–3, 239
Klein, Melanie 129–30, 132, 134

Lactantius, 41–2
law and criminal justice system
    and impartiality 166
    and intimate relationships 4,
        8–9, 94
    and the Transition 166, 205
    and victim impact
        statements 194–7
    as liberating individuals from
        the burden of dealing
        with wrongdoing 4–5, 94,
        135–6, 141, 170
    "closure" in 29, 196
    corrupt and unjust 211, 214, 221
    expressing Transition-Anger 179
    forward-looking 171, 178–9
    in the Middle Realm 7–8,
        140–1, 148
    scope 153, 164–5, 175
incarceration. *See also*
    punishment
    and racism 181–2
    anger as motivation for 182
    in a welfarist theory 192–3
    its failure to deter 177
    shame and dignity in 198
    the cost of 180–1
limits of 94, 135

mercy in 206–8
retributivist desires in 12, 29,
      136, 175, 178, 196, 249. *See
      also* retributivism
status injury in 176, 178
Lazarus, Richard 16, 18, 20–22
Lerner, Harriet 107–9, 116–8
lex talionis. See retributivism
Lloyd-Jones, Hugh 1
love, unconditional
   and mercy 209
   and the Prodigal Son 78–81
   compared to forgiveness 81
   in the case of Charleston Church
         shooting 77, 197
   in George Eliot's
         Middlemarch 119–20
   in Mahler's Resurrection
         Symphony 81–5
   in Philip Roth's *American
         Pastoral* 103–4, 106
Lucretius 40

magical thinking 24–7, 33–4, 38–9,
      54, 112n, 127, 178, 183–5.
      See also cosmic balance,
      ideas of
Mahler, Gustav
   Resurrection Symphony 81–5
Maimonides (Rabbi Moshe Ben
      Maimon) 60–3, 69
Mandela, Nelson
   and forgiveness 10, 12
   and forward-looking
         spirit 228–30
   and generosity 12, 226–32
   and Kobie Coet see 232–3
   and non-anger 39, 218, 225
   and non-violence 39, 212, 219
   and personal attachments 234
   and respect 227
   and status anxiety 227
   and the Anthem 233–4

and the rugby team 234–6
and the Transition 229–31
on status 226–7, 245–6
on violence 219
manliness 26, 44–5, 175, 254
Markel, Dan 189–90
marriage. *See* relationships,
      intimate
Medea. *See* Seneca
mercy
   and Transition mentality 207
   and criminal justice 207–9
   as combining *ex ante* and *ex post*
         perspectives 207
   compared to compassion 206
   compared to forgiveness 209
   egalitarian conception of 206
   God's 75, 78
   in Greco-Roman thought 205–6
   in Nietzsche 208
   "monarchical" conception of 206
Middle Realm, the
   and anger 139–40, 165
   and false social values
         139–40, 147
   and gratitude 160–4
   and grief 139–40, 164–5
   and status 147–8
   and Stoic thought 139–47
   and Transition Anger 140–1,
         148, 150, 153
   and the law 140–1, 164–7
   deterrence in 141, 148, 167
   harms involving
         stigmatization in 152
   harms involving false accusa-
         tions in 152–3
   forgiveness in 141, 149, 166–7
   nature of 7, 138–9
   performance of anger in 150
   provocation in 165–6
   the Middle of. *See*
         workplace, the

Mill, John Stuart 30, 174–6, 190,
        192, 200
Moore, Michael 184, 186–7
Morris, Herbert 130, 132,
        184–6, 188
Murphy, Jeffrie 10
Murray, Liz 110–2, 118, 136

narcissism
    and anger 21, 25, 28–30, 38,
        52–4, 95
    and forgiveness 12, 87–8
    and guilt 131
    in infants and children 45,
        130, 132
    in intimate relationships 97
    in religious outlooks 11
    in the Middle Realm 147, 159–60
    narcissistic error, the 29, 38
    of resentment 12
negative emotions. See emotions
New Testament. See Bible, the
Nietzsche, Friedrich 12, 58, 60,
        73–4, 131–2, 134, 208
non-anger
    as "feminine" and "weak" 44,
        46, 175, 220
    as not entailing nonviolence 39,
        218–220
    in ancient Greece and Rome 44
    in intimate relationships 122
    in the Middle-Realm 139, 149,
        151, 154, 159–60, 162
    in law and criminal justice
        system 174–5, 177, 193–4
    and victim impact
        statements 194–7
    and dignity 197–200
    and confrontation and
        reintegration 200–5
    in revolutionary justice 212–3,
        218–25, 236–7, 245, 248
    and Gandhi 212, 218–25

    and King 212, 218–9, 224,
    and Mandela 213, 218–9,
        224, 226–37
    in Stoicism 38, 44, 139, 142–5,
        161. See also Stoicism
    toward the self 146
nonviolence 39, 212, 218–20,
        225, 230

Orwell, George 98–9, 224–5, 248n3

payback wishes. See anger; cosmic
        balance, ideas of; magical
        thinking; retributivism
Paton, Alan
    Cry, the Beloved Country
        213–7, 222
prisons. See under law and crimi-
        nal justice system
privacy 256–7
Prodigal Son, the 79–81, 83,
        120, 235
provocation, reasonable 165–6, 176
punishment. See also law and
        criminal justice system;
        retributivism
    and anger 27, 145, 165–6, 172,
        176, 195
    and deterrence 27, 30, 42,
        167, 171
    and humiliation 27–8, 177–8,
        183, 195, 198–9
    and mercy 205–10
    and proportional suffering 178
    and rehabilitation 27
    and reintegration 200–5
    and retributivism. See
        retributivism
    and violence 199
    by God 68
    compared to ex ante methods of
        dealing with wrongdoing
        8, 179–81, 183

forward-looking concern of
171–2, 177, 179, 183,
187, 192
harsh 177, 181, 207
in Aeschylus 4, 165
in revolutionary justice 238, 240
indicating social failure 193
motivated by disgust and racism 182, 215
spirit of generosity in 172–3

Rawls, John 51n87, 173–4,
186, 249n 5
reactive attitudes. *See* emotions
relationships, intimate
and anger 92–3, 96–7, 105, 116
break-down scenarios 94–5
and flourishing 93
and gratitude 113–4
and grief 4, 7, 89, 113
and liking 95
and social norms 96–7,
115–6, 121–2
and status anxiety 97
and trust 94
and vulnerability 94
between lovers and spouses
and status anxiety 122
and the law 135–6
compared to parent-child
relationships 114–5
erotic betrayal in 120
forgiveness in 118–20, 124
involving grave
wrongdoing 135–6
involving status anxiety 116
the Transition in 118, 124–6
trust in 114–5
violence in 20, 23
vulnerability in 114
features of 93–5
involving hierarchy and status
97, 122

parent-child relationships
and forgiveness 105–6, 110–1
and grief 102
and the Transition 101–5
children's anger as
status-anger in 107
anger, separateness and
equality in 106–7
involving harm 101
involving vicarious ego
investment 101
religious models of 98–9
vulnerability in 99
trust in 99
future-directed focus of 100
readiness to change in 100
with adult children 100–1
with oneself
and moral dilemmas 134–5
distinguished from self-other
relationships 128
guilt. *See* guilt
self-anger 128–9
in our culture 133
self-forgiveness 132–3
similarities to self-other
relationships 127–8
Transition-Anger at
oneself 128
remorse 134–5, 134n60. *See
also* guilt
resentment. *See* anger
retaliation. *See* retributivism
retributivism
and helplessness 208
and ideas of cosmic balance
38–9. *See also* cosmic
balance, ideas of
as constitutive of anger 15, 17,
30–1. *See also* anger
borderline
Duff's 188–8
Markel's 189–90

retributivism (*Cont.*)
  expressive 190–1
  futility of 15, 31, 33, 38, 102, 129.
      See also anger
  in Aeschylus 1, 3–5
  in Christianity 72. *See also*
      Christian thought
  in forgiveness rituals 105
  in Greek thought 171
  its dominance in popular ideas
      of punishment 176
  its influence on incarceration
      discourse 181
  its tension with sympathetic
      understanding 54
  in the Middle Realm 140, 142
  Moore's 186–8
  Morris's 184–6
  not motivated by anger 183–8.
      See also Moore, Michael;
      Morris, Herbert
Road of payback 5, 28–30, 51, 77,
      93, 122
Road of status 5–6, 28–30, 50, 52,
      77, 93, 97, 105, 122–3
Roth, Philip
  American Pastoral 102–6

Santideva. *See* Buddhism
Scanlon, Thomas 165,
      258–60
self-help. *See* therapy and
      self-help
Seneca. *See also* Stoicism
  and the middle realm,
      140, 142–8
  departing from his view
      146–7, 152–5
  his advice 7, 56, 140, 144, 155,
      167–168
  his critique of anger 140,
      142–8, 150
  his definition of anger 20

  his struggle with his own anger
      7, 56, 137–8, 155, 167
  Medea 45, 91–3, 122–4, 127
  on mercy 205–6, 208–9
Shakespeare, William
  Hamlet 137, 153
  Measure for Measure 206
  The Merchant of Venice 206
shame
  and attention to status 45,
      199–200
  and punishment 197–203. *See also*
      Kahan, Dan
  in Braithwaite's
      thought 203–5
  and repentance 63, 71–2
  and retaliatory anger 199
  and stigma 199, 202–3
  anger and as aiming to inflict 197
  distinguished from guilt 128
Sher, George 258, 260
Smith, Adam 7, 11, 16, 30, 52–3, 139
Smith, Angela 258–60
Soloveitchik, Joseph Dov
      60–2, 64–5
status
  in culture 20, 30, 40, 45
  injury 28, 39
    and God 41, 74
    anger about 6, 21, 41, 51
    damages not involving 20
    defined 5–6, 20–1
    not justifying violence in most
        democracies 176
  relative
    distinguished from equal
        human dignity. *See*
        human dignity, equal
    normative problems in focusing
        on 5–6, 15, 27–8, 31, 183,
        197, 200
    restored by retaliation 26, 31,
        129, 197

Road of. *See* Road of Status
status error. *See* narcissism
status-focused anger 6, 21,
    41, 51
status-focused person 30
Stoicism. *See also*
        Chrysippus; Seneca
    and care for well-being 46,
        140, 248
    and Gandhi 223–4
    and inner acts 70n38
    and intimate relationships 7, 40,
        88–9, 92, 94–5, 97
    and Mandela 226, 228, 236
    and self-examination 146
    and the Middle Realm 7, 139,
        142–4, 161
    as comic 138, 164
    and the motivation to pursue
        justice 38
    its continuity with
        Christianity 89
    on anger 20, 142, 161, 261
    on gods 40–1
    on gratitude 113, 161
    on mercy 205–6
Strauss, Richard
    Elektra 4
Strawson, Peter F. 14–5, 258

Talmud, the 60, 85–8
Tertullian 67–8, 70, 72
therapy and self-help
    and anger 10, 17, 125–7,
        166–7
    and the criminal justice system
        15n9, 190, 207
Transition-Anger
    distinguished from hatred and
        contempt 50–1
    explained 6, 35–7, 262
    expressed by the justice system
        179, 207, 209

in parent-child relationships
    100–1, 104
in revolutionary justice 212,
    229, 240
in self-anger 128, 133
in the Middle Realm 140–1, 148,
    150, 153
leading to the Transition 35, 51
Transition, the
    aided by gentle temper and
        sympathy 52–4
    aided by playfulness and
        humor 55
    and acknowledgment 125,
        125, 136
    and forgiveness 33, 136
    and justice 33
    and mercy 209
    and unconditional
        forgiveness 77–8
    arising from initial anger 35–6,
        38, 42, 51
    as the goal of law 135
    explained 6, 31
    from self-anger 131, 133
    in American culture 33
    in intimate relationships 94, 96,
        100, 102, 105, 129
    in relation to
        Transition-Anger 35
    in revolutionary justice 31–2, 36,
        38–9, 212, 216–7, 222–3,
        229, 231, 236
    in the Middle Realm 139–41
    inhibited by status-focused
        anger and hatred 49–50
Trollope, Anthony 98–9, 121–2
trust
    among citizens in political com-
        munities 13, 173, 183, 188,
        192, 212–3, 232, 238
    and acknowledgment 135, 238,
        240, 243

trust (*Cont.*)
  and revolutionary justice
        212–4, 232–4, 236, 238,
        240–1, 243
  and vulnerability 94, 114,
        136, 173
  apology as a sign of
        trustworthiness 13
  betrayals of 119–21
  between parents and children
        99–100, 105
  distinguished from reliance 94
  in intimate relationships 4, 7–8,
        94, 98, 114–5, 173, 238–40
  in oneself 133
  in political institutions 173,
        177–8, 188, 196, 239
  its absence in the Middle Realm
        138, 154–5, 164–5
Truth and Reconciliation
        Commission, the
  and backward-looking forgive-
        ness rituals 244–5
  and respect 241
  and transactional forgiveness
        12–3, 241–3
  and Transition Anger 240
  their virtues 237–40
Tutu, Desmond 12, 59, 237–44.
        See also Truth and
        Reconciliation
        Commission, the

Utilitarianism 24, 30, 42, 134, 174,
        179–80, 192–3. *See also*
        welfarism
Utku people, the 43–4, 55, 150

victim impact statements. *See*
        law and criminal
        justice system
violence. *See also* nonviolence;
        wrongdoing

and forgiveness 72–3, 87–8
and racism 181–2
and the law 141, 175–6, 190
as not inherent to the content of
        anger 22
in a spirit of non-anger 39,
        212, 218–20
in intimate relationships 9, 20,
        23, 94, 123, 141, 204
increased by shame-based
        penalties 199
vulnerability
  acknowledging 88–9, 105
  and grief 105, 127, 136
  as a cause of anger 21, 29,
        54, 254
  caused by trust 94, 114, 136, 173
  in intimate personal relation-
        ships 94, 97, 99, 102,
        113–4, 173
  in relation to political
        institutions 173

Wallace, R. Jay 15, 258
welfarism
  and gratitude 47
  and guilt 133–4
  and moving beyond
        narcissism 53
  and speech rights 200
  and the non-status-focused
        person 30–1
  as alternative to anger 34, 36–7,
        42, 47, 93, 172
  expressive theory of 191
  in revolutionary justice 241
  nature of 6, 173–4, 188,
        192, 198–9
  on punishment 176, 180–4, 195,
        203, 207
Williams, Bernard 12, 96, 106,
        130–2, 134–5
Winnicott, Donald 55, 132

women. *See* gender
workplace, the. *See also* Middle
      Realm, the
   apologies in 157, 159–60
   comic aspects of 154–5, 159
   features of 154–6
   nature of relationships in 154–5
   non-anger in 159–60
   spirit of generosity in 155
   wrongdoing in 155. *See also*
      wrongdoing
wrongdoing
   acknowledging 125, 173, 177–8,
      192, 207, 238
   and racism 181–2
   as the focus of anger 37

   culpability vs. desert in 192
   distinguished from inconve-
      niences 148, 154
   distinguished from the
      wrongdoer 49–50, 57,
      201–2, 205
   false social values about 174–6
   intentional 177
   that touches on core values of
      the self 19
   the desire to see it punished 34.
      See also retributivism
   the suffering of the wrongdoer
      5, 84, 92–3, 129

Yonah of Gerona 60–4